November, 1978

Unequal Development

Unequal Development

An Essay on the
Social Formations of
Peripheral Capitalism

by Samir Amin

Translated by Brian Pearce

Monthly Review Press
New York and London

Originally published as *Le Développement inégal*
by Les Editions de Minuit, Paris, France,
copyright © 1973 by Les Editions de Minuit

Library of Congress Cataloging in Publication Data
Amin, Samir.
    Unequal development.
    Translation of Le Développement inégal.
    Bibliography: p. 387
    1. Capitalism. 2. Socialism. 3. Economic history.
4. Underdeveloped areas. I. Title.
HB501.A5913   330.9'172'4   75-15364
ISBN 0-85345-380-2

First printing

Monthly Review Press
62 West 14th Street, New York, N.Y. 10011
21 Theobalds Road, London WC1X 8SL

Contents

Unequal Development

Introduction

Only at the end of the nineteenth century did a worldwide civilization begin to take shape. During the first seventy years of the twentieth century, however, which have been marked by a speeding up of the historical process, the division of the world into "developed" and "underdeveloped" countries has not become less pronounced; on the contrary, the gap between them continues to grow larger and has brought about the first crises of a capitalist system that had only just begun to be a world system.

The Russian Revolution of 1917, the Chinese Revolution that took place between 1930 and 1950, the revolutions in Vietnam and Cuba are all so many stages in a process of development beyond capitalism, in the name of socialism. The fears that Marx expressed in the middle of the last century, to the effect that a socialist Europe might find itself up against a capitalism still on the upgrade in Asia, have not proved justified. The opposite, indeed, has occurred. At the very center of the system, however, in the advanced capitalist countries, an all-round challenging of this system has begun, through a thousand indirect and unexpected channels.

This challenge to the foundation of the system of values upon which the world capitalist system is based brings into question in turn the conventional social science of the "establishment" and the universities. Conventional sociology, whether functionalist or structuralist, having developed as a reply to historical materialism, has the same ideological foundation and seeks to justify the established order by demonstrating "universal harmonies." Political science wavers between journalism and formalism. As for social psychology, this continues to evade its real problem — how to build the bridge linking the individual to the social — with Wilhelm Reich constituting the exception, a pioneer whom few have followed. The weakness of the so-called "fundamental disciplines," conceived in mutual isolation, results in the weakness of their multidisciplinary combination, as geography and history. Geographers are content to juxtapose facts, while the basic question of their discipline — how natural conditions act upon social formations — remains almost unanswered. History continues to be anecdotal in character: if it cannot be everything, it is nothing. And if, amid this general insolvency, conventional economics seems the least poorly equipped of the social disciplines, it owes this advantage to two main reasons: in the first place, because the dominance of the economic instance in the capitalist mode of production makes "economism" the dominant ideology, and in the second place, because the management of the social system of capitalism is principally, and for this very reason, economic management.

It was criticism of development economics that led me to put forward the following thesis, according to which, when a system is outgrown and superseded, this process takes place not, in the first place, starting from its center, but from its periphery. Two examples are given to illustrate this thesis — the birth of capitalism in the periphery of the great precapitalist systems, and the present crisis of capitalism.

The first chapter deals with the genesis of capitalism, and the remaining four with that of socialism. Chapter 2 sets forth the laws of the central capitalist system and Chapter 3 those of peripheral capitalism. Armed with this twofold analysis, I show in

Chapter 4 the mechanisms of dependence and illuminate the process of the "development of underdevelopment," before drawing up, in Chapter 5, the balance sheet of the peripheral social formations of the capitalist world.

1

The Precapitalist
Formations

1. MODES OF PRODUCTION

The concept of "mode of production" is an abstract one, implying no historical order of sequence with respect to the entire period of the history of civilizations that stretches from the first differentiated formations right down to capitalism. I propose to distinguish between five modes of production: (1) the "primitive-communal" mode, which is anterior to all the others; (2) the "tribute-paying" mode, which adds to a still-existing village community a social and political apparatus for the exploitation of this community through the exaction of tribute; this tribute-paying mode of production is the most widespread form of precapitalist classes, and I distinguish between (a) its early and (b) its developed forms, such as the "feudal" mode of production, in which the village community loses its *dominium eminens* over the soil to the feudal lords, and this community continues as a community of families; (3) the "slaveowning" mode of production, which constitutes a less frequently encountered form, though it is found in a number of places; (4) the "simple petty-commodity" mode of production, which though a frequently found form practically never constitutes the

13

dominant mode of any social formation; and (5) the "capitalist" mode of production.

The communal modes of production constitute the first modes of production that provide a basis for an embryonic class distinction. They insure the transition from primitive communism to full-fledged class societies. This primitive communism is marked by "primitive negation," as Guy Dhoquois puts it, of the division of labor and of the surplus product. Because this transition from negative (absence of classes) to positive (class society) is slow and gradual, the communal modes of production are many and various, being determined by natural conditions. But the modes of production of the primitive community are all characterized by: (1) organization of labor partly on an individual basis (that of the "nuclear family") and partly on a collective basis (that of the "extended family," the clan, or the village), with the principal means of labor, the land, being collectively owned by the clan and its use freely granted to all the clan's members, but in accordance with precise rules (utilization of holdings distributed to families, etc.); (2) absence of commodity exchange; and, correlatively, (3) distribution of the product within the collectivity in accordance with rules that are closely bound up with kinship organization.

Access to the land is not necessarily on an equal basis for everyone in these communities. It is so in the most primitive of them, but in the others this access is hierarchical, with some families or clans having the right to better holdings — more conveniently situated, for example, or larger. It is at that stage that an embryonic distinction between classes is observed. Such privilege is, as a rule, closely connected with a hierarchy of political and religious authority. Black Africa offers a wide spectrum of modes of production of this kind — some, especially in the Bantu part, having only a slight element of hierarchy, while others are extremely unegalitarian, such as those found among the Toucouleurs in the Senegal valley, the Ashanti in Ghana, the Hausa in northern Nigeria, etc. In all of them, however, the peasant enjoys access to the land: by the mere fact of belonging to a clan he is entitled to a part of this clan's territory. Consequently, proletarianization, that is, the separation of the producer from the means of production, cannot take place.

The tribute-paying mode of production is marked by the sepa-

ration of society into two main classes: the peasantry, organized
in communities, and the ruling class, which monopolizes the functions of the given society's political organization and exacts a tribute
(not in commodity form) from the rural communities. This mode
of production, when it assumes an advanced form, almost always
tends to become feudal — that is, the ruling class ousts the community from *dominium eminens* of the soil.

The feudal mode of production implies: (1) organization of
society into two classes, that of the lords of the land (whose property is inalienable) and that of the serf-tenants; (2) appropriation
of the surplus by the lords of the land, as a matter of right ("dues")
and not through commodity relations; (3) absence of commodity
exchange inside the "domain," which constitutes the primary cell
of this kind of society. This mode of production is threatened
with disintegration if for any reason the feudal lord should rid
himself of some of his tenants, "freeing" his serfs — in other words,
proletarianizing them. The fundamental right of access to use of
the land that is possessed by every peasant who belongs to the
community under the tribute-paying mode of production renders
this disintegration impossible.

The slaveowning mode of production turns the worker, as a
slave, into the essential means of production. The product of this
slave labor may enter into the circuit of noncommodity transfers
specific to the community (patriarchal slavery) or into commodity
circuits (Greco-Roman slavery).

The simple commodity mode of production is marked, in its
pure state, by equality between free petty producers and the organization of commodity exchange between them. No society has
ever been based on the predominance of this mode of production.
Frequently, however, there has been a sphere governed by simple
commodity relations — in particular, the sphere of handicraft
production, when this has been sufficiently dissociated from agricultural production.

The tribute-paying mode of production is the form that most
normally succeeds the communal mode; it is the rule. Characteristic of this mode is the contradiction between the continued existence
of the community and the negation of the community by the state;
and also, as a result of this, the confusion of the higher class that

appropriates the surplus with the class that is dominant politically. This circumstance makes is impossible to reduce production relations to legal property relations, and compels us to see production relations in their full, original significance as social relations arising from the organization of production. This mode of production, sometimes inaccurately called the "Asiatic" mode, has existed in four continents: in Asia, of course (China, India, Indochina, Mesopotamia, and the Asia of Classical times), and in Africa (Egypt and Black Africa), in Europe (in the preclassical societies of Crete and Etruria), and in pre-Columbian America (Incas, Aztecs, etc.).

The feudal mode of production appears as a "borderline" case of the tributary mode, in which the community is especially degraded, since it loses the *dominium eminens* of the land. This borderline character entitles us to describe the feudal formations as "peripheral" in relation to the "central" tributary formations. The slaveowning mode of production is similarly situated on the borders of the tributary formations, appearing only by way of exception, in a sequence that is not central but peripheral, as is also the case with the simple petty-commodity mode of production.

2. SOCIAL FORMATIONS

None of these modes of production has ever existed in a pure state: the societies known to history are "formations" that on the one hand combine modes of production and on the other organize relations between the local society and other societies, expressed in the existence of long-distance trade relations.

Social formations are thus concrete, organized structures that are marked by a dominant mode of production and the articulation around this of a complex group of modes of production that are subordinate to it. Thus, one can observe the simple petty-commodity mode of production linked to a dominant tribute-paying mode of production (whether "early" or "feudal"), to a slaveowning mode of production, or even to a capitalist mode. Similarly, the slaveowning mode of production may be nondominant, which is the rule when it is linked to a dominant tribute-paying mode (or even to the capitalist mode, as in the United States until 1865), or, by way of exception, it may constitute the dominant mode (as in the formations of Classical Antiquity.)

All precapitalist societies are social formations combining the same elements, and marked by: (1) the predominance of a communal or tribute-paying mode of production; (2) the existence of simple commodity relations in limited spheres; and (3) the existence of long-distance trade relations. When the feudal mode of production is absent or embryonic and there are no simple commodity relations within the given society, the formation, thus reduced to the combination of an undeveloped communal or tribute-paying mode of production with long-distance trade relations, is of the "African" type.

Long-distance trade is not a mode of production but is the way in which independent formations are linked together. This is the difference between it and trade within a given social formation, which is constituted by the commodity exchanges typical of the simple petty-commodity or slaveowning modes of production, these being elements in the formation in question. Internal trade can also, however, be a prolongation of long-distance trade.

Long-distance trade brings into mutual relations societies that are ignorant of each other, that is to say, it brings together products whose cost of production in one society is not known in the other, and scarce goods for which substitutes cannot be found, so that the social groups that engage in this trade hold a monopoly position from which they profit. This long-distance trade plays a decisive role when the surplus that the local dominant classes can extract from the producers within the formation is limited, owing to the less advanced level of development of the productive forces, to difficult natural conditions, or to successful resistance by the village community. In these cases, long-distance trade makes possible, through the monopoly profit it permits, the transfer of part of the surplus from one society to another. For the society that benefits from such a transfer the latter may be vital, forming the main foundation of the wealth and power of its ruling classes. The civilization in question may depend entirely upon this trade, and a shift in trade routes may cause a whole region to fall into decline, or, contrariwise, may provide conditions for it to flourish without any significant advance or regression of the productive forces having occurred.

Analysis of a concrete social formation must therefore be organized around an analysis of the way in which the surplus is generated in this formation, the transfers of surplus that may be effected from or to other formations, and the internal distribution of this surplus among the various recipients (classes and social groups). The very condition of existence of a class-divided formation is that the development of the productive forces (and so the degree of division of labor accompanying it) shall be sufficient for a "surplus" to appear — in other words, an excess of production over the consumption needed in order to ensure the reconstitution of the labor force. This concept of "surplus" assumes different forms in different modes of production — noncommodity forms such as tribute, rent in kind, etc., or commodity forms. In the latter case the term "surplus value" is employed. Under the capitalist mode of production "profit" is the specific form assumed by surplus value when it is distributed in proportion to capital invested. Since a social formation is an organized complex involving several modes of production, the surplus generated in this formation is not homogeneous but is the sum of surpluses of differing origin. It is essential to know, in relation to any particular formation, what the predominant mode of production is, and thus the predominant form of the surplus. Then we need to know the extent to which the given society lives on the surplus that it produces for itself and the extent to which it depends on surplus transferred from another society (in other words, what is the relative importance of long-distance trade?). The distribution of this surplus among social classes that are defined in relation to the different modes of production characteristic of the formation, and the social groups whose existence is related to the ways in which these modes of production are linked together, provides us with the true "face" of the formation concerned.

Thus, analysis of a concrete formation demands that we discover how one mode of production predominates over the others, and how these modes of production are interconnected.

The family of formations that is most widespread in the history of precapitalist civilizations is that of the formations in which the tribute-paying mode predominates. On emerging from primitive communism, communities evolve toward hierarchical forms. It is this evolution that gives rise to the tribute-paying mode of production. The slaveowning and simple commodity modes are linked with the dominant tribute-paying mode, and occupy in the given society a place that is of greater or lesser importance depending on the relative importance of the surplus extracted in the form of tribute. If the natural and social conditions (the degree of development of the productive forces) are favorable, the tribute is large. The state-class that levies it, the royal court, redistributes a considerable proportion of it by providing a living for the craftsmen who supply it with the luxury goods it consumes. These craftsmen are often petty-commodity producers. Craft production may also be organized in enterprises in which the workers are slaves or free wage earners and which produce commodities. A class of merchants inserts itself between the state, the village communities, the craftsmen, and the entrepreneurs (whether slaveowners or not), and organizes these trade circuits. The linking of these secondary modes of production to the dominant tribute-paying mode has thus to be analyzed (as was done by François Quesnay) in terms of the circulation of the original surplus, to which is added the possible generation of secondary surpluses (in the case of enterprises in which the workers are slaves or wage earners). To this circulation of the surplus may also be added a surplus transferred from outside, if long-distance trade exists and is dominated by the merchants of the formation being considered. In a case where the tribute of internal origin is not great, a tribute-paying society may be expected to be poor: it may, however, be rich if the surplus of external origin from which it benefits is substantial. This is what happens with societies based on control over long-distance trade circuits. The existence and prosperity of such a society depends on monopoly control over the relations that other formations (in which an original surplus is generated and then transferred) maintain with each other through the mediation of this society. Here we have formations of the kind that may be called "tribute-paying and trading" formations. The relations can even be reversed: at the level of the formation the transferred surplus feeds the sec-

ondary circuits (of simple commodity production, etc.), and a tribute may be levied on this transferred surplus by the dominant
state-class.

The first subfamily of tribute-paying formations, that of the
rich tribute-paying formations (based on a large internal surplus),
is the one that embraces all the great, long-lasting civilizations,
especially Egypt and China. The second subfamily, that of the
poor tribute-paying formations (characterized by a small internal
surplus), embraces the bulk of the civilizations of Antiquity and
the Middle Ages. The third, the subfamily of the tribute-paying
and trading formations, appears here and there for periods of varying duration, depending on the vicissitudes of trade routes: ancient
Greece, the Arab world at its apogee, and some states of the Black
African savannah are the most striking examples.

In comparison with this group of formations, predominantly of
the tribute-paying type (with the tribute-paying and trading type
as a marginal case), the formations in which slaveowning and
simple commodity modes predominate appear as exceptions.

The type of formation in which the slaveowning mode is predominant is not universal and is practically nowhere found to be
at the origin of class differentiation. The slaveowning mode of
production acquires considerable scope only in connection with
the development of commodity exchange, in ancient Greece and
Rome. In Greece we find long-distance trade at the origin of
civilization. The profits of this trade made possible the organizing
of commodity production by slave labor, and this brought a shift
in the center of gravity of the formation. At first, the principal
surplus originated from outside; then, with the growth of slavery,
the internally produced surplus became increasingly important,
and some of the commodities produced by slaves came to be exported. Alexander's empire, and then its Roman successor, enlarged the geographical area in which this exceptional formation
prevailed. Its spread eastward, where it came up against solidly
established tribute-paying formations, proved difficult, and its center
of gravity shifted northward and westward to regions where the
tribute levied was smaller. Even in this imperial zone, in which
slavery, simple commodity production, and trade both internal
and external acquired exceptional dimensions, the communal mode

of production (in the West) and the tribute-paying mode (in the East) persisted. This formation's dependence on what lay outside it — its source of slaves — made it fragile. In comparison with the duration of the Egyptian and Chinese civilizations, the period covered by the Roman slaveowning civilization is brief. Out of the ruins of its destruction by the Barbarians a new tribute-paying formation emerged: that of feudal Europe.

Predominance of the simple commodity mode of production is even more exceptional. We find it only in New England between 1600 and 1750, in the South Africa of the Boers between 1600 and 1880, and in Australia and New Zealand from the beginning of white settlement to the rise of modern capitalism. These societies of small farmers and free craftsmen, where the simple commodity mode of production was not tacked on to tribute-paying or slave-owning modes but constituted the principal mode of social organization, would be inexplicable if one did not know that they were the by-product of the breakup of feudal relations in England (and, secondarily, in the Netherlands and France). The poor people proletarianized by this breakup emigrated, and the ideal model that they established in the new lands where they settled gave expression to this exceptional background. Such formations have a strong tendency to develop into full-fledged *capitalist* formations.

The concept of the social formation is thus indeed a historical concept. Technological progress — the level of development of the productive forces — is cumulative. As Darcy Ribeiro and Silva Michelena have shown, it takes place within the framework of a formation and enables us to mark the stages of history.

However, this historical sequence of formations is not unique. The principal, most common line of development shows us first a series of communal formations, then a series of tribute-paying ones. But this main line becomes relatively "blocked" in that technological progress may take place with the tribute-paying formation, even though slowly. A secondary, marginal line of development shows a succession of communal formations, and then of feudal formations (which are a borderline variety of the tribute-paying family) with a strong commodity element in them (slaveowning-commodity and/or nonslaveowning simple commodity), which testifies to the original, or in other words, peripheral, character of this line. Along this line, the development of the productive forces comes once more into conflict with social relations, and the formations of capitalism are the result.

The historical sequence of social formations, in contrast to the lack of sequence in the modes of production they combine, shows that it is absurd to draw any sort of analogy between identical modes of production integrated in formations belonging to different epochs — for example, between African or Roman slavery and that in nineteenth-century America.

Capitalist formations are all marked by the dominance of the capitalist mode of production. All products in these formations are commodities, whereas only products in which the surplus of earlier modes was incorporated could previously assume this form. In all the precapitalist modes, the means of subsistence were not objects of exchange (whence the description of "subsistence economies" applied to precapitalist formations) and the surplus was often transferred in other than commodity form (as tribute, or rent in kind). Moreover, whereas the precapitalist formations were marked by a stable coexistence of different modes, linked together and arranged hierarchically, the capitalist mode tends to become exclusive, destroying all the others. The condition, however, to which this tendency to exclusiveness is subject, is, as will be seen, that it be based on the widening and deepening of the internal market. This applies in the case of the central capitalist formations but not in that of the peripheral ones. In the latter, the capitalist mode, which is dominant, subjects the others and transforms them, depriving them of their distinctive functioning in order to subordinate them to its own, without, however, radically destroying them.

The predominance of the capitalist mode of production is also expressed on another plane. It constitutes a world system in which all the formations, central and peripheral alike, are arranged in a single system, organized and hierarchical. Thus, there are not two world markets, the capitalist and socialist, but only one, the capitalist world market, in which Eastern Europe participates marginally.

3. SOCIAL CLASSES:
THE ARTICULATION OF INSTANCES

Analysis of a social formation, which means clearing up the problems of the generation and circulation of the surplus within this formation, throws light on the question of "classes" and "social groups." Each class-divided mode of production determines a pair of classes that are both opposed and united in this mode: state-class and peasants in the tribute-paying mode, slaveowners and slaves in the slaveowning mode, feudal lords and serfs in the feudal mode, bourgeois and proletarians in the capitalist mode. Each of these classes is defined by the function it fulfils in production. This essential reference to the production process cannot be reduced to "ownership" of the means of production. The state-class in the tribute-paying mode does not own the land, which belongs to the community. The feudal lord enjoys only *dominium eminens* over the soil, with the community retaining the right to use it. But both the state-class and the feudal lord organize and plan production, and in this way "dominate" the production process. The communal and simple commodity modes of production each determine a class of producers, which is in fact a social class, that is, a group defined by reference to the production process: the class of those peasants belonging to the village community, and the class of free petty-commodity producers (peasants and craftsmen). By reference to the circulation process of the surplus, when this takes the commodity form one can define another class, the merchants. When the surplus does not circulate in commodity form, it is the dominant class of the given mode that assumes this function by levying tribute through the agents of the state-class or by requiring the peasants to pay rent in kind directly to their lord.

Since a formation is a group of modes of production, every society actually presents the picture of a complex group of more than two classes: feudal lords, serf-peasants, free peasants, commodity-producing craftsmen, and merchants in feudal Europe; imperial court and "gentry" officials, communal peasants, free petty craftsmen, wage-earning craftsmen employed by entrepreneurs to produce commodities, and merchants in imperial China; slave-owners and slaves, free or communal small peasants, and merchants in Classical Antiquity; bourgeois, proletarians, and petty-commodity producers in the modern capitalist world.

A society cannot be reduced to its infrastructure. The way the latter (in other words, its material life) is organized requires that certain political and ideological functions be carried out relevant to the dominant mode of production and the linking-together of the various modes that make up the given formation. These functions may be carried out directly by the classes that have been defined above, or else by social groups that are dependent upon them. The actual structure of the particular society will be strongly marked by these groups. The most important of them is the "bureaucracy," which ensures the operation of the state: it has a civil branch (tribute collectors, police, and judges), and other branches (military, religious, etc.). But a bureaucracy defined in this way must not be confused (even in a broad sense) with the state-class of the tribute-paying mode, or the "state bourgeoisie" of state capitalism. The bureaucracy does not fulfil functions of direct domination of the production process, whereas the state-class directs this process itself, planning and organizing production, as in China and Egypt. The same is true of state capitalism, in which the state bourgeoisie directs the enterprises, deciding what is to be produced and how. The internal struggles between "technocrats" and "bureaucrats" in Russia reflect this distinction.

This example of conflict between a class and the group that is supposed to be in its service shows that there is still another problem to be clarified, namely, that of the relations between the different "instances" of a mode of production. Since society cannot be reduced to its infrastructure, how are the relations defined between the latter (the economic instance) and the superstructure of society (the politico-ideological instance)? These relations are not the same in all modes of production. Of course, whatever the mode of production may be, the economic instance is the determining one in the last analysis, if we accept the fact that material life conditions all other aspects of social life — in other words, that the level of development of the productive forces, by determining the relative size of the surplus, conditions the level of civilization. Nevertheless, it is important to distinguish between this determination *in the last analysis* and the question of whether the economic or the politico-ideological instance is the dominant one in a given case.

In all precapitalist modes of production the generation and employment of the surplus are transparently obvious. The producers can therefore agree to levy from themselves this surplus that they produce, and know that they produce, only if they are "alienated," and believe such a levy to be necessary for the survival of the social and "natural" order. The politico-ideological instance thus necessarily assumes religious form and dominates social life. In cases of this kind, moreover, if the surplus levied is not used "correctly," that is, so as to maintain, reproduce, and develop the state and civilization, if it is "squandered" by plundering invaders or by a "bad king," the producers rise in revolt in order to impose a "just government," since natural order and divine laws have been violated. When the maintenance and development of this social order require that specific social groups, such as the civil or military bureaucracy, or the theocracy in the service of the tribute-levying state-class, shall function properly, then these groups occupy a central position in the political history of the given society. Empirical observers of this history who imagine that what they see is the outcome of ideological or political struggles are falling victim to the same alienation as the society that they are studying.

Under the capitalist mode of production, on the contrary, generation of the surplus takes place obscurely, opaquely. As Marx said, the main thing in *Capital* is its demonstration of how surplus value is transformed into profit. Narrow-minded "economists" have seen in this transformation a formal contradiction (the alleged contradiction between Volume I and Volume III of *Capital*). This simply shows that they are victims of economistic alienation. For the effect of the transformation shown by Marx is to cause the origin of profit in surplus value to vanish, and "capital," a social relation, to appear as a "thing" — the means of production in which this social power is embodied. This "thing" is endowed with supernatural power, being held to be "productive." The term "fetishism" that Marx applies to this process is highly appropriate. On the plane of appearances, under the capitalist mode, capital thus seems to be productive, just like labor. Wages seem to be the "fair" reward of labor (whereas in fact they represent the value of labor power), and profit to be compensation for "services" rendered by capital (risk, saving through abstinence, etc.). Society is no longer in control of the evolution of its material life: the latter appears as the result of "laws" that dominate it in the same way as physical, natural laws. "Economic laws" — supply and demand in relation to commodities, labor, capital, etc. — bear witness to this alienation. This is why "economic science" emerges as an ideology — the ideology of "universal harmonies" — reducing the "laws of society" to the status of laws of nature that are independent of social organization. While the economic instance is hidden in mystification, politics is demystified: it no longer takes the form of religion. The true religion of capitalist society is "economism," or, in everyday terms, the worship of money, the cult of consumption for its own sake without regard to needs. The entire crisis of present-day civilization lies here, insofar as this ideology shortens the time prospect of society, making it lose sight of its future. At the same time, politics becomes a domain where openly asserted rationality prevails. The social groups that carry out functions at the level of this instance are naturally and obviously in the service of society and never appear as its masters.

Analysis of the way the instances are linked together complements that of social formations. Taken together, these analyses enable us to understand the dynamic of classes and social groups. Empirical analysis detects social "categories" in numbers that are arbitrary: two (the "rich" and the "poor"), or three (adding the "in-betweens"), or fifteen or twenty (occupational categories, or income brackets). Taking this method to extremes, one arrives at one category per individual, thus conforming to the individualistic requirement of the ideology that takes the place of social science. The dynamic of society then becomes incomprehensible.

4. NATIONS AND ETHNIC GROUPS

Study of a social formation necessarily leads to consideration of the problem of the nation, of how to define the precisely outlined social group that constitutes a particular social formation. Conventional social science evades this problem, and the mystical foundation ascribed to the fact of nationality does not help us. Stalin confined this social reality to the modern capitalist world by laying down as one of the prerequisites for a nation's existence the presence of an integrated capitalist market. This formulation is unacceptable for it is clear that imperial China or ancient Egypt were not mere conglomerations of peoples but were in this regard quite different both from Barbarian Gaul or Germany and from civilized India.

I shall define two concepts: that of the "ethnic group" and that of the "nation." The former presupposes linguistic and cultural community and homogeneity of geographical territory; also, and above all, there is consciousness of this cultural homogeneity, even if this be imperfect, with dialects or religious cults differing between one "province" and another. The nation presupposes the ethnic group but goes beyond this. According to Saad Zahran, the nation appears when, over and above the features mentioned, a social class, controlling the central state machinery, ensures economic unity of the community's life — that is, when the organization by this dominant class of the generation, the circulation, and the distribution of the surplus, welds together into one the fates of the various provinces.

Thus in regions where control of irrigation necessitates administrative centralization and planning of production on a country-wide scale, the dominant state-class transforms an empire into a nation if it is already homogeneous. The case of China (despite that country's pronounced regional variations) and, even better, that of Egypt are the most cogent. If the condition of ethnic homogeneity is not fulfilled, or that of economic unity, then what we see is an empire, not a nation — as in India.

This state-class is not the only precapitalist class present at the origin of the national phenomenon. The class of merchants in tribute-paying and trading formations, or slaveowning and trading ones, may fulfill the same function. Unity is brought about in these cases through circulation of the surplus that this class controls. Ancient Greece or the Arab world constitute examples of nations of this type. In Greece we see a nation despite the lack of a central political authority, which existed only embryonically, expressed in the confederacies and alliances between the Greek cities. In the Arab world, ethnic homogeneity, that is, common language and culture (though with some minority enclaves inside the national empire), was reinforced by economic unity, manifested in the great days of that world through the circulation of goods, ideas, and men, under the leadership of the ruling class of merchants and the military courts, which formed a single class of merchant-warriors. An Arab nation did indeed come into existence.

Nations founded in this way upon the merchant class are unstable when the tribute-paying substratum is unstable. This is why it can be said that if the nation is a social phenomenon that can appear at any stage of history and is not necessarily associated with the capitalist mode of production, the national phenomenon is reversible; it can flourish or it can disappear, depending on whether the unifying class strengthens its power or loses it. In the latter case the given society regresses to become a conglomeration of ethnic groups that may become increasingly differentiated. Here, too, the case of the Arab world is illuminating. Because the bulk of the surplus came from the profits of long-distance trade and was not generated inside the society itself, the vicissitudes of this surplus proved to be those also of Arab civilization and the Arab nation. The decay of trade entailed that of the class of merchant-warriors. A series of major historical events marked the stages in this national regression: the Crusades and the transfer of the center of gravity of trade from the Arab cities to those of Italy; the fall of Baghdad under the blows of the Mongols in the thirteenth century; then the Ottoman conquest in the sixteenth century, with the transfer of trade from the Mediterranean to the Atlantic in the same period and, correlatively, the direct contact established by Europe with Monsoon Asia and Black Africa, which deprived the Arabs of their role as middlemen.

Similar phenomena are found in Black Africa. Throughout the savannah country along the southern edge of the Sahara, tribute-paying and trading formations underlay the great historical states of Ghana, Mali and Songhay, and the Hausa cities. Here was at least an embryonic stage of national development. But all of these formations were soon undone by the ending of trans-Sahara trade and the growth of the slave trade across the Atlantic.

The disappearance of the Arab nation gave back life to the nation that was able to live exclusively by the internal generation of a substantial surplus, namely, the eternal Egyptian nation. The social class in control of the rebirth of the Egyptian nation was the bureaucratic landowning aristocracy. In the eighteenth century, with Ali Bey, but especially in the nineteenth, with Mehemet Ali, this state-class resumed the functions of directing and planning the economy and organizing the circulation of the surplus it levied; in other words, it renewed its control over the forms of the nation's economic unity.

Elsewhere in the Arab world — in Morocco and Tunisia from the fifteenth century onward, in Algeria with Abdel Kader, in the nineteenth in the Sudan with Mahdism, in the Yemen or in the Lebanon — attempts to form nations did not get very far, in some cases because they fell beneath the blows of foreign intervention (in Algeria and the Sudan, for example), but mainly because the level of development of the local productive forces did not make possible the extraction of a surplus adequate to support a class that might undertake the constituting of a nation. The destiny of that class depended upon its capacity to acquire through large-scale trade a surplus of external origin — hence upon circumstances outside the given society. This surplus, amounting to very little, did not necessitate economic unification; it circulated to only a slight extent, and each of these societies remained a conglomerate of regions that were not sufficiently integrated to form a nation.

The same reason prevented the African states lying south of the Sahara from surviving, even as embryonic nations, after the disappearance of the Saharan trade.

The formations of feudal Europe did not become nations either. Here the internal surplus was relatively large, but it hardly circulated at all outside the limits of the fief where it originated, at least during the early Middle Ages. From the thirteenth century onward, however, and especially in and after the sixteenth century, in Atlantic Europe (England, France, Spain, and Portugal), long-distance trade increased the amount of the surplus by adding to it transferred values of external origin. Rent in kind yielded place to money rent, and this stimulated a prosperous simple commodity production by craftsmen, which added its effects to those of long-distance trade. The absolute monarchies of the four countries mentioned centralized an increasing proportion of the surplus, ensured its circulation with the aid of the merchants of the mercantilist era, and gathered together the lands of their realms to form nations.

While the nation is certainly older than capitalism, the capitalist mode of production thus plays, nevertheless, a considerable role in its development. The degree of economic centralization is brought, under this mode of production, to a level higher than before, as all production, and no longer merely the surplus, becomes commodity production. Labor power itself becomes a commodity, and this, through internal migration, causes the population to become more closely integrated. Capital in commodity form brings about integration of the market, with a centralized currency system and the circulation of wealth.

The existence of a nation thus implies that the dominant class can aspire to national hegemony within the given society, that it has taken shape as a class integrated on the national scale, with organization and hierarchy at that level, in contrast to those dominant classes that are made up of independent equals in juxtaposition. This integration has been seen in history as the state-class of the rich tribute-paying systems; in exceptional cases it has occurred in the merchant class in periods of great prosperity of the societies it has dominated; and, above all, it has happened to the bourgeoisie — at least in the central formations of capitalism.

5. LONG-DISTANCE TRADE AND THE BREAKUP OF FEUDAL RELATIONS

In the debate about the origins of capitalism two schools confront each other. For one of these, capitalism was born of the effects of the great discoveries of the sixteenth century and the Atlantic trade; for the other it was born of the breakup of feudal relations.

Actually, the conditions needed for the development of capitalism are essentially two in number: proletarianization and the accumulation of money-capital. While accumulation of money-capital occurred in all the trading societies of the East, of Antiquity, and of the feudal world, it never led to the development of capitalist relations, because a supply of free and available labor power was lacking. This process of proletarianization — that is, in practical terms, the exclusion from the village community of part of the rural population — is explained, so far as Europe is concerned, by the breakup of feudal relations. But these two conditions must *both* be present, and it is the absence of this conjunction that forbids us to speak of "capitalism in the Ancient World," or "capitalism in the Oriental Empires."

The expression "mercantilist capitalism" used to describe the period of Europe's history between the Renaissance and the Industrial Revolution (1600-1800) is perhaps responsible for many errors in analysis. It is an ambiguous expression, for this period was in reality one of transition. After the event, we can now see that it was transition *to capitalism*. But until the Industrial Revolution the capitalist mode of production did not yet really exist. The period in question was marked by: (1) the continued predominance of the feudal mode of production within the formations of that time; (2) the flourishing of long-distance trade (mainly the Atlantic trade); (3) the effect of this latter development upon the feudal mode of production, which disintegrated. It was this third feature alone that made the period one of transition. And it was because the feudal mode is a particular form of the tribute-paying mode that long-distance trade could cause it to disintegrate.

Money and trade are, of course, older than capitalism. They appeared as soon as the producers had a surplus available and when division of labor made possible exchange of the products in which this surplus was incorporated. But not all exchanges are commodity exchanges: in precapitalist times the bulk of the exchanges effected between petty producers (whether grouped in communities or independent) within a single society (peasants and craftsmen in the same village) took place without any specialized trader as intermediary, and often even without money playing any role.

However, as soon as a substantial part of the surplus had become centralized in the hands of powerful privileged classes (feudal lords, kings' courts, etc.), this could be used for long-distance trade — usually for exchange against luxury products originating in other societies. A merchant go-between then exploited his monopoly position to profit by his services in bringing different societies into contact. The profit he made, however, based upon the difference in subjective values (social utilities), evaluated unequally in two societies that were ignorant of each other — that is, societies exchanging scarce products without knowing their respective social costs of production — must not be confused with the profit made by (the return on) commercial capital.

Only under the capitalist mode of production does trade become a capitalistic activity like industrial production and, consequently, does commercial capital appear as a fraction of total capital. Thenceforth, commercial capital participates in the general equalization of profit. Commercial capital's profit thus arises from the redistribution of the surplus value generated within a formation, from the transformation of this surplus value in its specific form as profit on capital. The precapitalist merchant drew *his* profit from his possession of a monopoly. In long-distance trade this monopoly made it possible to transfer a surplus from one society to another. It was precisely because what was involved was a monopoly that this function was so often carried out by distinct social strata — specific castes or ethnic groups ("people-classes") that were specialized in this activity, like the Jews in medieval Europe or the Dioula in West Africa. Cities might constitute societies that fulfilled this function of intermediary between different formations more or less distant from each other: the Phoenician and Greek cities, those of Italy between the twelfth and sixteenth centuries, the Hansa towns, etc. When the merchants were not grouped in independent cities or in castes, or differentiated ethnically or by religion, they organized themselves into closed groups like the "merchant adventurers" in Europe or the corporations that existed in China.

This monopoly was the completer in proportion to the distance over which the trade was carried on and to the rarity of the goods involved. If there were commodity exchanges within the formation that were effected through specialized traders, the latter also tended to organize themselves in monopolies, but these were precarious, and failed to bring in the enormous profits obtainable through long-distance trade.

This trade always brought about a concentration of wealth in money form. But such concentration was not capitalism. Insofar as conventional historiography has confused money with capital, and trade with capitalism, it has discovered capitalism everywhere — in ancient China, among the Phoenicians, the Greeks, the Romans, the Arabs of the Middle Ages, and so on. Then the question arises: why did only "European capitalism" come to anything? And, to answer it, religion is invoked (Max Weber and the Protestant ethic), or else race (the specific qualities of democracy among the Germanic peoples, or more subtly, Europe's "Greek heritage").

In reality the concentration of money-wealth in the hands of merchants did not automatically lead to capitalism. For that to happen there was also needed a breakup of the dominant precapitalist mode in the formation to which the effects of long-distance trade had been added — a breakup such as to result in the proletarianization, that is, separation of the producers from their means of production so that the way to a free labor market was opened. This breakup took place in Europe but not in China or in the Arab world or anywhere else. Why and how was this so?

In order to answer the first of these questions we need to look more closely at the specific character of the feudal mode of production. Because Barbarian Europe was backward in relation to the areas of ancient civilization, a full-fledged tribute-paying mode of production did not become established there: feudalism took shape as an embryonic, incomplete form of this mode. The absence of a strong central authority to centralize the surplus left more direct power over the peasants to the local feudal lords. *Dominium eminens* over the soil became theirs, whereas in the fully developed tribute-paying system of the great civilizations, the state protected the village communities. In those civilizations it was only during periods of decline, when the central authority weakened, that society became feudalized, and this feudalization appeared as a regression, a deviation from the ideal model: peasant revolts re-established the tribute-paying system by reconstituting state centralization through destroying the feudal lords, thus putting an end to their "abuses."

The backward nature of feudal society also implied that the commercial sectors possessed greater independence. The peasants who fled from feudal tyranny, and later those whom the lords themselves evicted in order to modernize the organization of production, formed in the free cities a proletariat that was at the disposal of the merchants who controlled these cities. Commodity production by free craftsmen and by wage labor developed, both being dominated by the merchants.

The latter were able, therefore, to do more in the field of long-distance trade than their equivalents in the tribute-paying formations had achieved. From the sixteenth century onward, the Atlantic trade in America led to the creation of a periphery for the new mercantilist system. The trade no longer consisted merely in collecting the products that the local societies could offer; these societies were directly subjugated so that they might be organized to produce goods for sale in Europe. The merchants were accorded, in carrying out this aim, the backing of the nascent centralized monarchies, whose ambitions they supported, facilitating, through the financial possibilities their prosperity brought with it, the recruitment of professional armies and administrative centralization.

The influx of new wealth arising from this trade, based as it was upon dependent producers in America, had an effect in turn upon the feudal sectors of the formation, hastening the breakup of feudal relations. In order to obtain the new goods, the feudal lords were obliged to modernize their methods of exploitation, extracting a larger surplus and converting this into money. This modernization led them to drive off the land the excess population, as happened in the English enclosures. Rent in kind was gradually replaced by money rent.

Feudal agriculture evolved into capitalist agriculture, either by the feudal lords themselves becoming capitalist landowners or by the emancipation of the peasantry, enabling a new "kulak" class to arise.

All these important social phenomena taken together seem to confirm the view that it was the internal evolution of European rural society that gave rise to capitalism, without the Atlantic trade playing a decisive part in the process.

In order to understand the nature of these changes it is necessary to show, following P.-P. Rey, how the capitalist formations integrated property in land while transforming its significance. The capitalist mode of production in its pure form implies only two classes, bourgeois and proletarians, and the two corresponding forms of income, profit on capital and wages of labor — just as the feudal mode implies only two classes, landlords and working peasants, with two corresponding forms of income, rent and what the peasant keeps for himself. But the laws that determine how the elements of the social product are generated and distributed are not the same for these two modes of production. Profit presupposes capital, in other words, private appropriation of means of production that are themselves products of social labor; whereas rent is derived from exclusive control by one particular class of natural resources that are not products of social labor. Capital presupposes wage labor, in other words free labor, a labor market, the sale of labor power. Rent, on the contrary, presupposes a lack of freedom on the part of the working peasant, the fact that he is "bound to the soil" — which does not necessarily take the form of a legal restriction upon his freedom but more generally implies that he still has access to the land. Capital is essentially mobile, and Marx deduces from this the transformation of value into price of production, which ensures equal rewards for individual capitals, whereas the appropriation of natural resources is essentially static, and rent varies as between one piece of land and another. The capitalist mode of production in its pure form thus presupposes free access by the capitalists to natural resources, and Marx emphasizes (e.g., in his *Critique of the Gotha Programme*) the noncapitalist character of property in land. However, the capitalist formations have not developed in a vacuum, or out of nothing — they have taken shape first of all inside previously existing formations, in new (industrial) sectors that were not governed by the characteristic relationships of the earlier modes. Subsequently, when capitalism became dominant in the formation as a whole, it completed the transformation of agriculture, in which the ownership of land constituted a hindrance to it. Thereafter, the land-owner (or the function he fulfilled) ceased to play a determining role in agriculture, his place being taken by the capitalist farmer (or by the latter's function, when the landowner took this upon himself). In advanced capitalist formations there are no longer any "landowners" in the feudal, precapitalist sense of the term, but only agrarian capitalists.

Thus, the two elements — long-distance trade and the breakup of feudal relations — interacted with each other so as to engender the capitalist mode of production. The concentration of money-wealth at one pole created potential capital: it took place first among the merchants, then among the new rural capitalists. But this potential capital became real capital only because the breakup of feudal relations released a supply of labor power and proletar-ianized the peasantry. The latter became wage workers in the em-ployment of the new industrialists or of the capitalist landowners and farmers of the countryside.

6. THE BLOCKING OF THE DEVELOPMENT OF THE TRADING FORMATIONS: THE ARAB WORLD AND BLACK AFRICA

The significance of the process of interaction between long-distance trade and the breakup of precapitalist relations is more easily perceived if we compare the way Europe evolved with what happened to the other precapitalist formations.

The Arab world offers us the case of a formation in which long-distance trade played an exceptionally important role but that failed to develop an indigenous capitalism. Why was this?

The Arab world extends over several thousand miles of the semiarid borderland that stretches like a belt across the Old World, between the Atlantic and Monsoon Asia. It occupies in this region a zone that is separated from Europe by the Mediterranean, from Black Africa by the Sahara, and from the Turkish and Persian "worlds" by the mountain ranges of the Taurus, Kurdistan, and western Iran. It is not identical with the Islamic world, which, broadly speaking, occupies the whole of this semiarid belt and is divided between four groups of peoples — the Arabs, the Turks, the Persians, and the Indo-Afghans. This Islamic world has only marginally overflowed into Monsoon Asia (Bengal, Indonesia) and, in more recent times, into some parts of Black Africa (the West African savannah, and the East coast). The Arab world is not to be seen as an ethnoracial phenomenon, for the process of Arabization has mixed together a wide variety of peoples. The Arab world constituted a relatively centralized political entity for only a short period of its history, a mere two centuries, and during that period (the age of the Omayyads and the first Abbasids, between 750 and 950), linguistic unity was a great deal less advanced than it is today. The Arab world then broke up into comparatively stable regional political entities, which were not brought together again (and then only superficially) until they were subjected to the Ottoman yoke, that is, to a foreign ruler.

As regards the structures of their precolonial social formations, the Arab countries did not constitute a homogeneous whole. The Arab world was very different from medieval Europe. It was always divided into three zones that were very dissimilar in social structure and in political and economic organization: the East (*al Mashraq*), embracing Arabia, Syria (i.e., the present states of Syria, Lebanon, Jordan, and Israel), and Iraq; the Nile lands (Egypt and the Sudan); and the West (*al Maghreb*), extending from Libya to the Atlantic and embracing the modern countries of Libya, Tunisia, Algeria, Morocco, and Mauritania. In the whole region, Egypt alone, which divides the Arab world in two, has always been a peasant civilization. Elsewhere in this semiarid zone agricultural activity is always precarious and the surplus that can be levied from the agriculturists is on the whole very meager. Techniques of agricultural production are necessarily not very advanced, the productivity of agricultural labor is low, the standard of living of the agricultural community is close to subsistence level, and consequently the forms of social organization inevitably bear the mark of primitive collectivism. There is no sufficient basis for a surplus to be levied on a scale that would make possible a feudal class structure or even a brilliant civilization.

And yet the Mashraq (especially, but the Maghreb as well, although to a lesser extent) has been the scene of rich civilizations that, moreover, were definitely urban in character. How could this "miracle" have occurred? How are we to explain this apparent anomaly that wealthy Egypt, the only large oasis in this arid zone, has always been a peasant country, with comparatively little urban development until the modern period, even in the great ages of its ancient civilization, whereas the Mashraq, which has known equally brilliant epochs in its history, has always been an area of great cities?

In order to understand this, we must see the Arab world in its true context, as a great zone of passage, a sort of turntable between the major areas of civilization in the Old World. This semiarid zone separates three zones of agrarian civilization: Europe, Black Africa, Monsoon Asia. It has therefore always fulfilled a commercial function, bringing into contact, through its role as the only middleman, agricultural communities that had no direct awareness of each other. The social formations on the basis of which the Arab world's civilizations were erected were always commercial in character. This means that the surplus on which the cities lived was drawn in the main not from exploitation of the area's own rural inhabitants but from the profits of the long-distance trading activity that its monopoly role as intermediary ensured to it — that is, an income derived in the last analysis from the surpluses extracted from their peasantries by the ruling classes of the *other* civilizations.

This pattern of a trading formation was characteristic of the Mashraq down to the First World War. Thereafter, the integration of the region into the imperialist sphere, which had begun only superficially in the Ottoman period, brought about decisive changes in the class structure of Iraq but only minor ones in Syria and Palestine. At the other end of the Arab world, in the Maghreb, this pattern of society remained characteristic until the French colonial conquest. That colonization, which began earlier and went deeper than that to which the Mashraq was subjected, brought about decisive changes in the Maghreb of modern times. Between the two regions, Egypt continued to be the exception, as a tribute-paying peasant formation well integrated into the world capitalist system.

Islam was born in Arabia, in the desert, among a population of nomads who were organized to carry on large-scale trade between the Eastern Roman Empire and Persia on the one hand and South Arabia, Ethiopia, and India on the other. It was the profits obtained from this trade that made possible the existence of the urban merchant republics of the Hejaz. The domination exercised by these towns over the small rural oasis areas around them, which they exploited on a semiserf basis, was not at all the main source of income for the ruling merchant classes. As for the pastoral subsistence economy of the nomads, this existed side by side with the commercial activity, for which it supplied men and animals but to which it contributed no surplus. The desert civilization thus presupposed the civilizations of the Eastern Roman Empire and Monsoon Asia, which it linked together. If, for one reason or another, the surplus that fed the springs of the long-distance trade dried up or the trade routes shifted, the desert would die. This happened more than once in the course of history, and on each occasion the men of the desert endeavored to survive by becoming conquerors.

The first part of the "civilized world" to be conquered by the Arabs was the Fertile Crescent — the lands of Syria and Iraq, along the northern edge of the Arabian Desert. There the Arabs were in familiar territory, for the societies of the Ancient East had been very largely commercial communities of the same type as their own. There were, to be sure, some peasants in this semiarid zone, whereas there were hardly any to the south of it. But these were mountain peasants, clinging to the hillsides of the mountains of the Lebanon, the Jebel Ansariya, the Taurus, and Kurdistan, where the rainfall was just enough for them to be able to survive. These rural areas were too poor — despite the epithet "fertile" — to supply the surplus needed to support a brilliant civilization. They had therefore remained "primitive," organized in village communities and comparatively isolated, jealously defending their independence. Civilization had developed at the edges of the region in two exceptional areas: Mesopotamia and the Mediterranean coast. Mesopotamia had seen the development of the first genuine agricultural civilization thanks to the exceptional natural conditions provided by the Tigris and the Euphrates. An organization arose there that was similar to Egypt's, based upon the surplus levied by the cities from the neighboring countryside. Like all agricultural civilizations situated at the edge of deserts, it lived under the constant threat of destruction by the Barbarians. It was, indeed, crushed by the Turco-Mongol invasions of the tenth and eleventh centuries and was reborn only after 1918, under the aegis of the *Pax Britannica*. To the west, beside the sea, since the agricultural miracle was not possible, the city-states of Phoenicia and Syria never obtained their resources elsewhere than from long-distance trade, carried by ship or by caravan. The Arabs who had come out of the desert thus found themselves quite at home here, and by establishing their new capital, that of the Omayyad dynasty at Damascus, they transferred northward the trading civilization of Medina. Having in this way regained control of their trade routes, they once more enjoyed the profits of large-scale trade and revived their civilization.

The unity of the Fertile Crescent was not really disrupted until after the First World War. But it was always a unity in diversity: a diversity, however, that was never "cultural," still less, ethnic. The intermingling of peoples goes back so far in this region that it is futile to try to contrast one people with another on so fragile a basis. What is characteristic of a zone of civilization of this type, the essence of which is its commercial function of putting in touch two zones that it separates, is that it is dialectically both unifying and dismembering. It is unifying because it causes men to move around ceaselessly so that customs and religions are passed on and a travelers' *lingua franca* becomes the predominant speech. It is dismembering because it is based on competition between rival mercantile cities. The detailed course of events is not the main thing here: what is significant is the presence or absence of a single formal political authority. If such an authority is strong, it will, of course, set limits to the competition between the cities, often ensuring a pre-eminent position for the capital. Such was the state of the Omayyads, centered at Damascus, and then that of the Abbasids, centered at Baghdad. In order to maintain its rule, the state had to have at its disposal an army of mercenaries recruited from among the neighboring nomads. As for the peasants, they strove to remain isolated in their mountains and fell into semiservile dependence upon landlords, always town-dwelling absentees (merchants, courtiers, etc.) in areas near the cities — or, by way of exception, in Lower Iraq, which was organized into commodity-producing, slave-worked plantations of the "Roman" type. For twelve centuries, between 700 and 1900, the Fertile Crescent was thus both unified and divided, experiencing a succession of brilliant periods and periods of decadence, depending on the fate of the trade routes linking Byzantine and Western Europe with India and China.

The Fertile Crescent soon became Arabized. Already on the eve of the Islamic invasion, when it was Christian, it was unified linguistically through the triumph of the Aramaic tongue. Being itself a Semitic language, Aramaic could give way without difficulty to Arabic. The region's linguistic unity has been practically complete for centuries, if we do not treat as different languages ways of speech that differ only in accent and in a few colloquialisms. A very pure form of Arabic is spoken here, and from Jerusalem to the borders of Turkey the same "Syrian" accent is characteristic. Palestine is a fragment of this Mashraq, nothing more.

But the profound cultural unity of the Mashraq does not imply the absence of diversity, as between the various cities and the various little rural areas. The country districts have been isolated from each other for twelve centuries, and of little weight either economically or politically. They have resisted in arms and with religious dissidence the attempts of imperial authority to subject them. Thus, in the Mashraq, the only truly rural areas are all nonconformist in religion: the mountains of the Lebanon, divided between Maronite Christians and Shi'ite Moslems; the Jebel Ansariya, home of the Alaouites, and the Jebel-Druse, in Syria; and Lower Iraq, with its Shi'ite population. The Shi'a heresy, which divided the Moslem world very early on, found favorable soil in the free communities of the mountains. It developed in these conditions a much freer, more critical, and even egalitarian spirit than that of the "official" Sunni doctrine. This is likewise why it was the ideology of the peasant slaves who revolted in Lower Iraq (the Qarmathian rebellion).

We cannot speak of "feudalism" here, even if "semifeudal" forms did develop during periods when large-scale trade was in decline. In the flat country areas the townsmen could dominate more easily; they thus used to make up, by tribute extorted from the peasants, their loss of income from long-distance trade. The plains of the Bekaa, of Palestine, Homs, Hama, and Central Iraq were in this way sometimes brought under control by greedy landowners, especially during the Ottoman period (from 1500 onward), which was a long period of commercial decline. Much later, starting in the 1930s, the modern-style exploitation of agricultural areas, made possible by irrigation works, was to spread wider the zone occupied by latifundia.

What is essential here, however, is not the country but the town. Here were huge cities, truly of monstrous size when trade began to decline; they were among the most populous cities of Antiquity, the Middle Ages, and modern times before the capitalist period, being much more important than the cities of the West. Aleppo, Damascus, Baghdad, Basra, and Antioch had hundreds of thousands of inhabitants. In their best periods they embraced the majority of the population of the region, which exceeded five million inhabitants, a larger number than it was to contain at the beginning of the twentieth century. These were cities that were always centers of courts and merchants, with great numbers of craftsmen and clerks around them. They were merchant cities, like those of Italy, which echoed them in the medieval West, or like those of the Hanseatic League. The accumulation of wealth in these cities expressed the brilliance of their civilization. But this accumulation did not lead to capitalism, precisely because the country districts, isolated as they were, had not been "feudalized." Retaining thus their mercantile but not capitalist character, the cities of the Mashraq formed a set of little worlds competing with each other; the outlets for their very advanced craft production were the distant markets to which their merchants traveled. The cultural unity of this dominant urban world was pronounced. These cities were centers of Arabo-Islamic culture, citadels of Sunni orthodoxy.

At the other extremity of the Arab world, in the Maghreb, the same structures were to be found. There nomads and cultivators had struggled since time immemorial for possession of a narrow strip of territory squeezed between the sea, the mountains, and the great desert. The *Pax Romana*, by setting up a series of fortified posts all long the *limes*, the imperial frontier, had pushed further south the zone of the Berber cultivators, who encroached upon the lands over which roamed the nomads and seminomads who were also Berbers. Already before the coming of the Arabs, the decline of the Roman Empire had enabled the nomads to recover some of their territory from the cultivators.

When the Arabs arrived, they encountered among the agricultural population of the mountainous areas the same resistance that others had experienced before them. They, however, skirted these massifs and established cities in the plains. These cities, as in the East, could not have survived and prospered if they had not found in large-scale, long-distance trade the resources that were denied them by the difficulty of extracting surplus from the cultivators. The search for income from trade led the Arabs farther and farther afield, across the Mediterranean and across the Sahara, too. Toward the south they encountered Berber nomads who had the same interest as themselves, that of becoming the caravaneers of a flourishing commerce. These Berbers became Arabized much more quickly than the peasants, who had little interest in the urban civilization of the Arabs. Ibn Khaldun gave a perfect analysis of the nature of these social formations of the medieval Maghreb. With an intelligence and exactitude that might be envied by many historians and sociologists of the Arab world today, he analyzed these formations as being based not on a surplus levied from the peasants of the region but on the profits of large-scale trade. It was in this way that all the great states of the Maghreb were founded upon the trade in gold, the gold in question coming from West Africa. For centuries and until the discovery of America, West Africa was the chief supplier of the yellow metal to all the western part of the Old World — to the Roman Empire, to medieval Europe, to the Ancient East, and to the Arab world. This trade in gold nourished to the north of the Sahara the states of the Almoravides, the Almohades, and others, and to the south of the great desert the states of Ghana, Mali, and Songhay. The structures of these social formations were so alike that Ibn Khaldun, with the Arab travelers of the time (Ibn Batuta, for example), assimilated them all to the same pattern.

Alliance between the cities and the nomads, together with exclusion of the peasantry from the civilized state, are characteristic features of the civilization of the Maghreb, as of the Fertile Crescent. Ideologists of the French colonization of the Maghreb sought to explain these features in terms of the conflict between races — Berber peasants against Arab nomads — and to account for the decline of the Maghreb by the ravages of the Arab nomads, who had destroyed agriculture and the works that made it possible. Similar explanations have been given in relation to the Arab East, where decline was also ascribed to the devastation wrought by nomads. However, one observes that the brilliant ages of Arab civilization, in the East as in the Maghreb, were not marked by great achievements in the agricultural field but by the prosperity of trade and the cities, and often, in connection with the prosperity of trade, by the rule of great nomadic tribes to the detriment of the peasantry, who never counted for much in those parts.

Decline came to the Maghreb with the shifting of the trade routes. As these were displaced from West to East, we note a corresponding shift in the centers of civilization, both to the north of the Sahara and to the south of it. Thus, in the earliest period there were the states of Morocco in the north and Ghana and Mali in the south; later, the gold routes shifted toward Tunis, and later still toward Egypt, while the south saw the flowering of the Songhay and Hausa states. And in the Maghreb the peasant redoubts upheld their autonomy by clinging to the Berber language and culture, just as in the Arab East, having been Arabized so far as language was concerned, they sought to maintain their autonomy through religious dissidence.

Egypt's history was quite different. From one of the oldest peasant peoples in the world a huge surplus could be tapped by the ruling classes, thus providing the basis for civilization. State centralization imposed itself early here, and in an extreme form, both for "natural" reasons (the need to organize large-scale irrigation works) and in order to protect the Egyptian oasis against the danger from the nomads. In order to survive, Egypt has always tried to live retired within itself, relying on numbers to beat back the onslaughts of the nomads. When Egypt conquered territory outside the Nile valley, the motive was to better defend its peasant civilization by installing garrisons in the heart of the lands of the nomads and seminomads — to the east in Sinai and Syria, to the west in Libya. In Egypt, however, there were never, until the

Hellenistic period, any really great trading cities. The capitals of the Pharaohs were set up in the midst of the fields, in the densely populated countryside.

The very type of the traditional social formation in Egypt was thus constituted on foundations that were quite different from those of the Mashraq and the Maghreb. The peasant redoubts of both of the latter were autonomous, not much integrated into civilization, and with a very low level of development of the productive forces. The Mashraq and the Maghreb also remained to a large extent organized in village communities. The Egyptian peasantry left that stage behind them over four thousand years ago. The Egyptian formation was not of the type in which the towns and the merchants are predominant, but of the rural type, with a tribute-paying peasantry. This tribute-paying formation, in which the peasants are not oppressed in groups retaining the relative autonomy of their village community but individually, in small family units, thus evolves on its own toward a form of genuine feudalism. The latter, which I would prefer to call a developed tribute-paying formation, and which resembles that of China, differs from the feudalism of the West only in its state centralization, the ruling class that levies the surplus being strongly organized in a state.

After Alexander's invasion Egypt became a province, forming part of empires based on large-scale trade: this was its situation in the Hellenistic world, then in the Byzantine world, and eventually in the Arab world. During the brilliant periods of these empires, when long-distance trade was flourishing, Egypt experienced mercantile urban civilization. But this civilization remained something "foreign," established in cities of courts and merchants that did not really become Egyptianized until the long-distance trade by which they lived began to decline. Such was Alexandria in the Greek period, Fostat, and later Cairo, in the Arab period. The world of rural Egypt remained outside all that. So far as it was concerned, the only change was that the surplus it had paid to the national ruling class around the Pharaoh was now paid to foreign courts.

Nevertheless, Egypt became Arabized in the matter of language. This happened belatedly, however, just when the trading empire of the Arabs was losing its *raison d'être*. The country had then to turn in upon itself once more, and the Arab ruling classes had to Egyptianize themselves, taking more interest in the peasants. The latter adopted Islam, though this happened slowly, and the Arabic language, also slowly (several centuries had to pass before the Coptic language disappeared). In becoming Arabized, however, the Egyptian people kept a very firm sense of their distinctness. They never called themselves "Arabs," a word that remained for them synonymous with "barbarians," but always "Egyptians." And Egypt has retained its originality, not on the linguistic plane but on that of culture and values, which in Egypt are peasant values.

Southward from Egypt, the Sudan belongs both to Black Africa and to the Arab world. In its northern part, nomadic Arab tribes who came from the East, from the shores of the Red Sea, and inter-married with the black natives of the area, established a civilization of nomadic stockbreeders. In addition, these nomads, who not only became Moslems but also adopted the Arabic language, functioned as trading middlemen between Egypt and the lands to the south. The central regions of the Sudan, however, retained their traditional agrarian civilization, based on the village clan community common to all Black Africa. By way of exception, these black peoples adopted the Arabic language, though elsewhere, in West Africa, similar groups merely adopted Islam without becoming Arabized. This Arabization was doubtless due to the prolonged and thorough ascendancy exercised by the Arab nomads of the north over these communities. Later, in the nineteenth century, the Egyptian conquests, from the time of Mehemet Ali (1810-1848) and the Khedives who succeeded him down to the British occupation (1882) and the revolt led by the Mahdi (1882-1898), superimposed upon this ascendancy the domination of the Egyptian military bureaucracy. Here, however, the subject Arabized black peasants retained down to our own day their autonomous village organization, long since forgotten in Egypt. Only very much later, in certain areas of colonial exploitation, during the British period, especially in the Gezireh, was a real agrarian capitalism created; the peasantry was prole-tarianized, and the system benefited the nomad chieftains to whom the colonial power granted the lands brought under cultivation by irrigation works. Altogether, it was a process similar to what went on in Iraq in the same period, that of the British Mandate, giving rise to an agrarian economy that was modern (capitalist) and alien to tradition, both African and Arab.

The southern part of the Arabian peninsula is made up of a group of social formations that truly belong to the Arab tradition. Agriculture never played a decisive part in the development of civilization here: except on the heights of the Yemen, where the monsoon rains enabled a peasant community to exist, even if under rather arduous conditions, civilization in this area was urban and mercantile. The maritime "empire" of Muscat and Zanzibar provides the very pattern of it: an urban trading state drawing its revenues from its role as intermediary between the Mediterranean world, the eastern shores of Black Africa, and India. Encircled by nomads in the service of the maritime traders, the peasants of the Yemen, like those of the Fertile Crescent, safeguarded a limited degree of autonomy by taking refuge in religious dissidence: like the Alaouites in Syria, they are Shi'ites.

This, then, is the Arab world: basically a commercial grouping, with Egypt as the only great "peasant" exception. In this world the ruling class is urban, made up of court officials, merchants, religious leaders, and around them that little world of craftsmen and petty clerks that is typical of Eastern cities. The ruling class is the cement that binds the whole grouping together: everywhere it shares the same language and the same profoundly Islamic culture, which, moreover, is orthodox (Sunni). This class is highly mobile, being able to move from Tangier to Damascus without ceasing in the slightest to feel at home. It is this class that has created "Arab civilization." Its prosperity is bound up with that of long-distance trade. The latter is the basis of its alliance with the nomadic tribes, its caravan escorts. This explains the isolation of the agricultural areas, which retain personalities of their own, either linguistic (Berber) or religious (Shi'a), but play no important part in the civilization of the Arab world. Except in Egypt, the peasantry enters little into the system and is subjected only episodically and slightly to the levying of tribute. This Arab world is thus both diverse and profoundly unified — by its ruling class. It is not to be compared to feudal Europe of the Middle Ages, which was thoroughly "peasant" in character. This is doubtless why Europe was to evolve toward the formation of separate nations, for the ruling classes of Europe, living as they did on the surplus taken from peasant communities, were bound to emphasize the diversity of the peoples of Europe. In contrast to this, in the Arab world, because the peasants did not play this role, unity was preserved. For the same reason, however, Arab civilization was a fragile affair. It was enough for trade to fall off for the states to perish, along with the cities on which they were based — and for the wretchedness of a world of poverty-stricken nomads and of small, isolated peasant communities, also very poor, to present a picture of decay.

The example of Black Africa also shows that long-distance trade does not of itself give rise to capitalism.

Here the premercantilist period extends from the beginnings down to the seventeenth century. During this long period relations were established between Black Africa and the rest of the Old World, especially across the Sahara, from the savannah, which stretches between Dakar and the Red Sea, on the one side, and to the Mediterranean on the other. Social formations made their appearance, which cannot be understood unless they are placed in the setting of the whole constellation of social formations, in their relation to each other. In that period Africa as a whole does not give an appearance of inferiority and weakness as compared with the rest of the Old World. The inequalities of development within Africa corresponded to those observable north of the Sahara on both sides of the Mediterranean.

However, complex social formations, sometimes in the form of states, and in nearly every case based upon obvious social differentiation testifying that the process of degradation of the primitive village community had taken place long before, were already typical of Black Africa. If discussion of traditional African society is dominated by great confusion, there are many reasons for this, the four chief ones being: (1) shortage of documents and survivals from the past, which consist almost entirely of the accounts given by Arab travelers; (2) confusion that often obtains between the concept of mode of production and that of social formation; (3) confusion between the different periods of African history, especially between this premercantilist period and the mercantilist period that followed it; and, finally, (4) ideological prejudices against Africa, connected with colonialist racism.

The African formations of the premercantilist period developed independently, although this development followed a parallel course to that of the formations of the Mediterranean world, both Eastern and European. As we have seen, the semiarid zone that stretches as a belt across the Old World between the shores of the Atlantic and Central Asia separates three regions where natural conditions have been conducive to agriculture from its primitive stages: Monsoon Asia, Tropical Africa, and the temperate zone of Europe. This belt of land saw the rise of brilliant civilizations, almost all based on long-distance trade, such as Greece and the Arab empire. On either side of this belt the development of independent social formations (those of feudal Europe and some, at least, of those of Tropical Africa, especially in the Sudan-Sahel zone situated immediately south of the Sahara) proceeded along parallel lines. This part of Africa was thus fully integrated into world history in the same way as Europe.

In this connection the role played by trans-Sahara trade emerges clearly. This trade enabled the whole of the Old World — Mediterranean, Arab, and European — to obtain gold from what was the principal producing area before the discovery of America, namely, Upper Senegal and Ashanti. This trade was one of the essential bases of the organization of the societies of Tropical Africa. The mining of gold under the orders of the kings provided the ruling classes with a means of procuring from across the Sahara both scarce luxury articles (fabrics, drugs, and perfumes, dates and salt) and also, and especially, the articles they needed in order to establish and strengthen their social and political power (horses, copper, iron bars, weapons). This trade therefore fostered the development of social differentiation, the constitution of states and empires, and progress of the productive forces (improvement in the instruments of production, adaptation of techniques and products, etc.). In exchange, Africa supplied mainly its gold, together with some rare products such as gum and ivory, and some slaves. It is only recently that some European historians have tried to confuse this trade between equal and independent partners with the devastating trade in Negro slaves that developed in the mercantilist period:

the very slight black element in the population of the southern Maghreb (only a few hundred thousand), compared with the hundred million Negroes in America, is enough to show how ill-founded this view is. For this reason, moreover, the ideas that circulated along with the goods were accepted readily in this region — notably Islam, which appeared very early on the banks of the Senegal River. The importance of this trade, its nature as equal exchange, and the independence of the African formations all stand out clearly from the Arab writings of the time. It is easier to understand the admiring tone of the accounts written by the Arab travelers if we appreciate that the North African and West African formations were at much the same stage technologically; they were similar in their structures and in the place they occupied in the world system of the time. The link between the royal monopoly of the exploitation of gold and its marketing by Moslem merchants provides the key to the structure of these formations. The merchants in question were, as so often, organized in a sort of caste, forming here a religious minority.

For centuries the social formations of the Mediterranean world and those of Tropical Africa were thus closely related. The gradual shifting of the trade routes from West to East was reflected in a parallel shift of civilization and of powerful states both in North Africa and in the West African savannah lands, as we see in the successive might of Ghana, Mali, the Hausa cities, Bornu, Kanem, and Darfur. The shift in the center of nascent European mercantilist capitalism from the Mediterranean to the Atlantic also caused a crisis in Africa. This shift tolled, in the sixteenth century, the knell of the Italian cities, and at the same time it brought ruin to the Arab world and to the Black African states of the Sudan-Sahel zone. A few decades later the representatives of Atlantic Europe made their appearance on the shores of Africa. The shifting of the center of gravity of trade in Africa from the savannah hinterland to the coast was a direct consequence of the shift of the center of gravity in Europe from the Mediterranean to the Atlantic. However, the new exchanges between Europe and Africa were to serve a different function from those of the previous period and form part of the operation of mercantilist capitalism.

Obviously one cannot know what would have become of the

African formations if they had continued to evolve on their own after the seventeenth century. Integrated at an early stage (the mercantilist stage) in the nascent capitalist system, they were broken off at that stage and soon began to regress. It seems, however, that the large-scale trade of premercantilist Africa, remarkable though it was in some regions, being linked with relatively poor formations of the communal or tribute-paying types, would not have been able to generate by itself the capitalist mode of production.

7. THE BLOCKING OF THE DEVELOPMENT OF THE TRIBUTE-PAYING FORMATIONS

The examples of the Arab world and Black Africa show that large-scale trade does not engender capitalism and is not itself capitalist. Here were formations that were marked by a substantial development of long-distance trade together with a relatively small surplus produced within the agrarian society. Such was not the case with either China or Egypt, whose civilizations never depended on trade. The first attempt to understand why the development of these civilizations was blocked was made by Marx in his observations in the *Grundrisse* regarding the Asiatic mode of production. These observations show very deep insight, but Marxists have been content to go on repeating them without taking the trouble to correct the errors and shortcomings in them due to the state of knowledge in Marx's time. Today we know that the village communities of ancient Egypt and China subjected their members to no greater restrictions than did those of medieval Europe; that the Egyptian and Chinese communities were, for thousands of years, no less crushed than those of Europe of a few centuries ago; and that the model of communities that are still strong is rather to be sought in Black Africa than in Asia. It is therefore not possible to seek the cause of the obstructed development of the tribute-paying formations in the survival of the community and its exceptional resistance to degradation.

Civilization, in the Old World at any rate, seems to have appeared if not simultaneously then at least about the same time in four places: Egypt, Mesopotamia, the Indus valley, and the valley of the Yellow

River. It was not accidental that these were four river valleys located in relatively hot regions. The natural conditions played a determining role at the start. Irrigation made possible both greater productivity (in terms of the annual product of each peasant family) and a much higher density of population. It thus facilitated the first real concentrations of population, with the circulation of goods, people, and ideas.

In all four cases the form assumed by the given civilization was identical. It was the tribute-paying form: a state-class of the theocratic-bureaucratic type emerged from the communities and asserted itself as organizer of the political and economic life of society. We must conclude from this that the first kind of class-divided social formation was not the slaveowning but the tribute-paying kind.

The natural conditions were to cause these four civilizations to experience different destinies. Mesopotamia and the Indus valley were highly vulnerable: surrounded as they were by relatively well-populated zones, their wealth attracted attack by the nomads, seminomads, and settled mountain peoples of the zones where agriculture depended on rainfall. Several times destroyed, they were unable to progress in a systematic and continuous way, as regards either the technology of irrigation and industry or that of political and administrative organization. Egypt and China, on the contrary, enjoyed favorable conditions. Egypt is protected by deserts both on the west and on the east. China is situated not in the heart of the Old World but at its eastern limits and is comparatively isolated from what lies to the west of it by mountain barriers that are hard to cross, high rugged plateaus, and deserts. Egypt was thus able to develop its tribute-paying civilization in a sheltered setting and soon attained a fully developed form of this civilization. China enjoyed an additional advantage, being able to expand southward at the expense of primitive peoples who, equally isolated from the West, were incapable of becoming a threat to the Han people in the way the Indo-Europeans became for Mesopotamia and India. Not only did China soon reach, like Egypt, the heights of the tribute-paying type of civilization: it was also able to expand, establishing along the banks of its southern rivers new zones of agrarian civilization on the same pattern as the original one.

Some remarks are called for regarding these two centers of tribute-paying civilization. Firstly, these two civilizations were truly central, in the sense that they involved a considerable proportion of the world's population: nearly ten million in Egypt by the second millenium B.C., while China soon reached a population of a hundred million, at a time when the rest of mankind amounted to hardly the same number, scattered over millions of square miles. Secondly, in these two civilizations the village community quickly weakened and almost disappeared as state authority became more powerful. The community survived as a community of families, but lost the *dominium eminens* of the land, which passed to a broader and higher community that soon developed into a nation. Thirdly, the state-class that became organized on the national scale was not, despite widely held notions, particularly "despotic." As a national state-class, it took account of the public interest and organized useful large-scale public works. The pyramids are unimpressive compared with the works undertaken to harness the Nile, which required an amount of labor several hundred times larger. This class, organized in a state, remained comparatively open, and social mobility in access to it was considerable, as is shown by the Chinese system of the mandarinate. In comparison with the violent history of European feudalism, abuses were limited in these civilizations, which deserved the epithet "despotic" only occasionally, when Barbarian invaders took command of the state — and even in these cases the Barbarians soon became assimilated and civilized — or in troubled times when the state collapsed, giving way to independent feudal authorities, so that these civilizations came to resemble feudal Europe. Fourthly, the power of the state that was characteristic of these formations in their developed condition gave the tribute-paying mode a clear dominance within them: long-distance trade, craft production (whether carried on by free men or slaves), production in those sectors where wage labor existed — all were subject to close control by the state, which taxed them. It was, indeed, in relation to these sectors that society was despotic, and not in relation to the peasants. In feudal Europe the opposite was the case: the state, being weak, let the towns flourish "in freedom," while the feudal landlords, living close to their peasants, were free to oppress them without any restriction. Fifthly, these two well-developed models of the tribute-paying formation were able to digest the progress achieved by the productive forces. The production relations defined by the tribute-paying mode were compatible with a wide range of levels of development of the productive forces. The conflict between productive forces and production relations makes its appearance only when the capitalist mode has been introduced from outside. The historical duration of the fully developed tribute-paying mode was thus, in principle, very long. Nevertheless, this compatibility with progress meant relatively blocked development, in relation, that is, to the progress possible in less advanced, less developed formations, in which the conflict between production relations and productive forces manifests itself sooner, compelling an advance beyond precapitalist relations.

All the same, Egypt and China remain the two original models, the basic sources of science, technique, ideology, and organization.

Alongside these central tribute-paying formations, exchange between the three poles of tribute-paying civilization in the West led to the establishment of peripheral trading formations: the Phoenician, Syrian, and Arab cities. The seminomadic tribal kingdoms of western Asia and southern Europe sought to reproduce the model provided by Egypt, or Mesopotamia, or the Indus civilization — but without much success, for their material basis was a fragile one. The surplus they were able to levy was small, and for this reason the communities remained hardy and state centralization was poorly developed and constantly threatened by local autonomies. Greece, after learning from one of these kingdoms inspired by Egypt — namely, Crete — was to develop to the full the peripheral character of its formation. The exceptional growth of commercial functions in this Greek society, together with the difficulty of obtaining even a moderate agricultural surplus from inside the country, led Greece along a new path, that of the use of slave labor on a large scale. This use of slave labor presupposed manhunts carried on outside the limits of Greek society, and had the effect of enriching commodity production and enabling this society to outgrow its function as a mere trading intermediary, creating the conditions for it to reproduce itself:

production by slaves became the means whereby more slaves could be bought. Rome was to spread this formation over the whole of the Mediterranean basin.

This slaveowning formation lacked the elasticity of the tribute-paying formations because it presupposed the existence of a periphery from which manpower had to be obtained. The strong tribute-paying societies with which it entered into trade relations, and even relations of domination, did not sell their people. The periphery from which slaves had to be drawn was therefore the Barbarian periphery of Europe — Celtic, Germanic, Slav. It was not slave revolts that put an end to the Roman Empire but the blows struck by the Barbarians. The latter, having established themselves on the ruins of the Empire, superseded the slave-owning mode, setting up the feudal mode, a variant of the tribute-paying mode. The Barbarians, established first of all where natural conditions were favorable, thus ended by making their way (via the slaveowning mode) into new regions.

The feudal variant remained weak in comparison with the original, fully developed tribute-paying mode. This weakness, this peripheral character was to become its strength. At the beginning of the feudal order in Europe, it meant a surplus of modest size but also an absence of political, administrative, and economic centralization, the one going along with the other. This low level of centralizing capacity was to allow freedom to the commercial sectors, as yet only embryonic. Under their stimulus, agriculture made great progress, and the surplus produced by agriculture grew naturally, so that the dialectics of increasing trade and breakup of feudal relations could get under way, leading in turn to the rise of capitalism.

The parallel between this exceptional line of evolution in the west of the Old World and what happened at its eastern extremity is striking. The problem of the Japanese "miracle" has never been looked at in these terms of relations between center and periphery. And yet the analogy is impressive. In the region to which Japan belongs, China was the finished model in all respects — a model that was faithfully reproduced wherever natural conditions made this possible: in Vietnam, in Cambodia in the Khmer period, and in Korea. In Japan, however, the natural conditions presented serious obstacles: the feudal fragmentation of the country and the autonomy of the trading cities limited the degree of state central-ization so that there were great similarities between Japan and Europe, separated as they were by thousands of miles. True, Japanese society did not give rise to capitalism until it had received a jolt from without. But when the time came, it became capitalist with the greatest of ease. In fact, this evolution might not have taken place if Japan had been so unlucky as to become integrated in the periphery of the capitalist system. It did not suffer this fate, because it was a poor country. China, on the contrary, with its substantial centralized surplus, attracted the cupidity of Europe and the United States. Also, the fact that the launching of the process of the birth of capitalism was occasioned by a jolt from without caused it to assume special forms, in particular emphasizing the role played by the state.

The evolution of the Indian subcontinent likewise enters into this schema. The tribute-paying civilization of the Indus valley was destroyed in the distant past, but the Indo-Aryan invaders rebuilt it over a larger territory. The process was a slow one because the territory was so vast, and the Ganges valley had to be conquered gradually from nature and from the primitive inhabitants. This process was also disturbed by the opening of India to the west and the successive waves of invasion that this invited. In the *cul-de-sac* of southern India some tribute-paying formations were also gradually established. India thus arrived at the tribute-paying mode rather late, not long before it was brought under colonial rule. Here, by way of exception, in a few areas where the process was still young, the village communities continued to flourish, and it was these that often led observers to regard the survival of the community as a prerequisite of the tribute-paying mode.

Why did not *all* the peripheral societies of the tribute-paying mode give birth to capitalism? We have already seen what the reasons were in the Arab world and Black Africa. The Byzantine Empire and its Ottoman successor were also peripheral forma-tions — or, more precisely, groups of formations — of the tribute-paying system. Actually, the tribute-paying mode never succeeded in taking root in this area in a thorough way. Some parts of the area (in the Balkans, Caucasia, Syria, and North Africa) continued to be organized in solid communities, and the tribute levied by Constantinople and later by Istanbul was always in jeopardy from revolt by these communities. Other parts of the area stagnated because the slaveowning or commercial basis to which they had owed their former prosperity had shrunk: this happened with Greece and the Eastern cities. The commodity production of these parts was transferred to the capital, to which Greek, Egyptian, and Syrian craftsmen were deported by the thousand; in the capital alone could the centralization of the tribute levied from an immense empire sustain this commodity production. Here was a case of a tribute-paying formation that was trying to cut its way through an older substratum that offered effective resistance. It is comprehensible that a formation like this was unable to engender capitalism. In other regions of the world, in Iran and Central Asia, tribute-paying formations remained too poor, owing to natural conditions, and too much threatened by Barbarian invaders, to be capable of achieving capitalism.

As in the Old World, the class-divided formation that arose in pre-Columbian America was of the tribute-paying type. This was the case with the Incas, the Aztecs, and the Mayas. Evolving in isolation, without any danger from without, owing to the small population of their continent, these formations appear to have attained a high level of development, comparable to that of Egypt and China in the Old World. We cannot know how they might have evolved further, since from the sixteenth century onward these formations were violently subjected to conquest by Spain and then broken up, to give place to the specific formations on the periphery of mercantilist capitalism.

As for the special formations that were constituted on the basis of European immigration in new lands where there was no previously existing substratum (New England and Canada, Boer South Africa, Australia, and New Zealand), these belong neither to the category of the periphery, nor to that of the tribute-paying systems, nor to that of capitalism. They were exceptional formations that were constituted from the start in close connection with the genesis of European *central* capitalism. I shall refer to them as the "young centers."

It has been shown that the precapitalist formations, despite their variety, are made up of a dominant central form (the tribute-paying formation), and a series of peripheral forms (the slaveowning, feudal, and trading formations). The tribute-paying formation is accounted for essentially by its own inner dynamism. In this sense it is autocentric and constitutes the normal path of evolution. The peripheral precapitalist formations are due to the interaction between their own inner dynamism and the influence exercised upon them by the fully developed tribute-paying formations. In this sense they are not autocentric and constitute exceptional paths of evolution. Around two fully developed centers of the tribute-paying formation that appeared very early, namely, Egypt and China, and a third that arose later, namely, India, peripheral constellations of various types took shape and entered into relations with each other along their fluctuating frontiers. Thus one may list the Mediterranean and European peripheries (Greece, Rome, feudal Europe, the Arab and Ottoman world), those of Black Africa, Japan, etc. It was in one of these, Europe, that capitalism was born.

2

The Fundamental Laws of the Capitalist Mode of Production

1. PRODUCTIVE FORCES AND PRODUCTION RELATIONS IN THE CENTRAL CAPITALIST FORMATIONS

I have defined the capitalist mode of production as being characterized by the exclusive appropriation by one class of means of production that are themselves the product of social labor. This exclusive appropriation by a certain class, although it has historically taken the form of individual ownership of the means of production, may also take collective forms. Capitalism exists wherever means of production that have been produced by social labor are not managed by society as a whole but by a section of the latter, which then becomes a "bourgeoisie." Capitalism makes its appearance when the level of development of the productive forces is sufficiently advanced for these means of production, which are themselves products, to be no longer simple enough to be manageable by the individual producer. The traditional peasant and craftsman make their own tools. Industrial workers cannot make their own factories. Consequently, the center of gravity of the means of controlling society shifts from domination of the *natural* means of production to domination of those means of production that are themselves *products* — equipment, machinery, plant.

The capitalist mode of production is thus marked by three essential features: (1) the whole of social production takes the form of commodities; (2) labor power itself becomes a commodity, which means that the producer, having been separated from the means of production, becomes a proletarian; and (3) the means of production themselves become commodities, in which is materially embodied a social relationship, that of their exclusive appropriation by a particular class — in other words, they become capital.

Whereas in precapitalist societies economic life is in the main not concerned with commodities, under the capitalist mode the entire economy becomes a commodity economy. This situation is reflected in conventional economic theory, which takes as its point of departure "supply and demand," thus presupposing the existence of commodities and the market. This theory is supposed to constitute a universal economic science, not limited to any particular phase of history, whereas in fact it treats as common to all civilizations the characteristics of the capitalist mode, which is what it actually observes. By so doing it is prevented from understanding how the capitalist system originated and its laws of development. It loses its scientific character, becoming an ideology.

Extending the domain of value to the whole of economic life changes the very form in which the law of value is expressed. Within the precapitalist formations, in the sectors where commodity exchange prevails, the law of value is expressed in simple form: exchange relations (relative prices) correspond to the average quantities of social labor embodied in the products exchanged. The means of production, which are themselves products of social labor, are not very substantial and belong, in effect, to the producers themselves. Simple commodity production is the predominant form of commodity production, and, consequently, prices are equivalent to values.

In the capitalist mode, not only are the means of production that are produced by social labor substantial, but they are owned exclusively by one class, and so they play a predominant role in society. The surplus labor provided by the producers is distributed among the members of the dominant class in proportion to the importance of the latter, itself measured by the amount of their capital — the share of social capital that they control. The law of value thus finds expression at one remove, in a complex form, prices being deduced from values in a way that makes possible this redistribution of surplus social labor.

The system of relative prices that operates under capitalism can, indeed, be described without recourse to the "intermediary" of value, and this has been done by Piero Sraffa. Such a description takes the form of a system of equations reflecting the relations between different industries. The cost of each product is the sum of the cost of the constituent elements of constant capital (material inputs —that is, the physical quantities of each of the inputs consumed — multiplied by their respective prices); wages (quantities of labor multiplied by wage rates); and profits (proportional to the values of the inputs, which are the form in which "capital" is crystalized). Solution of this system of equations gives the vector of relative prices without the need to go through the intermediary stage of value. However, this system remains merely descriptive, since its composition assumes, on the one hand, that products and labor power are commodities — in other words, that surplus labor exists and its volume is determined — and, on the other, that this surplus labor is distributed in proportion to capital invested. The composition of the system of equations thus assumes the existence of the capitalist mode of production.

This description shows that capital is not a thing but a social relation, since the vector of relative prices depends on both the rate of wages and the rate of profit; it shows that economic rationality is not an absolute, that it stands no higher than the rationality of the social relation that determines the division of income between wages and profits, in other words, the division of social labor time into paid labor and surplus labor. The description does not, for all that, enable us to understand how the capitalist mode began and how it developed, since it assumes this mode as given.

The Marxist critique of political economy alone furnishes the system of concepts needed for *this* purpose, by approaching the task of explanation from the appropriate angle, which is not that of economics but of historical materialism. If the transformation of values into prices, as Marx analyzes this in Volume III of

Capital, can be criticized, it is only in so far as it constitutes merely a first sketch. The system of transformation is analyzed incompletely: the elements of constant capital are reckoned at their value instead of at their price (Volume III, which was published after Marx's death, was, in this respect, only a rough draft). A complete mathematical system of transformation of values into prices is possible, but only if it be accepted that the average rate of profit cannot be equal to the rate of surplus value.

The rate of profit is actually determined by the relation between the value of certain products (products A) and that of others (products B) in a system of prices that differs from one in which the rate of surplus value is defined as the relation between the value of products A (in physical quantities) and that of products B. This nonidentity constitutes the reason why the capitalist system conceals the origin of profit and causes capital to appear as a thing that itself possesses productivity. It is by becoming aware of this economistic alienation that we are able to grasp the essential laws of development of the capitalistic mode. Such awareness means taking into account the logic of the distribution of surplus labor in proportion to the fractions of social labor controlled by the various social groups making up the dominant class; and also of the rule of competition and mobility of capitals, which is the prerequisite for equalization of the rate of profit. This competition entails in its turn a distinctive feature of the capitalist mode, namely, the "endogenous" nature of the progress of the productive forces, in relation to the way the system works, so that when an entrepreneur introduces a more advanced technique, the other entrepreneurs are obliged to follow his example. This "endogeneity" of progress under capitalism makes it seem an "external datum," and so deprives society of control over its own process of development.

If we decline to analyze the transformation of value into price, we decline to undertake the recovery of this control by society over itself, which means declining to advance beyond capitalism and giving up the prospect of socialism. Already in the nineteenth century German social-democracy supposed that socialism would be similar to capitalism in its "rational" economic choices, once the initial expropriation of the capitalists had been carried out.

Marx in his *Critique of the Gotha Programme* and Engels in *Anti-Dühring*, protested against this reduction of socialism to a "capitalism without capitalists," which actually contained the germ of state capitalism.

The universalizing of the commodity form of profit and the transition from a simple to a complex expression of value reduce commercial profit to the common denominator of profit on capital. Commercial profit is, of course, a category older than capitalism, since it presupposes merely the existence of commodity production. Precapitalist commercial profit is an income derived from monopoly, and as such does not obey precise rules. When societies brought into contact by monopolist merchants are ignorant of each other, and in particular are unaware of the real social costs of production of the products they exchange, the profit derived from a trading monopoly can be very high. It corresponds to a transfer of surplus from one class (and sometimes from one society) to another class, a class of alien merchants — this original surplus being ground rent or, in more general terms, tribute. When the capitalist mode becomes predominant, the predominant form taken by the surplus is profit on capital. Commercial activity is no longer a monopoly but a capitalistic activity like others, its domain extending to *all* products. The capitalist producers know the social costs of production of these products. Competition thus causes capital invested in commerce to share in the general equalization of profit. Commercial profit becomes profit on commercial capital, which is rewarded like other capitals, with the average rate of profit. To be sure, the reward of commercial capital is still a transfer, having its source in surplus value created elsewhere: in production. But this transfer is henceforth limited by the average rate of profit, which depends, in the last analysis, on the rate of surplus value.

Similarly, the universalizing of the commodity form alters the field in which the other precapitalist activities function. Agriculture was the chief field of activity in the precapitalist period and was dominated by feudal relations. Ground rent was the predominant form assumed by the feudal surplus, and landownership by the dominant class of precapitalist society was the legal expression of these feudal relations. Marx showed that private property in land is a hindrance to the development of capitalism in agriculture, because it gives landowners, as monopolists, the means of ensuring that part of the surplus value produced elsewhere is transferred to them in the form of absolute rent. If, however, capitalism respects private ownership of land, this is not merely for political reasons (alliance between all the possessing classes of the old modes and the new capitalist mode alike, against the oppressed classes) but above all because it has a vital interest in this private landowner- ship. Capitalism cannot develop so long as the producers have not been excluded from this precapitalist mode and put at capital's disposal as proletarians. Private property in land fulfils this function during the transitional phase between feudalism and capitalism, the mercantilist phase. Stimulated by the spread of commodity exchange, the landowners themselves become commodity producers. The agricultural revolution that preceded the Industrial Revolu- tion, first in England and then on the continent of Europe, reflected this extension of commodity exchange to agricultural production, the substitution of money rent for rent in kind being merely the immediate expression of the process. Competition spread to agricultural production, and the modernization it entailed re- quired exclusion of the excessive quantity of peasant labor power, this being eliminated from production and proletarianized.

Is absolute rent, which Rey calls "the way in which the dominated feudal mode is linked with the dominating capitalist mode," subject to determination? In Volume III of *Capital*, Marx puts forward the idea that transfer of surplus value to landlords can take place because the organic composition of capital is higher in industry than in agriculture, so that with the same rate of surplus value the surplus value produced in agriculture is greater, for a given amount of capital invested, than it is in industry, agriculture being a "light" activity. Private property in land obstructs the spread of the equalization of profit to the field that it controls, and it is the surplus value thus retained, withheld from the mechanism of equalization, that determines rent. Actually, this explanation given by Marx does not seem to me to be necessary. Even if the organic composition of capital were the same in agriculture as the average prevailing in industry, or higher than that, monopoly landownership would make it possible for the price structure of agricultural products, relative to that of industrial products, to be such as to include a transfer of value — a real transfer, not a mere withholding from the equalization process — to the advantage of the monopoly owners of land, constituting their rent. This is determined not by the difference in comparative organic compositions of capital in agriculture and industry but merely by a social relation: the relation of strength determining the division of social and political power between the bourgeoisie and the landowners. Rent cannot be made to disappear unless ownership of land itself disappears. The bourgeoisie attacks private landownership by opening up to agricultural production new lands where there are no landlords, that is, by bringing into competition with the products of agriculture dominated by landownership the products of agriculture where access to the natural conditions of production is free, unrestricted by monopoly landownership: this was the significance of the opening of the British market to the wheat of North America during the nineteenth century. The bourgeoisie also brings into competition with the products of agriculture in the center of the system the products of peripheral agriculture, which is dominated by landownership, to be sure, but in which the reward of labor is lower and the rate of surplus value higher.

Rent, which continues to exist as long as private property in land continues, nevertheless assumes, owing to the predominance of capitalist relations, the form of a profit on capital — on the capital "invested" in the purchase of land. In the precapitalist formations, the land was a monopoly held by one class to the exclusion of another. In the capitalist formations it becomes subject to buying and selling. Its price — a new category — is the rent that it can yield, capitalized. Thenceforth, this rent appears as the reward of the capital sunk in purchasing the given piece of land.

In the advanced capitalist formations, agricultural production no longer occupies more than a restricted place in the social product. Agricultural land is thus subject to frequent and easy commercial transactions that are no longer hindered by the presence of a peasant class, for whom agriculture was not merely a field of production but also a way of life. Agricultural ground rent disappears, since the profit of the capitalist entrepreneurs in agriculture — the share of social surplus value to which they are entitled —

has to reward *all* the capital they have invested, including that which was devoted to purchasing land. Land continues to command a price because it is subject to monopoly.

Whenever access to the natural (or social) conditions of production is restricted by a monopoly, a problem of the transference of value arises. This is why it is not possible to grasp the problem directly on the basis of an analysis of prices.

While in the advanced capitalist systems the problem of agricultural rent has lost its acuteness in quantitative terms, at least, if not in terms of theory, *urban* ground rent becomes day by day of greater quantitative importance. The ideologists of the system claim that ground rent is the "rational" way to stop people from planting potatoes in the Champs-Elysées. In reality, it is quite clear that access to plots of land in the Champs-Elysées is not controlled by society but is a monopoly held by a certain social group, that of the owners of these plots. The volume of the transfer of value that takes place to their advantage as a result of this fact thus depends exclusively on their social power.

The same is true of "natural resources" in the form of minerals, forests, rivers, lakes, and seas, in so far as access to them is restricted by a social monopoly. In his *Critique of the Gotha Programme* Marx shows that social labor is the sole source of value, but not of *wealth*. The latter means the quantity of useful objects (useful from the social, not the individual standpoint) obtained with a given amount of social labor. This social labor is carried out not in a nonmaterial, abstract setting but under given natural conditions. The distinction between nature and society determines what is meant by social science, defining as it does mankind in contrast to the animal kingdom. If society controlled access to all natural conditions, it would be able to plan the use of them in a rational way: in other words, it would choose the ways and means to obtain, by exploiting these natural resources in accordance with a definite social time-prospect, the maximum of utilities in return for a given amount of social labor. In the capitalist system, this access to natural wealth is subject to extreme disorder. Some forms of natural wealth are freely accessible, and on this account are wasted, to the detriment of society's interests, as problems of the environment reveal (pollution of the atmosphere, of rivers, etc.). Freedom of access excludes the way these resources are used from the field of economic calculation: for the capitalist enterprise this constitutes an "external saving," whereas on the social scale the using-up of these resources signifies a real cost, namely, that of the "fight against pollution" (the expenses of cleaning work undertaken by the public authorities, extra expenditure on health services, forced movement of persons, etc.). Other natural resources are subject to ownership, and the price paid by the capitalist entrepreneur will depend on the social relations between the capitalist class and the group that monopolizes access to these resources. Where resources of the subsoil are concerned, for example, this price will vary widely, depending on whether the laws in force separate ownership of the surface from that of the subsoil, whether the land is privately or publicly owned, and so on — that is, depending on the social conditions that define the framework of economic activity.

A further step is taken when we consider the stages in the evolution of the productive forces and of production relations in the capitalist system. The mercantilist period, which was that which saw the formation of the system, defined by the establishment of the two poles of the capitalist mode (concentration of money-wealth and proletarianization), was a period of transition: on the one hand, the law of value was still expressed in its simple form, in the sector of petty-commodity production, but on the other the concentration of money-wealth was already taking place in a sector that was not governed by the law of value — that of the large-scale Atlantic trade organized in monopolies. The Industrial Revolution, that is, the coming together and merging of the two poles created during the mercantilist period, opened the way to the fully developed capitalist mode of production: money-wealth became capital, setting to work under its control the "released" labor power that became the proletariat. The nineteenth century, until approximately the 1880s, was marked by the industrial form of the central capitalist formations. The predominant form of capital was industrial capital, made up of independent units corresponding, as a rule, to separate enterprises, which were largely family businesses. Competition offered the law of value in its complex form the widest field of operation. But there were some hindrances to this operation, especially in agriculture, which because of private property in land continued to be subject to the social monopoly of the landlord class. Centralization of capital, progressing as a result of competition, brought about at the end of the century a qualitative change in the predominant character of the system. The generalizing of the monopoly form of capital showed that the level of development of the productive forces had now risen beyond that of the production relations. For monopoly is above all a hindrance to the equalization of profit. Prices therefore cease to be determined by a general law based on values. The field of operation of the law of value contracts. There is no longer any rationality, even apparent, in the price system. Prices are determined by social relations of strength within the dominant class, between the financial groups that dominate the various sectors of economic activity. Down to this time the social relations that played a part in determining relative prices were only those between the dominant capitalist class as a whole and the other classes and social groups. Thenceforth, there was no longer a single rate of profit, but at least two rates: the one governing the monopoly sectors and the one applying in the sectors where, despite domination by the monopoly sectors, competition still prevailed. Politics, that is, resort to intervention of the state in the economic field, acquired a new dimension.

The only way forward for capitalism — faced with the transcending of the system by socialism, with the contradiction between productive forces and production relations — is state capitalism. Centralization of all production on the national scale, through the replacement of ownership by social groups by *state* ownership, brings the production relations up to the level of development of the productive forces. It restores the social character of capital, which had been disguised by the parcelation of the latter into privately owned shares. It imposes social planning as a way of managing the economy. How is it possible now to define prices otherwise than as purely conventional, since the entire social product appears as a single commodity — with labor power as the only other commodity? It is on this last point that the frontier lies between state capitalism and socialism. It corresponds to a class frontier — that which divides the proletariat, which still sells its labor power, from the bourgeoisie, which has become a state-class, as in the days of the tribute-paying mode. To this renovation of capitalist society there also corresponds the maintenance of domination by the economic instance over the politico-ideological instance; the solution found by state capitalism to the problem of planning is a capitalist solution — the determination of "prices" that "reward" on an equal basis the "capital" (i.e., the fractions of capital) assigned to the different branches of the economy. When the Russian economists adopt this formula they are returning, in fact, to the "rationality" of the capitalist mode, which had been shaken by the rise of private monopolies.

Let us recapitulate. Capitalist calculation has no rationality *in itself*. Rationality is in fact always relative to a particular mode of production and never transcends the framework of social relations distinctive of that mode. In the capitalist mode, in its fully developed industrial form, this rationality is limited — on the one hand, by the essential social relation that defines the rate of surplus value, namely, the rate of exploitation of labor, and, on the other, by the secondary social relations that obtain between the bourgeoisie and the landowners who control access to certain natural resources. With the coming of private monopolies a third limitation appears — that which is caused by social relations within the dominant bourgeois class.

The result of economic calculation based on such foundations is irrational from the social point of view, and this irrationality becomes apparent as soon as the level of development of the productive forces requires that they be controlled by society as a whole. It is here that the content of the problem of the "environment" is to be found. The use of this (inaccurate) term testifies merely to the fact that the problem is felt by society as a sort of discomfort, without being understood scientifically. It covers two sets of facts, belonging to three planes on which the irrationality of the system is manifested: (1) the waste of "human resources"; (2) the waste of natural resources; and (3) the inevitably limited time-prospect of "economic calculation."

For the capitalist mode of production, people exist as labor power, a "work force," and not as ends in themselves: its immanent law is therefore to try to reduce the cost of this labor power, to maximize the rate of surplus value, to thrust out of the realm of economics — and into the field of "external savings" for the enterprise — what have been wrongly described as "social costs" or "human costs" (education, health, etc.), the economic alienation involved being reflected in the very choice of the term "costs" (like the term "human resources," which underlines the fact that humans are a "resource" . . . for capital). State capitalism is driven by the same law: labor power remains a commodity, and the economistic alienation persists. Socialism is defined by social command over the threefold relation between the social labor time assigned to reproducing the production cycle, the social labor time assigned to expanding this, and the time not devoted to labor. In this way socialism is able to dominate the process of accumulation, which, in the capitalist mode of production, on the contrary, dominates social development.

The capitalist mode of production either takes or fails to take into consideration the using-up of natural resources, depending on accidents of social relations that are not under social control. The "price" of products, which decides their relative use, either contains or does not contain, according to cases, the margin needed if society is to be able to maintain and renew its stock of these resources. Thus, high rates of accumulation, measured in the classical terms of national accounting, for example, and consequently rates of growth of the social product measured in these terms, are obtained at the expense of the future, through the exhaustion of natural resources.

A society that wishes to control its future must first and foremost take a long view — have a lengthy "time-prospect." This was the case with the precapitalist societies, in which the dominant instance was not the economic but the politico-ideological one. However, these societies had little power over nature, owing to the low level of development of the productive forces (hence their religious alienation). These societies built pyramids or cathedrals, in other words, monuments that were destined to last forever and the purpose of which was to serve not men but the gods. In capitalist society this claim is made no longer: but while capitalism has freed men from the gods, it has not freed them from themselves. All it can offer them is an alienating ideology, that of the "consumer society," a short-term prospect of "growth" of consumption without any reference to real human needs. This shortening of the time-prospect results from the dominant function of the rate of surplus value. It is this rate that determines the pace of accumulation, and so, ultimately, the "rate of discount" on the basis of which choices are made. It seems to give rationality to what is irrational. But we know that a rate of 7 to 15 percent means that the alternatives between which a choice has to be made become practically identical within a period of ten to fifteen years at the most. In fact, "economic calculation" is nothing more than an ideological justification of the way capitalist enterprises spontaneously behave. Even when it is transposed to the national or "social" scale and purged of its most harmful consequences by taking into consideration "reference prices," nothing has been done to alter its short-sighted outlook. The crisis of our civilization is wholly concentrated in this absurd contraction of human time. One of its aspects is the contradiction in which our civilization is trapped, between the "objectives" of education and those of the system of production. In a world that is progressing fast, education cannot content itself with teaching techniques that correspond to particular occupational capacities, which it is hardly possible to know will still be wanted in twenty years' time. Education ought therefore to form men with a capacity, later on and throughout their lives, for adapting themselves and progressing, and also, contrariwise, for adapting economic evolution to the pace they prefer. But this is not the purpose of "educational planning": a victim of economistic alienation, it tries to treat the formation of human beings as a cost (one of the capitalist enterprise's external savings) and therefore tries to adapt its products to the needs of the economy — needs that the system itself does not know for more than ten or twenty years ahead.

The rational economic calculation of a socialist society cannot be based on such principles as these. First, let us recall that, for society as a whole, only calculation in terms of value is meaningful — that is, in terms of social-labor time. Any accounting in prices that "equalize the rewards of capital" is meaningless. The organization of the social division of labor (between the production of "capital goods" and that of consumer goods) and the time needed for going over from a given structure of this division to a different structure, corresponding to a higher level of development of the productive forces (a period of time governed in the last resort by the time taken to train and transform men: technical training, reorganization of production, etc.) have to be considered from the standpoint of a single choice to be made — that of the solution capable of reducing to the minimum the necessary social-labor time within a given time-prospect. The latter has to be determined by society in accordance with its maximum power to know the future. As for the useful objects that have to be produced, these must bear an explicit and continuous relation to the needs expressed by society, without any reference to prices (and so to the market and to the distribution of income, necessarily unequal at that stage): only in this way can society choose between labor-time and nonlabor-time, instead of remaining trapped in the futile choice between different "goods," with labor-time — kept as long as possible — not a matter for discussion. For capitalism, indeed, the aim of the system is not to maximize production but to maximize surplus value; this is what determines the economistic alienation. Finally, natural resources must all be taken into consideration, and within a defined time-prospect a part of the product must be assigned to maintaining or reconstituting them. This part, to be kept as small as possible, dictates the choice to be made between alternatives; it will depend, however, on the prospects of scientific progress, justifying the exhaustion of a certain resource if there is a possibility in the future of producing goods to satisfy the same needs by drawing upon a different resource. This is what is meant by "reconstituting" natural resources. And this is how we are to understand Marx's observation that under a socialist regime the individual worker cannot "receive the undiminished proceeds of his labor," as naive socialists had supposed.

2. THE ACCUMULATION OF CAPITAL IN THE CENTRAL CAPITALIST FORMATIONS

The capitalist mode differs from all previous modes in that

here it is appropriation of means of production that are themselves products of social labor that governs the production process, and no longer appropriation of the natural means of production. This feature, which reflects a qualitative leap in the level of
development of the productive forces, is itself reflected in the
vulgar definition of "capital" as meaning material equipment
("capital goods") and in the unhappy expression "capitalistic
technique," which conventional economics uses to describe this
qualitative leap. Conventional economics claims to base its analysis on the fact that equipment is produced earlier in time than the
production of consumer goods, which it makes possible. The
"roundabout path" of production constitutes the basis of "marginalism" and enables Böhm-Bawerk to base the "productivity of
capital" on "the rate of discount for the future" ("the price of
time"). Actually, this is a meaningless notion. What is characteristic of the capitalist mode is the *simultaneous* production of
production goods and consumer goods, the social division of labor
between these two main branches of social production. It is an
analysis of the link between these two branches that needs to be
treated as central in an analysis of accumulation. In fact, this social
division of labor both governs and reflects the level of development of
the productive forces — the overall productivity of social labor (the
quantity of utilities obtained with a total quantity of labor distributed in a certain way) — just as it governs the distribution of
social income. The determining link in an autocentric capitalist
system is therefore that which connects the production of consumer
goods with the production of the production goods that are destined
to make it possible to produce these consumer goods. This link
has been a feature of the historical development of capitalism at
the center of the system, in Europe, North America, and Japan.
It provides the abstract definition of the capitalist mode of production in its "pure" form and is analyzed as such in Marx's
Capital. It could be shown that the process of development of the
USSR and also of China, are also based upon this link, although the
forms it assumes are in these cases (especially in that of China)
original ones.

Marx shows that in the capitalist mode of production there is
an objective, necessary relation between the rate of surplus value

and the level of development of the productive forces. The rate of surplus value is what basically determines the structure of the social distribution of the national income (its division between wages and surplus value, which takes the form of profit), and consequently, that of demand (wages constitute the bulk of demand for mass consumer goods, profits being either wholly or in part "saved" in order to be "invested"). The level of development of the productive forces is expressed in the social division of labor: the allotment of labor power in suitable proportions to Departments I and II of the reproduction model in Volume II of *Capital.* This objective relation, though fundamental to Marx's argument, has often been overlooked, as in the discussion concerning the tendency of the rate of profit to fall. The argument often put forward to the effect that an increase in the organic composition of capital may be compensated by an increase in the rate of surplus value collapses if we appreciate that the contradiction between the system's capacity to produce and its capacity to consume — which is immanent in the capitalist mode of production — is continually being overcome; that it is in this way that the objective character of the relation between the rate of surplus value and the level of development of the productive forces is expressed. This theoretical model of accumulation is much richer than all the empirical models constructed subsequently, for it shows that "real wages" cannot be fixed in an arbitrary way, and thus endows social relations of strength with objectivity.

This objective relationship is expressed in the conjunctural fluctuations of economic activity and unemployment. An increase in the rate of surplus value above the objectively necessary level results in a crisis, through the inadequacy of effective demand. A reduction in this rate slows down economic growth and creates the conditions for a labor market favorable to capital. The schema of this adjustment process — which corresponds to the history of accumulation from the Industrial Revolution to the crisis of the 1930s — is more complex, owing to the influence of the secondary effect of variations in wages upon choice of techniques, thereby reflecting the suboptimal character of the economic system. A tendency to full employment (which does not rule out but, on the contrary, implies a small margin of permanent unemployment) and big conjunctural fluctuations in unemployment represent the working of this system. The internal changes that have taken place in present-day capitalism have deprived this mechanism of adjustment of its functional role. The monopolization of capital, on the one hand, and labor organization on a nationwide scale, on the other, have made possible "planning" so as to reduce conjunctural fluctuations. If the working class agrees to stay within this framework, that of the system — in other words, concretely, if under the aegis of the state, capital and labor accept a "social contract" that links increases in real wages to increases in productivity, in proportions worked out by the "technocrats" — then a stable state of quasi-full employment can be assured. Except, of course, that some sectors of society may, by refusing to accept this "contract," cause disturbances: this may happen with the small and medium enterprises that are the victims of concentration, and that may possess a far from negligible power for political blackmail; and except, too, that external relations cannot be brought within the scope of this type of planning. The contradiction is growing between the worldwide character of production (shown in the increasing weight of the multinational corporations) and the still-national character of the institutions both of capital and of labor. The social-democratic ideology expressed in this type of social contract finds its limits at the frontiers of the national state.

This model reflects the essence of the system. It leaves out of account external relations, which means not that the development of capitalism takes place in a self-contained national framework but that the essential relations of the system can be grasped without taking account of these relations. Moreover, the external relations of the advanced regions, taken as a whole, with the periphery of the world system are quantitatively marginal in comparison with the flows that take place within the center; besides, as we shall see, these relations are a matter of primitive accumulation and not of expanded reproduction. The historically relative character of the distinction between mass consumer goods and luxury goods is also clearly seen here. Strictly speaking, those goods should be regarded as luxury goods the demand for which arises from the part of profit that is consumed. The demand that arises from wages increases with economic growth — the progress of the productive forces. While, at the start of the history of capitalism, this demand related almost wholly to essentials — food, clothing, and shelter — it relates ever more extensively at present to "consumer durables" such as automobiles, electrical appliances for domestic work, and so on. This historical succession in the type of "mass" goods is of decisive importance in understanding the problem that concerns us. The structure of demand in the first period of the system favored the agricultural revolution by providing an outlet for foodstuffs in the home market (historically, this transformation of agriculture took the form of agrarian capitalism). We know, moreover, the historical role played by the textile industry and by the growth of towns ("when the building industry is going well, everything goes well") in the accumulation process. Durable consumer goods, the production of which consumes a great deal of capital and of skilled labor, only make their appearance when productivity in agriculture and the industries that produce nondurable goods has already reached a high level.

This analysis plays a vital part in the demonstration of my argument. I will add to it three observations.

First, autocentric accumulation, that is, accumulation without external expansion of the system, is theoretically possible if real wages increase at a given, calculable rate. Now the immanent tendency of the system is to maintain constant the level of real wages, which do not increase unless, and to the extent that, the working class brings about an increase by means of trade-union struggles. If real wages do not increase at the necessary rate, accumulation requires, as compensation, a steady *external* expansion of the market. This is what underlies the necessary expansionism of the capitalist mode. Throughout the nineteenth century, until the 1880s, because real wages at the center did not increase sufficiently, a form of expansionism was necessary that conferred certain functions upon the periphery. Since the last decades of the nineteenth century, however, real wages at the center have increased at a faster rate, and this has caused the expansionism of the capitalist mode to assume new forms (imperialism and the export of capital) and has also given the periphery new functions to perform.

Second, autocentric accumulation gives the capitalist mode at the center of the system a tendency to become exclusive, that is, to destroy all the precapitalist modes. By way of exception among social formations, the central capitalist social formation tends to become identical with the mode of production that dominates it, whereas all previous formations were stable combinations of different modes.

Third, autocentric accumulation is the condition necessary for manifestation of the tendency of the rate of profit to fall. Monopolies and imperialism are the system's response to this tendency, putting an end to the equalization of profit. However, on the one hand, the "reparation" of profits from the periphery, where capital has gone in search of a better return, and, on the other, the steady decline in the rate of profit at the center, together with pursuit of the mechanisms of autocentric accumulation, aggravate the problem of how to absorb excess capital. The way in which the system overcomes this problem is through state monopoly capitalism, which organizes the absorption of the surplus. Analysis of this response by the system to its problems necessitates the introduction of a new concept, that of "surplus," which is wider than the concept of surplus value.

An example of the fundamental divergence that exists between this analysis and that made by dogmatic Marxism is provided by the discussion that took place around the book *Monopoly Capital,* by Baran and Sweezy. This work makes an important contribution, taking account of essential new facts relative to the way in which the system is today overcoming, at its center, the fundamental, permanent, and growing contradiction between capacity to produce and capacity to consume. The tendency for the surplus to increase, which results from the policy of the state and of the monopolies in the epoch of contemporary monopoly capitalism, does not contradict the tendency for the rate of profit to fall — on the contrary, it is the way the latter finds expression in the system as it exists in our time. Some commentators have raised objections to the work of Baran and Sweezy, because it shows that the system *can* function. They prefer the religious and comforting vision of an apocalyptic catastrophe, and a golden age miraculously reached, to the disturbing prospect of continually

changing conditions, which make it necessary continually to undertake fresh analyses.

3. THE CONDITIONS FOR AUTOCENTRIC ACCUMULATION: THE ROLE OF THE MONETARY SYSTEM

Monetary theory is the favored sphere of an "economic science"
that applies itself only to pseudo-problems. For money conceals
the essential relations, namely, production relations, and brings to
the forefront relations that are superficial, namely, exchange relations. In reality, the banking system fulfils only the passive function
of adjusting the quantity of money to need. True, it also fulfils an
active function in the mechanism of accumulation (in the process
of realizing surplus value), but precisely this function remains
unsuspected by current monetary theory.

The subjective theory of value can answer the question of the
value of money only in a tautological way: the value of money, it
says, is that of the goods it enables one to buy. Actually, money
fulfils four essential functions: it is the instrument by which value
is measured; it is the concrete instrument of circulation; it is the
licensed instrument of legal tender; and it is the instrument by
means of which value is stored. Marginalist theory emphasizes the
role of money as circulation medium, from which it derives all the
other functions. Keynesian theory emphasizes money's function as
"means of hoarding," regarding this as the most specific function
of money. Present-day economists (Lindahl, Myrdal, Lundberg,
Harrod) ascribe a complementary, though secondary, role to the
two functions in the mechanisms of accumulation, while the Chicago
school (Milton Friedman) goes back to the quantity theory. Marx
(whose position is shared to some extent by Joseph Schumpeter) is
the only economist to have opened the way to a real discussion on
the role of money in accumulation.

From Classical Thinking to Keynes and Milton Friedman

Paradoxically, the economic thinking called "classical" by Keynes attributes, like the Keynesian doctrine itself, a decisive role in the mechanisms of economic development to the rate of interest, and a quite negligible one to the banking system.

Saving and investment are, for the writers whom Keynes attacks, real factors in the economy. However, the monetary form in which these quantities are expressed adds a new cause of maladjustment to the real causes of possible disequilibrium. There is alleged to be a "natural" rate of interest that ensures economic equilibrium. The amount of saving made available, allowing for "preference for the present" is held to be, at this rate, equal to the amount of investment demanded, allowing for the productivity of capital.

Now, not only is this analysis tautological, since neither Fisher nor Böhm-Bawerk established the existence of the productivity of capital on any foundation other than "preference for the present," so that the so-called natural rate of interest is nothing more than the rate of depreciation of the future, but the mechanism of determination of the "natural" rate of interest, at the point where the curves of supply of saving and demand for saving intersect, actually explains nothing at all. Keynes showed this very clearly: when the demand for capital changes (some innovation calling for larger investments), then incomes change, and therefore likewise the supply of saving. By resorting to history in order to solve the problem — the supply of capital available today is said to be determined by the distribution and amount of income that existed yesterday — the logical difficulty is dodged.

In any case, the first marginalists paid no attention to monetary conditions. It "went without saying" for them that monetary conditions caused the rate of the money market to "tend" toward the "natural" rate. Wicksell opened a new era when he showed how cumulative processes in the banking mechanisms allowed the monetary rate to diverge from the natural rate. This analysis, taken up later by Myrdal, Keynes, and Cassel, served to explain economic cycles.

The underlying assumption here is that the rate of interest dictates the amount of saving as well as that of investment. But this is not so. Saving depends essentially on the absolute and relative amount of incomes from property. Investment responds only slightly to variations in the rate of interest: essentially, it depends on the degree to which capacity to produce corresponds to capacity to consume.

In Keynes the same contrast is found between the excessive role attributed to the rate of interest and the passive role attributed to the banking system. The imbalance between saving and investment is ultimately ascribed to liquidity preference, which prevents the rate of interest from falling below a minimum level: the rate of interest is determined by the state of liquidity preference, allowing for the volume of money supplied by the banks. Equilibrium forces then determine relative prices such that the marginal efficiency of different capitals is in every case equal to this rate. From that moment onward there is no longer any gap between the rate of interest and the efficiency of capital, and consequently there is no further net investment. The equilibrium state of the Swedish school has been attained, in which, the monetary rate being equal to the natural rate, profits are nil. But this equilibrium may well be an equilibrium of underemployment. Indeed, whatever the volume of money, the rate of interest cannot, owing to liquidity preference, fall below a certain level. The banking system is then quite helpless. This is why many Keynesians condemn the policy of monetary expansion, which when the rate of interest has reached its minimum level, cannot but engender inflation, even without full employment.

This analysis is based on the idea of liquidity preference, that is, of propensity to hoard. What is meant by the "need for liquidity"? On the one hand, it is the need to have cash in hand with which to finance current transactions. To what extent is an entrepreneur prepared to pay out the funds needed to keep his current production going? Clearly he will do this until the point is reached at which these charges reduce his profit to zero. On the other hand, it is the need to have cash to hoard. But in a capitalist society, once an entrepreneur has ensured the reserve savings he needs, he has no desire to hoard: he wants to save in order to *invest*. The question is thus not why the rate of interest cannot fall below a certain level but why the level of the marginal efficiency of capital *can* fall so low. On this point, Keynes's explanations remain vague.

What is especially disappointing in Keynes's theory, though, is that the banking system appears in it as being ineffectual not merely beyond a certain point — but at *all* levels. One might think that money plays a passive role, in the sense that its supply is adapted to the need for liquidity. Now, Keynes considers that this supply is rigid. It is this rigidity that, faced with a fluctuating demand, determines the current variations in the rate of interest. True, variations in this rate are sometimes due to the quantity of money becoming adapted to demand. But these difficulties are only temporary and cannot explain the average level at which this rate remains over a long period.

The Adjustment of Issue to Needs

The first question to be answered is how the adaptation of MV (quantity of money multiplied by velocity of circulation) to PT (level of prices multiplied by volume of transactions) takes place. Total saving does not constitute a homogeneous mass: we must distinguish the *creative saving* represented by the amount of money put on one side by entrepreneurs with a view to subsequent expansion of production from the *reserve saving* represented by the money put on one side either by consumers with a view to future expenditure on ultimate consumer goods, or by entrepreneurs in order to finance all the productive expenditure needed to ensure the present level of production and the normal disposal of this production.

It is this volume of liquidities that constitutes the primary social need for money. The banking system adjusts the amount of money in circulation to this need by means of short-term credit. It is at the request of entrepreneurs that commercial banks grant short-term credits to them. These credits serve merely to finance the current functioning of the economy, that is, to spread over a period of time the receipts and payments of entrepreneurs.

The whole question is whether or not this social need for money is predetermined: that is, if we assume habits of payment to be stable (which is true in the short run, though in the long run the improvement in banking techniques speeds up the circulation of money, in view of the increasing need for this to be done), whether or not the size of the national income is predetermined, or, in other words, whether or not the levels of economic activity and prices are predetermined. If, indeed, the banks *can* modify these levels by injections or withdrawals of money, then to say that the banking system "adjusts the quantity of money available to the need for it" is meaningless.

Here, too, we need to know whether, fundamentally, the level of activity and the level of prices are determined by the quantity of money, or whether these levels ultimately depend on other economic factors. Keynes says that the quantity of money supplied fulfils the function of an independent primary variable. This assumption is baseless. But a more serious question is this: what forces determine the level of marginal efficiency of capital? Keynes has nothing to say on that point. Actually, this efficiency, which is nothing but the profitability of investments, is directly bound up with the degree of correspondence between society's capacity to produce and its capacity to consume. If the capacity to produce ever became greater than the capacity to consume, the profitability of investments would soon sink to zero, so that, whatever the level of the rate of interest might be, economic activity would contract.

Fundamentally, then, the level of economic activity depends on something other than the quantity of money. Is this also true of the price level?

The quantity theory associated the value of money closely with the quantity of money. Although this mechanical connection as shown in Fisher's equation has today been abandoned, it does not follow that every trace of "quantitativism" has been eliminated from economic theory. There has even been an attempt to rescue the quantity theory by showing its link with the subjective theory of value. Thus, Von Mises declares that, when the quantity of money increases, this means that certain incomes have increased and, since the marginal utility of money declines for individuals when their incomes increase, prices increase in their turn. Is this reasoning well-founded? When the quantity of money increases, it is usually the case that production has increased, for the additional money has entered into the economy through concrete channels. To an increased demand there corresponds an increased supply.

Economic theory seems to have taken a quite new path, that of studying the function fulfilled by money of satisfying the "need for liquidity." Has liquidity analysis radically eliminated the quantity theory? There is reason to doubt this. In the Keynesian model, the supply of money and the rate of interest being given, the level of liquidity preference determines the proportion of money that will be hoarded (and, consequently, the proportion that will be "active"). As the rate of interest determines the volume of investment (because the marginal efficiency of capital is an independent variable that does not depend on the quantity of money) and thereby the volume of the national income, all the factors in the economic system are present except the general level of prices, which must be determined, according to the quantity-theory formula, by the ratio between the real national income and the quantity of active money. Keynes therefore remains, so to speak, a second-degree quantity theorist. This is why, when the effect of liquidity preference ceases to be felt, pure and simple quantitativism reasserts itself. This way of looking at the matter, in which the quantity of money is a factor to which the other factors adapt themselves (for Keynes the quantity of money determines both the level of the national income and that of prices, instead of determining the latter alone, as the "classicists" hold) rather than being itself a variable dependent on the demand for money (in other words, on the level of income and prices), has made it easy to integrate the Keynesian system into the classical system. This integration, carried out by Modigliani in a general model, is liable to all the reproaches directed by Nogaro at the quantity theory. An antiquantitativist position is, in fact, incompatible with any theory of general equilibrium, since there *has* to be an independent variable in the system. The Chicago school (Milton Friedman) has made this return to the quantity theory. It is then led, once the quantitativist assumption has been accepted, to orient all its investigations in the only direction open to an empiricism that condemns itself to seeing only appearances: seeking for direct correlations between the quantity of money and sundry variables of the system ("permanent income"), "psychological" analysis of the "desire for cash," and other pseudo-problems.

If, then, all forms of quantitativism are rejected, the problem of how the value of money is determined remains to be solved. This being so, we can distinguish between two cases: that of a currency convertible into gold and that of an inconvertible one. In the first case it is certain that the cost of production of gold plays a decisive role in the mechanism whereby the general price level is determined. If, however, the currency is inconvertible, then the safety barrier constituted by the value of gold is no longer present. Up to this point no expansion of credit could "exceed" the limit of needs because the credit offered would not have been asked for by the entrepreneurs. Only in the form of a distribution of purchasing power without any real backing (issue of paper money in wartime, for example) could the quantity of money be increased. The increase in prices, resulting from imbalance between income and production and not from the quantity of money, makes it necessary to abandon convertibility. When the banks no longer buy gold at a fixed price, the expansion of credit, or issue of purchasing power, can then take place without any limit, since the price of gold is drawn into the general upward movement. The fundamental dependence of the supply of money upon the demand for it seems therefore to have been eliminated.

Credit inflation has become possible, at least within the confines of an independent national monetary system. In fact, because inflation entails changes in the external balance of payments (usually causing a deficit), and on the scale of the worldwide capitalist system gold continues to be the ultimate means of payment, a country's national economic policy then runs the risk of clashing with that of other countries.

The Role of Money in the Process of Accumulation

The monetary system thus passively fulfils an important "technical" function: that of adjusting the supply of money to the need for it expressed in a "state of equilibrium," that is, on the assumption of simple reproduction. It also fulfils another function, much more decisive in character, although totally ignored by conventional theory — that of making expanded reproduction possible. This I call the "active" function of money, thereby directing attention to the role of the monetary institutions that fulfil the function of the planner who, looking to the future, adjusts supply to demand in a dynamic way.

Capitalist accumulation requires, in fact, an increasing quantity of money not just because the gross national product is increasing but also because in order that the transformation of saving into investment may take place, it is constantly necessary that new money be introduced into the circuit *before* the gross national product has increased. New investment has no outlet yet at the moment when it is made, since all the outlets existing at a given moment cannot exceed the volume of production at that moment. But new investment will soon create this new outlet by expanding production. In order to invest, however, the entrepreneur needs to possess a certain amount of money. It therefore seems that some previously existing outlet must enable him to sell that part of his product the value of which is destined to *expand* production, so as to "realize" in money form the "saving" he has accomplished, his extra capital. The problem appears insoluble, for the entrepreneur can find no such outlet, since the outlets available at the time when he wants to sell cannot exceed the volume of present production, and the entrepreneur has to find today an outlet equal to the volume of tomorrow's production. In reality, it is enough for an extra quantity of money equal to the value destined for accumulation (which will create its own outlet tomorrow) to be placed today in the entrepreneur's hands — from whatever source this money may come.

Analyzing Marx's schemas of expanded reproduction, Rosa Luxemburg thought she had discovered that dynamic equilibrium is possible only if external outlets (external, that is, to the capitalist mode) exist as a precondition, so that when the capitalist mode has conquered the whole world it must find itself up against an insurmountable obstacle, and so automatically collapse. Rosa Luxemburg's mistake was that she did not take account of the role played by money as the means of restoring dynamic equilibrium.

Let us take Marx's own example, with a model of expanded reproduction in which half of the surplus value produced in

Department I (production of means of production) and a fifth of that produced in Department II (production of consumer goods) is "saved" during the first phase, to be "invested" at the beginning of the second, by being added to constant capital (C) and variable capital (V) in proportions identical with those of the first phase. We thus have here an extensive model of expanded reproduction, without any technical progress (without any change in the organic composition [C/V] of any of the branches between one phase and the other), made possible through an increase in the labor power available.

For the first phase we have:

$$\text{I} \quad 4,000\,C_1 + 1,000\,V_1 + 1,000\,S_1 \; (400\,ScI + 100\,SvI + 500\,S'_1)$$
$$= 6,000\,M1$$

$$\text{II} \quad 1,000\,C_2 + 750\,V_2 + 750\,S_2 \; (100\,Sc_2 + 50\,Sv_2 + 600\,S'_2)$$
$$= 3,000\,M2.$$

I have broken down the surplus value generated in each branch into its three elements: that which is saved for the purpose of accumulation in the same branch, realized in the form of a further investment in means of production (Sc); that which is saved for the purpose of a subsequent purchase of additional labor power (Sv); and that which is consumed (S'). These elements are put between parentheses.

The production of means of production during this period (6,000) exceeds the demand expressed at the same time (4,000 + 1,500) by the amount of the surplus value produced in I and not consumed (500). Similarly, the production of consumer goods (3,000) exceeds the demand expressed during this period (1,000 + 750 + 500 + 600) by the amount of the surplus value produced in II and not consumed (150).

During the next phase, however, the equilibrium equations become:

$$\text{I} \quad 4,400\,C_1 + 1,100\,V_1 + 1,100\,S_1$$

$$\text{II} \quad 1,000\,C_2 + 800\,V_2 + 800\,S_2$$

Over and above simple renewal of the means of production, the demand for extension of the productive apparatus at the beginning of the second phase absorbs the excess production of I during the first phase. In fact, $(4,400 + 1,600) - (4,000 + 1,500) = 500$. Similarly, the demand for consumer goods that results, during the second phase, from an increase in the amount of labor power employed absorbs the excess production of the first phase, since $(1,100 + 800) - (1,000 + 750) = 150$.

Thus, part of the first phase's production is absorbed during the second phase, and so on.

The assumptions made in Marx's example — different rates of accumulation in the two Departments, and unchanged organic compositions — are not essential. Anne-Marie Laulagnet has shown that dynamic equilibrium is possible provided that certain proportions are observed, even if we assume an equal rate of accumulation in the two Departments and organic compositions that gradually increase from one phase to another.

This model shows that there is no problem of "necessary external outlets" but only one of *credit*. Entrepreneurs must have at their disposal, during a given phase, monetary means that they will not in fact cover until, during the next phase, their production can be realized. Such realization will be possible if certain proportions (between M_1 and M_2, C_1 and C_2, etc.) are observed from one phase to the next.

If these proportions are kept to during the second phase, the entrepreneurs will be able to pay back at the end of this phase the advances they had previously been given, provided that the monetary system makes them a fresh advance, bigger than the previous one, corresponding to the requirements for equilibrium during the third phase, and so on.

Dynamic equilibrium is possible without external outlets provided that a continually increasing amount of money (at constant prices) is injected into the system. This quantity of new money reaches the entrepreneur either through the production of gold or through the banks. Marx analyzed the channels whereby additional gold makes its way into the economy a century ago in *Capital* and *Critique of Political Economy*, and I shall not go over that ground again. I will merely say that new gold production makes possible a special kind of sale: the gold producer buys the products of other entrepreneurs out of his profits (which are in the form of gold), either in order to consume them or to expand his production. The entrepreneurs are thus able to sell their "surplus product" (in which their real saving is embodied) and to realize in money form the value destined for the development of their industries. With this money they can purchase means of production and hire workers. The outlet existed potentially, but a special monetary mechanism was needed in order that it might be realized. Today it is through the channel of credit that the quantity of extra money is created *ex nihilo* by the banks. Schumpeter has shown how this money put at the disposal of entrepreneurs enables production to be expanded.

Even this service rendered by the banking system is not, however, fundamental in character. It is, indeed, only when the investment has created its own outlet that the advance can be repaid. If this does not occur, the issuing of money does not solve the problem of the absence of any outlet for the extra production.

The monetary system thus fulfils a delicate task, taking care to keep entrepreneurs' expectations within "reasonable" limits and calculating the probabilities of dynamic equilibrium. It plays the role of a planner watching over the maintenance of dynamic sectoral equilibria. This is why the capitalist system devised, at its very start, the *centralization* of credit. Credit existed before capitalism, but it was capitalism that organized centralized banking, made universal the use of bank money, and instituted a centralized system of fiduciary issue on the national scale as an essential condition for accumulation.

The Conditions in Which the Contemporary Monetary System Functions: Creeping Inflation

The quantity theory claims that only an increase in the volume of money can bring about a general increase in prices. The facts of history, when hastily considered, do seem to justify this theory — though the fall in the real cost of production of gold due to the discovery of richer mines suffices to explain the great price movements of the nineteenth century. After 1914 Aftalion was to show that the rate of exchange can also determine general price movements. It is now accepted that a general rise can be caused by rigidity in supply due to some bottleneck in relation to expanding overall monetary demand. A situation like this is frequent in time of war, of war preparation, or of reconstruction, when the production of consumer goods is limited or operates in conditions of increasing costs, while incomes to which there is no real equivalent are distributed by the state. It is also maintained that the struggle waged between social groups over their share of the national income can, when the mechanisms of competition are functioning badly, create a climate of general increase in prices. In all these cases, monetary expansion follows the price rise and does not precede it.

This being so, economists, perhaps out of desire to break away from the quantity theory, have managed to forget the case that in former times specially interested them, namely, the one in which an issue of money in excess of needs choked the channels of circulation and brought about a price rise. This is the only case that deserves to be called inflation, for it is the only one in which the rise in prices has a monetary origin.

Inflation is impossible within the framework of convertibility into gold. There may well be general increases in prices under this system, as a result of a fall in the relative cost of producing gold or of a rise in the real cost of producing goods in general, but it is impossible to conceive that the channels of circulation should be choked in such cases. Credits are, in fact, granted by the banks in response to demand. These credits serve to finance new investment. This new investment either creates its own outlet — and the borrower is able to pay back the banker (and when this happens there is no increase in prices, because production has grown in the same proportion as the income distributed) — or else it does not do this, and there is a crisis. In so far as the bank does not wish to suspend convertibility, it will avoid granting credit beyond a certain limit, because it knows that, for real reasons of imbalance between production and consumption, new investment beyond a certain point can no longer create its own outlet, even if the borrower were prepared to pay a high rate of interest.

As for gold, this too is incapable of choking the channels of circulation. If the rate of production of new gold increases, then either the central bank, which buys this gold at a fixed price, sees its reserves increasing without any increase in the credit it makes available, or else hoarders buy this gold in order to meet their needs. In any case, gold is put into circulation by the producers, who sell it.

While in this case there is no inflation, the situation is not the same when convertibility is abolished.

Fundamentally, it is the changes that have occurred in the conditions of competition that have radically altered the course of the general movement of prices. During the nineteenth century, in so far as competition constituted the rule and monopoly the exception, an entrepreneur was unable to increase his prices, because he would have lost his customers. Under these conditions the banks could not issue "too much credit" because, on the one hand, since entrepreneurs did not expect an increase in prices, they had no need of extra liquidities, and, on the other, the central bank, concerned to safeguard convertibility, prevented the commercial banks from granting credits in excess of the need for liquidities. Convertibility could thus be suspended only in exceptional situations, when the state issued purchasing power in paper money without any real equivalent.

In addition to this, competition, by generalizing new techniques, brought about a fall in real costs that was reflected in a chronic tendency for prices to fall. This tendency was offset by shorter bouts of general price increase, which were due to sharp reductions in the cost of producing gold. If we study the curve of wholesale prices between 1800 and 1900 we do not observe that "long wave" that Kondratiev caused to emerge by means of a skillful manipulation of statistics. This does not mean that, in certain periods that were more frequently interrupted by wars, a tendency to increased prices did not sometimes offset the general downward tendency that formed the backdrop of the century as a whole. At other periods a mighty wave of innovations may have served, on the contrary, to *intensify* this downward movement of prices.

In the twentieth century conditions have changed. Monopolies dominate the principal branches of production. Now, monopolies are not obliged to lower their prices. Competition between them proceeds by other methods. It was thus the resistance of prices, in the new structural conditions, to any downward movement that made it impossible to get back to the gold standard after the First World War. The first wave of difficulties that occurred swept convertibility clean away.

Since then there has been no barrier to increase in prices. Does this mean that this increase will be continuous? No, for if entrepreneurs want to raise the price level, they have to apply to the banks for increases in the credits that the latter allow to them. Since convertibility has been abolished, the central bank is free to agree or to refuse to follow such a policy. In this limited sense, management of money and credit has become a reality unknown to the previous century.

But in the event that the central bank follows a policy that accords with the wishes of the entrepreneurs, will the increase in prices go on indefinitely? We may well ask why the monopolies do not wish to keep on raising prices, why the increase in prices has not been continuous since 1914, why periods of price stabilization succeed periods of sharp increase (apart, of course, from periods when the price increase is due not to the behavior of entrepreneurs but to real causes: increase in costs of production, or disproportion between money incomes distributed and actual production, such as occurs in wartime). If the increase in prices does not go on uninterruptedly, this is because there is a level of real wages that ensures the sale of what is produced at a price yielding the maximum profit. In the last century wages constituted a fixed datum, like prices, against which the entrepreneur, isolated from his competitors, could do nothing. Today the situation is not the same. The monopolist tries to influence these two formerly independent factors. To the extent that the workers refuse to allow their real income to be reduced so as to be adjusted to this level, "wage inflation" is inevitable. But who is to be blamed for the rise in prices? The workers who refuse to let their wages be adjusted to the level that best suits the entrepreneurs, or the entrepreneurs who refuse to adjust their profits to the level of wages acceptable to the workers?

The struggle between classes over the division of income goes forward today in a setting where the confrontation between monopolies and trade unions is given institutional form. In so far as the working class accepts the "rules of the game," in other words, the ideology of social-democracy, adjustment of real wages to a certain level calculated so as to ensure equilibrium in autocentric growth becomes the subject of a social contract. This adjustment is secured through regular increases in nominal wages. Only if these increases are too big do they induce price increases. "Creeping inflation" is thus the mode of expression of the fundamental laws governing equilibrium in autocentric growth in our time. The system demands the abolition of convertibility and adjustment of the external value of the currency when rates of inflation have been more rapid than in other countries.

4. THE FORM OF AUTOCENTRIC ACCUMULATION: FROM CYCLE TO CONJUNCTURE

Fluctuations in the conjuncture — whether they take cyclical form (as was the case until the Second World War) or not, as has been the case since then — are manifestations of the inherent contradiction between capacity to produce and capacity to consume, which is characteristic of the capitalist mode of production, a contradiction that is continually being overcome through extending the capitalist market ever wider and deeper. Current economic theory is sometimes able to grasp this dynamic of contradiction — in the narrowly "economistic" terms of the combined working of the "multiplier" and the "accelerator," which conceal the origin of the contradiction — when this theory proves capable of rising above the monetary appearances of phenomena. It then reproduces Marx's analysis in a mechanistic and simplified form.

The historical law of this inherent contradiction of the capitalist mode of production is that it tends to get worse, as was shown by the exceptional scale of the crisis of the 1930s. But this tendency does not lead to a "spontaneous catastrophic collapse" of the system, because the latter can always react by organizing monopolies and bringing in the state to absorb the increasing surplus. The historical conditions within which accumulation on the world scale proceeds are of vital importance from this standpoint. The scientific and technical revolution of our time, together with the gradual integration of Eastern Europe into the world capitalist system, will probably modify to a considerable extent the conditions surrounding this accumulation on the world scale. The extension of capitalism to the periphery, the adjustment of the structure of the periphery to the requirements of accumulation at the center (i.e., the forms assumed by "international specialization" between the center and the periphery) must also be accorded importance in analyzing the conjuncture.

The cyclical form assumed by accumulation became very early the subject of economic study. For a long time, however, because current economic theory had made an article of faith out of the "law of markets" (according to which investment of savings that have succeeded in assuming the money form, through which they are obliged to pass, takes place automatically thanks to the finance market), the "cause" of the cycle was sought in money, the psychology of the entrepreneur, or the technical conditions of production — in other words, in what have been called "external" or "independent" variables. This view was inevitably a superficial one. It gave rise to an efflorescence of "theories" about the cycle — with Malthus, Sismondi, and (above all) Marx as three impressive exceptions. But the validity of the "law of markets" was so little questioned that Marx's analyses remained uncomprehended, wrongly interpreted, and rejected without real examination by marginalist critics, who defined the value of money by its purchasing power.

At the end of last century Wicksell was obliged to challenge the dogmatic status of the "law of markets," as a result of his study of general price movements and his attempt to discover the reasons why total supply and total demand can be unequal. Myrdal, from 1930 onward, and Keynes already from 1928 onward, but especially in 1936, carried further this critique of the "law of markets." Thereafter, study of the cycle could rise above psychological and monetary commonplaces to engage in study of the mechanisms that adjust the saving derived from total income to the investment required for economic growth.

The historical development of capitalism has not proceeded

along a regular upward path. Rather it has followed the line of a series of cyclical fluctuations accompanying a *general* upward tendency. The possibility of continuous growth in a capitalist economy without an "external" outlet was proved by Marx, and then again by Lenin, arguing against Rosa Luxemburg. The saving derived from the income of a previous period can be invested and so create its own outlet during a subsequent period, deepening the capitalist market without widening it. In this sense the "law of markets" possesses relative validity, provided that it is not forgotten that the capitalist form of development implies dissociation in time between the act of "saving" and the act of "investment." Credit, and the momentary advantage constituted by the conquest of new external outlets, facilitate the fundamental operation — the real investment of saving in money form. Real saving derived from income during the previous period must, before being invested, assume the form of money. The production of gold in the nineteenth century and the banking system today make possible the carrying out of this preliminary operation.

But the essential claim made by the "law of markets" is mistaken. Investment *can* create its own market — but it can also fail to create it. The special function of the theory of the cycle is, precisely, to determine the conditions under which investment does not succeed in creating its own market.

Money certainly gives flexibility to the economic system, but it also makes it possible for the system to break down owing to an imbalance between total supply and total demand. By enabling the act of saving to be separated from the act of investment, money creates the possibility of crises. Does this mean that it is solely responsible for them? If this were so, it would have to be explained why this imbalance is a periodic and not a chronic phenomenon, why it is overcome on each occasion, and why the phenomenon of the cycle is distinctive of the capitalist mode of production alone, and not of other modes of production that use money, such as simple commodity economy. In fact, if the cycle is a "monetary" phenomenon in the capitalist mode of production, it is so no more and no less than all other economic phenomena. This is why all theories of the cycle based on study of credit mechanisms deal only superficially with the problem. In fact, money does not play an active role in exchange: the outlet (the market) has to exist already; money on its own cannot create it. All that money can do is facilitate a transition in time. Serious modern theories have ended by rallying to the view that the cycle was the specific form of development by which the regularly occurring disequilibrium between saving and investment was regularly overcome — the conception set out in Marx's analysis.

The "Pure Theory" of the Cycle: The Monetary Illusion

Keynes's analysis has been described as "metastatic." In *The General Theory*, the volume of investment determines, through the multiplier, the level of national income. The volume of this investment itself depends on two independent variables: the rate of interest, on the one hand, and, on the other, the marginal efficiency of capital. There is no reaction from income to investment — or, more precisely, investment is proportional only to income, not to the growth of income. The result is that the equilibrium established at the level of the national income at which saving and investment are equal is a stable equilibrium.

The General Theory does indeed contain a sketch for a theory of the cycle. A sudden fall in the marginal efficiency of capital is accompanied by a rise in the rate of interest, because it leads to an increase in liquidity preference. Investment suddenly slumps, and with it total demand: the national income shrinks to the point at which the amount of saving derived from this income no longer exceeds the diminished amount of investment. This analysis does not, however, take the theory of the cycle any further, because the sudden fall in the efficiency of capital remains unexplained.

Keynes turns to psychology, implying the impossibility of men entertaining indefinitely optimistic expectations where future return on capital is concerned. If, however, there were no objective reason why the level of this return should fall when a certain point was reached in development, such expectations *would* correspond to a real state of affairs.

At most, accidental "historical" causes might from time to time produce a psychological crisis, and so a contraction in total income. But the *regularity* of the cycle calls for an explanation rooted in the mechanism of the economic dynamic itself.

Abandoning Keynes's assumption of stable values of the propensities to save and to invest, Kaldor, Kalecki, and others have constructed models that take account of the possible generation of fluctuation in total income. Harrod, perhaps, is the writer who has best analyzed, up to now, the logical sequence linking all the factors that connect national income with investment, and vice versa. According to him, the imbalance in economic growth arises from the basic antinomy between actual saving, which essentially depends on the *level* of real income, and desirable saving, which essentially depends on the *rate of growth* of real income. In *The Trade Cycle* Harrod constructs a model of the cycle by making the multiplier and the accelerator function in the following way. An initial investment engenders an increase in national income, which itself determines a secondary investment (acceleration). The boom continues until the multiplier has lost magnitude sufficiently to annul the action of the accelerator. This is indeed what happens during prosperity: propensity to consume diminishes in proportion as income decreases, since the share of this income taken by profit increases faster than the share taken by wages.

There is no special chapter in *Capital* that brings together all the elements of a theory of the cycle, but, nevertheless, Marx revealed the essence of the process through his examination of the phenomena known today as the "multiplier" and the "accelerator." In Chapter 21 of Volume II he showed that it was possible for investment to create its own market through the spreading and deepening of capitalism. In this same chapter, however, he analyzed the mechanisms by which what is today known as "propensity to save" was linked with total income. As income increases, so, proportionately, does the share taken by profit — the income essentially destined to saving and investment. This phenomenon corresponds to the diminution of the multiplier in Harrod's account. The multiplier is, in fact, merely the ratio between investment and that part of income the distribution of which is connected with it, which is spent (and so, the whole of this income, less what is saved). When the volume of the national income increases, as the share taken by profits increases more rapidly than that taken by wages, the amount of expenditure engendered by a given investment diminishes. If Marx considered that this diminution of the multiplier (in the form of an imbalance between incomes spent, the source of ultimate demand, and production supplied, the source of this distribution of income) did not block development *from the very outset* this was because he had previously analyzed what has subsequently become known as the accelerator.

When examining the replacement of fixed capital, he had suggested that an increase in ultimate demand might in some circumstances (those that are found together precisely at the end of a depression) engender a sudden investment, which in turn, through the distribution of income it entailed, would create new possibilities for the investment of fixed capital. But Marx immediately denied that this phenomenon of replacement of fixed capital, analogous to the accelerator, owes its existence to the technical requirements of production: the need to build a machine that will last a long time, in order to respond to any increase, even a temporary one, in ultimate production. He ascribed this phenomenon to the essential laws of the capitalist mode of production. An increase in demand, even a slight one, due to the opening up of a new market (internal, in the case of a demand connected with technical progress, or else external) at the end of the depression, causes a possible investment in fixed capital to seem a profitable prospect once again. All hoarded saving therefore suddenly moves into such investment. The new production engenders a distribution of income that makes this investment profitable indeed. Marx thought that in a planned economy these constraints of technique would be reflected in fluctuations in the amount of reserve stocks but that they would in no way determine the level of investment, which would be freed from its present dependence on immediate profitability.

Marx's analysis is in reality more complex in that, besides analyzing the antinomy between "multiplier" and "accelerator," it deals with the secondary problem of the cyclical fluctuations in wages, and also in that it is grafted upon the theory of the tendency of the rate of profit to fall. During prosperity the amount of unemployment declines, real wages rise, and more intensive use is then made of machinery. During depression an opposite movement takes place. These two mechanisms intensify the duration of both depression and prosperity periods. Dobb attaches an importance to this phenomenon, examined in Volume I of *Capital*, which, in my opinion, is false to Marx's thinking. However, the tendency of the rate of profit to fall shows itself by way of the cycle. At the beginning of the period of prosperity, the "counter-tendencies" are stronger than the general tendency. At the end of this period, the counter-tendencies are exhausted: the increase in the rate of surplus value, which conceals the effect of the increase in the organic composition of capital, slows down. The rate of profit slumps. But although this law manifests itself through the cycle, it is not the *cause* of the cycle, which lies in the combined effect of the evolution of the capacity to consume, which does not increase as does the capacity to produce (owing to the increasing share of income taken by profit), and of the immediate prospect of profitability, which guides investment and which, thanks to the accelerator, delays the baneful effect of the diminution of the multiplier.

If, then, Harrod arrives, in his study of the cycle, at a description that seems correct, this is because he breaks with the Keynesian analysis on an essential point. Harrod has linked propensity to invest directly to income, without going through the double intermediary of the marginal efficiency of capital and the rate of interest. He has taken as the starting point for his construction simply the antinomy between capacity to produce (linked with the saving derived from previous production) and capacity to consume (linked with the distribution of income that production engenders). He completely ignores interest, which he considers incapable of seriously affecting investment. He also ignores psychological phenomena, which he sees as dependent variables.

Hicks, like Harrod a post-Keynesian but much more attached to the traditional rate of interest, has sought to throw a bridge between Harrod's analysis based on the mechanism that links propensity to invest with total income, and the Keynesian analysis based on the antinomy between interest and the marginal efficiency of capital. In his view, a fall in the rate of interest (if the marginal efficiency of capital remains stable) entails an increase in investment, and thereby in income. But an increase in income increases the volume of money required for transactions. If the supply of money remains fixed, and if liquidity preference remains unchanged, the increase in the demand for money for transactions will in its turn bring about a rise in the level of interest. The development in time of these mechanisms, given schematic form in the two curves of liquidity and of the equivalence between saving and investment, is nothing other than the cycle.

Are we not here back in Hawtrey's utopia? An adequate injection of money, together with the increase in income, would apparently make it possible, allowing for a stable level of liquidity preference, to satisfy the growing need for money for transactions without raising the rate of interest. Prosperity would be continuous, unless, of course, the efficiency of capital were to decline — something that would then have to be explained, as Harrod and Marx have explained it, exclusively by an imbalance between capacity to produce and capacity to consume.

Hicks accepts the Keynesian hypothesis that the point has been reached at which, whatever the amount of money injected, the rate of interest is already at such a low level that it cannot sink any lower. No monetary measures can then avert the crisis. This analysis is unable, however, to account for the cycle in the more general case, that of the nineteenth century, when the average rate of interest stood at a higher level than today. One could, of course, invoke the marginal efficiency of capital: the cycle would then be seen as engendered by the independent movement of this variable, with the level of interest remaining situated relatively stably at its lowest point throughout the whole process. Here, however, one would stumble over that very difficulty from which one had started out, namely: what is the origin of the sinusoidal "psychological" movement?

The Theory of Maturity and the Theory of the Surplus in Present-Day Monopoly Capitalism: From Cycle to Conjuncture

For a century the cycle thus constituted the necessary form assumed by the development of capitalism. The cyclical imbalance between investment and saving was dictated by the mechanism of growth, by the functioning of the accumulation of saving that periodically became too plentiful in relation to possibilities for investment. The outcome of cyclical development was growth. There was no superimposing of one phenomenon upon another, different in kind — the cycle, on the one hand, and, on the other, the century-long general tendency. Construction of a "pure" model of the cycle in which the end point would be the same as the starting point is a fantasy. The starting point of the movement — the sudden investment in fixed capital — is incomprehensible outside of the setting of *technical progress.*

In the absence of the opening of an external market, only the introduction of new techniques enables the market to be expanded. And even the conquest of an external market does not resolve the imbalance between supply and demand on the world scale. In order to explain world recovery, we must therefore analyze the effects of the implementation of new techniques. In a period of depression, the general stagnation furnishes a strong motive for technical improvements, for the enterprise that takes the initiative in introducing innovations recovers its lost profitability. The new method comes into general use and, since progress is usually expressed in the more intensive employment of machinery, a new demand appears. Production starts up again, thanks to the sudden investment called for by the production and installation of the new machines. The subsequent development then takes cyclical form, but at the end of this movement the national income stands at a level higher than at the beginning. Something new has happened: a new technique has become general. Consequently, the volume of production has increased. The capitalist market is constantly expanding by this means, and the cycle is thus a feature that inevitably runs all through the upward trend.

However, independent of the mechanism of cyclical imbalance

between saving and investment there are real causes that tend to make these two overall quantities more or less easily "adjustable" in the long run. In this sense, the long-term tendency retains a reality of its own, even though this reality manifests itself only through the cycle. If the imbalance between saving and investment becomes chronic, this is reflected, during the cycle, in a longer period of depression and a shorter period of prosperity. If, on the contrary, equilibrium is easy to achieve, this is reflected in a shorter period of depression and a longer one of prosperity.

What are these real reasons that cause equilibrium between saving and investment to be either easier or less easy? Much was said, in the years following the Great Crisis, about "chronic stagnation" and about the "maturity" of capitalism. Keynes discovered at that time the possibility of chronic underemployment. In fact, the analysis of maturity made from a Keynesian standpoint is ultimately monetary in character. It is impossible to accept the thesis of the blocking of growth for purely monetary reasons. This being so, must it be admitted that since Marx study of the development of capitalism has been given up for good? At the beginning of the nineteenth century Ricardo thought he could prophesy a "stationary era" on the basis of diminishing returns operating on a historic scale. Any conception of a stationary state is entirely alien to Marxism. The law of the tendency of the rate of profit to fall merely signifies that the contradiction between the capacity to produce and the capacity to consume must necessarily get worse and worse. The ultimate reason for the overall imbalance remains the contradiction between the division of income between wages and profit (and thereby the division of income between consumption and saving), on the one hand, and, on the other, the division of production between the production of capital goods and the production of consumer goods. A certain volume of ultimate production necessitates a certain volume of intermediate production. This latter quantity is merely a way of looking at the volume of investment required to produce the desired volume of ultimate goods. Harrod, by abandoning monetary analyses of the rate of interest and psychological analyses of the marginal efficiency of capital, in order to concentrate directly on the capital-output ratio (measuring the capital-intensity of production, that is, the ratio between the production of capital goods and that of ultimate goods), on the one hand, and on the division of total income between consumption and saving, on the other, comes remarkably close to Marx's analysis.

In the nineteenth century, the youth of capitalism, the huge possibilities offered by the breakup of the precapitalist economies were collected in a tendency favorable to adjustment between saving and investment. Depressions were then less deep and less prolonged than the one that occurred in the 1930s. But then, just at the moment when the theory of maturity was forecasting the "end of capitalism" and "permanent stagnation," at the very moment when a simplified version of Marxism was adopting, under the title of "the general crisis of capitalism," an apocalyptic vision that was in fact alien to Marxism, the rate of growth of Western capitalism became faster, and, furthermore, growth lost its cyclical character.

Marxist analysis brought up to date provides the only explanation of this development. Baran and Sweezy have begun such an analysis by examining in a new way the "law of the increase of the surplus" and the forms whereby this surplus is absorbed. At the same time, moreover, the theory of monopoly capitalism explains why the cycle has disappeared. The cycle was due only to the inability of capitalism to "plan" investment. Now, monopoly capitalism can do this, in a certain sense and within certain limits, given the active help of the state. As soon as capitalism is liberated from the uncontrolled effects of acceleration, the cycle is no more, and all that remains is a conjuncture that is followed and observed, with the action taken by the state and the monopolies (the former in the service of the latter) to mitigate its fluctuations.

It may be asked why the cycle in its classical form should disappear, to give place to conjunctural oscillations that are close together, irregular, and of smaller dimensions, only after the Second World War, whereas the monopolies had already come into being at the end of the last century; and why the crisis of the 1930s was the most violent in the history of capitalism, if the capitalism of the monopolies is capable of "planning" investment better than competitive capitalism was able to do. The answer must be sought in the way that the international system functions. The monopolies are indeed able to "plan" investment up to a certain point, on condition that the monetary system lends itself to this being done, which presupposes that convertibility into gold has been abandoned and that the monetary authorities, together with the entire economic policy of the state, work in this direction. The "concerted economy" — planning, Western-style — means nothing more than awareness of this new possibility. Now, not only has this awareness, like all awareness, lagged behind reality, but also, and above all, the framework within which it can be translated into action is *national*. The international system has remained, long after the formation of the monopolies, regulated by "automatic mechanisms." On the international plane, therefore, no "concerting" is possible. The attempt made by Great Britain and France, after the war of 1914-1918, to re-establish the gold standard in external relations, although it had been finally given up in the internal economy, reflected this hiatus between the internal and the international orders. By making practically impossible any concerted internal policy, the international automatisms were largely responsible for the exceptional gravity of the crisis of the 1930s. The monopolies, which make possible a conjunctural economic policy on the national plane, also cause the fluctuations of the cycle to be aggravated if this policy is not followed. Keynes understood this. The maintenance of external controls after the Second World War was to make national economic policies effective for the first time; and it was at that time that there began, for example, France's "concerted planning." The subsequent prosperity, with the Common Market and the liberalizing of external relations that has accompanied this prosperity, now jeopardize the effectiveness of these policies. This is why the question of the international order is again on the agenda. The "order" that was established after the war, symbolized by the International Monetary Fund, is not an order at all, for it remains based upon confidence in automatic mechanisms. This "confidence" plays into the hands of the most powerful country, the United States, which is why a world economic policy is almost impossible. This flaw in the system expresses a new contradiction that has matured between the demands of the economic order, which can no longer be secured by way of national economic policy alone (because capitalism now possesses an essential *world* dimension) and the still-national character of institutions and structures. If this contradiction is not overcome, it is impossible to rule out the possibility of extremely grave "conjunctural accidents."

5. INTERNATIONAL RELATIONS AND THE INTERLINKING OF THE NATIONAL FORMATIONS OF CENTRAL CAPITALISM

The Economic Theory of Equilibrium in the Balance of Payments

Equilibrium in the balance of payments, which, at best, exists only as a tendency, is dependent on a permanent adjustment of the international structures. Now these are, so far as relations between the developed and the underdeveloped parts of the world are concerned, structures of asymmetrical domination by the center of the world system over the periphery. External equilibrium — international order — is possible only because the structures of the periphery are shaped so as to meet the needs of accumulation at the center, that is, provided that the development of the center engenders and maintains the underdevelopment of the periphery. Refusal to perceive this essential fact betrays the ideological character of current economic theory, which is based upon the postulate of universal harmony.

Is a momentary deficit in a country's balance of payments, whatever its cause, whether transient or structural, capable of being reabsorbed on its own by influencing the level of the rate of exchange, prices, and economic activity? Economic theory answers this question in the affirmative.

Adam Smith allowed only the price mechanism to enter into the construction of international equilibrium. In this he was following, on the one hand, the old, mercantilist tradition of Bodin, Petty, Locke, and Cantillon, who had observed that disequilibrium in the trade balance was compensated by movements of gold, and, on the other, the quantity-theory tradition according to which it was the movement of gold that in turn determined the general price level. Disequilibrium ought therefore to become reabsorbed on its own. It was only one step from there to declaring that the only possible cause of external disequilibrium was "internal inflation" — a step that the Bullionists were to take, under Ricardo's leadership, at the beginning of the nineteenth century. The arguments of Bosanquet, who attributed disequilibrium of the balance to nonmonetary causes (export difficulties due to war, together with the payment of subsidies to foreign countries), failed to convince contemporaries.

It was Wicksell who brought out, at the end of the nineteenth century, the role played by changes in demand in the mechanism of international equilibrium. A deficit in the balance was analyzed as a transfer of purchasing power. This extra purchasing power would enable the foreign country concerned to increase its imports, while the deficitary country would have to reduce its imports. International equilibrium would be achieved without any alteration in prices. This revolutionary theory was taken up by Ohlin, who claimed, on this basis, that it was possible for German reparations to be paid. The extent to which the classical theory of price-effects (connected with the quantity theory) continued to be influential, however, can be appreciated from the fact that so eminent a thinker as Keynes refused to give up the old outlook. If he alleged that it was impossible for Germany to pay reparations, this was because he believed that the working of the price elasticities of German exports and imports would bring about a "perverse" rather than a "normal" effect. It was only the post-Keynesians who incorporated in the theory of international equilibrium the essence of the method inaugurated by Bosanquet.

These two ways of looking at the problem — the "price" way and the "income" way — are often presented as being mutually exclusive. Yet these are merely two aspects of the same phenomenon, namely, demand. Does demand depend on price, or on income? The entire construction of Walras's "general equilibrium" remains based upon the law of supply and demand. It was with the intention of replacing the labor theory of value by the utility theory that the first analysts of the market, Say in particular, put forward the law of demand. The responses of demand and supply to variations in prices are then explained by the diminishing marginal utility of goods. Equilibrium is obtained without any elements other than these responses playing a part. This construction remains fragile, because Say and Walras overlook the fundamental element in demand that is constituted by income. They make the law of supply and demand contribute more than it is capable of contributing. The law of the diminishing utility of goods may well explain that demand falls when prices rise, but only provided that the level of incomes remains unaltered. Now, the distribution of incomes is, in the theory of general equilibrium, dependent on the relative prices of goods. Any change in prices alters incomes. Recourse is then had to "periodic" analysis in order to escape from the vicious circle of marginalism: today's prices depend on yesterday's incomes, and yesterday's incomes on the prices of the day before yesterday. Actually, this resort to history constitutes a real admission of the impotence of marginalism.

Analyses of the price elasticities of external trade are of the same order as the former analyses of supply and demand. They assume that the national incomes of the partners in exchange are stable, and thereby they lose all power to explain the real movements of international trade.

The introduction of the responses of supply and demand to variations in income in general, and of the responses of external trade to variations in the national income in particular, was a veritable revolution. But economists are still content to note that, the level of incomes being so much at a certain period, the level of exchanges of a certain product is so much. It is noted that, at a later period, the incomes, prices, and quantities exchanged are different. This provides a description of the changes that take place, but does not explain them.

The theory of price-effects. The classical theory of price-effects was worked out at the beginning of the nineteenth century in the context of assumptions corresponding to the reality of that time (the gold standard) and on the basis of the quantity theory of money. Since any importer has a choice between buying foreign currency (foreign gold coins) and sending gold abroad (in the form of ingots), a deficit in the balance of payments cannot bring down the national rate of exchange to a sufficient extent to influence the terms of trade and favor exports. Therefore, disequilibrium can ultimately find reflection only in a drain of gold. The general decline in internal prices resulting from this drain, and, consequently, the decline in the prices of exports, as compared with the stability of foreign prices, and, consequently, the stability of the prices of imports, discourages the latter, favors the former, and enables equilibrium eventually to be restored. It is the worsening of the terms of trade that does this.

Recently it has been perceived that the alteration in the terms of trade, which, on the one hand, favored (or disfavored) exports, also lowered (or raised) their unit prices. An internal increase in prices, like a fall in these prices, may affect the state of the balance for better or for worse, depending on the level of elasticities. The same is true, but the other way around, where imports are concerned. Analysis of the effects of different combinations of price elasticities has become commonplace today. The best formulation has been given by Joan Robinson, who takes account of these four elasticities: that of the national supply of exports, that of the foreign supply of imports, that of the national demand for imports, and that of the foreign demand for exports. It should be recalled that, long before the Keynesians, Nogaro had criticized Augustin Cournot's theory of the exchange, which assumed what had to be proved, namely, that price elasticities are such that devaluation makes it possible to reabsorb the deficit.

If the economy is perfectly integrated, a change in the price of imports must entail a proportional change in all internal prices, and, consequently, in the price of exports. Is not the relatively higher price of imports bound to influence *all* prices in an upward direction? Aftalion showed that the level of the exchange itself had an effect, in some cases, on the internal price level. It ought not to be assumed that the rate of exchange affects only the prices of imported goods, through variations in cost, and that devaluation ultimately affects the prices of other goods only in so far as imported goods enter into their manufacture. Aftalion shows, by means of examples from history, that the rate of exchange does sometimes influence *all* prices through an increase in money incomes. Will the influence of an alteration in the rate of exchange upon the income of importers (through stocks of goods that have been acquired and paid for previously), upon the income of holders of foreign shares, and upon the income of exporters and producers for export always be capable of bringing about a general increase or decrease in prices proportional to this alteration in the rate of exchange? If the influence goes far enough, if the fluctuations in money income are not compensated by fluctuations in hoarding, and if, finally, the whole of money income comes on to the market (as demand), then this will probably happen. In that case, the balance of payments, after devaluation has exhausted its effects, will be exactly what it was before devaluation. The chronic disequilibrium, which had been temporarily reabsorbed, now reappears. Numerous examples of this type of mechanism are to be found in history, especially in the monetary history of Latin America. In the nineteenth century successive devaluations took place there that proved inoperative in the long run because they were followed by a general and proportionate increase in prices. These experiences prove that it is not possible to resolve a real disequilibrium of the external balance due to profound structural maladjustments by currency manipulations. They also show that the internal and external values of money cannot long remain different from each other. Despite the real existence of home-produced goods that do not figure in international trade, the "domestic" sector does eventually become subject to the influence of foreign prices, which is exerted through the channel of incomes. For example, the devaluation of the franc in Mali in 1967, which, according to the French experts, was going to restore equilibrium to Mali's external balance, resulted in a proportionate and almost immediate increase in all prices, despite the freezing of wages. Here we see an extreme example that shows how the structure of the dominant prices imposes itself upon a dominated economy.

True, it can be quoted on the other side that, during the nineteenth century in Europe, the gold standard and the compensatory monetary policy of manipulating discount rates proved effective. But, if this happened, was it not merely because in the long run the balance of payments was in equilibrium, with disequilibria never more than momentary, conjunctural incidents?

The theory of exchange-effect. Given the assumption of inconvertible currencies, the existence of a rate of exchange that can vary widely at the whim of the balance of payments, does this not bring us back to the price-effect without the quantity theory coming into the argument? In this case, indeed, the alteration in the rate of exchange entails an alteration in the price of imports, but there is no reason why the price of home-produced goods and the price of exports, which must relate to internal prices, should alter. This is because the quantity of money continues to be stationary, say the quantitativists. Others say it is because the rate of exchange does not always necessarily influence internal prices.

The analysis needs to be completed. On the one hand, depending on price elasticities, the alteration in the rate of exchange may have "normal" effects or "perverse" ones. On the other, the price of imports may, here, too, influence the level of internal prices, and thereby that of exports, and in the same way — via costs, via the behavior of the dominant income, and via the transmission of price structures.

Here, too, short-term capital movements may prevent alteration in the rate of exchange (and in prices), just as formerly it prevented the movement of gold (and of prices). If the central bank raises the interest rate, it attracts foreign short-term capital, just as under a gold system, and for the same reason. In the event of a temporary deficit in the balance it can thus prevent devaluation (and the consequent increase in prices), just as under a gold system it could prevent a drain of gold (and the consequent decrease in prices). But this action comes up against the same limit as before. If the deficit is structural, chronic, and profound, the inflow of foreign capital will not succeed in neutralizing it — all the less because the prospect of losing on the exchange in the event of devaluation does not attract many speculators ready to be content with a small profit due to the increase in the interest rate.

Finally, what are we to conclude from the analysis of price-effects? First, that there are no price-effects but only an exchange-effect. Disequilibrium in the external balance does not influence prices directly, through the quantity of money. It affects the rate of exchange, and this in turn affects all prices. It follows from this that alterations in the rate of exchange can never, whatever the price elasticities may be, resolve the difficulties of a structural disequilibrium, since at the end of a certain period things are back as they were at the start. Second, it must be realized that, even in the transition period, fluctuations in the exchange do not necessarily improve the situation of the external balance, owing to the existence of critical price elasticities.

If we consider that, in the countries of the periphery, the elasticity of demand for imports is slight owing to the impossibility of substituting local production for foreign production; that in these countries the incomes of exporters are all the more important in proportion to the degree of the country's integration; that the influence of these incomes on demand is supplemented by decisive psychological considerations that link the internal value of the currency to its external value; and that there is a mechanism whereby the price structure of the dominant economy is transmitted to the dominated one — then we may conclude that, in nine cases out of ten, devaluation will in no way resolve the chronic disequilibrium of the balance of payments, either in the short run or, *a fortiori*, in the long, but that on the contrary this devaluation will worsen the external situation in the short run.

The theory of income-effect. Wicksell and Ohlin presented the mechanism of the income-effect in a very simple form. The deficit in the external balance is settled by a transfer abroad of purchasing power. This fresh purchasing power must enable the economy that benefits from it to import more than before. On the other hand, the transfer obliges the deficit economy to reduce its demand for imports. As for the transfer of gold that takes place under the gold-standard system, this provides support for the transfer of purchasing power, and nothing more. Obviously if we assume that convertibility and flexible exchanges have been abandoned, then disequilibrium, which is on the one hand a transfer of purchasing power, has on the other an effect on the rate of exchange. These secondary effects of disequilibrium on the rate of exchange may obstruct the working of the re-equilibration mechanism — for instance, by canceling out the transfer of purchasing power through a price increase. But the mechanism remains essentially of the same nature as before.

The advantage of Ohlin's theory over the previous one is that it enables us to explain the re-equilibration that takes place in the balance, however the terms of trade may evolve. According to the classical theory it is the alteration in these terms in a certain direction that re-establishes equilibrium. Now, experience has proved many times over that re-equilibration has taken place despite a perverse evolution of the terms of trade. The theory of transfer of purchasing power also has the merit of bringing out the point that there is only a *tendency* for equilibrium to be restored. Nothing ensures that the increase in purchasing power resulting from a surplus in the external balance will be wholly concentrated on demand for imports.

Keynesian thinking, by putting in the forefront the multiplier effects of a primary increase in income, was to make possible the final perfecting of the theory. This was done by the post-Keynesians, in particular Metzler and Machlup. Reduced to its simplest terms, the mechanism is as follows. A positive net external balance operates like an independent demand; it determines, through the working of the multiplier mechanism, a greater increase in the national income, which, given the propensity to import, makes possible a readjustment of the external balance. Conversely, a negative net external balance determines a shrinkage in total income, which facilitates a reduction in imports, which then contributes to bringing the external balance back to equilibrium.

The models put forward by Machlup and Metzler enable one to take account simultaneously of the effects of variations in country A's balance upon country B, and of the reciprocal effects of B's balance upon that of A. Let me mention straight away an interesting case, namely, that in which the contraction of national income in the "paying" and "receiving" countries is such that the debtor country is unable to settle its debt: the possibility of international equilibrium thus depends in this case on the value of the propensities to consume and to invest in the two countries concerned. This example shows that equilibrium in the external balance merely reflects a structural adjustment of the economies that confront each other, the conditions for which it makes apparent. The question of what the different propensities are, together with the reasons why they are stable and the changes that affect them, is not a question of "empirical fact" but a fundamental theoretical question. What, in reality, is meant by the structural adjustment that conditions equilibrium in external payments? This adjustment is expressed precisely through changes in propensities, in particular propensities to import. We are therefore not free to imagine whatsoever "models" we may choose, in an arbitrary way — we need to know how and why propensities change.

In rejecting the multiplier analysis, modern writers have mostly gone back to the traditional price-effect, at least where the under-developed countries are concerned. During depression, the prices of exports fall, even though the local currency stands firm (in a case of monetary integration, for example). Should it not be concluded from this that the underdeveloped countries prove the possibility of a direct price-effect? That in these countries the fluctuations in the balance of payments entail fluctuations in prices through the intermediary of international currency move-ments? Not at all. Prices fluctuate at the mercy of demand in the underdeveloped countries just as in the developed ones. If the prices of the underdeveloped countries' exports fall, say, in a depression period, this is not due to the deficit in the external balance but to a decline in the demand for these goods, a demand that mainly lies abroad. The volume and the price of exports fall together and for the same reason. The deficit in the balance has nothing to do with *causing* this fall: on the contrary, it results from it.

The conclusions at which we arrive, where the theory of the readjustment of the balance of payments is concerned, are thus wholly negative. In the first place, despite appearances, the price-effect no more functions in the underdeveloped countries than it does in the developed ones. Secondly, the exchange-effect does not tend to restore equilibrium. Alterations in the rate of exchange are often, especially in the underdeveloped countries, effective only for a limited period, until the internal increase in prices has become general and proportional to the fall in the rate of exchange, and are often effective in a perverse direction (owing to the price elasticities). Thirdly, the income-effect is only a tendency, and implies the presence of a structural adjustment that constitutes the very essence of the problem. There is, then, no mechanism that automatically re-equilibrates the external balance. All that can be said for certain is that imports, in general, transfer pur-chasing power abroad in a precise monetary form, and that this transfer naturally tends to make possible subsequent exports. But this tendency is very general in character. It is similar to that by which, in a market economy, any purchase makes possible a subsequent sale. Just as the existence of this profound tendency does not justify the "law of markets," so it does not justify the construction of a theory of automatic international equilibrium.

Equilibrium exchange rate or structural adjustment? The real features of two economic systems in contact with each other may thus be such that the balance of payments cannot be equilibrated in the context of freedom of exchange. Since the automatic mechanisms do not function, it seems that in this situation there is no equilibrium rate of exchange. What is, in fact, called the equilibrium exchange rate is a rate that ensures equilibrium in the balance of payments without restrictions on imports and the "natural" movement of long-term capital. If it is said that the mechanisms that readjust incomes have only a *tendency* to operate, this amounts merely to saying that such a rate does not always exist. To put it more precisely, as the mechanisms of the exchange belong to the short term, whereas structural readjustment is a long-term matter, there is not always an equilibrium rate of exchange, and still less a "natural" and "spontaneous" one.

Yet one gets the impression that an equilibrium rate *did* exist throughout the nineteenth century. "Par" was certainly at that time, from one point of view, the "normal" rate of exchange between two currencies that were both convertible into gold. Buying and selling of gold by the banks of issue, at a fixed price and in unlimited amounts, confined the fluctuations of the exchange rate between the narrow limits of the gold points. Convertibility into gold gave the world system sufficient solidity for the mechanisms of structural adjustment to function. However, this structural adjustment, submitted to by the weak and imposed by the strong, had nothing harmoious about it; on the contrary, it reflected the gradual shaping of the world in an ever more uneven way.

What happens, though, to the theory of the exchange if convertibility is suspended? As the purpose of this theory is to explain the ratio that obtains between the values of two currencies, one's general conception regarding the value of money is what ultimately determines one's conception of the fundamental nature of the exchange. This is why marginalism, which defined the value of money as its purchasing power, arrived at the theory, on the question of the exchange, of the parity of purchasing powers. And just as it ended up with the quantity theory in the internal domain, so also was it to end up with an international quantity theory, determining an international distribution of gold that would ensure the equilibrium of the exchanges at the level of purchasing powers.

According to my analysis, in which I reject the quantity theory, it is necessary, when determining the internal value of money, to distinguish the case of convertibility from that of inconvertibility. In the former case, the real cost of gold production is what ultimately sets limits to variations in the value of money. In *this* sense, par did indeed constitute the normal rate of exchange. When convertibility is abandoned, so that the central bank is no longer buying and selling gold in unlimited amounts and at a fixed price, this price may itself be drawn into the general upward movement, so that sight is lost of the concatenation of mechanisms that now seem perfectly reversible. Just as there is no longer a normal price level, so there is no longer a normal rate of exchange. Where the currency is inconvertible, a structural deficit in the balance of payments makes it necessary to devalue.

The devaluation of an inconvertible currency gives rise in its turn to a wave of inflation that brings the situation back to where it was before. Once again it becomes clear that chronic disequilibrium cannot be avoided except by way of control over external trade and capital movements, by direct influence on real movements. When the currency has become inconvertible, the system no longer possesses the solidity it needs in order to wait for the income-effect to exhaust its consequences and for equilibrium to be restored. The tendency to disequilibrium entails permanent instability.

Some economists lay down an additional condition when defining the equilibrium exchange rate, namely, that it must ensure full employment. The connection established between the level of employment and the rate of exchange is, at bottom, highly artificial. It follows from an almost caricatural simplification of the Keynesian analysis. Joan Robinson links the level of the national income to the rate of interest in a mechanical way, so that, in her view, there is always a level of interest that ensures full employment — whereas Keynes rightly insisted on showing that it was possible for unemployment to become an insoluble problem. Mrs. Robinson then links, in an equally artificial way, the international movement of capital with the rate of interest — whereas these movements are dictated by the absolute and relative volume of incomes from property, and prospects of profitability of investment, which are largely independent of fluctuations in the rate of interest. She goes on to show how to each level of interest (and therefore of employment) there corresponds a level of the exchange that equilibrates the balance of payments. This way of considering that one of a group of variables can always be fixed arbitrarily because the others then adjust themselves to this arbitrary value is typical of the method employed by the analysts of "general equilibrium." It is liable to all the criticism that can be made of the empiricist method in economics. It is thoroughly formalist, and denies the existence of causal relations that are fundamentally irreversible.

In reality, such an "equilibrium" rate of exchange may very well be — and certainly is, in relations between developed and underdeveloped countries — an exchange rate of "domination." To each level of the exchange there correponds a certain distribution of relative profitability of investments in the different sectors. But, in reality, it is not the exchange that determines the volume of absorption of foreign capital by the underdeveloped country. On the contrary, capital flows in to the extent that the developed countries have free capital to dispose of, and that general "real" conditions make these external investments profitable; and, by weighing upon the balance of payments, they determine an "equilibrium" level of the exchange — in other words, a level that makes possible payment of interest on imported capital and payment for the volume of imports determined by the degree to which the underdeveloped countries are integrated into the international market: that is, determined by the demand for foreign goods that the volume of exports (bound up with this degree of integration) makes possible. In other words, the mechanism of the exchange enables the structure of the underdeveloped country to be adjusted to that of the dominant country. In this sense, a "better" equilibrium, meaning one that makes possible an alteration of this structure, necessitates restrictions on imports. Clearly, in this case, too, when the protection constituted by the gold standard has been removed, a passing change in conditions of trade or movement of capital entails an alteration in the rate of exchange which, by bringing about a different distribution of relative profitability between different sectors of the underdeveloped economy, influences the orientation of foreign investments and, consequently, the conditions of domination. But what always happens is an adjustment of the underdeveloped structure to the developed one.

The Economic Theory of International Transmission of the Conjuncture

The economic theory of "automatic equilibrium" of the balance of payments forms the basis upon which conventional economics has erected the theory of international transmission of the conjuncture.

This theory was first given systematic form by Haberler, who argues for three propositions, basing the distinctions he makes upon the monetary systems of the partners brought into relationship.

First, in the case in which the two countries, A and B, which are brought into contact with each other are subject to the gold-standard system, the transmission of fluctuations from one country to another is perfectly symmetrical. This transmission reduces the intensity of the fluctuations in the originating country by spreading wider the area over which the cycle exerts its effects. In a period of prosperity in country A, its imports develop more rapidly than its exports. This country has to face a drain of gold that reduces inflationary tendencies within it, while reinforcing them in country B.

Second, if country B has adopted the foreign-exchange standard system, the cycle will not be propagated from the dominated country to the dominant one, but in the opposite direction this effect is reinforced. In a period of prosperity in the country that is dominated monetarily, this country pays for the deficit in its balance of payments in the currency of country A. The volume of credit exerts no stimulating influence in the dominant country because no transfer of gold, the ultimate form of money, has taken place. But, on the other hand, the natural development of prosperity in the dominant economy is not checked by a drain of gold, whereas the influx of foreign currency into the dominated country is reflected in a real increase in advances of credit in this economy.

Third, in the case in which each of the two countries has an independent managed currency, cyclical fluctuations are no longer transmitted at all. A boom in one of the two economies in contact entails a disequilibrium in the balance of payments which, since it cannot be adjusted by an export of gold or foreign exchange, has to be adjusted by an alteration in the rate of exchange. This adjustment reduces excessive imports to the level of possible exports.

This is certainly an analysis of a narrowly monetarist type. In the nineteenth century, colonial and metropolitan countries used the same metallic currency. Yet the direction in which the cyclical movement was transmitted was always the same: from metropolis to colony.

The post-Keynesian school has abandoned this monetarist theory of transmission. It is now claimed that the fluctuations are transmitted not through the channel of the flow of gold and foreign exchange that they engender, but directly, through the channel of commodity movements. The cyclical oscillations in one country are, in fact, transmitted to another in a real movement of exports and imports. Prosperity in some countries, by resulting in imports that are greater than exports, directly fosters the development in others of the inflationary tendencies characteristic of economic euphoria. The deficit in the balance is settled by way of foreign credits alone. No movement of gold or foreign exchange is necessary. No alteration takes place in the rate of exchange. Under these conditions, the quantity-theory mechanism does not function.

This new way of looking at the matter has enjoyed a great vogue, thanks to the elaborated form given to it by the theory of the foreign-trade multiplier. Colin Clark's study of the Australian cycle is typical from this standpoint. The theory of the foreign-trade multiplier declares that a favorable trade balance (a surplus of exports) plays the same role as an independent inducement to investment. But this theory remains at the descriptive and mechanistic level. Actually, the state of the conjuncture does not have a clearly defined effect on the trade balance. Prosperity brings about a parallel growth in exports and imports. Its effect on the balance varies: sometimes it causes improvement, at other times deterioration. While it is true that the balance of payments (not that of goods) tends to be favorable for the developed countries in a depression period, this is due to the cessation of the export of capital far more than to improvement in the trade balance. Similarly, for the underdeveloped countries, it is this cessation of the flow of capital, not the worsening of the trade balance, that causes the balance of external payments to show a deficit. It is for this reason that the alternation that is clearly apparent in the twentieth century, between a deficit balance and a surplus balance, depending on the state of the conjuncture, did not exist in the nineteenth century, before the movement of capital had assumed the dimensions to which it later grew. Even at that time, however, it was never observed that a period of prosperity in Europe produced, through the appearance of a favorable balance for Europe (a perverse effect, but a frequent one), a depression in the lands beyond the seas — or vice versa.

The International Monetary System and the Present Crisis

Our epoch is marked by a new, growing contradiction between the worldwide character of the activities of the firms that are most decisive in economic life (the transnational companies) and the national character of the institutions, particularly the monetary institutions, within which the economic policies of states are determined. It is the development of this new contradiction that accounts for the specific form assumed by the present crisis of the system, that is, for its appearance in the monetary sphere.

The international liquidity crisis. Since the end of the Second World War, the international monetary system has been based on the employment of three types of reserves: gold; certain key currencies (the dollar and the pound sterling) together with, to a subordinate extent, other "hard" currencies; and the credits granted by the IMF, either conditionally or unconditionally.

Between 1951 and 1965 the total amount of international reserves defined in this way, for the world as a whole — excluding the Comecon countries, China, Vietnam, Korea, Albania, and Cuba — grew from $49 to $70 billion, at the rate of 2.6 percent per year. During this same period, international exchanges increased at the rate of 6 percent per year, reducing the relative amount of the reserves from 67 percent to 43 percent of the value of imports. After 1965, this tendency was intensified: the international reserves increased to $93 billion in 1970, but this amount no longer represented more than 33 percent of the volume of world trade.

Was this reduction in the relative amount of international reserves the cause of the crisis? Not necessarily, at least where the central capitalist countries are concerned, for three essential reasons, namely: (1) because the volume of reserves needed does not depend on that of the exchanges effected but on the balances that have to be settled, and while, immediately after the Second World War, the structure of international trade was very unbalanced, it is a great deal less so today; besides, in 1913, monetary reserves (which mainly consisted of gold) covered no more than 37 percent of world imports; (2) because it is not only the stock of international liquidities that has to be considered but also their velocity of circulation, just as with an internal monetary situation; and (3) because procedures have been devised that enable the amount of necessary reserves to be reduced, such as bilateral swap arrangements — the ceiling of mutual credits arranged in this way increased from $1.7 billion in 1961 to $16 billion in 1970.

In reality, the crisis has arisen from the growing disequilibrium in the proportion of the different component elements of the reserves. While the gold component, which was $34 billion in 1951, and $42 billion in 1965, fell to $37 billion in 1970, the dollar component increased from $4.2 billion in 1951 to $14.8 billion in 1965 and $32.8 billion in 1970, with an annual growth rate of 9.4 percent between 1951 and 1965 and 17.5 percent between 1965 and 1970 — a much higher rate of growth than that of the reserves as a whole. Between 1965 and 1970 the currency element in the international reserves (mostly consisting of dollars) increased from $23.8 billion (33 percent of the total) to $44.5 billion (48 percent). As for the reserves issued by the IMF, the third element in the system, these remained modest: $1.7 billion in 1951 (3.4 percent of the total), $5.4 billion in 1965 (7.6 percent), and $10.8 billion in 1970 (11.8 percent).

The increase in the amount of dollars held abroad gradually

weakened the position of the United States, whose gold reserves fell from $24.3 billion in 1951 to only $14.7 billion in 1965 and $11.1 billion in 1971. Along with this reduction, the gross external indebtedness of the United States increased from $8.3 billion in 1951 to $25.2 billion in 1965, and the country's net indebtedness (external debts offset by credits to foreign borrowers) increased from $6.9 to $13 billion. After 1965 the situation of the United States worsened at a more rapid rate. The country's current external liabilities increased from $29 billion in 1965 to $64 billion in 1971, while the short-term loans to its credit increased merely from $7.7 to $13.3 billion. In other words, whereas in 1951, the United States's holdings of gold represented 3.5 times the amount of the country's net short-term indebtedness, in 1971 these holdings covered no more than 22 percent of this external debt.

Thus, through the working of the international monetary system, the United States occupied a privileged position: its national currency being accepted as an international reserve, it did not have to worry about its balance of payments — in other words, the deficit in the country's balance of payments was automatically covered by a credit advanced to the United States by the rest of the world.

This asymmetrical working of the system to the advantage of the North American center was accepted so long as the United States held a position of strength in relation to the other developed capitalist countries. In fact, so long as the United States's industrial superiority in all fields was expressed in a permanent tendency for that country's external balance to show a surplus, a "hunger for dollars" was general in the world, and the system could function. Since then, however, Europe and Japan have made substantial progress, and in some fields have become competitors of the United States. Also, the United States has engaged in a worldwide policy of intervention that has exceeded its real strength, as is shown by the defeat of the Americans in Vietnam. These two factors have led to the United States's external balance becoming deficitary. Dollars are thus accumulating to the credit of foreigners in quantities far greater than the latter wish to hold. Placed in relation to the United States's holdings of gold, these credits are now seen to be plainly inconvertible, and even perhaps hard to recover in any way: confidence in the dollar has been shaken, and the international monetary system is crumbling.

Analysis of the causes to which the world monetary crisis has been attributed, and examination of the solutions advocated, provide valuable lessons. The best experts in the Western countries admit that the crisis is due not to an overall shortage of international liquidities but to the anarchy that reigned in the evolution of the different components of the international stock of reserves. They refrain, however, from analyzing the significance of this anarchy in terms of conflicts between the nations at the center of the capitalist system, conflicts that emerge whenever the equilibrium of relations of strength is challenged by the uneven development of the different capitalisms in question. The solutions they recommend are either ineffectual or else express pious wishes that assume the conflicts of interest have been settled.

The tendency for the United States's balance of payments to show a surplus in the period after the Second World War did not express a particularly "fortunate" structural equilibrium but rather a disequilibrium over which American domination had been imposed. The dollar as a universally accepted international reserve currency expressed this domination. In the last ten years this situation has been challenged by the rapid advance of Europe (particularly West Germany) and Japan. The new balance of forces is no more harmonious than the old, but it is different. It is also expressed in a tendency to disequilibrium in the external balances of the powers, but the other way around from previously: it is the balances of West Germany, Japan, and some other countries that now tend to show a surplus, while that of the United States shows a deficit. Defenders of the United States such as Kindleberger deny that the American balance of payments is "really" a deficit, considering that the deficit is only "apparent," merely a reflection of the use of the dollar as a reserve currency. If this were so, there would be no crisis. The fact that there is a crisis — expressed in the devaluation of the dollar in 1971 — proves that dollars are accumulating in excess of the desire for cash holdings of dollars on the part of the economic agents. Few experts acknowledge that the crisis reflects a reversal of the direction of the system's permanent structural disequilibrium, the balance having tipped the other way during the

1960s, because to do this would necessitate recognizing that the world system is based upon a structural adjustment of the weaker to the stronger.

Reversal of the tendency in the world balance of strength is not, of course, something that happens in an instant, and it would be a mistake to conclude that American capitalism has lost all its vitality. This is why the controversy regarding the evolution of the United States's balance of payments continues to be confused. It is not to be denied that the flow of American capital exported to Europe forms one of the elements in the American deficit, nor that this flow has been, at least in part, caused by the discriminatory measures taken by the European Economic Community and the European Free Trade Association against American goods, measures that have been got around by the installation of American firms in Europe itself. These measures constitute, however, a means by which Europe has re-established its position, a weapon from the Continent's arsenal brought into action in order to change the unfavorable balance of forces resulting from the war. It is a means that, in conjunction with others, has proved effective. The flow of capital originating from the United States does not testify only to the continued vitality of American capitalism but also to the difficulties facing accumulation within the United States, that is, the disequilibrium of the American economy. It ultimately results in a slowing down of growth in the United States and an acceleration of growth in Europe, and thus forms one element in the process of change in the balance of forces. What has shocked the Europeans is that the international monetary system, based on principles derived from a period now left behind, has enabled the Americans to finance their exports of capital so cheaply. Indeed, the use of the dollar as international currency has made it easy for them to borrow the capital with which they have financed their investments in Europe. Now, the rate of interest paid on these somewhat "forced" loans is a modest one (less than 3 percent), whereas the rate of profit realized thanks to the investment that they make possible is substantial (between 7 and 15 percent). This mechanism of transference of value toward the dominant center is classical, being no different from that which is normally expressed in relations between the center and the periphery, in a monetary zone of the colonial or neocolonial type. It is being challenged precisely because the way the balance of strength is evolving does not justify any longer such an excessive advantage in favor of the United States.

Refusal to consider the change in the relations of strength as what underlies the reversal in the direction of a permanent structural disequilibrium explains the disorderly and contradictory character, as well as the theoretical feebleness, of the solutions being recommended. These solutions all belong either to the category of flexible changes or to that of a universal currency. Those in the first category are ineffective; those in the second are impossible.

Flexible changes cannot be introduced if the system suffers from structural disequilibria, which is the case, for they bring about permanent disorder. "Creeping parities" or margins of fluctuation permitted to operate within the framework of a regime of fixed exchange rates constitute palliatives, not solutions. As for the adoption of a universal curency, that is, an instrument issued by a supranational authority, this assumes that the problem has already been solved, with the conflict of interests settled at the level of this supranational authority. The return to the gold standard — in other words, a concerted restoration of the value of gold — would in theory enable the volume of international liquidity to be increased, but the way these liquidities were distributed would still be inadequate, and the evolution of this distribution would remain subject to that of the balance of strength. Furthermore, the system would not rid the world of the practice of using the national currencies of the dominant countries as international reserves. It has been pointed out to those who look back nostalgically to the nineteenth century that the gold-standard system was also, *de facto*, a sterling-standard system, sterling being the national currency of the dominant country of that time. Any alteration in the international balance of forces would therefore result in the role of key currency being transferred from one currency to another. Moreover, it is hard to see what power would wish to initiate this worldwide revaluation of the yellow metal, since the two chief beneficiaries would be South Africa and the

USSR. If gold is revalued, it will happen only because the creeping inflation of our time demands this, so long as gold continues to be used as one of the means of international payment.

The idea of a universal credit money is not new. Keynes advocated it in 1945, with quasi-automatic issue of "bancors" in response to international disequilibria. Even though the granting of these credits would be subject to conditions, the system could operate only in cases where, because the disequilibria were transient, the monetary policies laid down by the issuing agency could be effective; or else in cases where, the disequilibria being structural, the agency was endowed with a considerable supranational authority, such as to enable it effectively to lay down the direction to be taken by the growth policies of the states concerned and to impose a worldwide policy of harmonious development. Triffin takes up this utopian scheme at the point at which Keynes abandoned it. The reconciliation he undertakes between the evolution of the international system and that of the national currency systems, formerly based on gold, to which are juxtaposed fiduciary currencies issued by a multitude of institutions that are gradually subordinated to a single center, the central bank, is not in itself an absurd idea. But the "one and only reserve center" that he proposes, on the world scale, which would be the bank for the central banks and would create reserves in such forms as to ensure that their volume and distribution were constantly adapted to the needs of world trade, assumes that conflicts between nations no longer take place.

The system has thus remained based upon gold and the key currencies. The drawing rights of the IMF are credits granted in these key currencies, and nothing more. So long as the dollar was the only key currency, the IMF was merely an executive agency of the U.S. Treasury. As soon as other currencies began to aspire to this role, the IMF became one of the scenes of conflict between these currencies and the dollar. The creation in 1969 of special drawing rights has not altered the situation at all. Triffin may well be scandalized by the rule according to which these special drawing rights are automatically distributed in accordance with quotas, so that 72 percent is reserved for the United States and Great Britain and less than 20 percent allotted as "manna" for eighty underdeveloped countries, just as he may find "revolting" the use of these credits to finance national policies (actually,

American war policy in Vietnam). But none of this ought to excite surprise, for the crisis is not an expression of some abstract conflict between a "palaeonationalist" ideology, equally shared by all nations, and the lofty ideal of a universal order. It expresses a concrete conflict, that which counterposes the dollar, inheritor of a dominant position with all its advantages, to the candidates for a "more equitable" sharing of these advantages — first and foremost, the German mark and the Japanese yen.

Europe's experience bears witness, moreover, to the nature of the conflict. After 1964 the EEC considered a system of free exchange rates, accompanied by measures of monetary solidarity secured by the operation of short-term stabilization policies. This type of "concertation" has proved effective, however, only where there has been no major conflict of interest. The crisis of 1968 put an end to illusions, and it is now accepted that a common currency — or, what comes to the same thing, unlimited convertibility at a fixed rate — necessitates a single decision-making center, ensuring the operation of a single economic and social policy on the scale of Europe as a whole.

While there is no supranational authority on the world or the European scale, there are, however, some transnational authorities, namely, the multinational corporations. But these constitute not a group with a single purpose but a variety of conflicting interests whose conflicts cross frontiers and are superimposed upon the conflicts between national capitalisms. This is why it is no longer possible to be satisfied, as was the case twenty years ago, with arguing in terms of national conflicts without examining the strategies of the multinational corporations. The appearance of "Eurodollars," first observed in 1957, the development of the market in these liquidities with the subsequent rise of similar markets for other currencies, namely, the mark and the yen, testify to the increasing role played by the multinational corporations. These assets, payable in dollars (and now in other currencies as well), held by nonresidents in the United States (or in the other relevant country), and deposited outside the United States (or other relevant country) are derived to a large extent from the treasuries of the great multinational corporations. These holdings, which are extremely mobile, are not those of a multitude of "small speculators," as was formerly the case with the bulk of floating capital.

Their mobility is due to their origin — the multinational corporations being able, by mere internal book entries, to transfer them
without any difficulty. The scale on which Eurodollars, Euromarks,
Euroyens, and so on enter into international reserves is considerable: in 1971 it was of the order of $12 billion. The communication
between the different currency markets they make possible certainly
undermines the effectiveness of national monetary policies, and
thereby introduces an additional factor of instability into the
system.

The international monetary crisis must therefore be interpreted
as the specific form taken in our epoch by a crisis of a deeper
kind. The phase of rapid growth that characterized the center as
a whole after 1950 is coming to an end. The slackening of growth
rates shows this, with "stagflation" (stagnation despite inflation)
replacing growth accompanied by inflation. Contradictions sharpen
between nations as between multinational groups and corporations,
and, with this development, the struggle for external markets
becomes a battle. At the same time, the balance of forces that
was characteristic of the postwar period, based on domination by
the United States, is changing fast. Hence the twofold crisis: the
underlying crisis in the equilibrium between production and consumption, and the superficial crisis of the international monetary
system.

*The underdeveloped countries and the international monetary
crisis.* The underdeveloped countries have no say in the matter of
the international monetary system. Formally, of course, they are
members of the IMF, but whereas in some other international
bodies they do occupy a few jump seats, so to speak, in the IMF
they are wholly supernumerary. The quota of each member-state
being paid (to the extent of at least three-quarters of the total
amount) in its own national currency, their contribution has only
symbolic significance — and the resources effectively utilizable by
the IMF are less than the total of the quotas consisting of these
valueless contributions, since their national currencies are not
means of international payment, as are the key currencies (the
dollar and the pound sterling), or the other hard currencies (the
mark, the yen, the Swiss franc, etc.), some of which aspire to join
the dominant group. This is why IMF policy is actually decided

by the more exclusive "Group of Ten," which constitutes the real international monetary system.

Admission of the underdeveloped countries to the IMF fulfils, in fact, two functions. The first is that of constituting a manoeuverable reserve force to which the advocates of different policies within the Group of Ten can appeal: at the 1967 Rio conference the United States secured acceptance of "special drawing rights" by making play with the fact that a small share in these rights would be available to those of the eighty "poor" members of the Fund who would submit to whatever policies the latter might recommend.

The second function of the IMF is, indeed, to keep the monetary behavior of the periphery within the bounds set by the needs of the international system. The colonial powers possessed, and sometimes still possess, much more effective instruments for this purpose — the currency zones (sterling, franc, escudo, etc.) and the network constituted by their commercial banks. Immediately after the Second World War, the whole of Africa and nearly the whole of Asia were still dominated by the pound sterling, and to a smaller extent by the French franc. This still-important authority possessed by the pound, out of proportion with the place of Great Britain in the world economy, was one of the main reasons why this currency was consecrated by the IMF as the second-ranking key currency. At that time, however, Latin America was still, as a whole, free from any formal monetary control from outside. Furthermore, the United States aimed to establish a footing in the parts of Asia and the Middle East that were becoming politically independent. The IMF provided the framework needed for the United States to proceed with this takeover. The policy proved successful: gradually, Latin America became drawn into the dollar area, while Asia and the Middle East left the sterling area. When, in 1960, large parts of Africa acquired political sovereignty, they could not be refused admission to the Fund, even though such membership meant little to those countries which, like those of the franc area, lacked the minimum of monetary independence that would enable them to pursue any sort of monetary policy of their own.

In order to understand how the Fund carries out this function for the system where the countries of the periphery are concerned, it is necessary to remember, first of all, that the underdeveloped countries suffer almost permanent difficulties in their external payments, reflecting the fundamental structural disequilibrium between center and periphery, and the systematic transfer of value from the latter to the former.

While we possess more or less adequate information on the volume and evolution of the reserves, both gross and net, held by the developed countries, we still know little about the situation in this respect of most of the underdeveloped countries. The gross reserves of the monetary system have been counted, but the degree of indebtedness of the underdeveloped countries is not well known. The distinction between short-term debts (the only kind that, to some extent, are recorded in bank records) and medium- and long-term debts is in this sphere a fluctuating one with little significance. A far from negligible part of long-term indebtedness serves, in fact, to cover the immediate needs of current consumption, which is largely made up of imported goods. The debts of the monetary system are thus supplemented by those of the state and of both private and public enterprises. Considerable sums, moreover, are represented by the holdings of "residents" (including nationals of these countries) illegally deposited abroad, which nevertheless do not form part of the nation's reserves, because in no case are these holdings destined for repatriation.

Observing the state and evolution of the gross reserves held by the Third World, as shown in IMF statistics, one may, therefore, get the impression that the underdeveloped countries do not, as a whole, suffer from a shortage of international liquidities.

As regards the Asian countries, the gross international reserves of twelve states that are not oil-producing, for which comparable statistics have been available since 1948, fell from $5.4 billion in 1948 to $3.7 billion in 1951 and $3.6 billion in 1966, while these countries' imports increased from $4.4 to $5.1 billion and then to $9.5 billion between these same dates. Asia, which after the war possessed considerable reserves, in particular the sterling balances held by India (amounting to more than £1.2 billion for India and Pakistan together), saw these reserves melt away rapidly between 1948 and 1951 (the ratio of reserves to imports fell from 122 percent to 73 percent), and then more slowly, but steadily, after that date (the ratio was 38 percent in 1966). The reserves of large countries such as India and Pakistan no longer cover more than a quarter's imports. The reserves of smaller states have behaved better, notably those of Thailand, which increased by $0.7 billion between 1948 and 1966. The reserves held by the oil-producing countries of the Middle East have markedly increased: those of Iran and Iraq from $0.3 billion in 1951 to $0.7 billion in 1966, while those of Kuwait (reserves of the Currency Board and the government) rose to the figure of $1.1 billion and those of Saudi Arabia (Saudi Arabia Monetary Agency) to $0.8 billion.

In Latin America calculations for sixteen countries for which we have comparable statistics show that the ratio of reserves to imports, which was about 50 percent in 1948 (when reserves amounted to $2.5 billion and imports to $5 billion) remained unchanged until 1953. Imports were then $5.9 billion and reserves $2.8 billion, Mexico having contributed almost single-handedly to this improvement in reserves. After 1953, however, the situation steadily worsened. In 1962 reserves did not exceed $2.3 billion while imports stood at $7.9 billion (so that the reserves-to-imports ratio had become less than 30 percent). True, between 1962 and 1967 the situation seems to have improved, since, although imports rose to $9.5 billion, reserves rose to $3.1 billion. This improvement came almost entirely from two sources: the increase in the reserves held by Venezuela, a large oil producer (an increase of $254 million in five years), and, especially, by Argentina (which rose from $132 million in 1966 to $625 million in 1967) as a result of that country's policy of deflation. Apart from these two countries, the reserves-imports ratio continued to decline, falling from 30 percent in 1962 to 23 percent in 1967 (reserves: $1.6 billion, imports: $5.1 billion).

As regards Africa the statistics for the twenty-eight countries for which we have comparable series from 1960 onward show a reduction in gross international reserves from $2.9 billion in 1960 to $2.2 billion in 1965, while their imports grew between these dates from $4 to $5.9 billion.

Between 1964 and 1970 the evolution of the ratio between gross reserves and imports seems to have been favorable to the underdeveloped countries. Gross reserves rose from $9.9 billion in 1964 ($2.2 billion being contributed by the chief oil-exporting countries) to $18.1 billion in 1970 ($4.2 billion being contributed by the oil-exporting countries), whereas their imports increased from 35.5 to 55.6 billion. These countries' gross reserves thus rose from 28 percent of their imports in 1964 to 32 percent in 1970.

If we look, however, at their net reserves, that is, their reserves after deduction of short-term external debts, we find a definite worsening of the situation between 1950 and 1970. For example, for the twenty-eight African countries under consideration, the ratio of net external reserves to imports fell from 60 percent in 1960 to 23 percent in 1965. The same is true of Asia and Latin America, where net reserves represent about two-thirds of gross reserves, with indebtedness increasing faster than the volume of gross reserves.

How, in these circumstances, have the underdeveloped countries managed to meet their external obligations? Partly it has been done by a mobilization of their "conditional reserves." Drawing rights on the IMF constitute the first type of reserves made available to certain countries of the Third World that have agreed to submit to the Fund's advice, embodied in "stabilization plans." The second type of conditional reserves results from bilateral agreements: these credits have been granted for purchases of goods (often specified in the agreement in question) to be made in the country that grants them. Although the figures concerning these agreements have not always been published in full and comparable form, we know that the volume of these conditional assets has considerably increased over the last decade. Finally, some countries have no problem, strictly speaking, as regards international liquidities. This is the case, for instance, with the African countries of the franc area, since any deficit that may occur in their balance of payments is automatically covered by the metropolitan country. On the other hand, however, these countries possess no means of managing their currencies, either internally or externally.

In general, any serious attempt at development made by a country of the periphery leads inevitably to difficulties in external payments. If powerful means of controlling these external relations and of guiding the strategy of transition are not brought into play in good time, the crisis thus caused gives an opportunity to the "great powers" and to the international institutions dependent on them to intervene and impose a "stabilization" that always deliberately sacrifices the purposes of development to the requirements of short-term solvency — in other words, to maintenance of the status quo.

For a Scientific Theory of the Structural Adjustments Between National Formations

Inspired by ideological concern to discover mechanisms that ensure harmonious equilibrium, conventional theory excludes from its field of investigation the real problem, which is that of the structural adjustment by which certain national formations are subjected to others, being shaped in accordance with the needs of these others. This problem of structural adjustment is seen to be fundamental when we examine relations between the center and the periphery, but also when we study the way relations between the different central formations evolve.

Conventional theory has proved to be bankrupt, for it cannot prove what it is supposed to prove, namely: (1) that a mechanism exists whereby the balance of payments tends toward a spontaneous equilibrium; (2) that to this equilibrium there corresponds one rate of exchange and only one; and (3) that this equilibrium, and the rate of exchange that corresponds to it, are independent of any structural changes that may take place in either of the partners. If, indeed, *different* equilibria are possible, depending on the structural conditions of the partners, then no "pure theory of international relations" is possible. The "economic policies" recommended that are based on this "theory" must therefore be ineffective — or, more precisely, the results achieved will be independent of the policies pursued, with successes, like failures, having their real causes elsewhere.

What then is left of the conventional economistic theory of international relations? Practically nothing. The ideological character of this pseudo-science is clearly perceived. Its mechanistic formalism prevents it from grasping the real problem: on the contrary, its function is to evade this real problem in order to provide justification for the international system based on inequality and to ascribe to it a harmony that it does not possess. François Perroux and Thomas Balogh have not hesitated to criticize severely the "international monetary policies" based upon this set of "non-scientific prejudices."

The real problem lies elsewhere — in historical analysis of the evolution of social formations; in the analysis of their respective dynamics and their specific contradictions; in the real, historical, concrete conditions of uneven development.

3

From Specialization to Dependence

1. THE FOUNDATIONS OF INTERNATIONAL SPECIALIZATION

The classical theory of international trade alleges that it is in the interest of each of the partners in an exchange to specialize, because this will raise the level of total income, in terms of use-values, in both countries. For the classical economists, labor is the source of all value. This is why Ricardo sees the exchange of two commodities as being, ultimately, the exchange of two equal amounts of labor crystalized in two products with differing use-values for the partners in the exchange. Whereas, however, in the sphere of internal exchange the law of value implies equivalence of the exchange-values of two commodities containing the same quantity of labor, in the sphere of external exchange the commodities exchanged contain unequal quantities of labor, reflecting uneven levels of productivity.

To take Ricardo's well-known example (but substituting "wheat" for "wine"), Portugal has more advantages than England both for the production of wheat (in which 80 hours of labor suffice to produce a unit of this commodity, as against 120 in England) and for that of cloth (in which 90 hours of labor produce in Portugal what 100 hours produce in England). But it has comparatively more advantages for producing wheat than for producing cloth. It is therefore to Portugal's interest to specialize in the first of these two lines of production and get its cloth from England, even though producing this cloth at home would cost Portugal less than England in absolute terms. The assertion that imports can be advantageous in terms of use-values even if the product imported could locally be produced more cheaply forms the main contribution made by Ricardo, as compared with Adam Smith.

All that this theory enables us to state is that, at a given moment, the distribution of levels of productivity being what it is, it is to the interest of the two countries to effect an exchange, even though it is unequal. Let us take Ricardo's example again, inverting the terms so as to bring it closer to reality:

Quantities of labor contained in a unit product

	In England	*In Portugal*	*Relative advantage held by England over Portugal*
one of cloth	80 hours	120 hours	1.50
one of wheat	90 hours	100 hours	1.11
Internal exchange ratio			
one of cloth =	0.89 of wheat	1.20 of wheat	

Let us suppose that Portugal agrees to specialize in wheat, and obtains its cloth from England. If the total available labor power in Portugal amounts to 1,000 hours, and the consumption of wheat remains fixed at five units, then Portugal will devote 500 hours' labor to producing wheat for its own consumption. It will have 500 hours at its disposal that it can employ either to produce its own cloth (500:120 = 4.2 units) or to produce five extra units of wheat with which to obtain five units of cloth, gaining 0.8 of a unit of cloth through the exchange. But, although it has gained in use-values, it will have expended 500 hours of labor in order to obtain five units of cloth that England would have produced in 400 hours. Its own Portuguese one hour of labor is exchanged for

0.8 of an English hour: an unequal exchange. The inequality of the exchange reflects the lower productivity of labor in Portugal.

This is why, if the inequality in productivity of labor is not natural but historical, the comparative advantage is modified when the backward economy makes progress. If Portugal is able, by modernizing itself, to attain the same productivity as England in all fields, in other words, to produce cloth in 80 hours and wheat in 90, it is worth its while to modernize. For then it will be producing its five units of wheat in 450 hours and will dispose of 550 hours with which to produce 6.9 units of cloth (550:80). No further exchange will occur, since costs are identical in both countries — but Portugal will have gained in comparison with the previous situation when there was exchange: $6.9 - 5 = 1.9$ of a unit of cloth.

If Portugal were to agree to specialize in wheat and devote all its efforts to catching up with England in this field, what would it gain? Henceforth it would have to devote 450 hours to producing five units of wheat for its own consumption (5 x 90); it would have 550 hours at its disposal with which it would produce 6.1 units of wheat (550:90), which would enable it to acquire 6.1 units of cloth. This choice is less good for Portugal because the potential progress in the cloth industry (reduction of cost from 120 to 80 hours) is greater than in the production of wheat (reduction of cost from 100 to 90 hours).

It is therefore more to the country's interest to develop those branches of production in which the greatest progress is possible, and to subject its choices where foreign trade is concerned to the priority requirements of this kind of development. The trading options thus decided on will have to be modified at each phase of development. This is certainly an aggressive conception of international relations; but it corresponds both to history and to the present situation.

Ricardo's analysis, being based on comparison between real productivities, provides the operational concepts needed in order to understand the nature of international specialization, that is, to appreciate the reasons for this specialization and draw conclusions from it that explain its dynamics. If, indeed, England needs to spend only 80 hours of labor on producing one unit of cloth, as against 120 hours needed in Portugal, then this is because English industry is more advanced than Portuguese, since what is involved here is total hours of labor, direct and indirect. In England the textile industry is mechanized, so that the 80 hours of labor needed are distributed in a certain way: for example, 20 hours of direct labor and 60 hours crystalized in the machinery, etc., used in this production. In Portugal, cloth is produced by craft techniques, so that the 120 hours needed are distributed in different proportions: less indirect labor and more direct labor (e.g., 90 of the latter and 30 of the former).

It should be noted in passing that, in Ricardo's example, real wages per hour are the same in both countries, being reduced to the physiological subsistence level. In their turn, subsistence goods are commodities that are subject to international exchange, and so can have only one and the same price (expressed in gold) in both countries. Gold prices of subsistence goods, nominal wages, and real wages are thus identical in England and Portugal. Specialization and exchange, by obtaining for the countries involved quantities of use-values larger than they would obtain in the absence of exchange, increase the volume of real profits realized in both countries.

The whole of Ricardo's argument amounts to asserting that, although Portugal is more backward in all spheres, it is nevertheless in that country's interest to specialize. Ricardo stops at this point in his proof, refraining from making use of the analytical tool he has discovered. What I have shown, in rendering Ricardo's analysis "dynamic," is that the immediate advantage derived from specialization will determine the direction of development as between the two countries in such a way that the one that agrees to specialize in the less dynamic branches of production will lose by doing so, in the long run.

The basis for unequal specialization cannot be understood except in relation to the objective theory of value. It was, however, the subjective theory of value that triumphed in economic science after 1870. By refusing to reduce all the costs in different "factors" to the common denominator of social labor, conventional economics deprives itself of any means of comparing productivities, and loses the sense of the essential concept of *level of development of the productive forces.* Relative advantage is thus to be measured by the ratio between prices, which depend on the relative rewards of the different factors and the relative use made of them in quantitative terms. The theory is thenceforth based upon a vicious circle and deprives the principle of comparative costs of its actual validity. For the most profitable technique (the most efficient combination of factors) depends upon the relative rates at which these factors are rewarded. Now, these rewards themselves vary according to the quantitative use made of the factors, and so, ultimately, according to the methods of production employed. It follows from this that the bearing the principle has is more restricted than in Ricardo's theory. In the classical theory the sequence of the movements of commodities was established. Here, on the contrary, every change in the movement of commodities alters the comparative advantages, because it affects the relative prices of the factors. We are thus caught in a vicious circle: each nation should specialize in whatever it has the biggest advantage in, knowing that this is so because it possesses in plenty a factor that is appropriate to this particular line of production.

Abandonment of the objective theory of value has thus transformed the nature of the theory of comparative advantages, giving it an apologetical-ideological character. For "advantage" no longer possesses any meaning: it is not contained *a priori* in objective reality. Empirical positivism is then obliged to invoke false theories (the quantity theory of money) or specious assumptions (no "perverse price-effects"), or else mistaken notions ("the factors of production — capital and labor — are given," whereas it is the social division of labor between Department I and Department II that is the content of these so-called "natural" endowments). Degeneration into apologetical ideology has continued with the modern formulation of exchange in terms of substitution. With Haberler, Lerner, and Leontief the theory came finally to assume its present form: the cost of one product is defined as equivalent to the renunciation of another. The compromise effected by Bastable, Marshall, Edgeworth, and Taussig, which consisted in assuming that, in each country, the cost of each product was made up of wages, profits, interest, and rent, in stable proportions (thus avoiding the problem of adding up the subjective utilities of different persons) was given up. I shall not recall here the details of the construction of the "collective indifference curves" obtained on the basis of the equivalence in utility of variable quantities of two different goods. Nor shall I recall the details of the construction of the "production possibility curves" obtained on the basis of the technical possibilities of producing variable quantities of two different goods with a constant stock of factors of production. The international exchange ratio was now situated between the two exchange ratios "in isolation" determined by the gradients of the tangents to the indifference curves at the points where these curves are themselves tangential to the production possibility curves. At these points, the rate of substitution of the products is the same for the consumer as for the producer. The necessary and sufficient condition of international exchange is then that the exchange ratios in isolation should be different as between one country and another. We are imprisoned in the basic tautology of all conventional subjectivist economics: exchange brings "advantage" to each party by the mere fact that it takes place. But this "theory" is perfectly useless. It prevents us from understanding history, because it avoids the question of the initial level and the dynamic of the development of the productive forces.

2. THE THEORY OF UNEQUAL EXCHANGE

A Fundamental Contribution

And so we see that specialization may be unequal. In what circumstances does international exchange also become unequal? It is to Arghiri Emmanuel, the author of *Unequal Exchange*, that we owe the first general formulation of the problem, which I shall recapitulate here, adding some points of my own.

The hypothesis of a capitalist mode of production implies mobility of labor (equalization of wages between one branch of capitalist economy and another, and between one country and another) and of capital (equalization of the rate of profit). This abstract hypothesis provides the frame within which both Ricardo and Marx reason when they study the capitalist mode of production. Marx refrains from tackling the question of international exchanges, since it has no special significance within this problematic. He is content to make a few passing observations on the possible consequences of imperfect mobility of labor or of capital, while emphasizing the analogy between this problem and that of the effects of a similar imperfection inside the nation.

Ricardo does deal with international trade, though in an ambiguous way. As an empiricist, he notes the relative immobility of labor and capital. This fact is not in itself questionable, at any rate for the period when Ricardo was writing — just as there is no question that any socioeconomic formation of capitalism at the center can be reduced to a pure capitalist mode of production, that the development of capitalism at the center is unevenly advanced in different countries, and that, consequently, organic compositions, productivities of labor, and values of labor power are not identical between one country and another. But Ricardo had no right to invoke in the same argument both these facts, which belong to the plane of concrete social formations, *and* the assumption that provides the framework of his thinking, namely, the capitalist mode of production in its pure state. What results is a theory that, since it assumes that real wages are equal in all countries, can base international exchange only upon the immobility of capital. Let us read what Arghiri Emmanuel says on this point (pp. 40-41): "As regards mobility of the factors, Ricardo is interested only in its effect, namely, the equalization of their rewards. This is why he speaks only of the equalization of profits, the only equalization that can be affected by immobility of the factors, particularly that of capital, since the equalization of wages is always ensured from below, through the working of the demographic regulator, whether or not there is mobility of the labor force. The nonequalization of profits is for Ricardo a necessary and sufficient condition for the working of the law of comparative costs, and this is an important point that does not seem to have been remarked upon until now."

If capital is mobile, and if we assume identical wages (equivalent to subsistence), exchange takes place only in the event that productivities are different. This can happen only through one or other of these two causes: either (1) different "natural" potentialities (with the same amount of labor, capital, and land it is possible to produce more wheat in Portugal than in England, owing to the climate); or (2) different organic compositions, reflecting unevenness in the development of capitalism. In the latter case, however, wages are not equal, because "there enters into the determination of the value of labor power a historical and moral element" (p. 150).

If the two factors, labor and capital, were perfectly mobile, there would be no trade (as Heckscher has shown). Emmanuel shows (p. xiii) that specialization represents only a relative optimum: "The absolute optimum would be, not for Portugal to specialize in wine and England in cloth, but for the English to move to Portugal with their capital in order to produce both wine and cloth."

One can observe, then, two forms of international exchange in which the products are not exchanged at their value. In the first case, wages (and rates of surplus value) are equal, but because the organic compositions are different the prices of production — which are implied by the equalization of the rate of profit — are such that the hour of total labor (direct and indirect) of the more advanced country (characterized by a higher organic composition) obtains more products on the international market than the hour of total labor of the less developed one. The following example illustrates this case:

	c Constant capital	v Variable capital	s Surplus value	V Value	p Profit	P Price of production
A	10	10	10	30	8	28
B	16	7	7	30	9	32

A = the less advanced country ($c/v = 1$)
B = the more advanced country ($c/v = 2.3$)
Rate of surplus value = 100 percent
Average rate of profit: $17/43 = 40$ percent

Emmanuel says (p. 164) that in this case, although exchange does not ensure the same quantity of products for an hour of total labor, it is nevertheless not unequal because "unequal" exchanges of this order are a feature of internal relations within the nation: "prices of production . . . are an element that is immanent in the competitive system."

And yet exchange is unequal, all the same, and this inequality reflects the inequality in productivity. For it is important to note that the two equations written here, which describe the conditions of production of one and the same product with different techniques — advanced in B, backward in A — are equations in terms of value: in hours of labor of A and B respectively, considered in isolation. In terms of use-values, the quantity of the product cannot be the same in A as in B, for the level of the productive forces is higher in B. With 30 hours of total labor (direct and indirect), equipped as this is in B, we get, for instance, 90 physical units of the product, whereas with the same number of hours of total labor equipped as it is in A we get only a smaller amount, say, 60 units. If A and B are integrated in the same world market, the product can have only one price, the price set by the more advanced country. In other words, 30 hours of A's labor are not worth 30 hours of B's: they are worth only 30 x $60/90 = 20$ hours. Additionally, if the product enters into working-class consumption, and has only one price (say, 10 francs per unit), then 30 hours of labor in B earn 90 x 10 = 900 francs, or 30 francs an hour, whereas in A these 30 hours are paid for at the rate of 20 francs an hour. If real wages are to be the same in A and in B, although their productivity differs, the rate of surplus value will have to be lower in A so as to make up for the lower productivity. The apportionment between variable capital and surplus value, instead of being equivalent to 10/10, must be equivalent to 15(10 x 90/60)/5.

As Charles Bettelheim has pointed out, exchange is, in fact, unequal in this case, mainly because the productivities are unequal (this inequality being connected with different organic compositions) and, secondarily, because the different organic compositions determine, through the working of the equalization of the rate of profit, prices of production that differ from values in isolation. It must be added that the problem is made still more complex by

the rates of surplus value, which are necessarily different in A and
B (in order to ensure an equivalent real reward of labor in A and B).

In reality, however, Emmanuel's argument is based on a different
case, in which the organic compositions of the products exchanged
are similar. Let us assume that production techniques are at the
same level of development (same organic composition), and, at
the beginning of our argument, that wages are the same (same
rate of surplus value). Exchange is then strictly equal. If now, for
one reason or another, while production techniques remain unchanged, wages in A are only one-fifth what they are in B, we
shall have the following situation:

	C Capital installed	c Constant capital employed	v Variable capital	s Surplus value	V Value	p Profit	P Price of production
A	70	10	2	18	30	14	26
B	70	10	10	10	30	14	34

A and B produce the same product (e.g., oil) with the same (up-
to-date) techniques, and sell this product on the world market. In
A, however, real wages are lower than in B. The product must
have a uniform price, that which prevails on the world market.
What does this price signify? What does it include, in terms of
transfers of value from one country to the other?

The greater rate of surplus value in A raises the average rate
of profit of A and B, taken together, from 14 to 20 percent. The
low-wage country (A) receives in international exchange, for an
equal quantity of labor (direct and indirect) of the same productivity, less than its partner B (exactly 76 percent). Emmanuel
describes this kind of exchange as really unequal exchange, as he
shows that the difference in rates of profit between one country
and another that have to be allowed in order to make up for the
inverse difference in wages would need to be very great. In the
example given above, for exchange to be equal, with wages in A
only one-fifth of wages in B, the rate of profit in A would have to
be 26 percent, as against 14 percent in B.

Now, this second case does actually correspond to the situation as it exists in reality. For the exports of the Third World are not, in the main, made up of agricultural products coming from backward sectors with low productivity. Out of an overall total of exports from the underdeveloped countries of the order of $35 billion (in 1966), the ultra-modern capitalist sector (oil, mining, and primary processing of minerals, modern plantations — like those of United Fruit in Central America, or of Unilever in Africa and Malaya) provides at least three-quarters, or $26 billion. If these products were provided by the advanced countries, with the same techniques — and so the same productivity — the average rate of profit being around 15 percent on capital installed, and the capital employed representing one-seventh of this (replaced after five to ten years, seven being the average), and with the rate of surplus value 100 percent (which therefore corresponds to a capital-output ratio of the order of 3.5) — their value would be at least $34 billion. The transfer of value from the periphery to the center under this heading alone would amount, at a modest estimate, to $8 billion.

As regards the other exports of the Third World, provided by the backward sectors, with low productivity (agricultural produce supplied by peasantries of the traditional type), is the situation less clear? Here the differences in the reward of labor (the term "wages" is out of place in this context) are accompanied by a lower productivity. How much lower? It is all the harder to say because the products involved are, as a rule, not comparable: tea, coffee, cocoa are produced only in the periphery. It can be safely suggested, however, that rewards are proportionately much lower in the periphery than are productivities. An African peasant obtains, for example, in return for 100 days of very hard work every year, a supply of imported manufactured goods the value of which amounts to barely twenty days of simple labor of a European skilled worker. If this peasant produced with modern European techniques (and we know, concretely, what this means, from the modernization projects drawn up by agronomists), he would work 300 days a year and obtain a product about six times as large in quantity: his productivity per hour would at best be doubled. Exchange is thus very unequal in this case: the value of these products, if the reward of labor were proportionate to its productivity, would not be of the order of $9 billion (which is what it is) but 2.5 times as much, that is, around $23 billion. The transfer of value from the periphery to the center is thus of the order of $14 billion. It is not surprising that this transfer is here proportionately much greater than that which arises from the products of modern industry. In the case of the latter, the content of imported capital goods is much greater, whereas this is negligible where the products of traditional agriculture are concerned, in which direct labor represents almost the whole of the value of the product.

Altogether, then, if exports from the periphery amount to about $35 billion, their value, if the rewards of labor were equivalent to what they are at the center, with the same productivity, would be about $57 billion. The hidden transfers of value from the periphery to the center, due to the mechanism of unequal exchange, are of the order of $22 billion, that is to say, twice the amount of the "aid" and the private capital that the periphery receives. One is certainly justified in talking of the plundering of the Third World.

The imports that the advanced countries of the West receive from the Third World represent, it is true, only 2 or 3 percent of their gross internal product, which was about $1.2 billion in 1966. But these exports from the underdeveloped countries represent 20 percent of *their* product, which was about $150 billion. The hidden transfer of value due to unequal exchange is thus of the order of 15 percent of this product, which is far from being negligible in relative terms, and is alone sufficient to account for the blocking of the growth of the periphery, and the increasing gap between it and the center. The contribution that this transfer makes is not negligible, either, when seen from the standpoint of the center, which benefits from it, since it comes to about 1.5 percent of the center's product. But this transfer is especially important for the giant firms that are its direct beneficiaries.

The thesis of unequal exchange has called forth three types of criticism. Bettelheim, while remaining within Emmanuel's framework of reasoning, nevertheless refrains from drawing the logical conclusion from the extension of Marx's models (of the transformation of values into prices of production) into the field of international relations and from his own assumption that the rate of surplus value is higher at the center: indeed, he ought to have deduced from this that it is the advanced countries that are the victims of unequal exchange! Other critics have claimed that wages are higher at the center because the productivity of labor is higher there, so that the inequality is "justified." Let us recall, as Emmanuel does, that for Marx the value of labor power is independent of its productivity. Apparently more subtle is the attitude of a third group of critics who deny that the expression "unequal exchange" possesses any meaning and claim that Emmanuel has no right to employ the value-transformation models. These models, they say, are significant *only* within the context of the capitalist mode of production, and cannot be applied to relations between different social formations. What they are doing, in fact, is denying that a single world capitalist system exists — in other words, they are, basically, denying the existence of imperialism itself! Of course the transformation models cannot be applied to any and every situation: for example, they could not be employed in analyzing trade relations between ancient Greece and Persia. But that is not the situation here: center and periphery are indeed parts of one and the same capitalist system.

Marx constructed the theory of the capitalist mode of production, defining in an abstract way three conditions for this mode of production: (1) generalization of the commodity form of the products (the generalized market); (2) generalization of the commodity form of labor power (the existence of a single labor market); and (3) generalization of competition between capitals (the existence of a single capital market, expressed in the equalization of the rate of profit). These three conditions reflect abstractly the reality of the capitalist mode of production that Marx studied, with mid-nineteenth-century England as its concrete model. The world capitalist system is *another* level of reality, which must also be defined abstractly if we are to analyze it theoretically. At this level, the world system is expressed in the existence of a world market for commodities and mobilization of capital on the world scale. Since there is a world commodity market, there is a problem concerning values on the international scale. And since this problem exists, we must use value-transformation models.

Is an Economic Theory of International Exchange Possible?

An economic theory must serve to analyze appearances, that is, to study the mechanisms whereby the capitalist mode of production functions. Marx, by revealing the essence of the capitalist mode of production, transcended economistic "science," subjecting it to a fundamental critique, and showed what must be the foundations of the only possible science, that of society.

It was because they remained economistic, and therefore alienated, in their way of thinking that Adam Smith and Ricardo sought to work out an economic theory of international exchange. In order to do this they had to assume the existence of a pure capitalist mode of production for both partners in exchange. But Smith already perceived the function of external trade that corresponds to the beginnings of capitalism ("the generation of a surplus restricted by the narrowness of the internal agricultural market"), just as Ricardo perceived its function for his time: "the generation of a surplus hindered by the diminishing returns of agriculture." Marx, as Christian Palloix has pointed out, synthesized Smith and Ricardo. If he went no further in this field, this was probably not because he failed to perceive the problem but, on the contrary, because he *did* perceive it. Since the theory of relations between different social formations cannot be an economistic one, international relations, which belong precisely to this context, cannot give rise to an "economic theory." What Marx says about these relations is in accordance with the questions that arose in his own time. Transfer of surplus from the periphery to the center at that time could not, indeed, be very substantial: the periphery was in those days exporting very little in absolute quantities, and, besides, rewards at the center were low — not very different, given equal productivity, from those at the periphery. It is not the same today, however, when 75 percent of exports from the periphery come from modern capitalist enterprises, and when the rates at which labor is rewarded at the center and at the periphery have diverged considerably.

The neoclassical form of the economistic theory of exchange, based on the subjective theory of value, represents, here as elsewhere, a step backward in comparison with Ricardo's economism

— for it can no longer be anything but tautological, since it has lost sight of the production relations. The real question is that of discovering what are the actual functions of international trade, as it has been and as it is, and how these functions have been fulfilled.

It is not certain that Marxists since Marx himself have always seen what the problem is. As an example, here is an argument used by Bukharin (p. 40):

> Corresponding to the movement of labour-power as one of the poles of capitalist relations is the movement of capital as another pole. As in the former case the movement is regulated by the law of equalisation of the wage scale, so in the latter case there takes place an international equalisation of the rates of profit.

Bukharin does not see that the world capitalist system is not homogeneous; that it cannot be seen as the capitalist mode of production on a world scale.

It was Rosa Luxemburg's great merit to have realized that relations between the center and the periphery depend on the mechanisms of primitive accumulation, because what is involved is not the economic mechanisms characteristic of the internal functioning of the capitalist mode of production but relations between this mode of production and formations that are different from it. Preobrazhensky wrote, in the same spirit, about these exchanges, that they are "the exchange of a smaller quantity of labor by one system of economy or one country for a larger quantity of labor furnished by another system of economy or another country" (p. 91). When that happens, unequal exchange is possible.

The dominant economistic theory, inspired by the Soviet Union, marks a step backward. Göncöl, Pavel, and Horovitz claim, according to Palloix, that "the value of the products supplied by the underdeveloped countries is determined by that of the advanced countries, sector by sector throughout production; and this value is practically zero, because the advanced countries would be able to produce for nothing a product that specialization has nevertheless assigned for production to the underdeveloped countries" (pp. 257-58). This argument will not stand up, for 75 percent of exports from the periphery come from modern enterprises with a very high productivity, and the rest — mainly exotic agricultural products — simply cannot be produced in the advanced countries. It is understandable that it should be a Romanian economist, Rachmuth, who has come out against this view; although, unfortunately, he invokes another economistic theory, namely, Ricardo's. International exchange based on comparative costs, he says, intensifies unevenness of development if "the advanced country specializes in activities that are susceptible to the biggest possible increase in productivity, whereas the less developed country is confined to specializing in the sectors in which increases in productivity are very limited." This is only partly true, since the specialized production of the periphery involves modern products to a considerable degree. Once again, the economistic theory of comparative advantages fails to answer the question: why are the underdeveloped countries restricted to this or that kind of specialization — in other words, what are the functions of international exchange?

The economistic theory of comparative advantages, even in its scientific Ricardian version, has only a limited validity; it describes exchange conditions at a given moment, but it does not allow for preference for some specialization, based on comparative productivities as these stand at a given moment, as against *development*, in other words, improvement in these productivities. It cannot account for the two essential facts that characterize the way world trade has developed in the setting of the capitalist system: (1) the development of trade between advanced countries that are of similar structure, and in which, therefore, the distribution of comparative productivities is similar — a development that seems to be more rapid than that of trade between advanced countries and underdeveloped ones, although the distribution of comparative productivities is more diverse in the latter case; and (2) the successive and varying forms assumed by specialization in the periphery, including its present forms, under which the periphery supplies raw materials that are mostly produced by modern capitalist enterprises with high productivity.

To explain these two phenomena, it is necessary to take note, first, of the theory of capitalism's inherent tendency to expand markets, and, second, of the theory of the domination of the periphery by the center.

Analysis of exchange between advanced countries and underdeveloped ones leads us to observe that exchange is unequal whenever labor of the same productivity is rewarded at a lower rate in the periphery. This fact cannot be explained without bringing in the policy followed by the capital that dominates in the periphery, as regards the organization of labor supply. How capital organizes proletarianization in the periphery, how the specializations that it imposes there give rise to a permanent and growing surplus of labor power in relation to demand — these are the real problems that have to be solved.

On the basis of the history of the development of the labor market in Rhodesia, Arrighi criticizes W. A. Lewis's theory of the dynamic of the supply of and demand for labor in the underdeveloped economies. Lewis postulates a potential surplus of labor power in the "traditional" sector ("concealed unemployment"), productivity being low in that sector — a surplus that is reduced as the "modern," high-productivity sector develops. It is this surplus that makes it possible to reward labor at a low rate in the modern sector, which is said to have an unlimited supply of labor power at its disposal. Arrighi shows that, in fact, the opposite has occurred in Rhodesia: the superabundance of the labor supply in the modern sector is *increasing*, being greater in the 1950s and 1960s than it had been in the early days of colonization, between 1896 and 1919 — because the superabundance is *organized* by the economic policy of the state and of capital (especially through the "reservations" policy). It is thus not the "laws of the market" that explain the way wages have evolved in the periphery (which is the basis of unequal exchange) but quite simply the policies of *primitive accumulation* that are practiced there.

Other Formulations and Aspects of Unequal Exchange

Formulation of the theory of unequal exchange in terms of the transformation of values into prices of production is essential in that it enables us to give the concept a scientific content, and thereby to define the conditions governing it, but it is not "practical." Indeed, the transformation of values into prices, in accordance with Marx's method, does not allow for the fact that the constituent elements of constant capital, the inputs, are themselves commodities, incorporated in the production process and for this purpose reckoned not at their values but at their prices. The same is true of the commodities consumed by the producers, which constitute the real content of wages. In order to take this general interdependence into consideration we need to stay at the level of immediate appearances, of prices, as Sraffa does. He arrives afresh, on the basis of an analysis carried out in positivistic empirical terms, at the essential conclusions that were drawn by Marx, namely, that the system of relative prices and the average rate of profit are determined by the level of real wages. This proof demolishes the entire edifice of subjectivist economics, depriving the "economic rationality" based upon subjective value of its claims to absolute validity, and reducing it to rational choice within a given system chiefly defined by a social relation that determines the value of labor power. What is of interest here is that Sraffa's system can be used to measure the degree of unequal exchange, as Oscar Braun has shown.

The latter assumes that two commodities, iron and wheat, are produced in a certain economy with the following technologies:

13 tons of iron + 2 tons of wheat + 10 man-years = 27 T of iron
10 tons of iron + 4 tons of wheat + 10 man-years = 12 T of wheat

If the rate of profit r is uniform, we have:

$$(13 p_1 + 2 p_2) (1 + r) + 10w = 27p_1$$

and

$$(10p_1 + 4 p_2) (1 + r) + 10w = 12 p_2$$

in which p_1 represents the price of a ton of iron and p_2 that of a ton of wheat, and w the wages paid per man-year.

Let us assume that the iron is produced by country A, an advanced country, in which wages are w_1, whereas the wheat is produced by country B, a dominated country, in which wages are w_2, less than w_1. If wages were the same in A and B — equal, say, to 0.56 — then the rate of profit would be 0.20 and the price of wheat 2.44, the price of iron being 1. If, however, wages in A were 0.70 and in B 0.12 (or 5.8 times less), then, with the same average rate of profit of 0.20, the price of wheat would fall to 1.83. A worsening of the terms of trade for country B (exporting wheat and importing iron) by 25 percent would imply, with an unaltered average rate of profit, a radical transformation in the respective wage levels: in A wages would increase by 25 percent, while in B they would fall to 17 percent of what they had been. Conversely, if wages were the same in A and B, with equal productivity (as is the case, since B produces wheat in accordance with the technique previously used in A), the international price of wheat would have been different from what it is when wages are lower in B. Which is cause and which is effect: the international prices, or the inequality in wage levels? The question is pointless. Inequality in wages, due to historical reasons (the difference between social formations), constitutes the basis of a specialization and a system of international prices that perpetuate this inequality.

Conventional economic theory remains fundamentally "microeconomic." In international relations it refuses to see anything but relations between individuals — the buyers and sellers. And yet the mercantilist experience contradicts this view of the matter: down to the belated victory of free trade, international economic relations were strictly subordinate to the policies of governments. The history of the chartered companies that operated within the framework of a monopoly of foreign trade shows this. Great Britain did not hesitate to employ political means in order to ruin possible competitors, as in the case of Indian industry. The doctrine of free trade has only ever been preached by the stronger, after they have established a dominant position by other means. A study of tariff policies leads one to consider the monopolistic character of international relations. According to the theory of comparative advantages, if a state sets up a protective tariff, its trading partners have no interest in replying in kind. For the newly established tariff is a "fact" that alters the distribution of relative prices inside the country that has established it. Other countries will continue to "maximize their satisfactions" by practicing free trade with this country and looking upon its internal price system — allowing for the customs duties — as a "datum." Reasons that might justify a reply in kind are excluded in advance from the theoretical assumption. These reasons are twofold: on the one hand, the purpose of the tariff is to create a monopoly, which improves the terms of trade, and, on the other, by protecting itself in this way, the country that does so makes it possible for certain industries to come into being behind the tariff barrier. In this manner it creates an advantage for itself in the future. The other countries ought, then, to do the same. Advocates of free trade answered by claiming that the reply-in-kind made by a country that increases its tariffs as the result of a similar action taken by its trading partners is based upon a miscalculation. On the one hand, to be sure, the country's terms of trade are improved; but, on the other, a nonoptimal distribution of resources is brought about. Taussig and Edgeworth affirmed, though without proving this, that the disadvantage so incurred was greater than the advantage gained. Actually, this was a pseudo-problem, for the theory of "optimal distribution of resources" is based on that of "factorial endowment," which is meaningless in the context of a dynamic view.

One trend in contemporary econometrics has proposed to "measure" the unevenness of monopoly in international relations by looking at *states* as the units in world trade. This trend measures the "comparative intensity" of the exports and imports of states, price elasticities and income from external trade, and elasticities of substitution. However, the contribution made by their work is of only secondary importance for understanding the relations between advanced countries and under-developed ones. Nations are seen as oligopolists of unequal strength. While this is true, theoretically, for relations between advanced countries, it is not the same for relations between advanced countries and underdeveloped ones. For the oligopolistic conception of international relations presupposes economic independence of the buyers and sellers. In relations between the advanced countries and the rest, however, the complementary character of the economies concerned, created by the mechanisms of specialization in the context of domination by the more highly developed economy, which adjusts the structure of the dependent country to suit its own needs, rules out this assumption of mutual independence. External analysis of bilateral monopolies or oligopolies will certainly be obliged one day to leave the domain of "games theory" in order to analyze social formations and the political relations between the different dominant classes within these social formations.

Instead of confining oneself to description of the phenomenon of inequality by carrying out econometric measurements of its outward manifestations (elasticities), what is needed is to analyze the place held by the monopolies in world trade. Today the greater part of the raw materials that are exported by the underdeveloped countries are controlled by the monopolies, either directly, at the stage of production, or else at the stage of world trade. The amount of profit realized by a monopoly is proportionate to the strength of this monopoly in relation to the producers it controls, and this strength is undoubtedly greater in the underdeveloped countries. To what extent will it be possible to effect a transfer of value? *A priori*, there is no means of determining the answer, for political considerations may not be without influence on the firm's attitude in the matter. Broadly, however, it is possible to say that this transfer can be effected up to the point at which the price of the product no longer covers more than the price of local production services (wages and rents), paid at the minimum rate, that is, so as to ensure subsistence for the wage earners and the amount of luxury consumption needed if the local property-owning classes are not to threaten the foreign monopoly with nationalization. The way these property-owning classes think is understandable, moreover. Nationalization does not only involve danger for them: besides the political difficulties it may engender, it cannot free the underdeveloped countries from the need to employ foreign technicians and foreign capital, which in such circumstances may require even higher remuneration.

Relative prices and comparative real rewards of labor do not constitute the only elements that enter into the theory of unequal exchange that we need, although they are its essential components. In the system of actual prices on the basis of which economic decisions are made, a special element is constituted by the cost of access to natural resources. We have seen that economic calculation based on the system of actual prices possesses no particular rationality, since some of these natural resources are subject to exclusive appropriation by a certain class, which introduces a factor of inequality, while others are free to all. Furthermore, these resources are distributed among different nations, and the conditions governing their appropriation are not everywhere the same.

In general, the "fair" international price of a product that necessitates consumption of a natural resource should include an element of *rent*, added to the equal reward of labor and the average profit, adequate to make possible the reconstitution of this resource. If what is involved is a resource that is self-renewing, like land, air, or water, then the price must make possible the satisfactory *maintenance* of this permanent resource. If what is involved is a resource that is liable to exhaustion, like hydrocarbons or minerals, then the price must make possible the development of a replacement activity of equal value to the nation.

This is rarely the case, however. The capitalist system makes use of the precapitalist forms of appropriation that are current in the countries of the periphery in order *not* to pay for the upkeep of the land. Systematic destruction of soils is a major factor of long-term impoverishment for the dependent economies. This destruction is to the advantage of the dominant economies, through prices that are lower than would be those of possible substitute products.

Technological dependence is another aspect of unequal exchange, the importance of which will doubtless increase. UNCTAD (the United Nations Committee for Trade and Development) has tried to work out the total amount of the transfers that the underdeveloped countries make to the advanced ones under this heading: royalties and payments for the use of patents, profits paid as a result of shares accorded to foreign capital in exchange for good will and know-how, super-prices paid by enterprises when they buy spare parts, fees for after-sales services, and so on. The minimum estimate, regarded as very much an underestimate by UNCTAD itself, was $1.5 billion in 1968. These transfers are increasing at the rate of 20 percent per year, and so in 1980 will amount to $9 billion or 20 percent of the probable exports of the underdeveloped world at the end of the present decade.

Here, too, we see a monopoly price — the price of what is certainly the most absolute of monopolies, that of technique. So long as production techniques were relatively simple, domination necessitated direct control of the means of production, that is, in practice, foreign ownership of capital. This direct form of appropriation tends to become pointless as soon as the time arrives when, through technology, central capital is in a position to dominate the industries of the Third World and draw substantial profits from them without even having to finance their installation.

3. THE EXPANSIONISM OF THE CAPITALIST MODE OF PRODUCTION

Precapitalist and Mercantilist Foreign Trade

"International" exchange is defined as exchange of products between different social formations. What is characteristic of precapitalist societies is the low intensity of internal exchanges. Inside the village community, the lord's estate, or the Oriental empire, the circulation of some products is well organized (payment of dues, exchange of gifts on certain occasions, circulation of dowries, etc.); this, however, is not commodity exchange but merely accompanies the fulfilment of social obligations of an extraeconomic kind. Nor is there much exchange *between* village communities or feudal lordships: each unit, resembling its neighbor, lives self-sufficiently. Hardly any of these societies, however, is unacquainted with long-distance trade. This trade procures for all of them exotic products whose cost of production they are unable to calculate.

The Chinese porcelain that has been found in Central Africa, the ostrich feathers that made their way to Europe, the famous "spices" — these bear witness to the nature of this long-distance trade. Whole societies (Phoenicia and ancient Greece, for example) were based upon this activity of bringing into contact worlds that were ignorant of each other. In many societies with a low level of differentiation, possessing only a slight surplus, control of products supplied by this trade was of vital importance in the organization of the social formation. But there was, strictly speaking, no international specialization, and, in that sense, long-distance trade remained marginal, since it did not enter as an essential element into the modes of production that were the partners in exchange.

The trade relations between the center in process of formation (Western Europe) and the new periphery that it was forming for itself in the mercantilist era constituted a fundamental element in the capitalist system that was taking shape. The international trade between Western Europe, on the one hand, and the New World and the trading stations of Asia and Africa on the other, made up, in quantitative terms, the bulk of world exchanges. A large proportion, probably the greater part, of internal exchanges at the center were moreover operations that redistributed products originating in the periphery: this was the role performed first by Italy (especially Venice) and the Hanseatic towns at the end of the Middle Ages, then by Spain and Portugal in the sixteenth century, and then by Holland and England from the seventeenth century onward. The center then imported luxury consumer goods that were either agricultural produce (eastern spices, sugar from the Americas) or the work of craftsmen (silks and cottons from the East). These products were obtained by the center either through simple exchange, through plundering, or through the organization of production established to this end. Simple exchange — with the East — was always in jeopardy because Europe had little to offer, apart from the precious metal that it procured from America. The constant danger of a drain of bullion was so serious that all the economic teaching of the age was based on the need to oppose this tendency. The forms of production established in America essentially fulfilled the function of providing the center with precious metals and with certain luxury goods. After a period of pure and simple plundering of Amerindian treasures, intensive mining enterprises were inaugurated, and had recourse to a tremendous squandering of human resources, as a condition for the profitability of their activity. At the same time a slaveowning mode of production was introduced in order to facilitate production of sugar, indigo, etc., in the Americas. The entire economy of the Americas was to revolve around these areas of development for the benefit of the center. The raising of livestock, for example, served the purpose of providing food for the mining areas and those where the slave-run plantations were located. The "triangular trade" that began with the seeking of slaves in Africa fulfilled this essential function: the accumulation of money-capital in the ports of Europe as the result of selling products of the periphery to members of the ruling classes, who were then stimulated to transform themselves from feudalists into agrarian capitalists.

Thus, the prehistory of capitalism, the epoch of merchant capital, which runs from the great discoveries (the sixteenth century) to the Industrial Revolution (the eighteenth and nineteenth centuries), assigned specific functions to the periphery (mainly America and Africa together with, later on, India under British rule). Capitalism in its fully developed, industrial form could come to flower only as a result of the exceptional encounter of the separate elements of the capitalist mode of production: one of these was a concentration of movable wealth, the other was proletarianization. While the second element appeared as the result of the internal disintegration of the feudal mode of production in Europe, the first was born of international exchange between the capitalist center in process of formation, on the one hand, and, on the other, its periphery and the independent social formations that were brought into contact with it. America, with its treasures of gold and silver, was at first subjected to brutal plundering. Then long-distance trade changed its character. First, it enabled the merchants of the Atlantic ports — Dutch, English, and French — to become rich. Then, for the benefit of this trade, plantations were organized in America, and these necessitated the slave trade, which was to play a vital part in the development of capitalism.

The International Flow of Capital in the Fully Developed Capitalist System

International trade changed its character when capitalism became a world system. For the first time in history it is possible to speak with justification of international specialization — in other words, exchange of products the value of which is *known.*

What are the structural features of the world capitalist system as it has taken shape during the nineteenth and twentieth centuries, as regards world trade and international capital movements? Starting from what is most obvious, we note first of all the disproportion (which is, moreover, increasing) between the economies concerned. The advanced world (North America, Western Europe, the USSR and Eastern Europe, Japan, Australia, and New Zealand) represented in 1938 about 800 million people, as against 1.3 billion in the "Three Continents" (including China, which had 400 million inhabitants at that time). It possessed 70 percent of the world's income. The average ratio of income per head was 1 to 4. Thirty years later, this ratio is 1 to 6 (China being excluded, as no longer forming part of the world market), the proportion of the world's population living in the underdeveloped countries (China still

excluded) having increased from 53 to 58 percent, while the proportion represented by their production has fallen from 20 to 18 percent.

The proportion of world trade contributed by trade between
center and periphery declines, while exchanges within the center
increase. At the end of the eighteenth century the foreign trade of
France, which came third after England and Holland, was of the
order of 550 to 600 million livres (gold francs), respectively for
exports and imports, of which 220 million represented direct
exchanges with the periphery (American colonies and the Levant),
excluding exports of slaves; while an important fraction of France's
imports from England and Holland (about 160 million altogether)
consisted of exotic products re-exported by those countries. Trade
with the periphery, direct and indirect, thus represented considerably
more than half of France's foreign trade. Around 1850, France's
foreign trade had doubled in comparison with the level of 1780
(which was recovered in 1825): 1.1 billion in imports and 1.2 billion
in exports. Extra-European trade accounted for 45 percent under
both headings and even if trade with the United States be excluded,
the figure was still more than 25 percent. In addition, a large
proportion of France's imports from England still consisted of
colonial products. Finally, it is to be observed that France's trade
with its industrial neighbors in Western Europe (England, West
Germany, Belgium) was not much greater than its trade with the
less developed countries of Europe (Russia, the Austrian empire,
Spain, and Italy). It can be said that 35 to 40 percent of France's
foreign trade was still with the periphery. These proportions were
not very different after the war of 1870, trade with the non-European
periphery, the United States excluded, being then of the order of 25
percent of all France's trade (which was worth about 4.5 billion, for
both exports and imports). On the eve of the First World War the
proportions had even evolved further in favor of trade with the
periphery: out of a total $7.7 billion in imports, over 30 percent
came from the "Three Continents," including the French colonies,
while 25 percent of exports (out of a total of 5.8 billion) went to those
countries. But trade with the advanced capitalist countries of
Europe and the United States had become much more important
than trade with the backward eastern and Mediterranean parts of
Europe — 6.5 times as important. Despite the extraordinary increase in

oil imports, trade with the periphery has fallen to less than 25 percent of all France's trade in recent years, the greater part of the country's exchanges now being carried on with other European countries (particularly those of the Common Market) and the United States. Britain's trade shows the same features in its evolution, but still more pronounced. The share of the periphery in the absorption of British manufactured goods (especially cottons) was preponderant down to 1850, at least. On the world scale, similarly, the proportion of internal exchanges within the developed group of countries, which was around 46 percent of world trade in 1928, had increased to 62 percent in 1965, while, correlatively, the proportion represented by exchanges between the center and the periphery decreased from 22 percent to 17 percent. In other words, the development of capitalism at the center has increased the relative intensity of the internal flows, but in the periphery it has increased only that of the external flows.

Another piece of evidence is provided by the increased degree of specialization in the exports of the underdeveloped countries — specialization in the export of a few "basic products," generally accompanied by a relative concentration of suppliers and customers. Certain oversimplifications must, however, be avoided.

In the first place, the underdeveloped countries have no monopoly of exports of "basic products" (i.e., primary products, agricultural, and mineral). There are *rich* countries that export basic products (Scandinavian timber, Australian wool, etc.) and there are "primary" products the trade in which is *mainly* carried on by advanced countries (wheat, for example). We shall see that the way the prices of these products behave is different from that of the exports of the underdeveloped countries. Identifying the underdeveloped countries with the exporters of basic products leads to a mistake in theory. The very nature of the products exchanged has evolved. In the initial stages, exotic agricultural products were exchanged for manufactured goods of current consumption (textiles, hardware, etc.): this was the situation in the age of the simple *économie de traite*. When an industry producing goods that took the place of imports was able to arise, through the expansion of the home market resulting from the commercialization of agriculture and the development of mining, trade evolved to a stage in which what were exchanged were basic products in return for consumer goods and the production goods (power, raw materials, semifinished goods, equipment) needed by the light industry that was replacing the former imports. At a further stage, the underdeveloped countries might become exporters of manufactured consumer goods, these being either exported from the more advanced to the less advanced of the countries concerned (this is already quite common), or even exported to the developed countries of the center — this is the policy recommended by certain international authorities.

The degree of integration into the world market can, in its turn, be measured. Crude observation, noting the ratio of exports to the gross domestic product, throws little light on this, for there is a wide "scatter" in this respect in the two groups of countries. If, however, we consider the exchanges between the advanced world and the underdeveloped world taken as wholes, we note that the relative importance of the products exchanged is greater for the under-developed economies than for the advanced ones. This is because the main part of the trade of the advanced countries is carried on by these countries among themselves. Whereas the advanced countries do about 80 percent of their trade among themselves and only 20 percent with the underdeveloped countries, the proportion is inverse for the countries of the periphery, which do 80 percent of their trade with the advanced countries. When we reach this point, the apparent confusion clears up. For the advanced countries, a strong negative correlation is observable between the economic stature of a given country and its ratio of exports to product. At the head of the list stand the "small countries" (Scandinavia, the Netherlands, Eastern European countries, etc.), with the "great powers" of Western Europe in the middle and the United States and the USSR at the end. This fact reflects the inherent tendency of capitalism to expand the market, which is overlooked by the theory of compara-tive advantages. For the underdeveloped countries, this element of economic stature is largely concealed by the degree to which they have been developed on the basis of external demand. Taken together, however, the underdeveloped countries can already be seen as highly integrated into the world market.

As regards the international flow of capital, six groups of

significant facts need to be included together in the explanatory model.

First, export of capital from the oldest centers of capitalism did not become really large-scale until after about 1880. Britain's exports of capital increased from £100 million in 1825-1830 to £210 million in 1854 and £1.3 billion in 1880, and then increased to £3.763 billion in 1913. In the case of France the leap was sudden: from 12-14 billion francs in 1870 to 45 billion in 1914. For Germany the figures are: 5 billion marks in 1883; 22-25 billion in 1914. And for the U.S.: $500 million in 1896; $1.5 billion in 1914; $18.583 billion in 1922; $25.202 billion in 1933.

Second, this export of capital has taken place principally from the old centers of capitalism to the new centers in process of formation, and only to a smaller extent to the underdeveloped countries. Thus, Russia, the United States, and the "white" Dominions of the British Empire were the principal outlets. In our own time the principal movement of capital is from the United States to Europe, Canada, Australia, and South Africa.

Third, export of capital has not replaced export of goods but, on the contrary, has given it a stimulus. The average rates of growth of world trade were 3.3 percent in 1840-1880, 14 percent in 1880-1913, 0 for the interwar period, and 7 percent for the period since 1950. The great period of capital export, 1880-1913, was also that which saw the biggest growth in world trade.

Fourth, the dynamic of the flow of investment of foreign capital and the back-flow of repatriated profit is very different in the case of relations between an old center and a new center in formation from what it is in relations between the center and the periphery. In the latter case, the periphery passes from the status of "young borrower" (the inflow of imported capital exceeding the outflow of exported income) to that of "old borrower" (the outflow of profits exceeding the inflow of new capital), and becomes stabilized at this stage. In relations between an old center and a new center in formation, the course of evolution is different: the new center itself becomes in its turn an exporter of capital (first "young lender," then "old lender").

Fifth, whereas in the new centers in formation wages tend to rise to the level prevailing in the old centers from which the capital comes (sometimes, even, their wage level is actually higher from the start), the gap between wages at the center and at the periphery, for the same productivities, tends, on the contrary, to become wider.

Sixth, and finally, the rate of profit in the periphery is higher than at the center. This difference is modest, however, in comparison with the relative gap in the rewards of labor. The gross yields of U.S. investments, for example, are about 15 to 22 percent in Latin America, as against 11 to 14 percent in the United States itself.

The Second World War did not merely overturn the relations of strength between the great powers, just as the First World War had done, it also established a new sort of hierarchy, with the United States playing thereafter a role that was quite out of proportion with the roles played by the other great powers of the West. This change was reflected in the absolute preponderance of the U.S. in the export of capital: that country's share grew from 6.3 percent in 1914 and 35.3 percent in 1930 to 59.1 percent in 1960, while that of Great Britain shrank from 50.3 percent to 43.8 percent and then to 24.5 percent, and the share of the two other principal exporters of capital (Germany and France) from 39.5 to 11 and then 5.8. However, the advanced countries have become by far the chief markets for American capital: in 1966 Europe absorbed 40.3 percent of it, Canada 34.8 percent, and Australia, Japan, and South Africa 7.2 percent, whereas the entire Third World received only 17.7 percent. The distribution of this capital between sectors of the economy is very different, depending on whether the country receiving it is of the advanced or of the underdeveloped category. In the total volume of direct American investment in 1964 the mining sector took 8 percent, oil production 32.4 percent, the processing industries 38 percent; public services, trade, and miscellaneous services 21.6 percent. If we consider American investments in different regions separately, however, we find that the share received by the processing industries rose to 54.3 percent in Europe, 44.8 percent in Canada, and 54.1 percent in Australia and New Zealand; whereas it fell to 24.3 percent in Latin America, 17.5 percent in Asia, and 13.8 percent in Africa. On the other hand, the share of investment that went into mining and oil production rose in the periphery to about 60 percent and 20 percent went into the tertiary sector. If we also consider that most of the American-owned industries in Europe produce for the European market (American capital controls 50 percent of the automobile industry in Britain, 40 percent of the oil industry in Germany, 40 percent of the industries producing electrical and electronic equipment in France, and nearly all the large-scale industries in Canada), whereas in the periphery most of the foreign-owned industries produce for the external market (processing of mineral products before they are exported), we can conclude that the bulk of the center's capital invested in the periphery is concerned with exporting activities (mining, oil, primary processing of mineral products), with the second place being occupied by tertiary activities connected with exports, and industry producing for the local market playing only a minor role.

The Question of the Terms of Trade

The movement of the net barter terms of trade altered after 1880. Between 1800 and 1880, Britain's terms of trade steadily worsened, passing from index 245 in 1801-1803 to 118 in 1843-1848, 110 in 1848-1856, and 100 in 1880. If we accept, what is broadly true, that Britain was in those days the principal supplier of manufactured goods and that its imports were largely made up of raw materials and agricultural produce originating in less advanced parts of the world, this meant that in 1880, with the same physical quantity of exports (of cotton, for example), the underdeveloped regions were receiving two and a half times as much in manufactured goods (in yards of cotton textiles, for instance) as in 1800, and 1.2 as much as in the middle of the century. After 1880 the movement went into reverse. The terms of trade worsened for suppliers of raw materials and agricultural produce, passing from index 163 in 1876-1880 to index 120 in 1926-1930 and 100 in 1938. This meant that in 1938 the underdeveloped countries could buy, with the same quantity of primary products exported, only 60 percent of the quantity of manufactured products they would have obtained in 1880.

The contemporary period falls into two subperiods. During the Second World War, and afterward until the end of the Korean War, around 1953-1955, the terms of trade substantially improved for the underdeveloped countries. The period of great prosperity into which the contemporary world entered thereafter, however, was marked by a serious worsening of the terms of trade, which, depending on the particular products exported by the underdeveloped countries, showed a divergence of between 5 and 15 percent at the least, and in some cases perhaps as much as between 8 and 25 percent.

In themselves, these changes in the terms of trade mean nothing. If progress in productivity is more rapid in one branch of production than in another, it is normal for the relative price of the products of the former branch to decline as compared with those of the latter. This is, indeed, the basis on which the theory of comparative costs founds its optimism. Let us have a look at what actually happens in relations between industrial and agricultural countries. If we assume that prices are fixed at the level of costs of production, and that a technical advance takes place in the industrial countries, then costs of production, and, with them, the prices of manufactured products, decline relatively to the prices of agricultural products. The terms of trade improve for the agricultural countries. The latter obtain more and more industrial goods in return for supplying the same quantity as before of agricultural produce, and thereby benefit from progress that has been made elsewhere.

This is what happened, apparently, in relations between Britain and the rest of the world between 1800 and 1880. But what happened after 1880? The worsening of the terms of trade for the producers of "primary" products would be normal if the progress of productivity had been greater in the export production of the under-developed world than in the exporting industries of the advanced world. In such a case it would be the advanced countries that would, thanks to international specialization, be reaping the benefits, along with the primary producing countries themselves, of the technical progress achieved in the latter. If, however, technical progress had been more rapid in the exporting branches of production in the advanced countries, then it would be necessary to explain by what mechanism the countries specializing in "primary" production had been deprived of the benefits of their specialization.

What do we learn from a comparison between the long-term progress in agriculture and industry, respectively, within a single economy?

Income per Head
[*in international units*]

			Increase percent	Annual growth rate
United States	(1850)	(1935)		
Agriculture	298	669	121	1.0
Industry	737	1,683	127	1.0
Great Britain	(1867)	(1930)		
Agriculture	581	827	42	0.6
Industry	418	1,151	175	1.6
France	(1860-1869)	(1930)		
Agriculture	435	500	15	0.2
Industry	468	1,373	193	1.8
Australia	(1886-1887)	(1935-1936)		
Agriculture	678	1,408	107	1.5
Industry	368	1,461	294	2.9

Progress in all these countries has been faster in industry — the most rapid progress in agriculture, that seen in Australia, being at about half the rate of industrial progress, even in the United States, where the faster pace of progress in industry has been very marked since 1935.

This faster rate of progress in industry is everywhere accompanied by a higher degree of accumulation of capital in industry as compared with agriculture.

When we move from the first group to the fourth, we find that the capital invested in agriculture has multiplied from three to five times, while the capital invested in other activities, mainly industrial, has multiplied from seven to eleven times. This shows the close correlation between capital-intensity and the level of productivity.

As regards the present period, the schema of technical progress seems to be undergoing profound change.

Evolution of the Accumulation of Capital

Income per head	Agriculture	Other activities
1st group: about 500 Japan, 1913 Scandinavia, 1880	100	400
2nd group: 1,000-2,000 Great Britain, 1865 Italy, 1913	100-300	700-1,400
3rd group: 3,000 Great Britain, 1885 Germany, 1913 France, 1913	300-400	2,300-3,400
4th group: 4,000-5,000 United States, 1913	300-500	3,400-5,100

Evolution of the Ratio Between Capital and Production

United States			Great Britain	
Years	Processing industries	Extractive industries	Years	National economy
1880	0.54	1.16	1875	3.51
1890	0.73	1.36	1895	3.72
1900	0.80	-	1909	3.80
1909	0.97	1.80	1914	3.40
1919	1.02	2.30	1928	3.53
1929	0.89	2.14	1938	2.68
1937	0.74	1.57	1953	2.55
1948	0.61	1.34		
1953	0.59	1.26		

The reversal of the century-long evolution of this ratio reflects the beginning of the scientific and technological revolution of our time. Based on automation, this is now causing the "residual factor" (science) to emerge as the factor that tends to become the essential one in technical progress, while the extensive factors (labor and capital) of the traditional production function contribute only a diminishing share. This revolution affects only the great advanced countries: it began in the United States in the 1920s and in Britain in the 1930s. It explains why, in the underdeveloped countries, where industrial accumulation of the classical type is still going on, the capital-output ratio tends to get heavier, whereas in the advanced countries it is getting lighter: it is already often heavier in some underdeveloped countries than in a number of advanced ones.

Generally speaking, if, in the advanced countries, during the classical accumulation process, agriculture has progressed less rapidly than industry — in countries where, nevertheless, mechanization *has* penetrated the countryside — it is clear, *a fortiori*, that progress in the export industry of the advanced countries has been greater than in the traditional export agriculture of the underdeveloped countries, where mechanization is still unknown. Proof of this is given by a growing divergence between production per head in industry (always, necessarily, modern in character) and in agriculture, a divergence that is growing faster in the underdeveloped countries than in the advanced ones. As we have seen, however, the underdeveloped countries are not mainly exporters of agricultural products coming from their traditional-type agriculture. We must therefore compare the progress made (1) in the industries of the advanced countries that export to the underdeveloped ones; (2) in the extractive industries (oil and other minerals) that export from the underdeveloped countries; (3) in the modern plantation agriculture of these countries; and (4) in the traditional export agriculture of these countries. This can be done if we compare the capital-output ratio for each of the four groups mentioned (since we lack the better indicator that their organic composition of capital would provide). We must also take care to estimate the capital invested and the product (value added: reward of labor and capital) in the same way. As regards capital, estimates in current values can be accepted as being homogeneous, because capital goods are supplied almost exclusively by the advanced countries. As regards the product, however, we must keep in mind the facts that, with equal productivity, wages are lower in the underdeveloped countries, and that part of the profit realized in these countries is transferred to the center, by way of the low prices of the products, through the worldwide equalization of the rate of profit. All things being equal, homogeneous comparisons ought to show lower figures for the capital-output ratio in the underdeveloped countries. How much lower? If, with equal productivity, real wages are only one-third in the underdeveloped countries of what they are in the advanced ones, if the average rate of profit before equalization is 30 percent, as compared with 15 percent in the advanced countries, and if wages represent 30 percent of the value added, then the capital-output ratios of the underdeveloped countries ought to be divided by two in order to be comparable with those of the advanced ones. Now, in the processing industries of the United States, which provide a valid sample of the exports of the advanced world, the capital-output ratio is of the order of 2 — whereas it is less than 3 in current estimates for the oil and mining industries of the underdeveloped countries, less than 1.5 for their modern plantation agriculture, and practically zero for their traditional agriculture: or, on the average (weighted by the relative importance of each of these groups of products in the exports of the underdeveloped world), of the order of 1.8, in current terms, for the exporting sectors of the periphery, and, in comparable terms, less than 1. In view of this, we are fully justified in concluding that progress in the export industries of the advanced countries has been faster than in those of the underdeveloped countries.

Precise analysis of the significance of the worsening of the terms of trade for the underdeveloped countries requires that systematic studies be undertaken in order to compare the evolution of relative prices (net barter terms of trade) with that of productivities. The concept of double factorial terms of trade answers to this need, as it is the quotient of the net barter terms of trade by the index of progress in comparative productivities. Unfortunately, very few studies have been devoted to evolution in the double factorial terms, which are the only terms that signify from the standpoint of the theory of unequal exchange.

In general, we can say that the double factorial terms, which, if exchange were equal, ought to have remained unaltered, have worsened for the underdeveloped countries since 1880. According to the theory of comparative advantages, the barter terms of trade ought therefore to have improved for the exporting underdeveloped countries, thus enabling these countries to profit by the more rapid progress achieved in the advanced industrial countries that supply them with manufactured goods. Yet this has not happened. How does conventional theory account for the fact?

From the subjectivist angle on value, price is determined by demand alone, regardless of any evolution that may take place in the cost of production. Some present-day economists are concerned to explain on this purely subjectivist basis the mechanism of the worsening of the terms of trade for the underdeveloped countries. They claim to be able to establish that the demand, and therefore the price, of "primary" products has undergone a systematic decline, at least in relative terms. The law of supply and demand does indeed say that price falls when demand falls, if income remains stable. But that is precisely what is not the case here, since the growth of demand runs parallel with that of income.

Raul Prebisch takes his stand on different grounds, by analyzing the comparative evolution, over the century, of technical progress and of the rewarding of the factors. He starts from the assumption that technical progress has been more rapid in the industry of the advanced countries than in the primary production of the under-developed ones. The benefits of technical progress can find expression in two ways: either prices fall, money incomes remaining the same, or else these incomes rise, prices remaining the same. If, in both types of country, prices fall as a result of progress, then changes in the terms of trade merely reflect the uneven spread of this progress. The same is true if incomes in both types of country rise together with productivity. It is *not* the same, however, if in one type of country progress brings about a fall in prices, while in the other type it brings about a rise in income without any fall in prices. Prebisch claims that this is just what has happened in international trade relations. In the industrialized world, the wage earners have obtained increases in wages, made possible by the increase in productivity. In the predominantly agricultural countries, however, the constant surplus of labor supply has prevented these incomes from sharing in the general prosperity. This observation impels us to bring in a new factor, which appeared about 1880, and which Prebisch has over-looked, namely, the transformation of capitalism at the center by the appearance of monopolies, a development that caused the economic system to resist the downward movement of prices. This is the reason why, all through the nineteenth century, technical progress was translated into a reduction in prices, whereas after 1880-1890 we find a steady rise in prices, and a faster rise in incomes (wages and profits together), as the reflection of progress. It was monopoly that made possible the rise in wages, competition being thenceforth manifested otherwise than through reductions in prices. This is why the worsening in the terms of trade for the underdeveloped countries began with the rise of monopolies, imperialism, and the "aristocracy of labor."

But what is, ultimately, the reason why the supply of labor is always excessive in the underdeveloped countries? Prebisch says that it is technical progress, which releases labor from production in these countries. Yet technical progress does exactly the same thing in the manufacturing industry. Actually, we need only consider the nature of the socioeconomic formations of peripheral capitalism to perceive that the reason for this permanent surplus of labor is quite obvious. These formations are characterized by the importance of rural reserves that are in process of disintegration, and that constitute the principal element in the labor market. In the formations of central capitalism such reserves no longer exist.

It must also be said that, in the advanced countries, although the supply of labor was relatively less excessive than in the underdeveloped ones, progress was not reflected until about 1880 in stable prices and increasing wages: throughout the nineteenth century prices went on falling at the center of the world system. In the formations of central capitalism the predominant form of income is capitalist profit, whereas in those of peripheral capitalism it is often the rent drawn by the landowners, who form the class that mainly benefits from integration into the international market. In a capitalist economy, profits constitute the elastic income that responds most readily to variations in the conjuncture. The exceptional profits realized in a period of prosperity are reinvested. The release of labor due to technical progress is partially compensated by the extra demand for

labor for producing capital goods. (Only partially, for the entrepreneur is interested in making an innovation only if the saving of
labor is greater than the additional expenditure of capital.) In an
agrarian economy integrated into the international market, the
situation is different. The rents of the landowners, which rise in a
period of prosperity, are not invested but spent (and, to a very large
extent, spent on imported goods). Progress in agricultural productivity
is not compensated, even partially, by an increasing demand for
labor for the making of capital goods. The latter, which are
imported, are paid for by part of additional exports they make
possible. The surplus of labor is therefore relatively larger. Added to
this fundamental cause of relative underemployment are other causes
closely connected with the nature of the system, such as the ruining
of craftsmen by foreign industry, a catastrophe that is not made up
for by the development of a local industry, so that the system has to
recover its balance by excluding a large proportion of the population
from production.

The Inherent Tendency of Capitalism to Expand Markets

The underlying reason for the expansion of the absolute and
relative sphere occupied by international trade must be sought in the
internal dynamic of capitalism, in its essential driving force, the
search for profit, and in the mechanisms that this sets working.
Between two precapitalist societies with relatively different structures
there are no exchanges because the driving force of societies of this
kind is the direct satisfaction of wants, and not the search for profit.
This satisfaction is obtained by producing at home, that is, in the
village, or on the great estate: the only things bought from outside
are the very few goods that are wanted but that it is quite impossible
to produce locally. The same reason that causes internal exchanges
to be infrequent causes external exchanges to be infrequent, too:
there is no seeking for profit, and no market. There may well be
differences in relative "real costs," but this does not mean there is
exchange.

In a capitalist economy the market expands continuously, because
the search for profit brings about competition, and this stimulates

each firm to accumulate, to grow bigger, and to seek farther off for cheaper raw materials and opportunities to sell more goods. The same mechanism that expanded the local market and created the national market impels the firm to sell abroad. It has been alleged that a firm has no call to sell abroad so long as it has not conquered the entire national market, and that, in order to conquer the national market, it would be necessary that its "optimum size" should be such that a single enterprise would suffice to satisfy all the nation's wants. This marginalist view is not valid, for the simple reason that there is no "optimum" size: a larger firm is always a stronger one, better able to compete. What, indeed, is the alleged optimum size related to? To the "enterprise" factor, the return on which is said to be at first an increasing and then a diminishing one. What we see here is the desire of the neoclassicists to construct a symmetrical theory for all the "factors." This, however, is highly artificial, for "enterprise" here means "administration." The single giant enterprise may well divide this administration into as many independent cells as are necessary in order that management may be optimal: the compartments into which this huge enterprise is divided will still possess a decisive advantage over smaller competitors of "optimum size," because they have at their command common financial resources.

Capitalism is thus always looking for new outlets, and there is active external trade, whether the structures are different or whether they are similar, for even in the latter case there will be, at any given moment, many products that are "specific," or regarded as such. These advantages are always changing, however, and the sphere of international exchange is always growing — not because each country is specializing to a greater extent, but, on the contrary, because production is becoming more diversified.

If the partners in exchange are at the same general level of development, then in theory there should be no comparative advantages. These do exist, however, but they are in constant change. If Germany can export Volkswagens to France, whereas France cannot export Renaults to Germany, this is not because the relative rewards of the factors and their relative utilization are different as between the two, but because the Volkswagen firm is technologically ahead of its competitor, Renault (this being in part due to its greater size), or because it commands greater financial resources. Should this superiority be canceled out through reorganization of the competing firm, the current will run the other way. If the partners in exchange are *not* at the same level of development, as in the case of exchange between the United States and Europe, it may be that the theory of comparative advantages can explain these exchanges, because the United States's superiority in productivity is distributed unevenly as between branches. It is also true that genuine "natural advantages" do exist, though in limited spheres (climatic reasons in the case of some agricultural products, or geological ones where mineral resources are concerned), and these explain why Italy exports citrus fruits to Norway and not vice versa, and why Ruhr coal is exchanged for Lorraine iron ore.

The problem we have been considering so far is different from that examined by Rosa Luxemburg. Expansion of markets, extending to the world scale, is in the very nature of capitalist development. It is not necessarily in order to solve a market problem, to realize surplus value, that this expansion takes place. The theory of the capitalist mode of production, as established by Marx and Lenin, tells us that the realization of surplus value does not necessitate extension of the market by disintegration of precapitalist societies. The only problem that exists where realization of surplus value is concerned is a monetary one — that of the adequate expansion of credit. Luxemburg raises a problem of a different order. She does not confine herself to the context of the capitalist mode of production (which is the context of *Capital*) but studies *another* problem, namely, the extension of capitalism over the whole world — the problem of relations between capitalist social formations (those of the center and those of the periphery) and of the transformation of these formations (disintegration of precapitalist societies). Parallel to the process of expanded reproduction through deepening of the market inside the capitalist mode of production, a simultaneous process of primitive accumulation was going on, as Luxemburg showed. Thus, the standing contradiction between the capacity to produce and the capacity to consume, which reflects the essential contradiction of the capitalist mode of production, is constantly being overcome both by deepening the internal (purely capitalist) market and by extending the market externally.

But this contradiction, which is constantly being overcome, is also *growing*. It thus shows itself in an increasing surplus of capital, while at the same time control of this capital becomes more highly concentrated and the capitalist market becomes worldwide. The export of capital on a large scale is therefore inevitable after a certain point has been reached in this development. If the theory of comparative advantages is assigned its rightful place, a secondary one, and it is recognized for what it really is — the theory of the apparent mechanisms of international trade — and not for what it is not — the theory of the essential forces that explain the international extension of capitalism — then the incompatibilities between the theory of international trade and that of the movement of capital will be found to disappear.

The inherent tendency to expand the market and constitute an international market is not a new phenomenon, characteristic only of the imperialist phase, in Lenin's sense of the latter expression. Oliver C. Cox has shown how, from its beginning in the mercantilist period, international trade played an essential part in the development of capitalism; how the dynamic, forward-moving, representative firm has always been deeply integrated into the essential networks of world trade, from the sixteenth century onward; and how today, despite the myth of self-sufficiency, world trade is of vital importance for the biggest American firms. By deducing that capitalism as a world system cannot be analyzed in terms of a pure capitalist mode of production in the setting of a closed system, Cox lines up with Luxemburg against Marx and Lenin. I do not agree with him on this point, because his argument that surplus value cannot be realized without an external, noncapitalist outlet is wrong: expanded reproduction is possible without noncapitalist milieus — the necessary outlet, nonexistent at the start, being created by the investment itself. And this point is essential for understanding the tendency of the capitalist mode of production to become exclusive when it is based upon the international market.

It remains true that this permanent tendency of capitalism to expand the market becomes transformed qualitatively in its forms of expression when concentration — another inherent tendency of capitalism — causes the system (at the center) to advance to the stage of monopoly. This is what Lenin appreciated when he made monopoly the principal axis of his new analysis of capitalism. For the small enterprise typical of the nineteenth century was incapable of exporting capital, and the tendency to expand the market was in those days necessarily manifested either in trade (export of goods) or in political intervention by the state, acting so as to subject the periphery to the objective requirements of the center. After 1880 the monopolies were to act directly on their own behalf, and the tendency to expand the market was to find a new form of expression: the export of capital.

The essential reason for the extension of world trade thus lies in the inherent tendency of capitalism to expand markets, and does not arise from any need for absorption of the surplus, either in the period of competition or in that of the monopolies. This was what Lenin said on the question of why a capitalist country needs a foreign market: "Certainly not because the product cannot be realized at all under the capitalist system. That is nonsense. A foreign market is needed because it is *inherent* in capitalist production to strive for *unlimited* expansion . . . " (p. 164).

International Flows of Capital

Current textbooks of political economy deal successively, and in contradictory terms, with trade in commodities and international capital movements. It is said, in connection with the latter, that they are due to the uneven distribution of the factors of production, which results in unequal rewarding of capital, whereas previously the same textbooks have said that the trade in commodities is due to this same unevenness in the distribution of factors, and even that the effect of exchange is to level out the rewarding of unevenly distributed factors.

Ricardo's theory of comparative advantages leads to the conclusion that international exchange does not affect real wages but increases the volume of profit realized in the two countries concerned without equalizing their rates of profit. This theory thus leaves room for a possible additional theory of movements of capital toward countries where the rate of profit is higher.

The adoption of the subjective theory of value led to Ricardo's thesis being abandoned. First it was thought, with Taussig, that international trade, as a consequence of unequal relative rewards of the factors, must bring about the absolute differences in these rewards. What Ricardo saw as true of profit alone, Taussig extended to wages and rent: exchange increases the productivity of all the factors, and therefore their real rewards, though without equalizing the rates of these rewards. Taking this line of argument further, Samuelson tries to show that exchange of commodities leads to absolute equalization of the rewards of the factors. But this thesis flies in the face of the most obvious facts. Besides, if trade and export of capital *both* constitute means by which international inequalities are compensated, how is it that one of these two means has not supplanted the other? How is it that export of, capital developed more rapidly only after a certain stage had been reached? How is it that the development of the export of capital has never acted so as to reduce, even partially, the export of goods but on the contrary has always given a fillip to the latter?

For the classical economists, a "superabundance" of saving was impossible by definition, since all saving was automatically invested. Keynes, by distinguishing between motive for saving and motive for investment, raised the question of possible overall disequilibrium. The post-Keynesians endeavored, on this basis, to define "maturity" in terms of a chronic surplus of saving. Harrod described technical progress as "neutral" if it kept the capital-output ratio (the ratio between the nation's capital and its income) stable, with a constant rate of interest. Given these conditions, progress did not alter distribution. This thesis of Harrod's involves the twofold assumption of a stable organic composition and an equally stable rate of surplus value. If progress were continuous, and still neutral, it would steadily increase the national income. For growth to be balanced, saving would have to increase no faster than income, or, in other words, the marginal propensity to save would have to be stable. But this propensity increases as income increases. For growth to remain balanced, therefore, the rate of interest would have to decrease all the time, which is impossible, owing to "liquidity preference." Thus, Harrod confines himself to studying the conditions of harmonious growth (from a marginalist standpoint) on the assumption of "neutral" technical progress. Joan Robinson has tried to complete this analysis. Inspired by Marx's views, she defines the neutrality of progress as meaning stability of the organic composition of capital. Then she studies the conditions of steady accumulation given certain assumptions: a constant rate of interest, neutrality of progress, stability of the division of net income between wages and profit. The two last assumptions, taken together, are equivalent to Marx's two assumptions (stability of the organic composition of capital and of the rate of surplus value) and to Harrod's definition of the neutrality of progress. Given these assumptions, accumulation can proceed steadily only if a constant fraction of net income is saved. It is thus for the same fundamental reason as Harrod gives — namely, the need for a stable and not an increasing amount of saving, with the rate of interest stable — that saving tends to become excessive in the advanced countries.

Thus, the post-Keynesians have claimed to rediscover the theory of the "general crisis" of "mature" economies. After a certain level of development has been reached, possibilities of saving become greater than investment needs (governed by the volume of consumption). We have here a general theory of underconsumption. The possibilities of saving have increased because average income is higher and the degree of inequality in the distribution of income has increased, while the need for new investment has remained stable, because, in the age we live in, the scientific and technical revolution is reflected in a fall in the capital-output ratio. This is why the beginnings of this revolution of our time (in the 1930s) were marked by the most violent economic crisis yet known. It remains true that, for a century, progress has not been "neutral" but *capital-using*. Steady increase in consumption therefore required an increasing rate of investment, to make up for the increasing amount of saving in relative terms. If there has been a tendency for capital to be superabundant since that period, is this not due, rather, to the fall in the rate of profit? Did not Keynes deplore the tendency of the marginal efficiency of capital to fall?

For Marx, technical progress is capital-using, in other words it raises the organic composition of capital (the ratio of constant capital to variable capital). On the plane of observed facts this is unquestionably correct, at least as regards the entire epoch of accumulation down to the technical and scientific revolution of our own day. Under these conditions, progress necessarily entails a falling rate of profit. This law of the tendency of the rate of profit to fall has been criticized, because the increase in organic composition that reflects the progress in productivity makes possible an increase in the rate of surplus value, the effect of which on the rate of profit is antagonistic to the alleged law. Some Marxists have thought fit to show that the tendency is stronger than this counter-tendency — either because, the increase in productivity being greater in the industries producing means of subsistence, although the rate of surplus value increases, this increase is less than that in the organic composition; or because, on the contrary, productivity rises to a greater extent in the *other* industries, in which case neither of the two ratios in question is affected on this account. A law that states a tendency bears within itself two contrary movements. This is the case here: increase in organic composition and increase in rate of surplus value go hand in hand, because the very forces that engender the increase in organic composition (technical progress) work in favor of an increase in the rate of surplus value as well. In actual fact, technical progress continually induces a surplus of labor, released by this progress, and this surplus makes itself felt on the labor market, facilitating increase in the rate of surplus value. However, the essential requirements of autocentric accumulation tend to stabilize the rate of surplus value in the advanced countries. Thereafter, the rate of profit has to decline in the fully developed economies. A search for new outlets becomes necessary, outlets where a better rate of profit can be secured: export of capital on a large scale makes its appearance. This outlet is naturally found in the new centers in process of formation, where the most up-to-date techniques can be extensively employed. Here, despite high wages — sometimes, even frequently, higher from the start than in the old centers — productivity is so much higher that the rate of profit is also improved. But the rate of profit is also improved in the countries of the system's periphery, for precisely the opposite reason, namely, because the rate of surplus value is higher there, wages being lower for the same productivity. Equalization of the rate of profit tends to become effective on the world scale in proportion as integration of commodities and capital into the world market becomes more thorough. This is why the differences observed and measured between rates of profit in advanced and underdeveloped countries, though manifest, are insufficient to make up for the massive transfer of value from the periphery to the center, which the differences in rates of surplus value make possible, through the mechanism of the worsening of the terms of trade.

The present age is distinguished by new tendencies. Monopoly does not imply merely a redistribution of profit to the advantage of the monopolies. Analysis of the conditions in which the contradiction between capacity to produce and capacity to consume — that permanent reflection of the basic contradiction of capitalism — finds expression in the present phase of the economy of "giant enterprises" has only recently been undertaken. Realization of the potential superprofits of monopoly dictates an increase in the "surplus" — a wider concept than that of surplus value, including nonproductive incomes and state revenues. Baran and Sweezy examine the ways in which this increasing surplus is absorbed. "Striving to sell" — competition between monopolies being no longer effected through prices — constitutes the inner law of the system: the lavish outlay on "selling costs" which accompanies monopoly makes possible the realization of monopoly profit while at the same time reducing the rate of this profit. Increased public expenditure, civil and military, which in the United States, for instance, has grown from 7 percent of the gross domestic product at the start of this century to 30 percent today, constitutes the other tendency inherent in the system of profit-realization. Thus, the surplus realized — all that can be measured: surplus value, waste, and surplus absorbed by the state — increased from 47 percent of the product in 1929 to 56 percent in 1963. But the whole of the potential surplus cannot be realized: underutilization of production capacity is permanent and the total of unemployed plus labor employed in the growing war-industry sector forms a high and undoubtedly increasing proportion of the labor force. This chronic underemployment reduces the actual rate of profit of the monopolies, determines the forms and particular conditions of technical progress, and ultimately impels the conquest of external markets that can provide a higher rate of profit. The examples given by Baran and Sweezy show the size of the superprofits of exported monopoly capital: "while two-thirds of Standard Oil of New Jersey's assets were located in North America, only one-third of its profits came from that region" (p. 194). True, what results from this gap between rates of profit is that, eventually, the centers of capitalism become huge *importers* of capital, for the backflow of profits is very much greater than the export of capital, as Baran and Sweezy point out, and so the export of capital represents no solution to the problem of how to absorb the surplus, but, on the contrary, worsens the conditions for this. The fact, however, does not stop the export of capital from seeming to the giant firm, at its microeconomic level, to be a solution to the problem of what to do with surplus profit.

The scientific and technological revolution of our time aggravates still further the basic contradiction of the system, for its main manifestation is to cause investment to be more efficient, in other words, to reduce the capital-output ratio, and so to make even more superfluous the unconsumed portion of profit. It thus reinforces the inherent tendency for capital to be exported, and is certainly what lies behind the recent flow of U.S. capital toward Europe.

The post-Keynesian "maturity" theory seeks to account for a real phenomenon: the difficulty of realizing surplus value in the age of monopoly. However, it goes in search of the causes where these cannot be found — in the monetary mechanism. Baran has shown how the law of the tendency for the rate of profit to fall is overcome in the age of monopoly by new forms of absorption of the surplus (waste and public expenditure). To do this, Baran had to invent a new scientific concept, the surplus, and, with Sweezy, to establish that in our time the potential surplus tends to be bigger than the actual surplus.

Like these two economists, I maintain that neither foreign trade nor export of capital really offers a means of overcoming the difficulties of realizing surplus value, for trade is equally balanced in the central regions of capitalism taken as a whole, and the export of capital gives rise to a return flow that tends to exceed it in volume. This is, moreover, the reason why the "excess surplus" is absorbed in other ways, through economic waste and public expenditure, especially certain contemporary forms of international relations — external military expenditure and state "aid" — which make possible a deficit in the balance of payments.

External trade thus corresponds to the same requirements of the system as formerly, but with tenfold force. It makes possible a reduction in the cost of labor power, in particular through the importing of agricultural products from the periphery, purchased under conditions of unequal exchange. This unequal exchange is itself possible thanks to the mechanisms that enable monopoly capitalism to ensure a steady increase in wages at the center (mechanisms bound up with the forms assumed by competition between monopolies), whereas the nature of the formations of the periphery makes it possible to keep the reward of labor there at a low level. External trade also enables the cost of raw materials to be reduced, thanks to the same mechanism of external exchange. The extraeconomic methods to which competitive capitalism had to have recourse have thus been replaced by strictly economic methods: this is one of the sources of "economism." At the same time the possibility, thanks to the monopolies, of exporting capital multiplies the means available for forcing upon the periphery the kinds of production that the center needs. The export of capital, while not enabling the surplus to be absorbed, serves to raise the rate of profit, since capital benefits from a rate of surplus value in the periphery that is higher than in its country of origin. But this transfer is largely concealed by the equalization of the rate of profit on the world scale, which constitutes the essence of unequal exchange.

We must not identify the function and mechanisms of trade and of capital export between countries of central capitalism, such as the United States and Europe, with the function performed by these relations between central and peripheral countries, for neither the nature of the products exchanged nor the direction taken by foreign investment, nor the dynamic of the return flow of profits are the same in these two cases. The uneven development as between the United States and the other countries of the center (Europe and Japan), which became accentuated during the Second World War, has made relations within the center especially important since 1945. It underlies the prosperity of this period, and has relegated relations with the periphery to a secondary role. Thereby, the world system has been transformed: a fundamental hierarchy has been established between the United States and the other countries, whereas previously the system had been marked by relative equilibrium between the powers. Now, the investment of U.S. capital in the other countries of the center does not fulfil the same function as the investment of this capital in the periphery. The search for raw materials plays a secondary role in it — the essential factors are access to the protection of licences and preferential markets, and, above all, technological superiority, rather than the lower level of wages.

State aid to the underdeveloped countries, which made its appearance after the Second World War, fulfils a variety of functions. Apart from its political significance, this aid enables the contradiction between the inflow of private investments and outflow of profits to be overcome — in other words, it serves the vital function of maintaining the *status quo*, which imposes an unequal form of international specialization upon the periphery. The transformations that followed the appearance of the monopolies did not create a new problem of surplus absorption. Marx pointed this out when he wrote in Volume III of *Capital* (p. 251): "If capital is sent abroad, this is not done because it absolutely could not be applied at home, but because it can be employed at a higher rate of profit in a foreign country."

The law of the tendency of the rate of profit to fall remains the essential, and therefore permanent, expression of the system's basic contradiction; and the function of trade in the struggle against this downward tendency is not confined to the competitive period of capitalism. The effectiveness with which it carries out this function is, on the contrary, reinforced by the monopolies, which make possible the export of capital. Unequal exchange between center and periphery also results from the rise of the monopolies at the center, which has made possible the development of the divergence between wages at the center and at the periphery, with equal productivity, and the organizing of a growing surplus of labor in the peripheral countries.

The Functions of the Periphery

With the Industrial Revolution, trade between the center and the periphery changes its function. This trade continues to be important quantitatively and to account for the major share of world trade, even though it starts to decline from 1830-1850 onward. For Great Britain, down to the middle of the nineteenth century, trade with America and the East (India, the Ottoman Empire, and, later, China) was predominant to such an extent that writings of this period consider only this type of trade whenever they endeavor to identify the mechanisms and work out the theory of overseas trade. For a long time Britain continued to serve as Europe's center for the redistribution of exotic produce. The center (first Great Britain, then Continental Europe and North America, and then, later, Japan) exported to the periphery manufactured goods for current consumption (e.g., textiles). It imported mainly agricultural products coming either from the traditional agriculture of the East (e.g., tea) or else — and especially — from the highly productive capitalist agriculture of the New World (wheat, meat, cotton). This was the period in which the international specialization between industrial and agricultural countries was decided. The center did not yet import mineral products from the periphery (production of which would require substantial investments and cheap means of transport), with the exception of the traditional precious metals. In proportion as new countries entered the industrial phase, their trade with Britain altered its character. At first they supplied agricultural products, receiving in return manufactured goods "made in England," just as the periphery did, or else exotic produce that came in via Britain. Since, however, though they were industrializing themselves, their level of industrialization was uneven — and also because they were endowed by nature with mineral wealth that was known and exploitable (coal and iron ore, for example) — relations of exchange of manufactured and mineral products for other manufactured and mineral products arose and developed between the countries of the center (e.g., France and Germany). The backward countries, such as Russia, remained exporters of agricultural products. Gradually world trade became split into two groups of exchanges with differing functions:

exchanges between the center and the periphery, and internal exchanges within the center.

In the age of competitive capitalism, then, extension of the market took place in the markets of the outside world in a context of competition between the enterprises of the metropolitan countries. Central capitalism nevertheless has some objective needs which result from (1) the inadequacy of the market, which is essentially agricultural in the first stages, restricted by the pace and scope of the progress of productivity in agriculture; and (2) the requirements for maximizing the rate of profit, which imply seeking abroad for cheaper goods for popular consumption (especially cereals), so that the cost of labor can be reduced, as well as for raw materials making it possible to reduce the value of the constant capital employed. Christian Palloix has thrown new light on the link between these objective needs and the stages in the formation of the theory of international trade, from Adam Smith to Marx. For Smith, coming at an early stage of capitalism: "(1) the external market serves as an outlet for surplus commodities, needed because of the narrowness of the internal market, in which the division of labor is limited during the phase of industrialization; (2) the external market, by itself, makes it possible to extend the division of labor within the nation, where, so long as only the internal market was available, this division was restricted." It was the relation between external trade and the generation of the surplus that concerned Ricardo, too. By his time, however, "the industrial sector possessed a base sufficiently large, contrary to Smith's expectations, to provide the enlargements of the respective markets needed for absorption of the industrial surplus; J.-B. Say's law of markets, which Ricardo was to support, gives definition to this prospect; and so the internal agricultural market plays only a minor role in the consumption of industrial products. . . . Though the agricultural sector no longer figures as the market for the absorption of the surplus, it nevertheless plays a part in restricting generation of surplus, in so far as . . . it threatens the very potentialities for this surplus to grow, through blocking profit's road to expansion by means of the law of diminishing returns, the cause of increasing wages. . . . The role of external trade . . . is to take the place of the internal agricultural market in furnishing the subsistence goods needed for labor power." Later, "Marx carried out a synthesis of the theoretical contributions made by Adam Smith and David Ricardo, reconciling the 'absorption' approach (stressing the export of manufactures) with the 'generation of surplus' approach (stressing the import of primary products)." External trade, in this sense, is a way of checking the fall in the rate of profit: "Since foreign trade partly cheapens capital and partly the necessities of life for which the variable capital is exchanged, it tends to raise the rate of profit by increasing the rate of surplus value and lowering the value of constant capital" (*Capital*, Volume III, p. 232).

These objective needs of central capitalism in the age of competition account for the economic policy followed by the states concerned in that period: colonial conquest and the opening of protected markets for the benefit of the metropolitan country, destruction of the crafts in the colonies, with recourse to political means for this purpose (the example of India is illuminating in this connection), encouragement of emigration and the opening up of land for producing wheat and meat in the North American West and in South America, etc.

In this period, the export of capital was still unknown as a means of expanding markets. This is why the predominant form it assumed, in the exceptional cases when it appeared at all, was still investment in the public debt, collected at the center by the most powerful finance houses, as with the loans made to the Khedive of Egypt.

Quite different were the forms in which this inherent tendency to market expansion was expressed in the age of monopoly. Thenceforth, the export of commodities was accompanied by that of capital. International economic relations (both trade and the export of capital) continued to serve the same functions so far as central capital was concerned, namely, to offset the tendency of the rate of profit to fall: (1) by enlarging markets and exploiting new regions where the rate of surplus value was higher than at the center; and (2) by reducing the cost of labor power and of constant capital.

Before that time there had been hardly any exporting of capital. The formation of monopolies made this possible on a huge scale from 1870-1890 onward. In this case, too, we must distinguish between foreign investments in the periphery and those destined for the young countries of the central type that were in process of formation (the United States and Canada, Russia and Austria-Hungary, Japan, Australia, South Africa). Neither in function nor in dynamic were these investments to be identical. The export of capital did not replace the export of goods; on the contrary, it gave the latter a fillip. It was to make possible changes in the way the periphery specialized. The periphery ceased to export agricultural products only and became an exporter of goods produced by modern capitalist enterprises with a very high productivity. Oil and crude minerals today make up more than 40 percent of the periphery's exports, while products resulting from initial processing of these materials (together with a few manufactured articles of importance chiefly for trade between peripheral countries at different levels of industrialization) account for more than 15 percent. Agricultural products — two-thirds of which are foodstuffs, but also including industrial raw materials such as cotton, rubber, etc., which make up the remaining third — constitute 40 percent at most of the exports of the Third World of today; and they are no longer supplied by traditional agriculture. At least half of these products come from modern capitalist plantations, such as those of Unilever or United Fruit. Thus, three-quarters of the periphery's exports come from modern high-productivity sectors that are the expression of capitalist development in the periphery — to a large extent the result of investment of capital by the center. This new specialization in the periphery is asymmetrical; so that the periphery does nearly 80 percent of its trade with the center, whereas the internal changes at the center proceeding parallel with this process have developed at a faster pace, with the consequence that 80 percent of the foreign trade of the central countries is carried on among themselves. These internal changes within the center are of a different type — mainly, industrial products being exchanged for other industrial products.

Between the Industrial Revolution and the complete conquest of the world (in 1880-1900), a century elapsed that was in the nature of a pause: the old forms (slave trade, plundering of the New World) gradually faded away; the new forms (the *économie de traite* and the exploitation of mineral wealth) took shape only slowly. We get the impression that Europe and the United States withdrew into themselves in this period, in order to accomplish the transition from the prehistoric forms of capitalism to its finished industrial form. During this period, products were exchanged at their value (or more precisely, at their price of production, in the Marxist sense); the rewards of labor at the center were very low, tending to be kept down to subsistence level; the terms of trade (of overseas produce in exchange for British manufactures) evolved in the direction conforming to the rule of equal exchange. It was this temporary situation that was responsible for Marx's assumption that India would become a capitalist country like Britain and, in general, for his neglect of the colonial question.

Imperialism, in Lenin's sense of the word, made its appearance when the possibilities of capitalist development on the old basis had been exhausted, through the completion of the first Industrial Revolution in Europe and North America. A fresh geographical extension of capitalism's domain then became necessary. The periphery as we know it today was created by way of colonial conquest. This conquest brought different social formations again into mutual contact, but in new forms; those of central capitalism and those of peripheral capitalism in process of constitution. The mechanism of primitive accumulation for the benefit of the center reappeared in a new form. The characteristic feature of primitive accumulation, in contrast to normal expanded reproduction, is unequal exchange, that is, the exchange of products whose prices of production, in the Marxist sense, are unequal. From that time onward the rewarding of labor became, in its turn, unequal. This new international specialization was to provide the basis for both the exchange of commodities ("basic products against manufactures," to give what is only a superficial description) and the movement of capital, since exhaustion of the possibilities of the first Industrial Revolution coincided with the formation of monopolies, which made this export of capital possible.

At every stage in the development of the world capitalist system the commercial and financial relations between the center and periphery thus serve the same twofold function: on the one hand, to facilitate, by extending the capitalist market at the expense of the precapitalist systems, the absorption of the surplus, and, on the other, to increase the average rate of profit. In the age of competition it was the first of these two functions that was vital, because keeping wages at the center at relatively low and stagnant levels (down to about 1860, at any rate) came into conflict with the objective requirement, in the model of autocentric accumulation, of a parallel growth of the reward of labor and the level of development of the productive forces. External extension of the capitalist market was therefore of prime importance as a means for realizing surplus value. After 1880 the monopolies created the conditions needed, first, for wages at the center to rise with the rise in productivity, as required for autocentric accumulation, with competition between firms no longer proceeding by way of price cuts, and, second, for the export of capital on a large scale to the periphery to become possible. The first of these changes reduced the role of the periphery in the mechanism of absorption. At the same time, however, it reinforced the second function, that of raising the level of the rate of profit, which was tending to decline faster at the center. This became possible through export of capital, which enabled forms of production to be established in the periphery which, although modern, nevertheless enjoyed the advantage of low wage-costs. It was then that unequal exchange appeared.

In other words, the fundamental contradiction of the capitalist mode of production — the tendency for capacity to produce to increase faster than capacity to consume, a tendency which is constantly being overcome, by means that reduce the rate of profit — was shifted from the center to the periphery, and transferred from the national formations of the center to the plane of the world capitalist system.

The imperialist epoch itself falls into two periods: from 1880 to 1945, and since 1945. Until the Second World War the colonial system imposed classical forms upon the international division of labor. The colonies provided the products of the *économie de traite* ("tropical" agricultural produce); European capital was invested in mining and in the tertiary sectors linked with this colonial exploitation (banking and trade, railways and ports, the public debt, etc.); the advanced centers supplied manufactured consumer goods. That such a system had a particularly impoverishing effect on the periphery and was bound to lead to a primary type of "blocked development" is obvious. Moreover, after an initial period that was euphoric but brief, between 1880 and 1914, capitalism was to experience one of its most stagnant periods, that between the two world wars. War preparation and war soon appeared as the only solution to the problem.

After the war of 1939-1945 a new period of dazzling growth began for capitalism in the center, based on the thorough modernization of Western Europe, which had lagged still further behind the United States during the war. At the same time, colonial subjection was shaken. Outside of Europe, establishment of groups of light industries was characteristic of this period: this expressed a policy of producing locally goods that had previously been imported. But everything continued to function within the framework of the world market, only the forms of international specialization being changed. In this case, too, a blocking of growth was inevitable. The present period is marked by three important structural changes in the capitalist system, namely: (1) the constitution of giant transnational firms that operate on the world scale, their activities being carried on through a large number of scattered establishments; (2) the impact of a technological revolution that transfers the center of gravity of the industries of the future toward new branches (atomic power, space research, electronics), and renders obsolete the classical modes of accumulation, characterized by increasing organic composition of capital; the "residual factor" — "gray matter" — becomes the principal factor in growth, and the ultra-modern industries are distinguished by an "organic composition of labor" that accords a much bigger place to highly skilled labor; and (3) the concentration of technological knowledge in these giant transnational firms.

This new form of monopoly entails important consequences for the periphery. Henceforth, the investment of physical capital loses its importance as a means of obtaining extra surplus value in order to increase the monopolies' rate of profit. Technological domination is increasingly adequate to accomplish this task. Accordingly, the return flow of profits from the periphery to the center is going to increase, and the underdeveloped countries are going to become sources of capital for the center. At the same time, technological revolution is going to make it possible for a new type of unequal international specialization to take shape.

This group of changes is what lies behind the dynamism of the capitalist system during the last twenty-five years. However, this dynamism is not synonymous with harmony. It has manifested itself in an increasingly wide gap between the center and the periphery and in a renewal of the antagonisms between national formations at the center. The hierarchy organized on the morrow of the Second World War, with the United States at the top, is being challenged now that Europe and Japan have succeeded, thanks to this long period of prosperity, in catching up. The world monetary crisis reflects this new development.

Is the period of great prosperity coming to an end? It seems so. In the countries of the periphery the possibilities of "import-substitution" are being exhausted, and this finds expression in a marked slowing down of industrialization and growth. In the Western countries of the center, the deflationary tensions of a semipermanent kind that are reappearing, together with the "international liquidity crisis," would seem to indicate a pause. But the world capitalist system can doubtless overcome this situation: it is looking for a solution in two directions, which will probably determine the future forms of international specialization.

The first of these directions is the integration of Eastern Europe into the internal exchange-network of the center, and its modernization, either under Soviet control or else through "independent" state policies (on the model of Yugoslavia, for instance). The second possible direction is the specializing of the Third World in industrial production of the classical type (including production of capital goods), while the center reserves for itself the ultra-modern branches of activity (automation, electronics, the conquest of space, atomic power). In other words, the periphery would accept a new form of unequal specialization, thus enabling the uneven development of the world system to get its second wind.

These are the different forms — past, present, and perhaps to come — of an unequal international specialization that always constitutes a mechanism of primitive accumulation to the advantage of the center. It is this mechanism that, finding expression in an increasing divergence in the rewards of labor, perpetuates and accentuates the underdevelopment of the periphery. At the same time, this "development of underdevelopment" expresses itself in aggravation of the internal contradictions characteristic of the peripheral formations: an increasing divergence between sectoral productivities within the economies of the periphery, which has to be reckoned with when analyzing the social formations of underdevelopment. At each of these stages capitalism reveals its expansionist tendency: the commercial expansionism of the first phase, then imperialism (in Lenin's sense of the word), and now postimperialism.

4. EXTRAVERTED ACCUMULATION AND DEPENDENCE

In studying the capitalist mode of production we have seen the central position occupied in the process of autocentric accumulation by the complementary relation between the production of means of production and that of consumer goods. This relation entails another, linking the level of development of the productive forces (the productivity of social labor) with the rate of surplus value (and so, the level of real wages). This latter relation is fundamental: it alone enables us to grasp the nature of the law of the tendency of the rate of profit to fall, and that of the concept of autocentric accumulation.

Autocentric accumulation does not mean autarchy. On the contrary, we have seen the decisive role played by external trade, not only in the origin of the capitalist mode of production, in the age of mercantilism, but also after the Industrial Revolution. However, external trade is here subordinated to the requirements of autocentric accumulation and constitutes a means to achieving this. In other words, autocentric economies impose a type of unequal international specialization for their own benefit.

If we examine this asymmetrical relation from the angle of the periphery, which is subjected to this unequal specialization, we shall discover a fundamentally different model of accumulation.

In the periphery we find, at the start, an exporting sector

destined to play a determining role in the creation and shaping of
the market. The capital of the central formation is not obliged to
emigrate owing to a shortage of outlets at the center: it will move
to the periphery only if it can find a better reward there. Equalization of the rate of profit will redistribute the benefits of this
better reward and reveal the export of capital as a way of combating
the tendency of the rate of profit to fall. The reason for creating
this exporting sector in the periphery is to obtain products that
constitute elements of constant capital (raw materials) or variable
capital (foodstuffs) at prices of production lower than those that
apply to the production of similar products at the center (or of
substitute products, when what are involved are specific products
such as coffee or tea).

The products exported by the periphery are of interest to
central capitalism in so far as — all other things being equal: that
is, with the same productivity — the reward of labor is lower
there than at the center. And it can be lower in so far as the
peripheral society is subordinated by all available means, economic
and extraeconomic, to this new function of supplying cheap labor
for the exporting sector.

When the given society has been subjected to this new function, it
loses its "traditional" character: indeed, it was not the function of
precapitalist societies to supply cheap labor to capitalism . . . The
principal articulation characteristic of the process of accumulation
at the center — the existence of an objective relation between the
rewarding of labor and the level of development of the productive
forces — is completely absent. Here the reward of labor in the
exporting sector will be as low as economic, social, and political
conditions permit. As for the level of development of the productive forces, it will be heterogeneous, whereas in the autocentric
model it was homogeneous: advanced (and sometimes very advanced)
in the exporting sector, backward in the rest of the economy —
this backwardness, maintained by the system, being the condition
that enables the exporting sector to benefit from cheap labor.

This being so, the internal market engendered by the development of the exporting sector will be restricted and distorted, and
consequently the periphery attracts only a limited amount of
capital from the center, even though it offers a better return. The

contradiction between the capacity to consume and the capacity to produce is overcome, on the scale of the world system as a whole, by the expansion of the market at the center, with the periphery serving only a marginal, subordinate, and limited function. This dynamic leads to an increasing polarization of wealth to the benefit of the center.

Nevertheless, after a certain level of growth of the exporting sector has been attained, an internal market does appear. As compared with the market created in the central process, this market favors demand for luxury consumer goods rather than for mass consumer goods. If *all* the capital invested in the exporting sector were foreign, and if *all* the profits of this capital were repatriated to the center, the internal market would consist entirely of a demand for mass consumer goods, as restricted as the reward of labor is low. But some of this capital is local. Furthermore, the methods employed so as to ensure that the reward of labor is low are based on strengthening those local parasitic social groups which function as transmission belts: latifundia-owners, kulaks, comprador trading bourgeoisie, state bureaucracy, etc. The internal market will thus be based mainly upon the demand of these social groups for luxury products.

A specific articulation, expressed in the link between the exporting sector and luxury consumption, is thus characteristic of this dependent, peripheral model of accumulation and economic and social development. Industrialization, producing goods to take the place of imports, thus begins at the end instead of at the beginning: in other words, with goods that correspond to the most advanced stages of development at the center, namely, consumer durables. Now, these goods require a lot of capital and of scarce resources. The result will be a significant distortion in the process of allocation of resources, in favor of these goods and to the detriment of the production of mass consumer goods. The latter will find little demand for its products and will attract no financial or human means to make its modernization possible. This accounts for the stagnation of subsistence agriculture. Any choice of a strategy of development that is based on "profitability" necessarily leads to such a distortion, the structures of income distribution, of relative prices, and of demand being what they are. The few industries established in this setting will not become poles of development but will, on the contrary, intensify the unevenness within the system, impoverishing the mass of the population (who, as producers, belong to the section that produces mass consumer goods) and at the same time enabling the minority to become more closely integrated into the world system.

Looked at from the social standpoint, this model leads to a specific phenomenon, namely, the "marginalization" of the masses — in other words, to a number of mechanisms of impoverishment: proletarianizing of the small agricultural and craft producers, rural semiproletarianization, and impoverishment without prole-tarianization of the peasants organized in village communities, urban-ization, and massive growth in both open unemployment and underemployment in the towns, etc. Underemployment will, in general, tend to increase, instead of remaining limited and stable, apart from fluctuations due to the conjuncture. The function of un-employment is thus different here from what it is in the central model: here, its pressure ensures a reward of labor that is minimal, and relatively rigid, and prevented from increasing, both in the exporting sector and in that which supplies luxury products. Wages appear here not as both a cost and an income that creates a demand essential for the working of the model, but merely as a cost, with demand originating elsewhere — either externally, or in the income of the privileged categories of society.

The "extraverted" origin of the development that perpetuates itself despite the increasing diversification, or industrialization, of the economy, is not external to the model of dependent peripheral accumulation. On the contrary, this model reproduces the social and economic conditions whereby it functions. The marginaliza-tion of the masses guarantees to the minority an increasing income that enables them to adopt European patterns of consumption. Extension of this pattern of consumption entails profitability of the sector that produces luxury goods, and intensifies the integra-tion — social, cultural, ideological, and political — of the privileged classes.

At this stage of diversification and the deepening of under-development there thus appear new mechanisms of domination and dependence. These are cultural and political, but also economic:

technological dependence and domination by the transnational firms. The exporting sector and that which supplies luxury products call for capital-using investments that only the big oligopolistic transnational firms can undertake, and which provide the material foundation for technological dependence.

Also, however, more complex forms of property structure and economic management make their appearance. The experience of history shows that private local capital often participates, even if only in a minor capacity, in the process of industrialization aimed at replacing imports by local production. It shows also that, in the big countries at any rate, an adequate market created by the development of the exporting sector and of that which supplies luxury products makes it possible to establish a sector producing production goods. This is often initiated by the state. However, the development of basic industry and of a public sector do not mean that the system is evolving toward a fully developed auto-centric form. For this production-goods producing sector is here in the service not of the development of production of mass consumer goods but of that of the exporting sector and that which produces luxury goods. The analysis thus obliges us to ask the fundamental question: development for whose benefit? A policy of development for the benefit of the masses would have to base itself upon a fundamental revision of priorities in the allocation of resources, implying rejection of the rules of profitability. That is what a strategy of transition would mean.

From another point of view, we see that, in the extraverted capitalist economies of the periphery, wages can be kept at very low levels without the process of extraverted development being hindered thereby. Where the capitalist mode of production is autocentric it tends to become exclusive, but extraversion restricts its development. This being so, what is the meaning of the "pair" constituted by the autocentric economy and the extraverted economy? It means that in the autocentric economy there is an organic relation between the two terms of the social contradiction — bourgeoisie and proletariat — that both are integrated into one and the same reality, the nation. And it means that, on the contrary, in an extraverted economy, this unity of opposites cannot be grasped within the national framework but only on the world plane.

Differential analysis of the essential laws of the functioning of the world system and of the capitalist mode of production necessarily leads to conclusions that call in question the entire problematic of the future of capitalism. It is not possible to reduce the bearing of these laws to the economic domain alone, depriving them of any political significance, without thereby denying the determining role that is played, in the last analysis, by the production relations.

The first conclusion to be drawn, which is on the directly economic level, is the existence of unequal exchange, meaning simply the transfer of value. To say that this is meaningless because what is involved is relations between different formations would signify treating as absurd Marx's analysis of primitive accumulation, which also dealt with relations between different formations. To say that the theory of unequal exchange means that "the workers at the center exploit those at the periphery" is meaningless, since only ownership of capital makes exploitation possible. (This also implies accepting a mechanistic relation between standard of living and political attitude, and so reducing the dialectic of the infrastructure and the superstructure to direct economistic determination.) To say, from a different standpoint, that it means that the bourgeoisie of the periphery is, like its proletariat, interested in shaking off the domination of the center, signifies that one has simply forgotten that this bourgeoisie has been formed from the outset in the wake of the bourgeoisie of the center.

Unequal exchange means, rather, that the problem of the class struggle needs to be looked at on the world scale, and that national problems cannot be treated as mere epiphenomena accompanying the essential problem of the "pure" class struggle. It means that the bourgeoisie of the center, the only one that exists on the scale of the world system, exploits the proletariat everywhere, at the center and at the periphery, but that it exploits the proletariat of the periphery even more brutally, and that this is possible because the objective mechanism upon which is based the unity that links it to its own proletariat, in an autocentric economy, and which restricts the degree of exploitation it carries out at the center, does not function at the extraverted periphery.

The constitution of a world system, with the characteristics that this possesses, has not only made possible the development of socialist trends at the periphery, but has also shifted the principal nucleus of the forces of socialism from the center to the periphery. It is a fact that transformations in a socialist direction have broken through only at the periphery of the system. To deny this is to deny the changes that have occurred in the world system, ultimately to deny the existence of a world system, and to forget that the periphery, integrated into the world system, has been very largely proletarianized. Charles Bettelheim wrote in his *Letter to Rossana Rossanda:* "I think it very important to draw . . . an extremely sharp line of demarcation between Mao Tse-tung's ideas and the 'Third World' tendencies which see in the so-called underdeveloped countries those which have been 'left on the shelf' by development, or merely *backward* countries, whereas in fact they are the product of imperialist domination, which has transformed them and integrated them into the imperialist system, in which they serve a quite definite function, namely, that of a reserve of raw materials and cheap labor. It is this function that renders the masses of these countries ready for revolution, whether the masses in question are proletarian in the strict sense of the word, or whether they are proletarianized, and thereby capable of being agents of a proletarian policy."

4

The Origin
and Development of
Underdevelopment

1. A THEORY OF THE TRANSITION TO
PERIPHERAL CAPITALISM

Marx's writings on non-European societies are not extensive: little more than four hundred pages, mostly consisting of articles for the *New York Daily Tribune*, focused on topical matters — the Sepoy mutiny in India and the Taiping rebellion in China, the opium trade, etc. — and often looked at merely from the standpoint of British domestic politics. Marx discusses only in a subordinate way the problems of Asiatic society and of the transformation of this society as a result of colonial subjection. Three types of problems are in fact touched on by him.

From time to time Marx discusses the nature of precolonial "Asiatic" society, notably in the passage in the *Grundrisse* where he formulates the concept of the Asiatic mode of production. He emphasizes the obstacle that the village community — in other words, the absence of private ownership of land — puts in the way of the development of capitalism. Here he reveals brilliant insight, when we recall the state of knowledge about non-European societies at that time.

Discussing the transformation that colonial rule was bringing to these societies, especially in India, Marx claimed that this would lead the East to full capitalist development. True, he noted that colonial policy was opposed to this, forbidding the establishment of modern industry in the colonies after having destroyed the crafts. But he considered that no power would be able to hinder for long the local development of capitalism on the European model. The article devoted to "The Future Results of British Rule in India" is explicit on this point: the plundering of India by the British aristocracy and merchant capital will be followed by industrialization carried out by the bourgeoisie of the metropolitan country; the railways will give rise to autocentric industries. Marx is so certain of this that he fears lest a developed bourgeois East may eventually prevent victory of the socialist revolution in Europe. He writes in a letter to Engels (in Avineri, p. 464): "On the Continent the revolution is imminent and will immediately assume a socialist character. Is it not bound to be crushed in this little corner, considering that in a far greater territory the movement of bourgeois society is still in the ascendant?"

In fact, the monopolies, the rise of which Marx could not imagine, were to prevent any local capitalism that might arise from competing. The development of capitalism in the periphery was to remain extraverted, based on the external market, and could therefore not lead to a full flowering of the capitalist mode of production in the periphery. Writing as he was in this early period of colonialism, Marx perceived only those mechanisms of primitive accumulation for the benefit of the center that belonged to the mercantilist phase and were coming to an end, and which he therefore regarded as belonging to the prehistory of capital.

Marx did, however, glimpse another possible outcome — Eastern society proletarianized for the benefit of the center, with the latter, proletariat included, becoming "bourgeoisified," and the periphery emerging as the main revolutionary force. In *The Poverty of Philosophy* (p. 35) he writes of "millions of workers who had to perish in the East Indies so as to procure for the million and a half workers employed in England in the same industry, three years' prosperity out of ten."

For my part, I put forward, as regards the theory of the transition to peripheral capitalist economy, the following nine theses:

1. Economic theory interests itself occasionally in the problems of "transition from a subsistence economy to a money economy." In reality, however, the pattern of transition to peripheral capitalism is fundamentally different from that of transition to central capitalism. The onslaught from without, by means of trade, carried out by the capitalist mode of production upon the precapitalist formations, causes certain crucial retrogressions to take place, such as the ruin of the crafts without their being replaced by local industrial production. The agrarian crisis of the Third World of today is largely the result of these setbacks. The subsequent investment of foreign capital does not have the effect of correcting these retrogressive changes, owing to the extravert orientation of the industries that this capital establishes in the periphery.

2. Unequal international specialization is manifested in three kinds of distortion in the direction taken by the development of the periphery. The distortion toward export activities (extraversion), which is the decisive one, does not result from "inadequacy of the home market" but from the superior productivity of the center in all fields, which compels the periphery to confine itself to the role of complementary supplier of products for the production of which it possesses a natural advantage: exotic agricultural produce and minerals. When, as a result of this distortion, the level of wages in the periphery has become lower, for the same productivity, than at the center, a limited development of industries focused on the home market of the periphery will have become possible, while at the same time exchange will have become unequal. The subsequent pattern of industrialization through import-substitution, together with the (as yet embryonic) effects of the new international division of labor inside the transnational firm, do not alter the essential conditions of extraversion, even if they alter the forms that it takes.

3. This initial distortion brings another in its train: the hypertrophy of the tertiary sector in the periphery, which neither the evolution of the structure of demand nor that of productivities can explain. At the center, hypertrophy of the tertiary sector reflects the difficulties in realizing surplus value that are inherent in the advanced monopoly phase, whereas in the periphery it is from the beginning a result of the limitations and contradictions characteristic of peripheral development: inadequate industrialization and increasing

unemployment, strengthening of the position of ground rent, etc. A fetter on accumulation, this hypertrophy of unproductive activities, expressed especially in the excessive growth of administrative expenditure, is manifested in the Third World of today by the quasi-permanent crisis of government finance.

4. Unequal international specialization also underlies the distortion in the periphery toward light branches of activity, together with the employment of modern production techniques in these branches. This distortion is the source of special problems that dictate development policies in the periphery that are different from those on which the development of the West was based.

5. The theory of the multiplier effects of investment cannot be extended in a mechanical way to the periphery. The significance of the Keynesian multiplier does indeed correspond to the situation at the center in the phase of advanced monopoly, characterized by difficulties in realizing the surplus. Neither hoarding nor imports constitute, in the periphery, "leaks" that reduce the multiplier effect. What annuls this effect is the exporting of the profits of foreign capital. Furthermore, unequal specialization, and the marked propensity to import that follows from this, have the effect of transferring the effects of the multiplier mechanisms connected with the phenomenon known as the "accelerator" from the periphery to the center.

6. Analysis of the strategies of foreign monopolies in the underdeveloped countries shows that, so long as the dogma of the periphery's integration in the world market is not challenged, the periphery is without economic means of action in relation to the monopolies.

7. Underdevelopment is manifested not in level of production per head, but in certain characteristic structural features that oblige us not to confuse the underdeveloped countries with the now-advanced countries as they were at an earlier stage of their development. These features are: (1) the extreme unevenness that is typical of the distribution of productivities in the periphery, and in the system of prices transmitted to it from the center, which results from the distinctive nature of the peripheral formations and largely dictates the structure of the distribution of income in these formations; (2) the disarticulation due to the adjustment of the orientation of

production in the periphery to the needs of the center, which prevents the transmission of the benefits of economic progress from the poles of development to the economy as a whole; and (3) economic domination by the center, which is expressed in the forms of international specialization (the structures of world trade in which the center shapes the periphery in accordance with its own needs) and in the dependence of the structures whereby growth in the periphery is financed (the dynamic of the accumulation of foreign capital).

8. The accentuation of the features of underdevelopment, in proportion as the economic growth of the periphery proceeds, necessarily results in the blocking of growth, in other words, the impossibility, whatever the level of production per head that may be obtained, of going over to autocentric and autodynamic growth.

9. While at the center the capitalist mode of production tends to become exclusive, the same is not true of the periphery. Consequently, the peripheral formations are fundamentally different from those of the center. The forms assumed by these peripheral formations depend, on the one hand, upon the nature of the precapitalist formations that were there previously, and, on the other, upon the forms and epochs in which they were integrated into the world system. This analysis enables us to grasp the essential difference that contrasts the peripheral formations to the "young central formations" — the latter, based on predominance of the simple commodity mode of production, possessing for this reason a capacity for independent evolution toward a fully developed capitalist mode of production. Whatever their differences of origin, the peripheral formations all tend to converge upon a typical model, characterized by the dominance of agrarian capital and ancillary (comprador) commercial capital. The domination by central capital over the system as a whole, and the vital mechanisms of primitive accumulation for its benefit which express this domination, subject the development of peripheral national capitalism to strict limitations, which are ultimately dependent upon political relations. The mutilated nature of the national community in the periphery confers an apparent relative weight and special functions upon the local bureaucracy that are not the same as those of the bureaucratic and technocratic social groups at the center. The contradictions typical

of the development of underdevelopment, and the rise of petty-bourgeois strata reflecting these contradictions, explain the present tendency to state capitalism. This new path of development for capitalism in the periphery does not constitute a mode of transition to socialism but rather expresses the future form in which new relations will be organized between center and periphery.

2. THE EXTRAVERSION OF THE UNDERDEVELOPED ECONOMIES

Extraversion must not be reduced to the quantitative importance of exporting activities in the underdeveloped economies: with "import-substitution" industrialization, extraversion assumes new forms. Nevertheless, hitherto, this quantitative predominance of the exporting activities has remained, on the plane of immediate facts, typical of the underdeveloped world. We have seen that if we take the advanced countries as a whole and the underdeveloped countries as a whole, the commercial exchanges they carry on between them represent a high proportion of income for the latter and a low proportion for the former. But this empirical approach is inadequate. The distortion toward exporting activities in the allocation of both financial resources (direct investments, the infrastructure created to serve the exporting areas and sectors, etc.) and human ones (orientation of training and education in accordance with the needs of integration into the world capitalist market, etc.) gives extra-version a qualitative dimension and asserts the dominance of the exporting sector over the economic structure as a whole, which is subjected to and shaped by the requirements of the external market.

The Historical Origin of Extraversion

Colonial trade. The Industrial Revolution was preceded in Europe by an agricultural revolution that released part of the labor force from the countryside, created the proletariat, and at the same time established the conditions for autocentric industrialization with the surplus that provided sustenance for the towns. The new industry ruined the old handicrafts, but at the same time recruited its labor force from them. Although this twofold process was accompanied by poverty and unemployment, it nevertheless represented an advance in the development of the productive forces, and the new socioeconomic equilibrium emerging from this process of transition to central capitalism was a higher equilibrium than that of the precapitalist society that existed previously.

The transition to peripheral capitalism follows a different pattern. Transformation of a natural subsistence economy into a commodity economy is never a spontaneous consequence of the introduction of new manufactured goods, causing the peasants to produce agricultural products for export in order to satisfy new wants. As the works of Rey and Meillassoux have shown, strictly economic mechanisms do not suffice, because the traditional social structures hinder the spread of commodity exchange: the vitality of the village community, for example (persistence of the right of all villagers to use of the land), makes ineffective the simple mechanisms of competition that played a determining role in the transition from feudalism to central capitalist economy in Europe. This is why the political authority — in this case, a colonial authority — concerns itself with stimulating "monetarization of the primitive economy," as the conventional expression has it. What is meant here is the use of methods that are purely and simply methods of violence, and therefore methods of primitive accumulation. The obligation to pay taxes in money form is the most widespread device employed. In the same connection, however, we should not forget "compulsory crops": in Tropical Africa, for example, the "commandant's fields," with the obligation to grow export crops. In extreme cases the cultivators have been simply expropriated: the creation of inadequate "native reserves," so that the African peasants are obliged to go and sell their labor power to the mines, factories, or plantations owned by the Europeans, belongs in this context. It has played a determining role in South Africa, Rhodesia, and Kenya. Rey gives the name of "colonial mode of production" to the totality of economic and political relations at this stage of transition.

Specific distortions make their appearance, altering the original society and depriving it of its traditional character. In general, the "prestige goods" in which the surplus of the traditional mode was embodied can henceforth be bought. This is the case, for example, with the total property accompanying exchanges of women between social groups. This mercantilization of precapitalist relations becomes a powerful factor in the penetration of capitalist relations. It compels people to go in search of money, and so either to become commodity producers or to sell their labor power. The land itself tends to become an object of private appropriation, to become a commodity, and ground rent makes its appearance.

The transition to commodity economy in Europe was accompanied by an advance of the productive forces, for it resulted from an improvement in the productivity of labor in agriculture. In the cases we are now considering, however, it is most often found that an increase in production per man is accompanied by an increase in the amount of labor put in. This is so in the agriculture of Tropical Africa, where, almost always, the growing of export crops is *added* to that of traditional subsistence crops, and does not take their place. Thus, a civilization based on a certain annual contribution of labor is superseded by one based on a larger contribution. This transition is painful and sometimes resisted by those involved: hence the use of extraeconomic methods like compulsory cultivation of certain crops. Large-scale landowners have favored the transition from subsistence to commodity-producing agriculture, and have to a large extent annexed the profits arising, without much improvement in agricultural productivity. This being so, the primary money income acquired gives rise to only a modest demand for local products, and affects mainly the demand for imported goods. Extension of the domain of commodity exchange where local products are concerned is thus a slow process.

This distortion of the traditional mode evicts part of the population from the land, proletarianizing it, but without creating a demand such as to provide employment for this surplus of population caused by the subjecting of the precapitalist structures to the requirements of foreign capital. This lack of a way forward through autocentric industrialization accounts for the increased "pressure on the land" that is so frequently to be observed in the Third World. The increase in the density of population in the countryside leads to a retrogression in agricultural technique, for progress in agriculture is usually expressed in the use of more capital and fewer men per hectare. The concentration of landownership and increase in the rate of ground rent reflect this agrarian crisis, perpetuating and reinforcing it. Thus, the extraverted orientation of the economy dooms agriculture to stagnation, sometimes even to retrogression.

Where a prosperous body of local craftsmen existed, its destruction through competition from imported manufactures brings about a second retrogression, to be contrasted with the progress that the destruction of the crafts by local industry represented in Europe. The history of the ruin of the crafts in India and Egypt has been written by Dutt, Clairmonte, and Issawi. Whereas in Europe society found a new equilibrium that ensured employment for its labor force, what we see here is a regressive equilibrium that casts a part of the labor force right out of the productive system.

Foreign investment. The conditions for unequal exchange — that is, for the reproduction of underdevelopment — are thus gradually assembled. The distortion of precapitalist agrarian relations and the ruin of the crafts bring about urbanization without industrialization. The low level of the reward of labor, at one pole, and the concentration of capital, at the other, encourage foreign capital to establish modern sectors in the periphery, producing for export.

To be sure, unlike private U.S. investments, which during the last two decades have been channeled, to the extent of more than 50 percent, into oilfields and mining, only a third of British capital abroad is invested in direct export activities: public services, railways, trade, and finance constitute together a much larger fraction of this capital invested outside Britain. For France the proportion of investments in tertiary activities is even bigger: during the nineteenth century the bulk of capital invested abroad went into loans to governments, public services, trade, railways, and banking. However, it quickly becomes apparent that the (mainly tertiary) sectors that have received, along with the plantations and mines, the major part of the capital originating from the center are to a very large extent grafted upon the exporting economy, to which they form a necessary complement. This is so with most of the means of transport (railways, harbors, etc.) and with commerce and banking. What is certain, in any case, is that this capital has been hardly attracted at all into the industries that work for the home market: the share of foreign investment assigned to these sectors is about 15 percent of the total foreign investment in the underdeveloped world.

In some capitalist countries of the periphery — the oil-producing and mining countries and some of those with a plantation economy — the bulk of foreign investment has gone directly into the export sectors. In others, where the principal exporting activity is indigenous agriculture, this investment is concentrated in the "ancillary" tertiary sector. Consequently there is great unevenness in the degree of penetration by foreign capital. Thus, Cuba before the nationalization measures (a typical plantation economy), and Zaïre, Zambia, and Chile (typical mining economies) received, per head, between five and thirty times as much capital as Brazil, Indonesia, Senegal, India, or Egypt; and the oil-producing countries received even more.

While in the second type of countries of the periphery a large proportion of local capital has been invested in export activities, the amount of these investments is often underassessed when they take the form of scattered investments in land improvement. Thus, in Egypt, agriculture, the chief source of exports, absorbed 30 percent of the nation's gross investment between 1882 and 1914, 12 percent between 1914 and 1937, 14 percent between 1937 and 1947, 4 percent between 1947 and 1960, and a higher percentage since then, with the building of the Aswan High Dam. These investments played a decisive part in growth, at any rate down to the First World War, after which the development of light industries producing goods previously imported took over the function of economic driving force: in 1882 agriculture absorbed 58 percent of national capital, in 1914 it absorbed 48 percent, and still 21 percent in 1960. The agriculture of the settlers in French North Africa, another export agriculture, absorbed a large, even though decreasing, share of investment: from 50 to 20 percent in Algeria between 1880 and 1955, from 45 to 22 percent in Tunisia between 1910 and 1955, from 26 to 13 percent in Morocco between 1920 and 1955. Even in Tropical Africa, where investment in agricultural development has remained relatively modest as compared with investment in the infrastructure, local capital has made an important contribution in this field. In the Ivory Coast, for example, between 1950 and 1965, export agriculture absorbed 17 percent of investments in money, leaving out of account the traditional investment in reclamation work.

Before the First World War a considerable part of the capital exported from the old centers of Europe was invested in the public debt of other countries. On the eve of the Second World War the proportion of the public debt of the colonial and semicolonial countries held in the great finance markets of Europe and North America ranged from 40 to 100 percent of the total amount of this debt, and accounted for between 15 and 70 percent of foreign investment. This investment corresponded largely to public expenditure on the infrastructure, occasioned by the integration of the periphery into the world market, an example being the great irrigation works undertaken by the Khedive Ismail in Egypt.

After the Second World War, the direction given to the use of what was thenceforth called "aid," while varying from country to country, tended to result in more attention to the financing of industry, including industry working for the home market. Soviet policy has played an important role in this connection, leading the West to revise its own attitude. It remains the case, however, that the doctrine laid down by the International Bank of Reconstruction and Development stipulates that investment must facilitate an improvement in the balance of payments such as to ensure repayment of the loan, together with the interest on it. The USSR itself has been moving toward this attitude for some years now. This confers a new dimension on the distortion toward the external market, within the context of an international specialization that concedes to the countries of the periphery certain industrial activities hitherto denied them.

At the outset, when contact was first established between the center and the periphery, if real wages (or real rewards of labor) were equal, the center, whose productivity was higher, could export, whereas the periphery was not competitive in any sphere, and could export nothing but exotic agricultural products or crude minerals. It was in that form that international exchange began — first with exotic agricultural products, then, later, when the cost of intercontinental transport had been sufficiently reduced, with crude mineral products, which required investment of foreign capital on a scale unknown until then.

Following in the wake of colonial trade, the creation of enclaves of foreign capital, especially in the mining sector, engendered no greater monetary demand for local products than had arisen from previous colonial exchange, for the primary income distributed by this type of enterprise largely evaporated in external "leaks." A substantial proportion of the expenditure of the foreign enterprises went directly into the foreign market — for the purchase of plant and for the payment of exported profits. Furthermore, part of the wages paid locally made its way out of the country, when the manufactured goods sought by the new workers were imported. Only part of this wage fund entered into local demand (mainly for foodstuffs); this made an important contribution to the spreading of commodity relations.

In the case of the exploitation of bauxite in Guinea by the Fria complex, for instance, only 12 percent of the total investment costs and barely 25 percent of the total value of the alumina exported remain within the country. As regards the exploitation of the oilfield in the Algerian Sahara, local expenditure occasioned by investment did not exceed 44 percent of the total, and then half of this local expenditure subsequently transformed itself into imports. The proportion represented by local costs in the value of the current exports of oil is even less — hardly 22 percent.

In the case of large-scale mining or oilfield exploitation, the major part of the fraction of "primary monetary" expenditure that remains inside the country is ultimately represented by the income the state takes, either in the form of royalties or as taxes, direct and indirect.

Industrialization by import-substitution. The industrialization of the Third World conforms to a pattern of import-substitution, which follows a process that "climbs up" from the light consumer-goods industries to the industries producing semifinished goods, and then to the industries producing equipment, whereas at the center the process of industrialization embraced all forms of industry at the same time, when it did not "descend" from the heavy equipment-producing industries to the consumer-goods industries downstream.

This industrialization of the periphery occurred late in the day — between the two world wars, in the case of Latin America, and after 1945 in that of Asia and Africa. The delay cannot be attributed to the meagerness of markets, owing to the low reward of labor, for this does not in itself constitute an obstacle to industrialization. The market is not composed of consumer goods alone: production goods play a big role there. Low wages mean high profits, and so it is possible for entrepreneurs to save and invest, that is, to create a market. In Europe industrialization took place on the basis of very low wages, to begin with, and the same is true of Japan. When productivity in the enterprises established in the periphery is similar to that in the countries of the center, lower wages make possible a higher rate of profit there. But the divergence between the rewards of labor became sufficient to matter only at a period when the concentration of industry at the center was itself well advanced. Under these conditions, it was the same monopolies that exported commodities to overseas countries that invested capital in those countries. They endeavored to maximize their profit on the whole of their activities, at the center and in the periphery, and this led them to prefer investing in the periphery in production for export. As for local capital, this was insufficiently centralized, and did not exist on a scale enabling it to compete with the foreign monopolies, and so chose, where possible, to go into sectors that were not competitive but complementary, such as comprador trade, or services.

In so far as there existed an industry focused on the local market, this faced a market that was distorted in character, owing to the low level of wages, and developed in response to the demand of the privileged strata, neglecting that of the masses. Moreover, the import-substitution industries employed modern techniques that were too capital-using to absorb the unemployment caused by the aggression of the capitalist mode of production, and so reproduced the conditions of a market in which abundant labor supply kept wages low.

The generalizing of the pattern of import-substitution industrialization opened up new opportunities for foreign capital without essentially affecting the extraversion of the economy. Beginning with the production of consumer goods that had previously been imported, the country was content to replace these imports by imports of capital goods and intermediate goods. An autocentric strategy must base itself simultaneously upon the production of consumer goods and capital goods. External trade then involves, as regards exports and imports alike, both consumer goods and equipment goods, so establishing the conditions of equal exchange.

The international division of labor within the multinational firm. The transnational firm, which appeared after the Second World War, is characterized by the scattering of its production activities across the world. It is made up of establishments distributed among the five continents, thus realizing a model of vertical integration that is often total. These establishments supply various items of a category of products the growing demand for which is typical of the "age of consumption." These are durable goods (domestic appliances, electrical and electronic devices, vehicles, etc.), always sharply distinguished by a particular trademark and the organization needed for after-sales service. The international dispersion of the different stages of production of these goods is a sign of the birth of a world production process in the full sense of the term: the old international division of labor, materialized in the exchange of products, is being replaced by a division inside the firm.

The choice of locations for these integrated activities is based on comparisons between wages for the same productivity. In East Asia the hourly wage in the textile industry varies from $.10 to $.30, as against $2.40 (or between eight and twenty-four times as much) in the United States, for the same productivity; and in the electronics industry the ratio is 1:7. It is thus to the firms' interest to establish those "links" in their production that demand relatively the largest amount of labor in the countries where labor is cheap.

From the standpoint of the international division of labor, this dispersion leads to a new form of inequality between nations. At the center are gathered the strategic activities, those which the jargon calls "software" (technological research and innovation, management), the "gray matter" in one form or another, and the production of the most complex types of essential equipment, those that require highly skilled labor. To the periphery falls the "hardware" — the production of those elements which, given the help of imported equipment, require only ordinary labor. For, despite the name given to it, the transnational firm remains national in its origins and in its top management. It is usually American, and less frequently Japanese, British, or German. The old division of labor, in which the underdeveloped countries supplied the raw materials and the advanced countries supplied the manufactured goods, is being replaced by a different division, in which the former supply the primary products *and* the manufactures, while the second supply the equipment and the "software." This division reinforces the functions of the centralization of decision-making authority and technological innovation. Thereby it reproduces its own conditions, splitting the world labor market into watertight national markets with big differences in rewards. It deepens unequal exchange by internalizing this in the firm.

The effects of this new inequality are several. In the first place, the international division of labor deprives the periphery of any initiative in its own development, and thereby reduces to nil all chances not merely of "catching up" in terms of consumption but even of aspiration to some sort of autonomy, if only of a cultural and political order. Then, it adds to the transfers of values from the periphery to the center. The visible transfers alone, in the forms of reward of capital and payments for "software," and arising from the monopoly of specific kinds of equipment, are enormous. UNCTAD, which associates these transfers with technological domination, estimates their annual increase at 20 percent. This division of labor disintegrates the economies and societies of the periphery. The missing links in them are multiplied through the centralization of the directing links at the center and the dispersion of the dependent links among many different locations, so as to bring about competition between the "little nations" and weaken their negotiating power. The transnational firm intensifies competition between underdeveloped countries, reproducing in them parallel structures that make impossible the development of integrating complementarities within broader structured economic spaces, which is the condition necessary for an independent development of these countries. On the plane of unevenness between regions, sectors, and labor markets, concentration in a few towns, where the "external savings" are greatest, aggravates existing distortions, especially as between town and country. Employing little labor, and preventing the transformation of agriculture and the backward sectors in the underdeveloped economy, these implantations contribute no solution to the unemployment problem: on the contrary, they worsen it by accelerating the disarticulation of the society in which they make their appearance.

These new tendencies in the international division of labor are as yet not very visible in the Third World as a whole. Only in

East Asia (South Korea, Taiwan, Hong Kong, and Singapore) and in Mexico is it possible already to study its effects. The installation of "runaway industries," originating in the United States, Japan, and Britain, in these territories has been sufficiently systematic to ensure, during the 1960s, a growth of manufacturing industry at exceptional rates — between 16 and 35 percent per year — and an overall growth in production, based on this type of industrialization, at rates varying from 7 to 10 percent per year. These five countries represent on their own nearly three-quarters of all the exports of manufactured goods from the Third World, which amount to about $4.4 billion. Their industries export to the advanced countries, especially the American market. They are, in the main, light industries (textiles, apparel, and leather goods, $1.6 billion; food and drink industries, $0.8 billion; wooden goods and furniture, $0.4 billion; etc.). But the very fact that they are concentrated in *a few* underdeveloped countries rules out the possibility of this being a development that could be extended to *all* the countries of the Third World.

The five countries mentioned above have nevertheless been put forward by the West as a model for the Third World, in reply to Chinese communism and Latin American nationalism. However, these hopes have already been dashed. Despite a big increase in exports, the balances of payments of the countries concerned have remained very vulnerable. First, because the exclusive allocation of investments to industries of this type has been made at the expense of agriculture and the industries aiming at the home market, so that there has been a rapid growth in imports in those sectors. Second, because imports of equipment and semifinished goods have increased at the same pace as industrialization. Finally, and above all, because transfers of profits, visible and invisible, largely wipe out the benefits of exports. The external balance worsens when the rate of inflow of new capital slows down, reproducing the familiar pattern of the blocking of independent growth. Although they have achieved high growth rates, none of these countries has approached the stage of independent and self-maintained growth, dear to the theory of "take-off." On the contrary, they are even more dependent than they were twenty years ago.

Looked at from another angle, this type of industry engenders a "semiaristocracy" of labor — few in numbers, badly paid by Western standards, for the same productivity, yet privileged by virtue of its security of employment in comparison with the proletarianized masses doomed to unemployment and casual work. This privileged situation ensures the docility of the proletariat, a condition for the reproduction of the system. The pattern of these industries rules out, moreover, any technical advancement, since the center keeps for itself those links that require skilled labor. Finally, the strengthened domination of central capital forbids any formation of a bourgeoisie of national entrepreneurs. These industries do, however, engender a middle class of salaried professionals — executives, engineers, office staff — who cleave to the patterns of consumption and ideology of the world system to which they organically belong. The "elitist" ideology that is grafted onto this type of dependence, and the degeneration of the national culture, lead to acceptance of a reduction in the sphere in which decisions are taken by the nation itself.

While these tendencies are also to be seen in the West, they do not have the same decisive implications as in the Third World, because they are grafted upon a different historical substratum. The flight of American (and also British) industries to Continental Europe, particularly Italy, does not alter the fundamental social structures already established there, and is often carried out in association with the local bourgeoisie. Moreover, this flight has already effectively slowed down the rate of growth both in the United States and Britain and created zones of depression and unemployment. Thereby it includes its own limitation. It ensured the U.S. domination over Europe for a certain period, but at the same time it created the conditions for a challenge to itself to arise. Indeed, the rapid growth of Europe and Japan in recent years is due in part to this redistribution of industry. Because the historical conditions are not those of the Third World, this revival has set in motion a wave of progress and technological innovations, especially in Japan and Germany, which have finally put an end to American domination. It is not possible to equate the asymmetrical processes of domination and dependence that characterize the relations between the center and the periphery with the uneven process of development inside the center.

Sectoral Unevenness in Productivity and Transmission of the Price Structure from Center to Periphery

If we break down production (value added), on the one hand, and the occupied labor force, on the other, into sectors, and compare the average sectoral product per head in the advanced countries and the underdeveloped ones, we are struck by the relative concentration of product-per-head around their national average in the countries of the center, and their very marked dispersion in the countries of the periphery, as is shown in the table below, compiled by Aníbal Pinto:

Gross Product per Occupied Person (1960)

	Latin America				United States	Great Britain
	Modern sector	Intermed- iate sector	Primitive	Total		
Agriculture	260	60	18	77	47	93
Extraction industries	1,060	99	16	521	133	90
Manufactur- ing industries	480	172	16	271	125	97
Building	208	68	22	87	120	99
Essential services	352	140	30	165	147	128
Other services	428	80	31	96	90	98
Total	388	98	18	100	100	100

In Latin America the extreme ratios of productivity observed, at the level of aggregation employed, are 1:11, between agriculture and extraction industry, as compared with only 1:1.4 for Britain and 1:3 for the United States.

Actually, this phenomenon is due to what I shall call "sectoral unevenness in productivity." It is not, of course, possible to compare productivities in the strict sense of the word except between two enterprises that produce the same product: the productivity of one will be said to be higher than that of the other if the total amount of labor (direct and indirect) necessary to ensure the production of one physical unit of the same product is less in the former case. Between one branch and another one can speak only of different *profitabilities,* as Emmanuel has reminded us. All the same, if, with a given price structure, conditions are such that labor, or capital, or both, cannot be rewarded in one branch at the same rate as in another, I say that productivity is lower in that branch. In the capitalist mode of production, distinguished as it is by the mobility of the factors, that is, the existence of a market for labor and for capital, the effective tendency is for labor and capital to be rewarded in all branches at the same rates. If, however, this price structure, corresponding at the center to homogeneous rewards for labor and capital, is transferred to the periphery, the result will be that the factors cannot be rewarded at the same rate in the different branches if the technical conditions (and so the productivity) are distributed otherwise than at the center. Direct comparisons of productivity are sometimes possible if the product is, if not exactly identical, then at least comparable as regards its use-value and the techniques that can be employed to produce it. If, for example, a quintal of wheat, produced at the center, requires a certain total quantity of labor (direct and indirect), and if a quintal of millet — a product of the periphery that is comparable both in use-value (a grain crop with the same nutritional potential) and in respect of the techniques that can be used to produce it — requires a larger quantity of labor, then this is because the production techniques in the periphery are backward. We are justified in speaking of a difference in productivity. In contrast to this, productivity will be the same at the center and in the periphery in the textile industries, where techniques are similar. For other products, of course, direct comparison of productivities is not possible: for example, for coffee, which is produced only in the periphery and cannot be compared to any product of the center.

Now, the price structure of the center is, in fact, transferred to the periphery. For there is a world market through which transference is inevitably effected to the periphery of the essential structures of relative prices that prevail at the center.

There is no reason why product per head should be the same in the different branches of a central capitalist economy. For this product is made up of two components, the reward of labor and the reward of capital, and, for product per head to be identical, five conditions would have to be fulfilled: (1) that the quantity of labor provided per occupied person (per annum, for instance) be the same; (2) that the organic composition of labor (Emmanuel's expression), meaning the proportion of kinds of labor with differing levels of skill, be the same; (3) that the rates of reward of labor (with the same skill) be the same; (4) that the amount of capital used, per worker (the organic composition of capital), be the same; and (5) that the rate of reward of capital be the same.

There is, however, a tendency in the capitalist mode of production toward the fulfilment of precisely these conditions. Capitalism does in fact tend to make labor-time uniform, to reduce it to its simplest, least skilled category, and reward it at a uniform rate, just as it tends toward equalization of the rate of profit. Furthermore, there is a tendency toward intensive use of capital in all branches of the economy; this constitutes the way in which productivity is increased. True, between one branch and another the organic composition of capital is different, and the higher the degree of disaggregation in the analysis, the wider is the range, with the new dynamic industries having the organic composition that increases most rapidly. It is this "scatter" of organic compositions that explains the fact that sectoral productivity is unevenly distributed at the center. But this "scatter" is even more pronounced in the periphery. If we break down the national economy into about ten branches, we find that the organic compositions at the center range from 1 to 4, and so, with an average rate of profit of 15 to 20 percent, productivities vary from 1 to 2, whereas in the periphery, with the same breakdown, the range of organic compositions extends from 1 to 35, and that of productivities from 1 to 10. Such a big divergence for the organic compositions of capital in the periphery is possible only if the capitalist mode of production has not taken hold of all the branches of production, as it has at the center. It is this circumstance that accounts for the sectoral differences in reward, and constitutes the principal aspect of the problem of unevenness in the distribution of income in the Third World.

To this main cause of unevenness in the distribution of income must be added some other causes which are also important, and which are connected with the incomplete extent of the development of capitalism: a low level of uniformization of labor-time (especially between agriculture, where capitalist forms of organization do not prevail, and the urban sector), different rates of profit for foreign monopoly capital and dependent national capital, etc. There are also some factors of a secondary order, such as: (1) the respective levels of employment in the rural and urban areas, which have a determining influence in the division of income between wages and incomes of enterprise and of ownership; (2) the structures of distribution of ownership of capital and enterprise, which mainly determine the way income of enterprise is distributed in the urban areas; (3) the structures of distribution of landownership and of the way the land is exploited which mainly determine the distribution of nonwage incomes in the rural areas; and (4) the distribution of the labor supply in accordance with the levels of skill and degree of trade-union and political organization of the different groups, which is what largely determines the structure of the distribution of wages.

The considerable divergences that are sometimes to be seen in the underdeveloped countries, between the average wage and the average income of the most deprived strata, especially the peasantry, are the inevitable consequence of the juxtaposition of two economic systems that belong to different epochs, and whose levels of productivity are not to be compared. It would be wrong to draw the hasty conclusion that one of the aims of economic policy must be to reduce the level of wages. In fact, a higher level of productivity not only makes possible higher wages but also, to a large extent, *demands* this. The Marxist conception of the value of labor power brings out this connection. This is why comparisons between standards of living, when types of income are too different, become dubiously valid — not to mention comparisons between standards of satisfaction, welfare, or happiness, which often lure economists beyond the realm of science. Such comparisons overlook price levels, which differ markedly between rural and urban areas in the underdeveloped countries; the foodstuffs provided by a food-gathering economy, which very easily are gathered in some parts of Tropical Africa, but which can be sold at high prices in the towns; the high cost of housing in the urban centers, even in the shanty-towns; the products of the food-gathering economy and of hunting, which do not figure in the national accounts; the different way of life in the towns, which entails new demands — fares, entertainment that has to be paid for, etc. The intensity of labor also has to be taken into consideration. It is often forgotten that the income of the traditional peasant corresponds to a hundred working days per annum, whereas that of the town worker corresponds to three hundred working days. If we allow for all these factors in the problem, the difference between recorded incomes, which is sometimes of the order of 1:10, often loses its dramatic character.

The problem of the "privileged wage earners" lies elsewhere. The hierarchy of wage levels is usually more pronounced in the underdeveloped countries than in the central economies. In the modern sector of the economy, both the plantations and the towns, the mass of unskilled workers, relatively more numerous, make up the most deprived group in the nation. It is in relation to this mass, and especially where unemployment in the towns and the underemployment of the landless peasants attain vast proportions, in relation to this mass of underemployed persons, who are mainly unskilled, that the wages of the skilled workers (both manual workers and office workers) confer a sense of privilege. The same applies to the groups employed in public service, especially where there is a widespread feeling that their numbers are too large and that recruitment is governed by the pressures of the "little society of the town," anxious for jobs. If, in addition, incomes of national capitalist enterprise are not present, then the privileged situation of these groups of workers acquires political significance.

It is generally supposed that there is bound to be an increasing divergence in the underdeveloped countries between the average income of the mass of the workers, the growth of which can only follow the very slow growth of the national product, and that of the more highly skilled categories, which will follow the income of similar workers in the advanced countries. Actually, these imitation effects are confined to the most highly skilled categories, the ones who are in a position to emigrate from their own country: this is what is called the "brain drain." The few data available for assessing long-term movements give cause to think that the gap was very large from the outset, perhaps just as large as today, especially wherever the heterogeneity of the two worlds, the traditional one and the modern one installed by colonization, caused the supply of labor to be inadequate in the new sector. Gradually the gap becomes narrower for the mass of unskilled workers in the modern sector, as emigration from the country to the towns develops, whereas it widens for the more highly skilled categories.

In the advanced countries, wage earners constitute the great bulk of the working people, between 60 and 90 percent of the occupied population. Consequently, in the long run the average wage cannot evolve very differently from the national product per head. Again, in the industrialized countries, the working class is, broadly speaking, fairly solid as regards unity in struggle, through its organization in trade unions — except where, as a result of racial differences (as with the black and white workers in the United States, for instance) or national ones (as with native and immigrant workers in some European countries), this solidarity is broken or at least impaired. The growth of wages therefore tends to be fixed at a uniform rate for workers in all branches of the economy, around the average growth rate of productivity, rather than around the varying growth rates of productivity in each separate branch. This being so, wages policy is a fundamental element in national policy on income distribution.

The situation is different in the underdeveloped countries, where wage earners make up only a small part of the occupied population — between 1 percent and a maximum of 30 percent — and where solidarity is not so strong, owing to the backward state of trade-union organization and the gap that exists between the worlds of the country people and those of the towns. There is therefore no obvious relation between the long-term evolution of wages and that of the national product. We find that in some countries in some recent periods a very low, or medium, growth of the national product (between 0.2 and 3 percent) was accompanied by a marked growth of real wages (over 6 percent per year in Jamaica and in Colombia; 4.5 percent in Ceylon; over 8 percent in Zambia, Rhodesia, Nigeria, and Tanzania), or else, contrariwise, very low rates of growth of real wages, even negative rates, in cases where the growth of production per head was relatively better (Taiwan, Burma, South Korea, India, Philippines, etc.). Phenomena like this are not open to simple explanations, for there is not the slightest correlation between the movement of wages and the pace of industrialization, or even the movement of profits. Cases are known (Belgian Congo, Puerto Rico) where a steady increase in wages has stimulated enterprises to choose more efficient methods of production. As regards response to chronic inflation, we find every possible case: belated adjustment of wages, steady advance of real wages, or, on the contrary, steady reduction of real wages. Elastic behavior by wages, upward or downward in real terms, is only possible because the problem of wages does not constitute the main axis of income distribution in the given country.

The large divergences, both absolute and relative, in the levels of remuneration of the different categories of working people in the underdeveloped countries — between those in the countryside and those in the towns, between the skilled and the unskilled, between those employed by certain large enterprises and the rest — even if explicable on strictly economic grounds, constitute an obstacle to the building of a coherent nation. It is conceivable that an economic policy of development might aim to work systematically *against* the "natural laws" of the economy, seeking to reduce these divergences in order to ensure national cohesion. But this policy can be justified only if the reduction in the rewards of the privileged categories of workers that it undertakes to achieve is *not* effected for the benefit of other categories of income, such as incomes of private enterprise, whether national or foreign, but for that of the community as a whole, and provided that the categories affected by this policy are clearly aware that this is so.

An egalitarian policy of this sort is politically rational, since the aim of national cohesion is essential for development. It means, however, that a price system must be adopted that differs from that of market prices. The actual price system in the under-developed countries, which is largely determined by that prevailing in the advanced countries, as a result of international competition and the substitution of some products for others, corresponds to a relatively uniform distribution of productivities. In view of the much wider "scatter" of productivities, in the underdeveloped economies, the rewarding of labor and of capital, respectively, on a uniform basis would result in a system of prices that would not be rational from the standpoint of economic calculation when it came to choosing the sectors of the economy to be developed. Two price systems would therefore be adopted, with rationalities situated on different planes: a system of actual prices intended to "iron out" inequalities in rewards and ensure national cohesion, and a system of reference prices serving the needs of economic calculation. Only in the course of development would the unevenness between productivities be reduced and the two systems draw close together.

The nature of the political relations between foreign capital, the local business bourgeoisie, the privileged strata of wage earners, and the administrative bureaucracy is what ultimately determines important aspects of the evolution of this social distribution of income. When there is no business bourgeoisie, as is often the case in Black Africa, the privileged wage-earning strata may become, along with the administrative bureaucracy, the principal transmission belt of domination from without. But this does not always happen. In Zaïre, for instance, between 1960 and 1968 it was the bureaucracy that grabbed the lion's share, while the condition of the working class, along with that of the peasantry, was worsened.

In the capitalist mode of production, the equilibrium prices that ensure supply is adapted to demand are prices of production in the Marxist sense. These prices presuppose equal rewards of labor in all branches (a single labor market) and an equal rate of profit on capital (equalization of the rate of profit). Consequently, if the same fraction of profit has to be saved in order to ensure expanded reproduction in all branches (let us say, for simplicity's sake, if all the profit is reinvested, eliminating consumption by the capitalists), the structure of growth — the sharing of investment between the different branches — is determined by the structure of prices. If there were no capital market to ensure the circulation of capital from one branch to another, there would be no guarantee of coherence between the structure of growth and that of demand, modified in its proportions by this very growth. The circulation of capital is therefore a necessary law of the way the capitalist mode of production functions. But this circulation comes up against a permanent obstacle: the *ownership* of capital. The enterprises and branches that are called upon to grow faster, as a result of the evolution of demand, are afraid, should they need, in order to finance their investments, to draw upon external capital to too large an extent, that they may lose control of their affairs. They therefore try to include in their prices a margin large enough to make possible an adequate volume of self-financing. The circumstances of competition make such an operation possible, more or less. A price system that would be rational from the standpoint of growth would imply (leaving out of account any consumption by the capitalists) a structure of prices by which each branch could finance its own growth, in accordance with demand, without calling in external capital, and so different rates of profit, or else, on the contrary, an equal rate of profit and a perfect circulation of capital. The actual price system in the capitalist countries is neither the one nor the other, but something in between; the margins for self-financing vary widely, depending on many factors — including, for instance, the degree to which the given branch is monopolized. To this must be added the distortions that uneven indirect taxation causes in the price system.

It will be said that an enterprise or a branch has a higher productivity than others if it ensures, with equal rewards of labor, a higher rate of profit; and this is indeed the tendency if the branch has to have a bigger growth rate in order to meet a change in the size of demand.

Now, the price structure at the center is largely transmitted to the periphery for the reasons that also explain the mechanisms of transmission of the value of the dominant currency: psychological mechanisms connected with consumption models, competition by imported goods with local products that are more or less subject to substitution, etc.

This transmission of the price structure of the center determines in the periphery unevennesses of productivity between branches that express the uneven degree of modernization — of penetration by the capitalist mode of production. These unevennesses of productivity are often reflected in unequal rates of profit, but also in unequal rewards of labor, especially where sectors that do not belong to the capitalist mode are concerned, as is often the case with rural production. This price structure has, therefore, nothing rational about it from the standpoint of the needs of a growth organized in order to put an end to the historical lagging-behind — uneven between one sector and another — which is characteristic of the periphery.

The transmitted price system is seen to be even more irrational if we consider that, with the generalization of monopoly in the central capitalist economies, the tendency to equalization of the rate of profit is continuously under challenge. The marginalist theory of general equilibrium was constructed on the basis of an assumption of perfect competition. Taking the hypothesis of sudden cartelization of an economy in a state of competitive equilibrium, Joan Robinson drew the twofold conclusion that the national income would be redistributed in favor of the entrepreneurs and that the orientation of production would be altered. If, indeed, we assume that elasticity of total demand for products varies from one branch to another, just as elasticity of the supply of the factors varies, then it follows that more products for which the demand is less elastic will be manufactured than products for which the demand is more elastic; while, similarly, those sectors where the supply of labor is highly elastic will develop, whereas those where it is less so will decline.

It must be added that increasing the degree of monopoly in the economy does not increase the volume of saving in the apparent proportion resulting from Joan Robinson's analysis, according to which what is lost by the factors of production is gained by the entrepreneurs. Indeed, when distribution is altered to the advantage of profit, the technique of production utilized tends to become more primitive, as Sraffa has shown. The level of the national product thus declines, and the entrepreneurs do not recover everything that the factors lose. Full development of the productive forces is fettered. Furthermore, this more uneven distribution of income aggravates the contradiction between the capacity to produce and the capacity to consume — a contradiction that becomes a supplementary reason for an equilibrium of underemployment. Baran and Sweezy show that in monopoly capitalism the actual surplus is less than the potential surplus.

Analysis of the phenomenon of monopolization in terms of elasticity of the demand for products is, of course, far from satisfactory. The overall conception of the degree of monopoly in the economy takes into account the fact that every system contains, potentially, a certain degree of monopoly. There is always a curve of total demand for every commodity, whether this commodity be produced by a single enterprise or by an infinity of enterprises. The hypothesis of complete cartelization merely reveals the degree of internal monopoly in the economy, and renders this effective. The method would theoretically enable us to measure the degree of monopoly in an economy in which production was entirely in the hands of the monopolies. It does not enable us to follow *the actual evolution* of the process of concentration. Now, analysis of this evolution, and of the distribution of monopoly superprofit — uneven as between different branches — is of decisive significance for the theory of prices. While analysis of the elasticity of demand enables us to understand the extent to which transfer of the profits of one branch to another can take place, it is in terms of the overall strategies of the firms concerned that we need to analyze the struggle — by means of prices and by other means (investments, purchase of blocks of shares, monopoly of trade-marks, etc.) — which goes on between monopolies in one and the same branch.

Looked at in another way, the world system of relative prices is, in part, the result of unequal exchange. This exchange — and the unequal specialization on which it is based — serves a function, namely, to increase the rate of profit on the scale of the system as a whole. It is in these terms that we need to interpret the results of Kalecki's analysis of the effects of monopoly. He believed he could define the reasons why the share of the national income obtained by labor had remained stable in the advanced countries in the course of history: the progressive increase in the degree of monopoly had been balanced by an evolution in the terms of trade to the disadvantage of raw materials.

It needs to be added that the price of a raw material becomes purely conventional if its processing is carried out by firms that are integrated with those providing this raw material. This is the case, for instance, with the bauxite produced in Jamaica, Guinea, and elsewhere by the same groups that control its transformation into alumina in Cameroon and into aluminum in Canada or Ghana. Depending on whether the group's interest lies in localizing its profits in the periphery or in the center, it will fix high or low prices for the bauxite or the alumina.

The view that the system of declared (book) prices constitutes an objective criterion by means of which the rationality of economic choices can be judged is without any scientific validity. The techniques for evaluating projects, based on calculations of profitability that rely on such a price system, which are advocated by the World Bank belong to the realm of pure ideology.

The Choice of Production Techniques in the Periphery: The Irrationality of the System

Marginalist theory claims that choice of technique is dictated by endowment in factors and that the economic system is rational, that is, that it ought to lead to light techniques being chosen in the underdeveloped countries. It is a matter of observation, however, that this is not so. Why not?

Does investment, under the particular conditions of the international integration of the underdeveloped economies, take the direction that is most favorable to maximizing the pace of accumulation? The problem has three aspects. (1) The question of the total rate of investment: What is the mechanism that determines the division of the national income between consumption and investment? Does this mechanism, under conditions of underdevelopment, determine a division that is particularly favorable to investment? Is it possible to determine *a priori* the proportion of the national income that it would be rational to devote to investment? In other words, up to what point is the restriction of consumption advantageous to a society which wants to speed up the rate of capital formation? (2) The question of the choice of investments: What are the mechanisms that guide investments toward one industry rather than another, differing in capital-intensity, and toward the use of one technique rather than another? What are the effects on the rate of development of these mechanisms as they function in the setting of underdeveloped economies? Is it possible to establish *a priori* an order of priority among useful investments? (3) The question of international specialization from the standpoint of the differing capital-intensity of industries: What are the mechanisms that guide a country's production mainly toward light industry or mainly toward heavy industry, when this country is integrated in the world market? Are the results of these mechanisms of international specialization favorable, in the case of the underdeveloped countries, to development at the most rapid pace? To what extent should organized investment-effort be based on the internal economy, and to what extent should it depend upon international exchange?

Marginalism considers that it is the rate of interest, and that alone, which determines the direction taken by investments — that is its theoretical position. It considers, moreover, that only a rate of interest freely arrived at on the money market is capable of guiding investment in a rational way and determining the rate of growth that conforms to individual preferences — that is its doctrinal position. As the marginalists see the matter, the rate of interest is what adjusts the supply of capital to the demand for it. Now, production methods that are more capital-intensive cause the process of production to be prolonged and require a sacrifice from the consumer, who regularly prefers present consumption to consumption of an equal quantity in the future. The money market thus makes possible, through rates of interest, adjustment of the division of income between consumption and investment in accordance with the rate of "subjective underestimation of the future." It determines the general rate of development that conforms to individual preferences. Furthermore, it is held, the rate of interest determines, besides the general rate of formation of saving, optimum distribution of investments between branches of production and optimum choice of production techniques. It is the rate of interest that ensures that no capital is invested in any branch beyond the point at which the increase in productivity resulting from the additional investment becomes less than it would be in other branches. Interest is, in fact (say the marginalists), not merely the yardstick of preference for the present but also that of the marginal productivity in value terms of the capital factor.

Does the rate of interest really play the decisive part in determining the total amount of investment and the direction taken by capital? No, it does not. In the context of the capitalist mode of production, the division between consumption and investment is determined by the level of real wages (the rate of surplus value) and not by individuals' preference for the present.

Indeed, how does Böhm-Bawerk set about proving that this division conforms to "individual time-preferences"? He starts from the principle that more intensive use of capital goods always makes possible increased production, but also requires a lengthening of the production period. This "length of the production process" is only a clumsy way of measuring the "capital-intensity" of production, something that the Marxist concept of the organic composition of capital expresses more clearly. This being so, Böhm-Bawerk's claim is no different from Marx's, namely, that the techniques that are most capital-intensive are also the most productive. The consequence of Böhm-Bawerk's argument, however, seems less pertinent. Since the longer the production process, the more productive it is, the production of intermediate goods ought to develop *ad infinitum*. Yet this is clearly not the case. Why not? Because, Böhm-Bawerk tells us, owing to the subjective underestimation of the future, although the physical volume of production can be increased indefinitely if we lengthen the duration of production, the value of this production, increasingly large in volume, but also increasingly distant in time, first grows and then shrinks, so that there is an optimum duration of production. For this to be so, however, we must presuppose, *a priori*, that the rate of subjective underestimation of the future is higher than the rate of growth of physical productivity when the production process is lengthened. To get out of this difficulty, Böhm-Bawerk then puts forward another proposition: the period of production *cannot* be lengthened indefinitely because the means of subsistence needed by the workers who make the instruments of production have to be produced. What does this new proposition mean? That the labor force can be divided into two categories: one engaged in producing consumer goods, the other in producing equipment for production. Böhm-Bawerk's new proposition means that it is not possible to reduce the fraction of the labor force engaged in ultimate production below the number needed to produce consumer goods equivalent to the wages distributed. The pace of development then appears as being fundamentally dictated not by the rate of subjective underestimation of the future, but by the rate of surplus value.

And so here we come once more upon Marx's fundamental proposition. Sraffa proves how the social relation that dictates the level of real wages (the value of labor power) determines at the same time the average rate of profit and the system of relative prices. This "rediscovery" finally exposes the ideological character of the marginalist analysis and strips the practice of economic choice under capitalism of all rationality — or, more precicely, reduces this rationality to what it really amounts to: the means of reproducing capitalism's own social conditions of reproduction.

The division of available income between immediate consumption and investment, or, in other words, the growth of future consumption, is thus a social choice. It is governed, in the capitalist mode of production, by the social relation between bourgeoisie and proletariat. In a rational society it can be governed only by a collective choice, effected on the basis of long-term considerations related to society's aims (which go far beyond the time-prospect of capitalist economic calculation). This is the answer to the first question.

Where choice of production techniques is concerned, current theory still resorts to a type of marginalist analysis. A certain kind of production can be carried on equally well with various combinations of factors. If the rewards of the factors are given, it will be possible to choose from among the different possible techniques the one which, with a given stock of factors of production, weighted in accordance with their relative rewards, makes it possible to maximize immediate production.

The employment of a more advanced technique, characterized by a higher capital-intensity, is accompanied by an increase in the productivity of labor. Two cases can then arise. In the first, the improvement in the productivity of labor is less than proportional to the increase in capital-intensity. In this case, the productivity of capital diminishes. Here we have the classical hypothesis: if, in order to make one unit of the product, one can employ less labor, then one must necessarily employ more capital. In the second case, the improvement in the productivity of labor is more than proportional to the increase in capital-intensity. In this case, obviously, the productivity of capital is also improved. The first case enables one to choose between different "efficient" techniques, while the second enables one to eliminate the "inefficient" ones, that is, those that are inferior, whatever the relative rewards of the factors may be.

What policy should be recommended in an underdeveloped country suffering from a substantial degree of structural unemployment — in other words, where shortage of capital is the factor limiting growth, whereas labor is available in unlimited quantity? The techniques that, though the lightest, are inefficient in the sense defined above must, of course, be ruled out. Among the efficient techniques, it is often recommended that the one be chosen that is most economical of the scarce factor, and that therefore maximizes the productivity of capital. This amounts to saying: the lightest technique among all the possible efficient techniques. Choice of a zero reference for wages leads regularly to preferences such as this.

This line of reasoning is highly questionable, even if we accept the assumption that the labor factor is indeed available in unlimited quantity. For, among a variety of efficient techniques, a less light technique may, at the prevailing rates of reward of the factors, enable a surplus to be produced which, allotted to investment, will provide the condition for growth later on. Calculation based on a zero reference price for wages rules out this choice, since it amounts to ignoring the fact that, in reality, wages are distributed that, being allotted to consumption, reduce the nation's capacity to obtain a surplus to be allotted to investment. The rule will thus be that the heaviest technique will remain preferable, because the improvement in the productivity of labor that goes with it provides a surplus that, when invested, makes possible growth at the rate desired by the community. Competition drives entrepreneurs to choose the technique that maximizes surplus. This is doubtless why, in economic life, in the present-day world of business, the choices made are not very different in the underdeveloped countries from what they are in the industrialized ones. Often, when different choices are made, this happens more for reasons connected with the size of the market than for reasons connected with the level of wages. In any case, these choices are almost always — and fortunately — remote from those that would be dictated by a calculation based on a zero reference price for wages. This reveals that the problem of the choice of techniques is a pseudo-problem, as often happens with marginalism. The real problem is that of the choice of branches.

The surplus can be allotted in its entirety to investment, or it can be consumed, wholly or in part. If one regards the growth of wages as the ultimate objective of development, one will endeavor to ensure a parallel growth of the surplus and of wages. Given that the surplus available for investment will grow more slowly in proportion as the rate of wages is authorized to grow faster, and that growth of employment depends on growth of the surplus reinvested, it will be possible to define a social optimum-function that will enable that combination of rates of growth of the surplus and of wages to be chosen that will maximize the wage bill not at the end of a period but during the whole period, of ten or fifteen years, for example.

These arguments are not of merely theoretical interest. The countries that began to industrialize later than others have indeed experienced rapid rates of growth both of productivity and of employment whenever they have granted priority in their development to the most up-to-date industries, using the most advanced techniques. As a general rule there are no grounds, in an underdeveloped economy, for making choices different from those that would be made in a country that was already well industrialized: it is necessary to choose the most efficient technique, the one that maximizes surplus, at the rate of rewards of the factors that actually prevails. In fact, accelerated accumulation in the modern sector will be accompanied by an improvement in wages, whereas in the traditional sector, where productivity is relatively stagnant, rewards will increase more slowly, if they increase at all. There is therefore no reason to be surprised if average incomes in the two sectors are very much out of line with each other, and if this unevenness becomes still more marked as development progresses.

Although the spontaneous movement proceeds along this path of increasing differences in the rewards of labor, it is to be considered that, during the long transitional period, a genuine policy of development will not be able to tolerate this increasing inequality, for this breaks up national unity, the very precondition of development. The state must, then, plan prices and wages so as to ensure national cohesion. In order to do this, the local price system will have to be isolated from the world system. But it must be appreciated, at the same time, that planning — the choice of the sectors to be developed — can then not be based upon the system of prices chosen, the rationality of which (the political necessity for solidarity between the workers in sectors with differing productivities) lies elsewhere. It will be necessary to have a system of reference prices, for economic calculation purposes, such that the choices made lead to the development of modern branches. In proportion as the traditional sector is encroached upon and reduced, the system of prices that is rational from the standpoint of political cohesion will approach closer to the system that is rational from the standpoint of economic choices.

We still have to answer the third question, regarding the way in which unequal international specialization takes shape. In a closed economy, a certain level of national income, accompanied by a certain distribution of this income, entails a particular orientation of demand and in consequence requires a particular orientation of production in conformity with this demand. The first industries established in Europe depended on techniques that were relatively light, because these were more profitable. But the development of an industry (e.g., textiles) necessitated increased production in other branches (e.g., the making of machines). The most profitable technique in these branches might be the heaviest. Marx examined this problem when studying the mechanism of the equalization of profit. Equilibrium is obtained when the orientation of production conforms to social demand, on the one hand, and on the other ensures equal reward of all capitals. The tendency for capital to prefer to go into light industry is thus limited by the necessary development of complementary industries.

It should be noted that this definition is quite different from that which identifies light industry with the making of consumer goods and heavy industry with the production of capital goods. Production of coal, for example, uses more labor per unit of capital than production of plastic objects, or of beer. Nevertheless, there is a link between the two phenomena: if, in any sector or industry, a more modern technique is put into effect, then the national production becomes "heavier" on the average. But then the production of capital goods has increased more than that of consumer goods. The increasing heaviness of techniques runs parallel with the shifting of the productive forces from ultimate production toward intermediate production. Under conditions of international integration, however, when capitalism is developing in a framework dominated by external exchange, the complementary goods may be imported.

It is the search for profit, and that alone, that leads central capital to establish light rather than heavy industries in the periphery. With the same productivity, wages are lower in the periphery than at the center. In a given branch of production, using the same techniques, the increase in profit resulting from emigration of capital from the center to the periphery will be the greater in proportion to the "lightness" of this branch. It is this force that accounts for unequal specialization.

Unequal International Specialization, Domination by Foreign Capital, and Transference of the Multiplier Mechanisms. Disarticulation

In distinguishing between the primary effects produced by an initial independent change in an economic magnitude from the successive waves of secondary and tertiary effects that it induces, theory has brought out the *cumulative* character of the majority of economic processes. Between the values of the different magnitudes considered in the initial situation, on the one hand, and, on the other, at the end of the infinite series of decreasing waves induced by the initial change, simple mathematical procedures enable us to reveal the multipliers that epitomize the volume of the change effected, and so the inducing power of the initial change.

We have seen the role played by two of these multiplier mech-

anisms in the origin of the economic cycle: the multiplier that
measures the relation between the inducing investment and the
growth of income induced, and the accelerator that measures the
relation between the growth of the inducing income and the
induced investment.

Keynes's analysis of the multiplier assumes the setting of an
advanced capitalist economy paralyzed by the inadequacy of demand,
and possessing an installed production capacity that has to be set to
work. In this setting Keynes assumes that supply responds at once
to the solicitations of demand — that is, that production can be
increased without any fresh investment. Any initial independent
demand (not only an independent investment, but also the creation
ex nihilo of an initial demand by the state, or a surplus in the
trade balance, etc.) makes it possible to reanimate the productive
system.

In cases in which expansion of production in order to meet the
pressure of demand requires an investment, we leave the strict
framework of Keynes's analysis. If, in order to bring about this
expansion, *all* the income saved during the first period has to be
invested, we are back in the "classical" case — in other words,
the multiplier no longer makes sense, its "value" becoming infinite.
But if only *part* of this saving has to be invested in order to bring
about this expansion, the multiplier recovers a finite value, Keynes's
"propensity to save" being replaced by a propensity to hoard, or
the propensity to consume by a propensity to consume *and* to
invest. If we accept that wages are destined to feed the demand
for consumer goods, and profits to supply saving (with a view to
investment), we shall have an inherent disequilibrium in the very
mechanism of accumulation when the ratio of profits to wages
increases faster than the ratio between the volume of equipment
needed in order to ensure a given increase in consumption and
the volume of this increase in consumption. In this case the
hoarding of part of the saving occurs not, as in Keynes's doctrine,
through some alleged "liquidity preference" but because of the
impossibility of investing profitably the *whole* of the saving taken
from income — a gap that expresses a contradiction between
society's capacity to produce and its capacity to consume. Hoarding
arises from the fact that the new demand requires, in order to

create its own supply, that only part of the saving be invested. In this case, investment of the entire saving is not profitable. The bridge between the theory of hoarding and analysis of the requirements of production is established without the need to bring in this psychological factor, the marginal efficiency of capital, which constitutes the weakest point of the Keynesian theory, and without bringing in the rate of interest and of "liquidity preference," which compel Keynes to accept the quantity theory of money.

Hoarding in the underdeveloped economies is a totally different phenomenon from this forced hoarding, which reflects the capitalist mode of production's inherent contradiction between capacity to produce and capacity to consume. In the precapitalist economies, hoarding arises from the social fact that the dominant classes appropriate the surplus in a setting in which they are not at all obliged to invest a saving in order to guarantee their future income. When integrated into the world capitalist system, these economies retain precapitalist forms of appropriation of the surplus, such as ground rent. Hoarding, which used to take the form of an accumulation of "real values" (gold and land), now takes the form of accumulating the local currency. The hoarding of precious metals must be identified with luxury consumption, since gold has to be produced, or paid for with real exports. If the hoarders buy land, the sums that are spent in this way pass into the hands of other individuals: demand is shifted but not sterilized. Nevertheless, this attraction to land does increase the inequality of distribution of wealth and income. If, finally, hoarding takes the form of an accumulation of currency, the quantity of money adjusts itself automatically to economic need, so that this hoarding is sterilized as regards its effect on the level of economic activity while retaining its function for the hoarder himself, namely, accumulation of potential purchasing power, reinforcement of his social effectiveness.

Since expansion of production under the conditions of the underdeveloped world obviously necessitates investment, and the specific forms of precapitalist hoarding do not constitute a leak or drain, in the Keynesian sense, the multiplier effects of an independent investment ought to be maximal. But they are not, and this for two reasons.

The chief reason is that the profits on invested capital are to a large extent exported, since this capital is foreign-owned. Now, it is profit that constitutes the income destined essentially to finance induced investments. Export of profits thus transfers to the center the driving power of the primary investment.

The second reason for this poor capacity to generate a cumulative process reflects the specific contradiction of peripheral capitalism. If, in the periphery, wages are low but the techniques employed are advanced (similar to those employed in the advanced countries), then overall equilibrium between society's capacity to produce and capacity to consume will not be achieved: profits, which will be high in these countries, will not be reinvested, for lack of outlets.

Turning now to the accelerator, let us recall that its effect is to increase induced investment — the increase in demand for capital goods being more than proportional to that for consumer goods — because modern production techniques require the installation of durable plant that takes many years to depreciate. We have seen that, at the beginning of the cycle, the accelerator helps to slow down the effects of the multiplier, but also to intensify the fluctuations in overall demand.

Once the accelerator has been transferred to the place where the equipment goods are produced, then if, as is the case, the unequal international division of labor assigns this branch of production to the center of the system, it will be at the center that the reinforcement effects that speed up the pace of accumulation will be felt.

This transference of the cumulative effects of investment results in making the underdeveloped economy that disjointed type of economy that has been depicted in inter-industrial tables for the last twenty years. Here, too, structural comparison between advanced and underdeveloped economies has meaning only if these tables, when compared, are compiled at the same levels of aggregation. A qualitative difference in structure is then perceived, which can be summarized by saying that the inter-industrial tables of the underdeveloped countries are "empty," or that the "technical coefficients" are negligible. For a level of aggregation that retains fifteen sectors, the total of inputs (those of diagonal being excluded) represents over twice the value added in the advanced economies of the West, and less than half that for the average underdeveloped countries (those where product per head is between $100 and $200). This means, if imports (or exports) represent in both cases about 20 percent of the gross domestic product, that at this level of aggregation, external exchanges make up, in the advanced countries, about 6 percent of all exchanges, internal and external, as against 12 percent in the underdeveloped countries. If we exclude ultimate exchanges, both internal and external — that is, the spending of income on ultimate goods (both for consumption and for investment), local and foreign alike — and if we accept that ultimate goods represent about half of imports, then external intermediate exchanges amount to 5 percent of the total intermediate exchanges (internal and external) of the advanced countries, as against 16 percent in the case of the underdeveloped ones. The higher the level of disaggregation, the bigger the range becomes. At the level of sixty branches, the range is between 3 percent and 15 percent. Although moderate at the overall level, the percentages are, of course, much higher for the main branches of processing industry (here the range is between 10 percent and 60 percent), and are probably even higher still in the case of certain especially important firms.

This means that the advanced economy is an integrated whole, a feature of which is a very dense flow of internal exchanges, the flow of external exchanges of the atoms that make up this whole being, by and large, marginal as compared with that of internal exchanges. In contrast to this, the underdeveloped economy is made up of atoms that are relatively juxtaposed and not integrated, the density of the flow of external exchanges of these atoms being much greater, and that of the flow of internal exchanges very much less.

The consequences that follow from this disarticulation are crucial. In a structured autocentric economy, any progress that begins at any point is spread throughout the entire organism by many convergent mechanisms. Contemporary analysis has stressed the "leading" effects of an increase in primary demand. Formerly, analysis emphasized other channels of diffusion: the reduction in prices resulting from progress, and so, along with this, the change in the structure of relative prices, of demand, and of real income, the possible increase in profits and change in the distribution of investments. If the economy is extraverted, all these effects are limited, being largely transferred abroad. Any progress realized in the oil industry will, for instance, be without the slightest effect on the economy of Kuwait, since nomad stockbreeding sells nothing to and buys nothing from the oil sector. This progress will be diffused in the West, in all the countries that consume oil.

In this sense, one ought not to speak of underdeveloped *national* economies, but to reserve the adjective "national" to the auto-centric advanced economies, each of which alone constitutes a true, structured economic space, within which progress is diffused from industries that can be regarded as poles of development. The underdeveloped economy is made up of sectors, of firms that are juxtaposed and not highly integrated among themselves, but are each of them strongly integrated into entities the centers of gravity of which lie in the centers of the capitalist world. What we have here is not a nation, in the economic sense of the word, with an integrated internal market. Depending on its geographical size and the variety of its exports, the underdeveloped economy may appear as being made up of several "atoms" of this type, all independent of each other (as with Brazil, or India) or of a single "atom" (e.g., Senegal, which is entirely organized around the groundnut economy).

The consequence is that the false, nonstructured economic spaces of the underdeveloped world can be broken up and divided into microspaces without serious danger, something that cannot be done without intolerable retrogression in the case of the integrated spaces of the advanced countries. The weakness of national cohesion in the Third World is often a reflection of this fact, which is also the source of micronationalism: the area interested in the export economy has no need for the rest of the country, which rather constitutes a burden upon it.

The effects of this disarticulation are plainly to be seen in the historical geography of the Third World. The areas interested in an export product that is comparatively important for the develop-ment of capitalism at the center experience brilliant periods of very rapid growth. But because no autocentric integrated entity is formed, as soon as the product in question ceases to be of interest to the center, the region falls into decline: its economy stagnates, and even retrogresses. Thus, Northeastern Brazil was, in the seventeenth century, the scene of an "economic miracle" that led nowhere — the moment that the sugar-growing economy lost its importance, the region fell into a state of lethargy, to become later on the famine area that it is today. Even in little Senegal, the river region was a prosperous one in the days of the gum trade. When gum was replaced by synthetic products, the region became an exporter of cheap labor, this being the only livelihood available to its population. When the iron ore of Lorraine is eventually worked out, this may create a difficult reconversion problem for the region, but it will be able to overcome these difficulties, for an infrastructure of integrated industries has been formed on the basis of the mineral, which could be imported from elsewhere. But when the iron ore of Mauritania is worked out, that country will go back to the desert.

3. MARGINALIZATION

Hypertrophy of the Tertiary Sector

The tertiary sector (commerce, services, administration, etc.) provides between 40 and 50 percent of the product in the advanced capitalist countries, whereas in the underdeveloped ones it represents between 30 and 60 percent: around 30 percent in the countries least integrated in the world market (countries in the interior of Africa, Afghanistan, etc.), and more than 50 percent (often a great deal more) in those where the degree of integration is high. Moreover, in the advanced countries the share of the secondary sector is close to that of the tertiary, whereas in all the underdeveloped countries it is much smaller. We find the same distortion in the way the occupied population is distributed between sectors. In the advanced countries it is distributed more or less equally between the secondary and tertiary sectors, with a tendency for the occupied population engaged in the tertiary sector to increase as the average product per head increases, whereas in all the underdeveloped countries the proportion of the labor force engaged in tertiary activities is very much greater than that engaged in secondary-sector occupations. Thus, paradoxically, so far as the place held by the tertiary sector in the economy is concerned, the under-developed countries seem to be closer to the United States than to Western Europe, and even more advanced than the United States, if only one pattern of development is recognized.

If, however, we look at the comparative historical evolution of these proportions in the formations of the center and in those of the periphery, we find a very different dynamic in the two cases. In the advanced countries, the movement of transference of the occupied population from one sector to another is not linear: between 1820 and 1880-1890 a transfer took place from agriculture into both of the other two sectors in proportions more or less equal and unchanging. In the twentieth century the decline in the agricultural population proceeded faster, but it was now more and more (especially after 1920) the tertiary sector that benefited from this population transfer. The evolution of the share contributed by each sector to the national product was approximately parallel, except that in the twentieth century the share of the tertiary sector in comparison with that of the secondary increased at an even faster rate than as regards the labor force employed in these two sectors.

In the Third World, on the contrary, the occupied section of the nonagricultural population went into the tertiary rather than the secondary sector, and this happened from the beginning of the process of modern urban growth, in connection with integration into the world capitalist system. The proportion of the population engaged in the secondary sector declined, even in this so-called initial stage of industrialization. In Egypt between 1914 and 1958 the percentage of the population employed in industry, building, and construction work generally fell from 34 to 25 percent of the nonagricultural employed population. In the Maghreb, around 1955, industry, the crafts, and building employed 45 percent of all urban labor, as against 55 percent engaged in commerce, transport, services, and administration. In the Ivory Coast, around 1965, the secondary sector employed only 33 percent of non-agricultural labor.

In other words, in the central model, industry, as it develops, provides work for a larger number of workers than the number of craftsmen that it ruins. Industry recruits from declining agriculture and from the natural increase in the population. In the periphery industry employs workers in fewer numbers than those of the craftsmen it ruins and the peasants who are "released" from agriculture. The effect of competition from foreign industry is obvious. Thus, urban growth is accompanied in the Third World by an increase, both absolute and relative, in unemployment, such as did not occur in the West except during brief periods, situated mainly (apart from the time of the great crisis of the 1930s) between 1820 and 1870. In Egypt, for example, the percentage of the employed population in the towns fell from 32 percent in 1914 to 22 percent in 1960. In the Maghreb and West Africa the unemployed accounted in and around 1965 for between 15 and 20 percent of the urban labor force.

The hypertrophy of administrative activities in the underdeveloped countries is now one of the commonplaces of "underdevelopment." An analysis that seeks to go beyond mere description of the problem needs to answer a whole series of questions in this connection. On the general plane, first of all, what are the comparative rates of growth of public expenditure and of the material basis of the economy, at the center and in the periphery? Is the tendency to distortion toward administrative activities a deep-rooted and long-established tendency of the periphery (apparent in the colonial period, for instance) or is it a recent tendency (connected with the political structures that have emerged from decolonization)? Is this distortion more pronounced, in the present period, in the periphery than it is at the center? Still on the general plane, how is this public expenditure financed: what in particular is the dynamic of its sources of finance (local taxes, local loans and external loans, inflation), as compared with the dynamic at the center? On the sectoral plane, we need to analyze the comparative structure of public expenditure in the periphery and at the center (productive and unproductive expenditure), and also the comparative structure of the way this expenditure is financed (what categories of income ultimately pay for this expenditure?

In Egypt the rate of growth of the administrative services (4.7 percent per annum between 1914 and 1960) was much higher than that of the production base of the economy (1.8 percent). To

Unequal Development

this expenditure were added very considerable investments in the irrigation infrastructure (especially between 1882 and 1914). Broadly, it was the demands of the world market (development of the cultivation of cotton on irrigated land) and extended schooling that were the chief causes of this evolution. All these forms of public expenditure were financed strictly without any inflation or external aid, which appeared only recently (from 1957 onward), with a regressive and rigid fiscal structure based on customs duties and indirect taxation. The tax burden increased steadily, from a very low level (about 7 percent in 1914) to a very high one (about 30 percent in 1960). In the Maghreb a progressive increase in public expenditure has been observed, affecting both current administrative charges and the equipment of the countries concerned, an increase proceeding, in percentages of the gross internal product, from 12 percent and 4 percent, respectively, in 1880, to 18 percent and 9 percent in 1955, in Algeria; from 11 and 3 percent in 1910 to 17 and 8 percent in 1955 in Tunisia; and from 10 and 3 percent in 1920 to 12 and 5 percent in 1955 in Morocco. Financed exclusively out of local resources until the time of the Second World War, this development is now financed from abroad to the extent of 40, 35, and 40 percent respectively of the local resources of these three countries as they were around 1955. For the countries of West Africa as a whole, current administrative expenditure increased from 12 percent of the gross domestic product in 1950 to 18 percent in 1970. For the countries of Central Africa as a whole, total public expenditure (on the civil service and on equipment) increased from 15 to 20 percent of the gross domestic product between 1960 and 1968, and the deficit in their treasuries increased from 5 to 6 percent of total expenditure.

Development, Underdevelopment, and Unproductive Activities

Basing themselves on the classical division of economic activities into three sectors — primary (agriculture and mining), secondary (industry and building), and tertiary (transport, commerce, services, administration) — Colin Clark and Fourastié formulated a general theory of the phases of evolution, which can be summarized as follows: in the first phase, development of the secondary sector takes place at the expense of the primary sector; in the second phase the tertiary sector takes over from the secondary, and its relative share in economic activity as a whole increases more and more rapidly, reducing the relative proportions of the primary and even of the secondary sector.

Actually, this classification forms a bad instrument of analysis, because it is based on a narrow "positivist-empiricist" approach. As for strictly economistic theory, this is unable to account for the specific functions of the tertiary sector at the center and in the periphery of the contemporary world capitalist system.

The distinction between the primary and secondary sectors was originally put forward by the Physiocrats. Do primary activities "extract" more from nature than the activities that are described as "processing"? Despite the reply given by Ricardo to Adam Smith, it is possible to consider that there is some truth in this distinction. Appropriation of the soil, before the capitalist mode of production appeared, constituted the basis of precapitalist modes of production — in Europe, of the feudal mode. This appropriation, respected by capitalism, has hindered the penetration of capitalism into agriculture: the position occupied by ground rent reflects this historical peculiarity. Nevertheless, with the penetration of the capitalist mode into agriculture, capital comes to occupy an increasingly important position in this activity. The capitalistic nature of production has been marked from the outset in mining activity, which it seems, for this reason, less artificial to include in the *secondary* sector, along with the processing industry and building.

But the artificiality of the threefold classification becomes especially obvious when one looks at the content of the tertiary sector. Here we find, along with activities, such as crafts, that produce services (hairdressing, for example), the activities of those liberal professions that have to a greater or lesser extent been turned into "public services" (teachers, doctors and nurses in state hospitals, lawyers, and judges, who all play the same economic role), and the capitalistic production of commercial and banking services, or even the capitalistic production of services similar to those that the crafts and the liberal professions provide (e.g., a hairdressing salon or a barrister's chambers). A predominant role is not commonly played by labor in all these activities, either from the social standpoint (predominant income) or from that of technique (share of wages in the value of the finished product). In banking and commerce it is *capital* that predominates, even if this factor does not mainly take the form of machinery, but rather that of monetary reserves or stocks of goods.

This being so, a return to the classical tradition, as deepened by Marx's analysis, is not so useless as marginalism has supposed. This tradition makes a fundamental distinction between productive and unproductive labor. The sphere of productive activity provides society with material products in the places where they are to be consumed. It can be subdivided into two sectors: the primary, in which landed property has played, historically at least, the dominant role (agriculture), and the secondary, in which it is capital that plays this historical role (industries in the strict sense, together with mining and transport). In contrast to this, unproductive activity extracts nothing from nature — which does not mean that it is useless. This approach is profoundly sociological: it corresponds to the fact that, in order to extract a certain amount of wealth from nature, men are organized in society and are obliged to devote part of their time not to direct production but to social tasks.

The concepts of productive and unproductive activity are relative to a given mode of production — here, the capitalist mode. Productive means here productive of profit, which is functionally destined to accumulation, that is, to the widening and deepening of the field of action of the capitalist mode of production. As Adam Smith observed, one becomes poorer by employing servants, but richer by employing workers. Any attempt to identify this problem with that of the utility "in itself" of any activity, regardless of the mode of production in which this activity takes place, proceeds from an unhistorical outlook. It is ultimately pointless to inquire whether the building of the pyramids, or of the cathedrals of the Middle Ages, was or was not useful for mankind, or whether, in the ideal society of the future, labor-time will be progressively reduced in favor of activities that do not constitute "labor," because they lack the latter's *compulsory* character: leisure, education, sport, etc.

An explanation of the rapid and recent growth of the tertiary sector in the advanced capitalist countries must take into account the internal dynamic of capitalism, the conditions in which surplus value is realized: the system cannot function unless surplus value is spent in its entirety. In order to overcome the fall in the rate of profit, one can try to increase the rate of surplus value. But such an increase — whether at the center or in the periphery — aggravates the inequality in the distribution of income and deprives investment of its outlet: the contradiction is intensified in society between the capacity to save and the possibility of investing new capital profitably. All that remains is to "squander" surplus value.

The changed conditions of competition, associated with the appearance of monopolies, themselves lead to this squandering. Selling costs, to which Chamberlin drew attention for the first time in the 1930s, both reflect the sharpening of competition between monopolies and also offer a solution to the problem. Furthermore, competition between states becomes more acute, and militarization, the consequence of this, has, since 1914, brought a valuable contribution. State intervention, which Keynes called for, constitutes the third source of waste, even though some of the state's activities may result in civil expenditure of a useful kind (education, social services). Baran and Sweezy have shown that the amount, both absolute and relative, of this wasted surplus cannot but go on increasing.

Where the underdeveloped countries are concerned, however, neither Colin Clark's apologetical thesis nor the Marxist analysis of Baran and Sweezy enables us to find the answer to the question presented by the hypertrophy of the tertiary sector. This answer lies in the conditions governing the integration of precapitalist societies into the international capitalist market, an integration that entails three main consequences.

First, competition by the industries of the dominant centers prevents the local capital that is accumulated from making its way into investment in *industry*, and diverts this capital into complementary activities connected with the export economy, especially commerce.

Second, the hypertrophy of certain tertiary activities with low productivity (small-scale retail trade, including itinerant trade, various services, etc.) is a manifestation of concealed unemployment, resulting from the processes of marginalization that are specific to the development of peripheral capitalism.

Third, the strengthening of the position of ground rent, a characteristic result of the international integration of the peripheral formations, also entails a particular orientation of the spending of income, marked by a distortion in favor of certain tertiary activities (personal services, for example). In the formations of central capitalism, landed property has lost its predominant position in the economy and in society, in favor of capital. In the periphery, however, the intensification of external exchanges — in the framework of a specialization based at the outset upon the export of agricultural produce — has strengthened the predominance of ground rent wherever an unequal distribution of landownership, either pre-existent or arising as a consequence of the commercializing of production, has made this possible. Now, ground rent does not necessarily have to be saved, as profit on capital must be, in order to be invested in the modernization that competition makes necessary, for it is an income derived from monopoly, and can therefore be spent in its entirety. Such spending is a luxury expenditure that is focused, so far as material goods are concerned, upon imported goods and, so far as local products are concerned, upon services (servants, leisure services, etc.).

The hypertrophy of the tertiary sector is therefore merely the manifestation of a specific law of overpopulation of the periphery, which itself results from the extraversion of the peripheral economy and the mechanisms that exclude from production an increasing section of these countries' labor power.

4. DEPENDENCE

Commercial, Financial, and Technological Dependence

So far as commercial exchanges are concerned, domination by the center is not a consequence of the fact that the periphery's exports are made up of basic products, but of the fact that the peripheral economies are *only* producers of basic products — in other words, that this production is not integrated into an autocentric industrial structure. What results from this is that, taken as a whole, the periphery does most of its trade with the center, whereas the central economies do most of their trade among themselves.

Domination is also expressed in the structure of the financing of the economy. At the center, capitalism being national, this financing is internal; but in the periphery it comes to a large extent from foreign capital, at least so far as productive investments are concerned. Now, if productive investments are financed by foreign capital, they must inevitably lead, sooner or later, to an outflow of profits, so that growth is blocked. External aid (public and free of charge, or partly so) then becomes a necessary condition for the system of "international specialization" to function. The effect of this is that responsibility for the direction that development is to take lies with those who provide the funds. It intensifies the mechanisms of economic domination, in addition to those of direct political domination.

There is not much information about the movement of exported profits. The balance of payments of a large number of underdeveloped countries are not well-documented, and in some cases (including several African countries) the information is totally imaginary. The official figures for the export of profits reveal a wide "scatter" of the underdeveloped countries from this standpoint: exported profits represent from 2 to 25 percent of the gross domestic product, and from 8 to 70 percent of exports. These are very high proportions for the countries belonging to the upper categories, such as certain oil-producing or mining countries. The way this burden has evolved during the process of colonial development is hardly open to question, even though scientific studies of the subject are very few. It is easier to appreciate this movement if we start by looking at the balance of payments of the advanced countries. For Britain, income originating abroad increased from 4 percent of the national income in 1880-1884 to 10 percent in 1910-1913; in France, from 2.5 to 5 percent; in the United States, income of external origin increased between 1915 and 1934 about 2.5 times as fast as the national income. Between 1950 and 1965 income from American investments abroad increased 2.3 times as fast as income from internal investments, with the proportion represented by the former rising from 8.8 percent to 17.8 percent of the total profits of American companies.

All these figures are inclined to err by underestimation, and they are only partly indicative of the decisive role played by foreign capital in the periphery. The statistics of the balance of payments cover, in the best of cases, only the profits that are actually exported. In Egypt, for instance, between 1945 and 1952 the profits of foreign capital represented 20 to 30 percent of the total amount of the reward of capital, and exported profits represented 15 percent. Export of the profits of foreign capital reduced Egypt's growth rate between 1882 and 1914 from 3.7 percent per annum (the potential rate if these profits had been reinvested) to 1.7 (the actual rate), and, similarly, from 3 or 4 percent to 1.4 percent in the period between 1914 and 1950. In the Ivory Coast private transfers increased from 7.3 billion CFA francs in 1950 to 25.2 billion in 1965, amounting to much more than the public aid and private capital that flowed in between the same years (from 4.6 to 15.4 billion). For the five franc-area countries of Central Africa the outflow of profits amounted as an annual average between 1960 and 1968 to 44.2 billion CFA francs, while public aid and foreign investment flowing into these countries did not exceed 34.4 billion. Gross exportable profits came to 13 percent of the gross domestic product in the Ivory Coast, and 13 percent also for all the countries of the UDEAC taken together. For nine countries of West Africa, during the ten years 1960-1970, the outflow of profits (92 billion CFA francs, or 10 percent of the gross domestic product) was greater than the inflow of private capital together with public aid.

Harry Magdoff has shown that the information available to us understates the significance of the phenomenon. The accumulation abroad of the profits of American enterprises has been so great that it has made them, in the course of twenty years, the third economic power in the world. It needs to be added that the available information shows only what these flows amount to *at market prices,* and the latter already contain a massive transference of value.

History shows that the dynamic of foreign investment leads to a reversal in the balance of flows, with the backflow of profits eventually exceeding the inflow of capital. It also shows that the dynamic of foreign investment is very different in the young capitalist countries, namely, the new central formations in process of development — in the nineteenth century the United States, Japan, Germany, Russia, and later Canada, Australia, South Africa — from what it is in the peripheral formations.

The young capitalist countries on the road to independent development — in other words, autocentric and to a large extent autodynamic development — were able to receive substantial amounts of foreign capital. This flow nevertheless played, in their case, only an auxiliary role, secondary in quantitative terms, and also of diminishing importance. Thus, in the United States the proportion of foreign capital in the national wealth declined steadily from 10 percent in 1790 to 5 percent in 1850-1870, to fall to 1 percent in 1920 and disappear altogether thereafter, and the experience of Sweden, Canada, Germany, Japan, and Australia was similar. In these countries investment as a whole, foreign and local alike, induced a growth that was rapid because autocentric. Under these conditions, the problem of the flow of exported profits became of secondary significance. These countries, having begun as borrowers, themselves became lenders, exporting capital in their turn, like the old metropolitan centers (Britain and France, later Germany).

This was not the situation of the countries of the periphery, which never arrived at the stage of exporting capital, but only passed from being "young borrowers" (with the inflow of capital exceeding the outflow of profits) to being "old borrowers" (with the outflow of profits exceeding the inflow of capital). The date at which the turning point was reached varied, of course, from country to country. For the old peripheral countries, such as Argentina, it had already occurred at the end of the nineteenth century. Broadly speaking, Latin America and the Asian countries that were reduced to colonial status long ago (India and Indonesia) became "old borrowers" several decades, and in some cases half a century, ago; whereas Tropical Africa is only now reaching this state. The development of new wealth, of interest to foreign capital, such as the oil of the Middle East since the Second World War, may temporarily set moving a new wave of investment and thereby revive the situation of "young borrower" for the countries concerned. But for all that, it cannot make possible an escape from this process.

What is true of the balance of private capital is also true of that of public funds. Although in this sphere the conditions are regarded as being particularly favorable (substantial proportion of gifts, favorable interest rates for loans, etc.), depreciation of the public debt absorbed, already in 1965-1967: 73 percent of the flow of new public contributions in Africa; 52 percent in East Asia; 40 percent in Southern Asia and the Middle East; 87 percent in Latin America. According to the calculations of the IBRD, if the amount of new loans stays at the present level for another ten years, in 1977 these proportions will be, respectively, 121, 134, 97, and 130 percent for the regions mentioned.

From these historical experiences of the periphery we can conclude that as development — that is, the development of underdevelopment — proceeds, the balance of payments of the periphery tends to worsen, both because the periphery passes from the "young borrower" to the "old borrower" stage and because the increasing commercialization of the economy, in the setting of unequal international specialization, gives rise to growing waves of imports, induced, indirect, and secondary.

The reversal of the balance of financial flows is delayed so long as the profits of foreign capital can be systematically reinvested, which is what happens during the prosperous periods of colonial development. But the national wealth then passes increasingly into the control of foreign capital, and the profits of development are to an increasing extent annexed by foreigners. To this basic mechanism is added the increasing competitive power of the foreign capitalist sector that, in some cases, ousts the local capital constituted in the first stages of integration into the international markets. This was what happened in Senegal, the bourgeoisie of which country, who had played their part in the *économie de traite* in the nineteenth century, were ruined between 1900 and 1940. The gradual transfer of the national wealth into foreign hands may attain, as in Black Africa, very high proportions: 15 to 80 percent of the gross domestic product (in money terms) of the countries of Black Africa comes from the foreign-owned sector. In the Ivory Coast in 1965 foreign income accounted for 47 percent of the country's nonagricultural product and 32 percent of the gross domestic product. In the Maghreb, then a "colony of settlement," these two proportions were in 1955 respectively 70 and 57 percent.

Forces exist, of course, which hinder the geometrical progression of foreign profits from attaining the astronomical levels that calculation designates. These are the same forces as those that prevent the total income from capital from accounting for an increasing share of income within an economy. All these forces — apart from monetary accidents (inflation) or political ones (nationalizations) — arise from the fall in the rate of profit. For if the reward of capital were stable, its accumulation would lead to an increase in the share of profit in the national income. It remains true that, in the model of prosperous underdeveloped countries, such as Rhodesia or South Africa, the polarization of control of the national wealth in the hands of minorities becomes extreme.

Appropriation by central capital of the surplus generated in the periphery results directly from appropriation by this capital of the principal means of production. Is this direct appropriation a necessary condition for transfer of the surplus? Certainly not. There is reason to think that technological dependence will gradually tend to replace domination through direct appropriation. Monopoly of the supply of specific types of equipment, after-sales services and the supply of spare parts, patents, and all the various forms of "good will" will make it increasingly possible to exact a substantial share of the surplus value generated in an enterprise without even being its legal owner. It is possible today to conceive a wholly dependent economy in which industry would still be national, and even publicly owned.

The Tendency to Deficit in the External Balance of Payments of the Periphery

The history of the periphery shows two phases in quick succession: a first phase marked by a surplus in the balance of payments, corresponding to the opening up of a country as a colony, the establishment of the underdeveloped economy, the development of underdevelopment, followed by a phase of chronic tendency to deficit, corresponding to the crisis of this system, the blocking of growth based upon external demand. The foreign-exchange standard conceals for a time this tendency toward external deficit; sooner or later, however, this obliges the underdeveloped countries to go in for monetary independence — an independence that cannot represent a real solution of the problem, but can only give rise to additional monetary disorders.

Since the underdeveloped economies are extraverted, all their problems emerge in the balance of payments. Every considerable economic change that occurs in the course of development has an effect on the various elements in the balance of payments. Can the same be said of the advanced countries? There, too, it is hard to imagine any big change that would be without effect on the conditions governing relations between the national economy and foreign countries. But the two problems are different in kind. It is possible to construct a valid model of the development of capitalist economy without bringing international relations into the schema of this development: capitalist economy forms a coherent entity that is self-sufficient. Such an entity is inconceivable in relation to an underdeveloped country, which, by definition, cannot be isolated from the international market.

The problem therefore does not consist in discovering whether there are mechanisms that ensure spontaneous equilibrium in the external balance in general, and in particular in relations between the dominant advanced center and the dominated underdeveloped periphery: such mechanisms obviously do not exist, at least not in a form that would ensure automatic equilibrium. The problem is to discover why, despite the absence of such mechanisms, the system does nevertheless function. Now, function it does, and ensures a relative equilibrium in the relations between the advanced capitalist countries, as in relations between these countries and those of the system's periphery. If, as regards relations between advanced countries, the system works, it does so through continual crises, which make up the history of the development of capitalism: the classical cyclical crises of the nineteenth century and the first third of the twentieth, external monetary and political crises of particular states, the "dollar shortage" crisis of the period after the Second World War, and then the crisis of the international monetary system. Permanent structural adjustment forms the backdrop of this history — an adjustment that is always characterized by unevenness, asymmetry, and domination (yesterday by Britain, today by the United States).

As regards relations between the center and the periphery, adjustment that is fundamentally unequal in character takes place through a permanent tendency to external deficit on the part of the underdeveloped countries, a tendency that is continually being overcome, thanks precisely to this structural adjustment. The periphery is so shaped as to conform to the needs of accumulation at the center, the price structures and the distribution of relative profitability being established in such a way that the development of capitalism in the periphery remains peripheral, that is, based essentially upon the external market. The adjustment is therefore accompanied by a chronic tendency toward deficit in the periphery's external balance. Attempts to explain the phenomenon of asymmetry in the balance of payments without referring to the structural adjustment (that is, to the mechanism of international specialization) can only be partial and descriptive. This is true of explanations that describe the state and movement of "elasticities" and "propensities" that are as they are just because they express the deepest mechanisms of structural adjustment.

How the phenomenon is manifested. If we assume a stable exchange (gold standard or foreign-exchange standard), the tendency to deficit is constantly being overcome by the slowing down of potential growth. It is very hard to register this phenomenon in statistical terms: it operates as an underlying tendency that does not show itself in obvious outward symptoms. When, however, the exchange is allowed to fluctuate freely, the tendency to disequilibrium is constantly reflected in devaluation of the currency. It is therefore easier in this case to register the phenomenon, even though the devaluation may have been caused by internal inflation and not by disequilibrium of the external balance. Only a knowledge of the actual history of the issuing of money enables one to place responsibility where it belongs. One may also try to disclose the phenomenon by observing the movement of the international reserves (in gold and foreign currency) held by the underdeveloped countries.

From what date, approximately, did the balance of payments of the periphery become chronically deficitary? It is hard to say, for the reversal of the situation seems to have occurred at different periods in different countries. It seems that the balance of real payments of Cuba and of the French and British colonies in Africa, for example, was for a long time chronically in surplus, a fact that caused some to say, mistakenly, that the import of monetary liquidities must have been paid for by real exports. Already in the nineteenth century, however, the rate of exchange of nearly all the states of Latin America was regularly lowered. In the case of Brazil, the deficit in the external balance was no less responsible for this than was the inflationary issue of paper money. The same thing happened in Argentina between 1880 and 1900. This means that probably the external balance of these countries — big suppliers of basic products, they were more fully integrated into the international market than the recently colonized countries of Africa and Asia — was already in the nineteenth century chronically deficitary.

For the twentieth century there can be no doubt about it. The gold value of the different currencies fell everywhere between 1929 and 1937; but its fall was noticeably greater in the case of the underdeveloped countries than in that of the advanced ones. If some of the former retained unaltered their rate of exchange with the metropolitan country (French, Belgian, Portuguese, Spanish, British colonies, and colonial members of the sterling area), this was not because they experienced no difficulty in keeping their balance even. Rather it was in spite of these difficulties that the metropolitan countries acted in this way, so as to allow the income mechanism to exhaust its effects. We have seen that their reserves in foreign currency (which for them take the place of gold as international currency) were less in 1937 than they had been in 1929, which shows that the tendency to deficit was chronic. The situation in Latin America also reflects such a deficit. For even at the depreciated rates that these countries adopted, the deficit persisted, as is shown by the fall in their central reserves of gold currency between 1927 and 1937 (an entire cycle), as well as in their currency reserves generally. For the advanced countries, on the contrary, all these reserves increased during the same period.

After the Second World War a system of relatively rigid rates took the place of the fluctuating exchanges of former times. Nevertheless, devaluations have occurred very frequently in the underdeveloped countries, with the approval and even on the recommendation of the IMF. They have sometimes been necessitated by previous internal inflation, but often also by the chronic external deficit, this having merely been reinforced by inflation. At the same time, the periphery's international reserves have diminished. It is true that the immediate postwar period was also marked by an external deficit in several of the advanced countries: the system was then — during the reconstruction period — almost exclusively to the advantage of the United States. The center (the United States, Europe, Japan) was not, as a whole, to recover its traditional position until this first stage had been passed, and not without serious problems of readjustment between the separate advanced countries themselves. However, between 1948 and 1967 the currencies of Europe lost only 5.2 percent of their value in relation to the dollar — as against a loss of 38.4 percent suffered by the currencies of the Middle East; 46.1 percent by those of the rest of Asia (Japan excluded); 47.6 percent by those of Africa; and 62.2 percent by those of Latin America.

Asymmetry in international relations: current explanations. Kindleberger seems to have been the first writer to try to give a systematic explanation of the asymmetry in the behavior of the external balances of trading partners. It was not, to be sure, with regard to the problem of relations between the underdeveloped countries and the advanced ones that he made his analysis, but in connection with the problem of relations between Europe and the United States in the years following the Second World War. Harrod, defending British interests, blamed the "dollar famine" on the policy of the United States, and in particular on the overvaluation of the dollar in relation to gold, together with the American customs tariff, which he considered too high. Kindleberger answered Harrod in the terms of a general theory. He started from the observation that the mechanism that causes the underdeveloped countries to be victims of the conjuncture in all its phases is similar to the mechanism that now operates in relations between Europe and the United States. In 1949 even a minor recession in the United States resulted in European exports to that country falling by about 50 percent. Kindleberger considers that for the effects of a variation in the national income in the United States and in Europe on international economic relations to be symmetrical, five conditions need to be fulfilled: (1) the degree of dependence by one region upon another (measured by the ratio of exports to national income in each of the two countries) must be of the same order of magnitude; (2) inflationary and deflationary pressures must work in the same direction of both countries; (3) price elasticities must be the same for the exports of both countries; (4) innovations must not always originate in the same country; and (5) in both countries the response of supply to the urgings of demand must be the same.

Now, in the relations between the United States and Europe, just as in the relations between the advanced countries in general and the underdeveloped countries, these five conditions are not present. There is therefore asymmetry in the balance of payments. The listing of these five conditions constitutes, however, only a description of the phenomenon, but not an explanation.

The same applies to Raul Prebisch's thesis regarding the asymmetry between center and periphery. According to this, fluctuations in income are assumed to have been greater in the nineteenth century in the advanced countries (mainly Britain) than in the under-developed ones. During depression periods the fall in the national income, which was relatively more serious in Britain than in the countries of the periphery, entailed a fall in the imports of the dominant center of that time that was relatively greater than the fall in the imports of the peripheral countries. Britain then attracted the gold of these countries to itself, since the balance (assumed to be in equilibrium over the period of the cycle as a whole) was, during depression, unfavorable to the underdeveloped countries. On the contrary, however, during periods of prosperity, the symmetry of the phenomenon caused gold to flow back to the underdeveloped countries: the relatively greater expansion of the national income of Great Britain entailed an increase in the level of British imports that was greater than that of the imports into the underdeveloped countries. In the twentieth century, Prebisch considers, the phenomenon has lost its symmetry because the United States's propensity to import has been continually falling, while that of Britain has remained stable.

Prebisch's proposition to the effect that the balance of the under-developed countries was in equilibrium over a long period in the nineteenth century, and is today chronically unfavorable, is not based on the relative size of the fluctuations at the center and in the periphery of the system, nor on the absolute size of the propensities to import, but exclusively on the movement of the center's propensity to import. What, then, does his thesis signify? Quite simply, that the development of the center is based on the internal market (that constituted by the advanced countries as a whole), whereas the development of the periphery is based on the external market (the advanced countries). It is this fundamental asymmetry in the structure that explains the evolution of the ratio of propensities to import. But this movement is not peculiar to the twentieth century. It dates from the integration of the periphery into the world market. How, then, are we to explain why the chronic tendency of the periphery's external balance to show a deficit has appeared only late in the day? By bringing in the factor that Prebisch neglects in his analysis, namely, the movement of capital. Prebisch takes into account only the trade balance, ignoring the other items in the balance of payments. The chronic tendency of the trade balance of the underdeveloped countries to be unfavorable can be offset by the influx of foreign capital. This influx, at certain periods only of the cycle (those of prosperity), may indeed cause the fluctuations in the balance of these countries to be greater, but it nevertheless contributes to equalizing the surpluses and deficits over the cycle as a whole. It is true that this inflow carries the implication of a backflow of profits that must eventually exceed it in volume. It is this backflow of profits, growing bigger and bigger, that in the end becomes responsible, together with the movement of the trade balance already analyzed, for the chronic deficit in the balance of the under-developed countries in our time. During the nineteenth century the increasing flow of foreign capital, exceeding the backflow of profits, made up for the progressive worsening in the trade balance. In the twentieth century the increasing backflow of profits, exceeding the inflow of new capital, is added to the progressive worsening of the trade balance, and so makes the overall balance of payments even less favorable.

Kindleberger's analysis remains restricted to the sphere of the trade balance, and therefore needs to be completed in the same way as Prebisch's. Furthermore, this analysis, too, remains purely descriptive. *Why* is the developed countries' propensity to import what it is and that of the underdeveloped countries what it is? *Why* are the price elasticities and the responses of supply to the pressures of demand what they are?

The answer is forced upon us: it is the place of the external market in the development of peripheral capitalism that explains the way these propensities move. Thus, the degree of dependence upon external trade is the product of a historical change the stages of which we have traced; what are called "deflationary" pressures are accounted for by the state of maturity, the price elasticities by the degree of monopolization of the economy — monopolized industrial production resists a fall in prices more firmly than agricultural production, which has remained competitive. As for innovations, obviously they must come from the advanced countries, not the underdeveloped ones. These innovations and the "demonstration effects" they engender in the underdeveloped countries reinforce the propensity to import by diverting demand from local goods toward imports. Finally, supply is markedly elastic in a capitalist structure in which the dynamic entrepreneur runs ahead of demand, but not very elastic in a structure in which the enterprise follows demand (itself external). This situation intensifies the effect of the difference in the degree of monopolization of production upon the relative elasticity of prices.

The causes of asymmetry in international relations: dependence. It is the center that takes the initiative in trading relations — the center that imposes upon the periphery the particular forms its specialization assumes. This asymmetry, which reflects the commercial dependence of the periphery, is shown in the anteriority of the center's exports in relation to its imports (the exports of the periphery, which has submitted to the forms of specialization required by the center).

The periphery's commercial dependence is aggravated by its financial dependence. The basic reason for this is that the investments of foreign capital in the underdeveloped countries automatically engender a reverse flow of profit transfers. At the average rates of reward of capital, which range between 15 and 20 percent, the back-flow of profits does not take long to become bigger than the inflow of capital investment, and, after a certain level has been reached, the balance of external payments tips. This reversal reflects the transition from the phase in which the territory newly made accessible to capital is being "opened up" to the phase in which it is being exploited "at cruising speed." The absence of stimulating side effects of foreign investment in an underdeveloped country means that such investment does not play the role of catalyst of the process of accumulation that can be played by foreign investment in countries with a capitalist structure.

Under the conditions of foreign investment in an underdeveloped country, equilibrium in the balance of payments necessitates a *rapid* growth of exports — not only more rapid than the growth of the gross domestic product but also more rapid than the growth of imports. Now, there are many forces that tend to hasten the growth of imports into the underdeveloped countries, the principal ones being: (1) urban development, together with inadequate increase in agricultural production of foodstuffs, which make necessary increasing imports of basic food products (wheat, rice, etc.); (2) increase in administrative expenditure, out of proportion with the possibilities of the local economy; (3) change in the structures of income distribution, with "Europeanization" of the way of life and consumer habits of the privileged strata (demonstration effects); and (4) inadequate industrial development and disequilibrium in the industrial structures (excessive predominance of consumer-goods industries), which necessitate imports of production goods and intermediate goods. The combined working of these forces renders the underdeveloped countries dependent on external aid, which tends to become permanent.

The dialectic of this specific contradiction between the tendency to external deficit and the resorption of this deficit through structural adjustment of the periphery to the center's needs for accumulation explains why the history of the periphery consists of a series of "economic miracles" — brief periods of very rapid growth while the system is being established, followed by periods of blocked development, stagnation, and even regression: miracles without any future and take-offs that have failed.

The foreign-exchange standard, with integration of the periphery into monetary systems dominated by the central metropolitan countries, eliminates the temporary difficulties that result from disequilibrium in the balance of payments, even if this is persistent: this disequilibrium is bound eventually to be resorbed by the working of the income mechanism. Adoption of the foreign-exchange standard enables the system to recover equilibrium by slowing down the growth of the underdeveloped country through acceptance of a "domination" rate of exchange, which facilitates the structural readjustment.

If this monetary integration is abandoned and independent monetary systems are established in the periphery, does this affect the mechanisms of structural adjustment? Not automatically. If we continue to think of development merely in terms of increasing international specialization — that is, development, first and foremost, of production for export on the world market — then external equilibrium can be obtained only at the cost of checking development, even peripheral development. The underlying tendencies to disequilibrium continue to operate, and sooner or later control proves ineffectual and it is necessary to devalue the currency.

The Role of the Monetary Systems of the Periphery in the Shaping of Dependence

The alleged "perverse mechanisms" of issue. Most of the underdeveloped countries now have an independent monetary system, that is, a central bank that is empowered to aid the national treasury and that manages the country's external holdings, in accordance with principles similar to those that apply in the advanced countries. Control of exchange and transfers is practiced, usually with a hope that liberalization may become possible: control is looked upon as a sad necessity due to the difficulties of the balance of payments, rather than as a regular instrument of economic policy.

None of the national currencies of the Third World can aspire to play the role of a key currency in the international monetary system, even though some of them are strong, because the external balances of these countries are unfavorable. Thus the external holdings of the Third World countries consist largely of foreign currency, meaning key currencies (the dollar first and foremost, followed by the pound sterling) and the currencies of the other advanced countries, particularly the old metropolitan centers. In this sense, all these countries live under a foreign-exchange standard regime. The term is used more narrowly when speaking of an organism that agrees to exchange its local currency at a fixed rate and in unlimited quantity (without any control) for the dominant currency, and vice versa.

Systems based on this principle were until recent times characteristic of almost all the countries of the periphery. The most straightforward is certainly the Currency Boards system, in which an issue of the local currency is backed only by an equivalent deposit of sterling. Actually, this local currency has no existence of its own — it is sterling that circulates under a special denomination. In the monetary system of the French colonies, the mechanisms of which still govern the African countries of the franc area, the same situation prevails, despite appearances to the contrary; the central banks of these countries are in fact merely outposts of the Bank of France, which is the only real central bank of the franc area. It alone is empowered to give public support — and only to the French treasury, moreover — and it alone manages the external holdings of the area as a whole. Transfers being free and unlimited, at a fixed rate, and the network of commercial banks consisting of branches of the metropolitan banks, the various masses of currency are in practice all one mass. The "franc area" might well be called, instead, the "area of the *French* franc." There can be no talk of a monetary area here except where the partners possess a certain degree of independence in monetary policy, that is, when their central banks are equally endowed with the general powers that are characteristic of such institutions, while undertaking to supply each other with their respective currencies at a fixed rate. In this case, the monetary institutions of the center of the area agree to supply advances to those of the periphery, if need be. This is the case with Mali, the only country that really belongs to the "franc area."

This margin of freedom can be expanded to the point at which there is almost an independent national monetary system. Even then, however, it is to be observed that, among the three possible forms of backing for issue of currency (external holdings, aid to the economy, aid to the public treasury), the first-mentioned, the external element, plays a larger part than in the advanced countries. This fact reflects the extraverted character of economic activity.

However, it enables economists of the classical school to put forward a new thesis, that of the "perverse mechanisms" of issue, according to which issue is not, in these countries, in conformity with need defined as the second member of the quantitative equation (PT: level of prices multiplied by volume of transactions), being determined automatically by the external balance. (This thesis, upheld by Chabert, has been refuted by Newlyn and Rowan and also by Ida Greaves.) The consequence is said to be that issue is excessive in periods of prosperity, when the external balance is favorable, and this sets off local inflation, whereas in depression periods, the balance being unfavorable, it is inadequate, and this delays recovery.

Let us assume that the balance is favorable. An importer obtains foreign currency, which he exchanges for local notes and deposits in a (foreign-owned) commercial bank. The cash-in-hand of this bank having increased, it is in a position to grant more credit to the local economy. If advances are in fact asked for, and if the bank agrees to grant these, so that the coefficient of liquidity is restored to its previous level, the volume of liquid assets in money form will have increased by a multiple of the difference in the balance, if there is a fixed ratio between the use of fiduciary money and that of representative money, determining a rigid coefficient of liquidity. Contrariwise, says this thesis, if the external balance is unfavorable, the banks are obliged to restrict the volume of credit. If local producers were to ask their bank to grant them more credit, the bank would not be able to do so. This is just where the mistake in the argument lies.

Let us take a concrete example. In Southern Rhodesia, between 1946 and 1951, the external balance was unfavorable. On the one hand, therefore, local currency was taken to the Currency Board to be changed into sterling for payment of the deficit. On the other, however, the banks changed sterling (their own) into Rhodesian notes in order to finance a considerable expansion of their local credits. Some will then say that the deficit in the balance was covered by an influx of short-term credit from abroad. The formulation is unacceptable because of its ambiguity: it implies that this inflow of credit is induced by the disequilibrium in the balance and that it is necessarily equal to the latter.

It is important to distinguish between what I call the balance of real payments — made up of exports and the flow of capital intended for long-term investment, constituting the credit side, and imports and the backflow of profits from foreign investments, constituting the debit side — and the balance of movements of bank capital (import and export of funds by the banks on their own account, and not as representatives of a client).

The balance of real payments is whatever it is. I have said that there is a tendency toward long-term equilibrium of this balance through the income-effect (a deficit constitutes a transfer of purchasing power) but that the deficit is not reabsorbed automatically — especially given that the rate of exchange is rigid and transfers are unlimited. In the case of independent currencies, there is in addition to this income-effect also an exchange-effect (disequilibrium leads to devaluation, which acts upon the balance in either a favorable or a perverse direction, depending on the elasticities) and this sometimes contributes to bringing about short-term re-equilibration.

As for the balance of movements of bank capital, this is independent and not induced by the balance of real payments. Therefore, although the balance of real payments automatically affects circulation, this effect is without importance, since it can be either counterbalanced or not by the movement of bank capital, which is always determined solely by the economy's need for money, and is limited by nothing else.

This is why it is possible for the volume of liquid assets in money, and even the volume of circulation, to increase although the balance of payments shows a deficit. There is no proof that imports and exports of money are induced by external payments; this is the finding of the best empirical studies that have been made of the working of monetary systems based on the foreign-exchange standard.

This analysis leads us to the real problem, namely, how the network of commercial banks is constituted, and what economic activities (extraverted or autocentric) it serves. If the network is made up of branches of the metropolitan banks, then the thesis of perverse mechanisms loses all validity. But this applies also, to a large extent, if the banking network is national. In this case, if a need for money is felt — a demand for internal credit — the external deficit merely leads to a reduction in the foreign-exchange cover, a reduction that reflects a diminution in the extraverted character of the economy.

Concomitance between the movements of the external balance, of the volume of money, and of prices confers no greater scientific validity upon the quantity-theory explanation. It is normal for prices to fall in a period of depression (especially the prices of raw materials), for the volume of money to shrink, and for the external balance of the underdeveloped countries to worsen. But it is the fall in prices that causes the external deficit, not the other way round.

The foreign-exchange standard system, which is typical of the underdeveloped countries, was not introduced without protracted preliminary tentative measures. True, it was introduced without its theory having been worked out beforehand: thus, for a long time, cash vouchers circulated in the West Indies that were not convertible into gold but *were* convertible into bills on the metropolitan country. The exchange fluctuated with the state of the external balance, because there was no organ that ensured exchange at a fixed rate and in unlimited amounts.

In general, all through the nineteenth century, the colonies, the countries of the East, and those of Latin America made use of gold, or more commonly silver, coins (China, India, Dutch East Indies, Persia, and Latin America with the exception of Brazil). Only gradually was the foreign-exchange standard system introduced, beginning in 1898 in India and then becoming widespread at the beginning of the twentieth century, especially in the colonies. A direct gold-exchange standard was introduced in Argentina in 1899, when the Conversion Office undertook to exchange gold for the local currency and vice versa. The same system was introduced in Brazil a little later. China alone continued to use its silver coins and its ingots of the same metal. As for Latin America, that was all through the nineteenth century the region *par excellence* of paper money, which circulated alongside silver coins that were more or less at a premium, depending on the volume of issue. Mexico moved belatedly from this situation, in which the rate of exchange fluctuated with the price of silver, to the foreign-exchange standard. The other states hesitated to take this decision, and only in the twentieth century did they at last stabilize their currencies by setting up central systems of the modern type (inconvertible credit money).

The experience of Latin America, where paper money issued by the state treasuries circulated, is worth some attention. Money, here introduced into the economy not by way of commercial bank credit but through the budget, may prove to be excessive in quantity. In the case of a budget deficit, money incomes are created without any real counterpart. Let us assume that the budget is balanced. A mere disequilibrium of the external balance results in a fall in the rate of exchange. This brings in its train price inflation through the increased price of imports. If the disequilibrium of the external balance is part of a permanent tendency, as is the case with the underdeveloped countries unless exchange control is applied, then what occurs is an endless series of devaluations, price increases, and fresh devaluations. Let us now assume that the balance of real external payments is, like the budget, in equilibrium. The money in circulation may prove to be insufficient. Money being introduced into the economy only by way of state expenditure, a trader who finds himself momentarily short of liquidities applies to the foreign-owned commercial banks. In order to respond to his application, the latter need an extra quantity of the local paper money that is legal tender in the given country. They import funds that belong to them, and buy local currency on the exchange market. This transaction tends to raise the rate of exchange, which in turn causes prices to fall. In this case the amount of money does indeed adjust itself to requirements, but only at the cost of continual upsets in the level of the exchange rate and of prices.

Independent monetary systems have been established in Latin America on the basis of the paper-money system previously obtaining there, and in Asia, the Middle East, and the English-speaking countries of Africa on the basis of the previous foreign-exchange standard system. Only the French-speaking countries of Africa remain outside this movement.

Freedom to fix the rate of exchange does not mean that the latter ceases to be determined by the cover and by the state of the external balance. If the cover of the money issued still consists of foreign exchange, fluctuations in the value of the foreign currency will continue to be transmitted. As for the external balance, this operates via the rate of exchange to influence the market — whether free, official, or black. Only exchange control is capable, by imposing equilibrium on the country's balance, of keeping its currency in good condition.

Under the foreign-exchange standard system, local issue is controlled, just like issue in the metropolitan country, by the central bank of the metropolitan country. This means control of credit, the importance of which economists tend to exaggerate. Generally speaking, those who have shown that circulation has adapted itself to needs have rejected the possibility of real *management* of the issuing of money. All the same, it has been said that, with the abolition of convertibility into gold, on the one hand, and the development of the monopolies, on the other, an inflationary issue (with the agreement of the central bank) has become a real possibility. In this sense, management of credit (checking or agreeing to this issue) has become significant, even though it is limited by the impossibility of issuing currency if the economy does not require this.

Does the creation of an independent monetary system in a dependent peripheral economy give the central bank a similar power to control credit? If we assume that freedom of transfer is maintained, the central bank remains powerless, since the (foreign-owned) commercial banks can refuse to submit to the discipline of a restriction on credit, and appeal to their head offices. The central authorities are thus in danger of clashing with the foreign-owned commercial banks if there is disagreement on general policy. In this struggle the government possesses, of course, one effective means of coercion, namely, possible control of transfers. All the methods by which the foreign banks may try to get around the regulation of credit by the central bank are liable to be neutralized by control of transfers. But this means, for an underdeveloped country, necessarily excluding itself from the international capital market. How, indeed, is it possible to distinguish between the capital that comes in to be invested and the capital that the banks import in order to supply the economic system with the liquidities necessitated by development? The central bank can now dictate to the expatriate banks. This advantage is nevertheless bought at a very high price, since, henceforth, (1) the fluctuations in the balance affect issue directly; (2) the foreign-exchange backing of the currency is paid for in real exports; and (3) the foreign-owned commercial banks make the economy pay for a service they can no longer render — providing advances backed by the guarantee of a stable and widely accepted currency.

The fluctuations in the volume of reserves that constitute the cover of the local issue compel the banks to regulate the volume of credit in accordance with the vicissitudes of the balance of payments. A deficit in the balance may thus lead them to restrict the volume of credit allowed. Restriction of the volume of activity risks aggravating the external deficit. Conversely, a surplus in the external balance brings no advantage to the local economy. Not only may the banks find themselves in a situation such that, no additional credit being asked for by the local producers (because the volume of exports, already considerable, cannot be increased), the surplus of foreign exchange rendered is sterile, but also, should an injection of credit actually take place, it is possible that the tendency to increased prices that it entails (together with other effects, such as the excessive demand pressing upon the local market, as a result of the country's prosperous condition following a successful export drive) may prevent the volume of exports from growing, or even reduce this volume, with the consequence that the country will soon lose its favorable situation in relations with the outside world.

It must be added that monetary independence implies a real cost for the underdeveloped systems. The foreign exchange that forms the cover for the local currency is hence forth obtained by means of a real surplus of exports over imports, which was not the case with a foreign-exchange standard: then the cover was provided, if necessary free of charge, by an import of capital through the foreign-owned commercial banks. It is only because they do not distinguish between the balance of real payments and the balance of bank flows that conventional economists are able to claim that the foreign-exchange standard system is equivalent to a 100 percent system of gold circulation.

With the establishment of control over transfers and consequently the ending of these bank flows, does the service rendered by the foreign-owned banking system to local economic activity justify what it costs? This question raises a serious problem indeed, that of the real cost of the banking system to the economy. The interest paid to the banks by the rest of the economic system for the service constituted by short-term loans destined to ensure the normal functioning of the economy constitutes a transfer of income the explanation of which is to be sought in history. If all the entrepreneurs of the nineteenth century had possessed an initial stock of gold equal to the volume of necessary liquidities, and if the production of new gold had kept in step with the pace of economic growth, then short-term credit would not perhaps have developed in the way it has. But, in fact, gold circulated in quantities that were increasingly inadequate, although it was the only currency acceptable in the society of those days. The banks were able to use this situation in order to issue fiduciary money: the convertible note, or representative money, in return for the payment of interest. They then ran the risk, to be sure, that was implicit in convertibility, since at any moment the entrepreneur might demand metal coins. It may be claimed that since convertibility has been abandoned, this risk no longer applies. It is true that the commercial banks do still run a certain risk, since the receiver of credit may always ask for banknotes. But if these banks accept the discipline of the central bank they are in practically no danger. Interest no longer appears as corresponding to risk. The central bank has become a public service providing the economy with instruments of payment. Interest is no longer the reward for this service but a convenient device for restricting demand for money (which may account for Keynes's attempt to explain theoretically the role of interest on these grounds). There are other ways of restricting the supply of money: the quantitative and qualitative control of credit has multiplied these techniques. In any case, the payment of interest by borrowers of bank credit does not impoverish the economy in the least, since it passes from the hands of those for whom it would have constituted additional profit (the entrepreneurs) into the hands of those for whom it will constitute the same kind of income (bankers' profit), even though this does have an effect on the pace of development and the direction taken by it.

It is not at all the same in the underdeveloped countries, where this payment represents a real loss for the economy. In so far as the banking network is foreign-owned and can transfer freely the funds that move from or to its head offices, this cost can be justified by reference to the advantage constituted by making a reliable currency available to borrowers. As soon as control over transfers is established, however, no special guarantee is provided from outside the economy.

This is why the underdeveloped countries have been led to go further. So long as an extraverted economic structure is accepted there is no reason to reject the foreign-exchange standard. This certainly does make impossible any local control over credit — but such control is pointless except in an autocentric economy. And what it actually comes down to is the possibility for the central bank to refuse to accept a price increase desired by the monopolies as a means of redistributing income in their favor, and considered unacceptable by the state, either for reasons of economic equilibrium or even for political reasons. But this problem of planning does not exist for a dependent peripheral economy.

If monetary independence, which implies nationalizing the foreign-owned banks, is a necessity, this is because bank credit must be made to serve a different policy — a policy of structural transformations aimed at strengthening the autocentric character of the economy.

The functions and orientation of bank credit in the dependent peripheral economies. The criticism leveled at the monetary system of the underdeveloped countries, to the effect that it supplies the economy alternately with too much money or not enough, is therefore without foundation. The monetary and banking system, even when foreign-controlled, supplies the economy with as much money as it requires. But to *whose* requirements does the activity of the expatriate commercial banks correspond? That is the real question. Alienated economists, especially those of the monetary school, pretend to be unaware of the structural relations that exist between the world of business and that of finance. Now, the banks never serve the economy "in general" but a specific group of economic activities.

In the underdeveloped countries the banks have a history that is closely linked with the history of the installation of peripheral capitalism in these countries. The European banks established branches there when international trade had attained large-scale dimensions, and with the aim of facilitating this trade. Gradually, starting from this extraverted sector, banking activity spread to the branches of capitalist production directed toward the home market, in the context of the import-substitution industrialization of recent decades. It is important to note, however, that a large part of these activities, often the major part, is controlled by the big multinational companies. These possess substantial financial resources, scattered all over the world. Depending on the difference in the rates of interest prevailing in this place or that, they will draw upon bank credit in one center of their activity in order to finance

operations located in another center. By internal book entries —
the conventional prices at which their various establishments sell
each other their products — they will be able to transfer their
financial resources in disregard of any controls over transfers that
there may be. Thus the policy of local control of credit increasingly
ceases to matter to them: in fact, control over these companies, to
be effective, would have to be international in scope.

From another angle, when a sector of national capitalism has
come into existence it has been obliged to set up its own financial
institutions, because the foreign banks confined their support to
the foreign capital with which they were connected. The example of
Bank Misr in Egypt is typical. In Tropical Africa local private
capital complains that the foreign banks regularly refuse to give it
support.

If this is so, it is because the function of the monetary system
cannot be reduced to putting short-term liquidities at the disposal
of economic activity. Besides this passive function it has an active
one, which is essential to the working of the mechanism of accumulation. Without the intervention of credit it is impossible to realize
surplus value. The ways in which short-term saving is transformed
into long-term investment, to use the financial jargon, are indeed
various. But this indispensable transformation has always been
carried out in the autocentric economies, either by the banks, or by
specialized institutions, or by the public treasury. Whereas in the
autocentric economies the financial institutions have facilitated the
transformation of reserve saving into long-term investments, in the
underdeveloped countries everything tends to foster the use of
savings, including sums the saver would like to invest on a long-
term basis, either for short-term financing of the economy (in so
far as this saving, deposited in the banks, is used to finance
external trade operations) or for financing state expenditure, much
of which, unproductive for the economy, is productive only of
interest for the holders of state bonds. Here the transforming
mechanism works in reverse.

The efforts made in recent times by many states to create a
monetary and financial market, the promotion by the state of
financial institutions of a public or semipublic character — stock
markets, saving banks, industrial and mortgage credit — have

produced only poor results. The cause of these setbacks lies in the actual situation of the underdeveloped economy. The creation of financial institutions may well favor the mobilization and centralization of capital: these funds will nevertheless lie unused if local industry fails to come into being as a result of foreign competition.

Monetary disorders and inflation in the periphery of the world system. Critics of the foreign-exchange standard not only charge this system with insusceptibility to management in accordance with local needs but also declare that it favors the automatic transmission of fluctuations in the value of the dominant currency.

True, as Bloch-Lainé writes (p. 39): "When products are freely exchanged and the different masses of money are in practice all one mass, the price level necessarily tends to be the same everywhere; if this is not so, the disparities are to be imputed to structural causes (cost of transport, of labor, or of power, for example) that are immune to monetary manipulation." In cases, however, where unlimited exchange at a fixed rate has been abolished, and where there is a managed currency backed by foreign exchange, this one-way influence nevertheless remains basically the same: if the value of all the foreign exchange is reduced, so that the cover possessed by the local currency declines in value, this currency itself very soon loses its initial value, because it owes this, to a large extent, to public confidence.

It is not only because imports become dearer that the local currency loses value. One might well suppose that the rise in internal prices would be localized in the international sector, while the domestic sector remained unaffected. This is what usually happens in relations between advanced countries when exchange rates are readjusted. Here we have an apparently paradoxical situation: in the advanced countries, in which all the sectors of activity "hold together," a price rise can be restricted to a single sector, whereas in the underdeveloped countries, where two sectors coexist without interpenetrating and the economy does not form an integral unity, a rise in prices in the capitalist sector linked with the international market is passed on in full to the native sector, which seems to be independent of it.

Perhaps the explanation of this phenomenon should be sought through analysis of human behavior. There are people who endeavor merely to adapt their nominal income to the level of prices. They follow the economic movement. Their behavior is neutral. Others, on the contrary — and these are the economically dominant categories — are constantly engaged in trying to discover what the value of money is going to be. As they have reserves of money at their disposal, and as a large fiduciary element enters into the determination of this value, they exert a serious influence on the way it evolves. In an underdeveloped country the individual who possesses a big income is often a landowner. He dreams of how he will spend his income, and he knows that he has to buy the luxury goods he wants from abroad. The value of money means for him the value of the relevant foreign currency. In an advanced country, on the contrary, the individual possessing a big income is normally an entrepreneur. He dreams of *investing* his money, and he knows that most of his production expenses — purchase of machinery, payment of wages — will be paid out in the country where he is. The devaluation of the currency abroad does not devalue the local currency, to his way of thinking, except, and only except, in so far as foreign trade supplies his country's internal market. Condillac devoted a chapter of his *Essay on the Nature of Commerce* to studying the mechanisms by which the tastes of the ruling class determined all prices and the amounts in which goods were produced.

The continuous creeping inflation that characterizes the functioning of the capitalist system in the age of monopoly (and which is responsible for the abandonment of convertibility into gold, as it provides the framework of monetary policy), thus transmits the climate of permanent price increases from the center of the system to its periphery.

The development of capitalism in Europe and in the United States proceeded in a climate of monetary stability and declining prices (the fall in prices being itself brought about by development, which was reflected in a steady reduction in real costs). In the underdeveloped countries, however, the current development of peripheral capitalism is proceeding in a climate of price increases transmitted from outside.

It has often been maintained that inflation favors forced saving at the expense of free saving. This is true only when the state, the promoter of inflation, uses the purchasing power it has created for productive investment. More generally, inflation is a way of redistributing income. In the underdeveloped countries the price rise transmitted from without enables the profits of the foreign monopolies to bite into the share of the weaker national sector. This transfer is not in the least a mere theoretical mechanism. The Africanization of certain sectors of activity (road transport, forestry, building, etc.), in most of the countries of Black Africa where this has taken place in the last twenty years, has been accompanied by a marked lowering in the profitability of these activities, to the advantage of those, whether upstream or downstream, which are controlled by foreign capital. This lowering of profitability has been greatly facilitated by the increase in prices, which has been uneven as between sectors. The other powerful element in an underdeveloped economy often consists of the landlords. They spend their extra income, due to inflation, upon luxury imports. Furthermore, in the general increase in prices, the ratio of wages to profits behaves very differently in the advanced and in the underdeveloped countries. In the former, wages, broadly speaking, follow the rise in prices, and the gains in productivity due to technical progress are thus constantly shared and shared again between the two categories of income. Over a long period experience shows that the share going to wages remains more or less the same. In the underdeveloped countries wages follow the rise in prices much less consistently, for deep structural reasons and in the first place because of the pressure of the excess supply of labor resulting from the breakup of the precapitalist rural milieus. At best, real wages manage to remain steady, despite improved productivity. What applies to wages applies also to the income earned by the peasants who produce commodities, especially for export. Creeping inflation constitutes a principal factor in the worsening of the double factoral terms of trade, a steady reinforcement of unequal exchange.

Transmission of the creeping inflation in the advanced centers to the world system as a whole is clearly not the only cause of inflation and monetary disorder in the periphery. According to Eli Lobel, three types of disorder need to be distinguished. The first two (disproportionate increase in consumption, public or private, and strains connected with industrialization) originate within the economy and may have effects on the external balance, while the third originates in the external balance itself.

Increase in consumption, public or private, at a rate that exceeds the growth rate of the productive economy, with its manifestations either in a budget deficit or in disproportionate credits for consumption purposes, or to cover the structural deficits of enterprises, constitutes the most familiar example of disequilibrium of internal origin. In such a case it may be necessary to devalue the currency: this will have effects comparable to an increase in the amount taken by taxes and the subsequent reduction in demand, although these effects will be less selective.

Some strains can set off a price spiral without total supply and demand being thrown off balance. This assumes a balanced budget, a neutral credit policy (the liquidities created not exceeding the desired increases in cash in hand), an equally neutral wage policy (wages rising in step with productivity), and no difficulties as regards the balance of payments. Nevertheless, a policy of accelerated industrialization may result in inflationary strain if the production of consumer goods, and especially foodstuffs, develops more slowly than industrial employment, which risks bringing about an increase in the prices of agricultural products, and so an increase in wages, and so of *all* prices, a subsequent deficit in the public finances caused by increased rewards together with delay in receipts, and strains in the external balance, because the price increase restricts export possibilities, and eventually has repercussions in the monetary sphere. There is in practice no way of avoiding strains of this kind, which necessarily accompany accelerated development: they can only be contained by means of constant readjustments (e.g., of the state's financial structures). It is clear that in this case inflation makes the situation worse.

A policy of industrialization based on "import-substitution," even if we assume that the quantity of agricultural products available keeps pace with industrial employment, may have the same effects if the infant industries produce at higher cost than the prices of the imported goods they replace. In such a case though, the currency may have to be devalued, which will have the same effect as a protective tariff for the infant industries. It would have to be selective, however (multiple exchange rates), if it is desired to avoid a general increase of internal prices.

Analysis of the imbalances originating in the external balance of payments starts from the case that is simplest but also certainly the most fundamental: the flooding in of an external inflation, by way of a pilot currency, which is what happens to countries that are integrated in a currency area, or that, though not so integrated, have an essentially bilateral foreign-trade structure. Here the rigidity of the system does not allow of much adjustment. On the world scale something like this happens when inflation spreads from countries whose national currency serves as reserve currency for others in the outside world.

The fall in the price of exports causes — quite apart from any action that may be taken to alter the rate of exchange, if this entails a disturbance in the external balance — a necessary contraction in imports, which is not always parallel to the fall in the income of exporters, and, consequently, sectoral imbalances between the supply and demand of different products, and spiral increases similar to the preceding ones. What is essential here is rather to combat possible speculative movements by trying to maintain key supplies at a satisfactory level; but this cannot always be done.

The increase in export prices does not always, however, produce symmetrical inverse effects. On the contrary, we see here a tendency for internal prices to become aligned with external ones, and a spiral of continuous increase may occur if the excess income encounters a feeble elasticity of supply. This is how this situation, which theoretically provides the possibility of accelerated accumulation, very often prevents this potential extra accumulation from being realized.

The structural conditions of underdevelopment reduce very considerably the possibility of mastering external relations and putting them at the service of a development policy. It is therefore important not to confuse "development inflation," which has been effectively carried out by some countries at certain periods, with "inflation without development," which constitutes the experience of the underdeveloped countries.

Inflationary experiences in the Third World, which were practically confined to Latin America down to the Second World War, have become a common factor during the last twenty years. Inflation in Zaïre resulted from the sudden coming to power of a new social class, the state bureaucracy, who sought to annex a part of the national income but were unable either to encroach seriously upon the share taken by foreign capital (owing to the outward orientation of some of the activities of this capital, or even, as regards the autocentric industrial groups of Kinshasa, because these foreign-owned enterprises were strong enough to be able to adapt themselves to inflation) or to levy tribute directly from the peasant masses (who resisted, either by open rebellion or by passive resistance through ceasing production for export). With the aid of the United States and the IMF an equilibrium was restored after eight years of inflation, marked by very considerable changes in relative prices and real incomes in Zaïre as compared with the situation in 1960, reflecting a transfer of income from the peasants and lower-paid wage earners (the real wages of the working class were cut by half) to the new ruling class. This equilibrium, a regressive one, has a content that is more biased toward consumption by the new privileged strata, so that the equilibrium of the public finances and that of the balance of payments (on which the former is based) are extremely fragile.

Most of the inflation in the Third World of today is of this type — for example, that in the Indonesia of Sukarno, that in Mali, or that in a number of countries of Latin America. In some cases there is juxtaposed to this type of inflation a process of credit inflation associated with a disordered process of industrialization, mediocre in its effect, for the same reasons of predominance by the new bureaucracy.

These particular processes of adjustment lie behind the structuralist thesis regarding inflation. But the same results can be secured without inflation. Thus, in the former French colonies of Black Africa, where the monetary system forbids any budgetary inflation, a progressive increase in the tax burden in the form of indirect taxes has reduced the real income of the agricultural producers and the wage earners in the towns, for the benefit of the same social strata as in the previously mentioned cases.

Quite different is inflation employed as a method of forced saving, in the context of a national policy of systematic autocentric development, such as occurred in Japan between 1877 and 1914. Here the state's aid to the old merchant families who, around 1870, became transformed into industrialists, was effected by way of loans without security. These advances weighed heavily on the market, causing prices to rise, and thus made possible a transfer of purchasing power from the peasant masses to the new bourgeoisie, who used this purchasing power to pay for the machinery they imported from abroad. This deliberate inflation of credit made investment possible before real saving had been obtained from production. The issue of currency, always ahead of requirements, certainly entailed a secondary price increase, but basically it made possible an increase in the level of economic activity. Part of the purchasing power created by the state for the benefit of the entrepreneurs found its way on to the external market, as it was necessary to import large quantities of machinery. These imports were paid for by liquidating the nation's stocks of gold and silver. In the Japanese case, the surplus of imports over exports was due to a sudden increase in imports of investment goods, and *not* to an increase in imports of luxury goods resulting from a transfer of income to the parasitical rich classes, as in the case of the underdeveloped countries. It was not external demand in general that had risen but only the level of demand for investment goods. The difficulties of the external balance were thus, in this case, the *result* of the acceleration of growth through internal inflation and not the *cause* of the increase in prices.

It is interesting to compare this pattern of development-inflation with that of the inflation and price rise in the underdeveloped countries during the Second World War. Here, the price increase, though internal in origin, was nevertheless closely bound up with the balance of payments. However, it occurred in a special war situation, so that some of its negative effects on accumulation were unable to take concrete form.

Indeed, since the demand of Great Britain and the United States increased during the war, as in a period of prosperity, and since the need, as well as the possibility, for these countries to export manufactured goods declined during this period, these circumstances resulted in an improvement in the terms of trade for the overseas countries, which favored local accumulation. A large part of this surplus income realized through the improvement in the balance of payments would in normal times have been spent on luxury imports. This surplus income thus constituted in part a forced saving that soon found investment locally, all the more so because the absence of foreign competition and the acute reduction in imports favored the creation of local industries. It is true that some contrary forces worked against this development, such as the decline in the productivity of agriculture due to the impossibility of importing fertilizers, and the difficulty in getting machinery from Europe and America. Accordingly, part of this surplus income was directed into the local market for luxury goods (building of luxury villas, etc.), where it caused a price increase. This unrestrained consumption of luxury products resulted, moreover, in investment in fast-food outlets, which served as a pole of development for local luxury expenditure. Part of the deficit in the balance of the Allied countries was paid for by liquidating gold reserves, and also, especially, by transferring foreign investments to local ownership — starting with the least profitable of these investments. In this way the war contributed to the formation of local capital, if only by this transfer of ownership, the consequence of which was to be that the profits subsequently realized would no longer be exported. Later, the deficit in the European balance was paid for either in depreciating currency or in "war debt" (sterling credits, for example), which also depreciated as the European currencies were inflated. European inflation was thus transmitted to the overseas countries, where it was intensified by the expenditure of the foreign armies.

The final outcome, despite the particularly favorable conditions for local development, was rather meager. Inflation was reflected in increased gross investment, but at the same time the war involved such a squandering of capital (nonreplacement of worn-out equipment, as in the case of railways, roads, harbors, etc.) that it is very hard to decide whether, ultimately, net investment was positive. Altogether, this type of inflation seems to have been negative in its effect. What did play a positive role was not the inflation itself but the momentary disappearance of foreign competition.

Thus, monetary structures are not the main thing in underdevelopment. Whatever these structures may be, the value of money at the periphery of the system cannot differ from that of the dominant currencies of the center.

The Functions of the Periphery
in the Movement of the World Conjuncture

Current economic theory, which identifies the underdeveloped countries with the advanced countries as they were at an earlier stage of their development, fails to take account of the conjunctural phenomena that are peculiar to the periphery. It takes refuge in a mechanistic theory of the conjuncture transmitted from the advanced countries to the underdeveloped ones either through the channel of monetary mechanisms or else through that of the external-trade multiplier. Actually, the economies of the system's periphery have no real conjunctural phenomena of their own, even transmitted from outside, because they are without any internal dynamism of their own.

The periphery does nevertheless occupy a position that can be important in the development of the cycle, or of the fluctuations in the conjuncture, on the world scale. It provides a field of possible extension for the capitalist mode of production at the expense of precapitalist milieus. Although this extension of the capitalist mode of production is not essential to the working of the mechanism of accumulation, it does play the role of a catalyst and an accelerator of growth at the center. It certainly played an important role from this standpoint in the initial period of colonization. It seems to have lost this importance in the present period, but may perhaps recover it in the setting of a new structure of international specialization.

Critique of economic theories of transmission. Contrary to the schemas put forward by Haberler and Clark, the economic oscillations experienced by the underdeveloped countries bear little resemblance to a cycle. When the conjuncture is favorable in the advanced countries, the level of exports from the underdeveloped countries goes up.

The incomes that benefit first and foremost in these countries consist mainly of ground rent. Most of the profits of enterprises of the capitalist type are exported, and wages may be assumed to be relatively stable. The elasticity of the rents drawn by the landowners, however, enables this income to absorb the supplement engendered by the increased price and volume of exports of agricultural produce. The small peasants also benefit to some extent from this prosperity (though less than the landowners, because they have to deal through intermediaries, in the shape of merchants who may absorb part of the extra income). This prosperity of ground rents finds reflection in a marked increase in imports of luxury goods and to a lesser extent in the level of imports of the cheap manufactured goods that the small peasants buy. Conversely, if the conjuncture is unfavorable in the advanced countries, primary products are sold in smaller quantities and at lower prices. The whole economy of the underdeveloped country suffers from this, but wages, being relatively rigid, are less affected than rents. As for profits, the volume of which also diminishes, they are still by definition exported and so do not affect the situation in the underdeveloped country. If, however, exports decline, and with them ground rents, then imports of luxury goods and goods for consumption by the peasantry will soon suffer the same fate.

The cycle is therefore not in the least transmitted by way of the balance of payments. The latter continues to be kept in equilibrium, in periods of prosperity and depression alike, since exports, rents, and imports all vary together in the same direction. Haberler's analysis, which might have some validity in the case of relations between countries with a central capitalist structure, has none in the case of relations between countries with such profoundly different structures as those of the center and the periphery.

Can we say that the cycle is transmitted directly by fluctuations in the volume of exchanges? No, for the special role of analysis of the foreign-trade multiplier is to show that the primary fluctuations in the volume of external exchanges (fluctuations due to the state of the conjuncture abroad, constituting an independent datum) give rise to secondary internal fluctuations. Here we have nothing of that kind. It is in this sense that it can be said that there is no true cycle in the underdeveloped economies. The fact that rent constitutes the elastic income in these economies means that the multiplier does not function there. The increased purchasing power available as a result of the increased value of exports is not mainly spent and partly saved — it is spent in its entirety. The increased demand does not here give rise to induced investments. As the accelerator is transferred abroad, there is no true cycle, not even a transmitted one, but only a sinusoidal oscillation of total income.

A study of the history of the world conjuncture leads to the following observations:

(1) Fluctuations in the total real income seem to be less marked in the underdeveloped countries, taken as a whole, than in the advanced countries, at least in the twentieth century — which does not mean that they may not have been *more* marked in *certain* underdeveloped countries. Furthermore, while the magnitude of conjunctural fluctuations is comparable between the different advanced countries, the "scatter" in the underdeveloped countries in this respect is very considerable. Fluctuations are more violent in proportion to the degree in which the country is integrated into the international market. In a country that is well integrated they may be no less violent than in the most advanced countries.

(2) Fluctuations in the unit value of export prices for primary products varied between 5 and 21 percent, depending on the particular product, between 1900 and 1970. The magnitude of these fluctuations increased by successive stages during the three peacetime periods: 11 percent per annum for 1901-1914; 13 to 15 percent from 1920 to 1939; and 18 percent from 1946 to 1965. Cyclical fluctuations in prices averaged 27 percent. Annual fluctuations in the volume of exports averaged 19 percent. After 1945 they amounted to 24 percent. Cyclical fluctuations in the volume of exports have been, on the average, of the same magnitude as those of prices. Finally, fluctuations in receipts from exports (cumulative effects of fluctuations in price and in volume) have amounted to 22 percent, both annually and cyclically. This magnitude gets bigger as time goes by: 19 percent in 1901-1913; 21 percent in 1920-1939; and 30 percent in 1946-1965. The variations in real values (obtained by dividing these variations in nominal values by the index of prices of British manufactured exports) show that the variations in real values (13.5 percent for the period 1902-1960) have been the same as the variations in nominal values (13.7 percent).

(3) There are no precise rules for the way the trade balance behaves, either in the advanced countries or in the underdeveloped ones, for exports and imports vary in the same direction and in similar proportions. Even so, there is a certain tendency for the imports of the underdeveloped countries to shrink less sharply than their exports.

(4) The contraction in the trade of the advanced countries is due

mainly to contraction in the *volume* of *both* their exports and their imports. The contraction in the trade of the underdeveloped countries, however, is due mainly to the fall in *the prices of their exports,* to the deterioration in their terms of trade that this expresses, and to the weakening of their real capacity to import that results from it.

(5) The cyclical movement of the balance of payments is due to that of *capital* far more than to that of the trade balance. The fluctuations in the value of exports are not compensated by equal and inverse fluctuations in the movement of capital. On the contrary, these oscillations reinforce the first-mentioned ones. It is during depression periods that least foreign capital flows into the periphery. While, therefore, the fluctuations in the total value of exports are compensated by equal fluctuations in imports (connected with the movement of ground rent), the oscillations in the movement of capital, which reinforce the terms of the trade balance, have the effect of periodically upsetting the balance of external payments, in one direction or the other. True, the outward movement of the exported profits of foreign capital serves to mitigate this disturbance. In fact, it is in a period of prosperity, when foreign capital is flowing in, that the volume of profits exported is also greatest. However, the magnitude of the fluctuation in capital movements often proves greater than that in the movement of profits.

(6) Fluctuations in national income increased sharply after 1914, both in the advanced countries and in the underdeveloped ones, as did fluctuations in exports and imports and in prices. Since the Second World War, fluctuations have lost their regular cyclical character, giving place to a shifting conjuncture with movements of limited magnitude.

(7) Fluctuations in industrial production in the underdeveloped countries depend on the destination of its products and on the degree of the given country's dependence on foreign trade. Fluctuations in agricultural income in the underdeveloped countries depend on the same factors, that is, on the extraverted or autocentric character of economic activity.

(8) Fluctuations in the total real income of the underdeveloped countries are often smaller than those that occur in the advanced ones. Fluctuations in income *in current prices* are, however, notably bigger, owing to the great volatility of prices in these countries.

From these observations I deduce the following four propositions:

1. The cycle is not transmitted through fluctuations in the quantity of money. While it is true that, the balance of payments being positive for the underdeveloped countries in a prosperity period and negative in a depression period, these countries see their resources in international liquidities alternately increasing and decreasing, internal circulation remains neutral, that is, proportional to money income (real income multiplied by the price level).

2. Nor is the cycle transmitted by the trade balance, through the working of the multiplier. The behavior of the trade balance is in fact extremely variable, both in different periods and in different countries. It must be added that even when the balance is positive in an underdeveloped country, we do not observe a wave of induced secondary investments engendered by this net surplus.

3. The cycle is, then, quite simply the cyclical aspect of the movement in the income of those agriculturists who live by exporting, which takes the form of a cyclical deterioration in the terms of trade for their exports. This oscillation has secondary effects on industrial production destined for the local market, as also on services as a whole; but these effects are rather weak, in so far as the oscillation parallels the general movement of imports. The cycle of the underdeveloped countries is merely the cycle of their capacity to import.

4. In the international cycle, the underdeveloped countries play an important role at the moment of recovery, because they provide supplementary outlets for the exports of the advanced countries, through the possible breakup of precapitalist milieus. In a period of recession, trade between the advanced and the underdeveloped countries often declines less than that between the advanced countries themselves, and often the imports of the advanced countries increase during depression (as was particularly the case in the nineteenth century).

The role of the periphery in the world conjuncture. The periphery plays a role which is far from negligible in the mechanism of international recovery. The point is that, however deep a depression may be, it can come to an end sooner in the underdeveloped countries than in the central capitalist economies, because it is more superficial in the former. During a depression in the advanced countries a considerable mass of labor is thrown out of employment. All incomes contract — profits first and foremost, but wages, too. During the preceding period of prosperity, new enterprises were set up, which are now working at a reduced rate. The burden of unutilized productive capacity weighs heavily, making recovery all the more difficult. In the underdeveloped countries, on the other hand, while oscillations in the predominant form of income, ground rent, are very considerable, this is not true of the mixed incomes of the bulk of the population, and especially of income from subsistence economy. From a certain moment onward, the relative rigidity of the underdeveloped markets may thus constitute a factor of recovery. The existence of exchange relations between the periphery and the center of the system offers the latter the possibility of finding new external markets through the disintegration of the indigenous precapitalist economy.

The further disintegration of primitive indigenous production at the end of the depression is reflected in a new wave of exports from the advanced countries. However, the money incomes distributed as a result of this imply a future increase in imports. This is why the opening of new external outlets does not constitute a final solution of the problem. In theory, this opening of a new field for the extension of capital is not needed in order that recovery may take place. This recovery is due very largely to a deepening of the internal market caused by the generalizing of a new, more capital-intensive technique. Nevertheless, we observe, after each depression at the center, the opening of new outlets in the periphery, which thus play an active role in the mechanism of international recovery.

The same thing happens during the cumulative process that is characteristic of the prosperity period. For the development of prosperity, marked by the growth of total income, is reflected in an increase in the share taken by profits, and consequently in an increase in the relative volume of saving that is accumulated. The relative share taken by wages decreases. Accordingly, capacity to consume falls farther and farther behind capacity to produce. The new equipment created by investment of the additional saving is not long in throwing on to the market a mass of consumer goods

that cannot be absorbed. The working of the accelerator maintains
for a time the illusion of the profitability of the new equipment
made necessary by the increase in the absolute volume of consumption.
There is thus overproduction of consumer goods, since the purchasing
power distributed and destined for purchase of these goods (mainly
wages) is less than the total value of this production. Trade
between the advanced and underdeveloped countries continues,
also, to conceal this imbalance, and so contributes to protracting
the periods of prosperity. Exchange between advanced and underdeveloped countries in no way constitutes, of course, the solution to
alleged general overproduction by the capitalist countries. Development of the capitalist countries is perfectly possible even when
there are no precapitalist milieus to be disintegrated. But the
advanced countries, which are always ahead of their backward
partners in exchange, take the offensive by exporting to them. Only
later does the structure of the underdeveloped countries become
modified, adapting itself to the evolution of production in the
advanced countries so as to make possible the export of primary
products to them. Imbalance is therefore a permanent feature of
trade relations between the center and the periphery of the system.
This permanent imbalance is, however, always being corrected. It
therefore plays, in the development of the most advanced countries,
only the role of a catalyst, comparable to credit. It is the products
that tend to be overproduced during the prosperity phase that are
the first to seek an outlet in the economies of the periphery —
namely, manufactured consumer goods. Contrariwise, the growing
demand of the advanced countries, during the prosperity phase, for
those products that are relatively least plentiful leads to adjustment
of the structure of the underdeveloped countries to the needs of the
most advanced economies. The underdeveloped economies specialize
in producing goods the supply of which tends to be less than the
demand for them in the advanced countries during the prosperity
phase: primary products that contribute to the equipment of the
advanced countries — in the main, raw materials. Exchange of
consumer goods, in respect of which supply is greater than demand,
for intermediate goods, in respect of which, on the contrary, demand is
greater than supply, thus facilitates the upward trend in the advanced

countries. We can now appreciate better the real place occupied by
the periphery in the world conjuncture. Although the extension of
the capitalist mode of production to the periphery is not essential
to the working of the mechanism of accumulation, this extension
plays the role of a catalyst and an accelerator of growth at the
center.

This is so, for example, in the present period. Capitalism has
been experiencing, since the end of the Second World War, a
period of brilliant growth, in which the Third World has played
only a very secondary part. It is the modernization of Western
Europe that has been the essential factor in this "miracle." Modernization means deepening (not spreading) the capitalist market, a
solution which — always possible, as Marx and Lenin showed —
has become real through the conjunction of elements situated on
different planes (such as the political plane, e.g., fear of communism),
so that any mechanistic "economistic" interpretation is ruled out.
The European Common Market and the influx of American capital
into Europe constitute the most obvious expressions of this phenomenon.

Nevertheless, although during this period the extension of capitalism to the periphery has not played an important role, this does
not mean that it has always been so, nor that it will always be so in
the future. In the past, the extraordinary wave of extension of the
capitalist market to the colonies during the nineteenth century very
certainly played an important part in the relatively peaceful course
taken by accumulation at the center. This first wave determined an
initial series of forms of international specialization between center
and periphery, the latter, of course, adapting itself to the requirements of the former. These forms of adaptation implied, after a
certain level had been reached, a relative blocking of the mechanism of
the extension of capitalism — whence the crisis of the 1930s.

The type of growth that the capitalist world has known since
1945 is tending in its turn to exhaust its possibilities. The world
monetary crisis is perhaps a symptom of this. What will take over
the role of ensuring the growth of capitalism? I see three possibilities.
First, progressive integration of the countries of Eastern Europe
into the world market, and their modernization. Second, the
contemporary scientific and technical revolution, which along with

automation, the conquest of the atom, and the conquest of space, may open up substantial possibilities for deepening the market. Third and last, a new wave of extension of capitalism to the Third World, based on a new type of international specialization made possible by the technical revolution of our time. In this context, the countries of the center would specialize in ultra-modern activities, while forms of classical industry that had hitherto been reserved for them would be transferred to the periphery. Once again, by adapting itself to the requirements of the center, the periphery will have played an important role in the mechanism of accumulation on the world scale.

5. THE BLOCKING OF TRANSITION

The capitalist mode of production possesses three means of checking the tendency of the rate of profit to fall — means that constitute the three profound tendencies of this mode's dynamic of accumulation. The first, which Marx studies at length in *Capital*, is increasing the rate of surplus value; in other words, aggravating the conditions of capitalist exploitation at the center of the system, which implies relative impoverishment. The second means is spreading the capitalist mode of production to new regions where the rate of surplus value is higher and where it is therefore possible to obtain a superprofit through unequal exchange. The third means consists in developing various forms of waste: selling costs, military expenditure, or luxury consumption, making it possible for profits that cannot be reinvested owing to the inadequacy of the rate of profit to be spent nevertheless. This third means was only glimpsed by Marx, its large-scale development being a feature of our own time.

Only the expansion of the sphere embraced by capitalism falls within our purview here. What needs to be grasped is that this extension is the work of central capitalism, which strives in this way to find a solution to its own problems. It is because central capitalism holds the initiative in this extension that relations between center and periphery continue to be asymmetrical — indeed, this is why a periphery exists and is continually being renewed.

The transition to peripheral capitalism already reveals this asymmetry, reflecting the fact that the source of the initiative is the center. The process of development of peripheral capitalism goes forward within a framework of competition (in the broadest sense of the word) from the center, which is responsible for the distinctive structure assumed by the periphery, as something complementary and dominated. It is this competition that determines three types of distortion in the development of peripheral capitalism as compared with capitalism at the center of the system: (1) a crucial distortion toward export activities, which absorb the major part of the capital arriving from the center; (2) a distortion toward tertiary activities, which arises both from the special contradictions of peripheral capitalism and from the original structures of the peripheral formations; and (3) a distortion in the choice of branches of industry, toward light branches, together with the utilization of modern techniques in these branches. This threefold distortion reflects the asymmetrical way in which the periphery is integrated in the world market. It means, in economistic terms, the transfer from the periphery to the center of the multiplier mechanisms, which cause accumulation at the center to be a cumulative process. From this transfer results the conspicuous disarticulation of the underdeveloped economy, the dualism of this economy, and, in the end, the blocking of the economy's growth.

It is the distortion toward export activities that constitutes the main reason for the blocking of a dependent and limited form of development. The fact is that the center's needs for primary products (agricultural and mineral) from the periphery follow, broadly speaking, the average rate of growth of the center. The countries of the periphery have to pay for their increasing imports with exports that need to increase at a faster rate so as to ensure that the profits exported by foreign capital are covered. The rate of growth of the center thus dictates that of the periphery. This blocking is, of course, only relative. Theoretically, it is not insurmountable. There are no vicious circles of poverty rendering impossible any genuine autocentric development, breaking with the orientation that is biased toward export activities. Large-scale organized investment would create its own market, by expanding the domestic market. But that would imply breaking with the rule of profitability.

Economists want to stay within the setting of respect for profitability, as they decline to reject the requirements for investment of foreign capital. For this capital, local investment directed toward the domestic market aggravates the external disequilibrium if it does not enable the volume of exports to be increased (or the volume of imports to be reduced) by the amount needed in order to export the profits made. Since a transformation of the economy based on large-scale imports of foreign capital entails substantial secondary waves of induced imports, direct and indirect, the requirement of external equilibrium gravely restricts the possibilities of autocentric development financed from without.

Experience shows that the development of underdevelopment is neither regular nor cumulative, in contrast to the development of capitalism at the center. On the contrary, it is jerky and made up of phases of extremely rapid growth, followed by sudden blockages. These are manifested in a double crisis, of external payments and of public finances.

Let us assume a growth rate of 7 percent per annum in a peripheral economy. For a capital-output ratio of about 3 (a modest estimate), investments should represent 20 percent, approximately, of the gross domestic product. Let us assume that half of these investments are financed by foreign capital rewarded at rates of 15 percent (again, a modest estimate). If imports increase at the same rate as the product, it will be possible for the balance of external payments to be kept level only if exports can grow at a rate much greater than 12 percent per annum. The following table shows the factors in this dynamic of growth.

	Year 0	Year 10	Year 20
General economic equilibrium			
Gross domestic product	100	200	400
+ imports	25	50	100
— exports	15	53	135
= Liquid assets	110	197	365

[*continued on page 290*]

	Year 0	Year 10	Year 20
Consumption, private and public	90	157	285
+ annual investment	20	40	80
(of which, external financing)	(10)	(20)	(40)
(accumulated foreign capital)	(0)	(150)	(550)
Balance of payments			
Exports	15	53	135
+ flow of foreign capital	10	20	40
= Total	25	73	175
Imports	25	50	100
+ backflow of profits	0	23	75

Furthermore, if the tax burden is at its maximum and is constant (say, 22 percent of distributed income, assumed to be spent wholly on consumer goods), allowing for the needs of financing public investments (the other half of investments), equilibrium in public finance would require that the advance of current public consumption should grow at a lower rate (4 or 5 percent only), that is, that current public expenditure should make up a decreasing proportion of the gross domestic product, as shown in the following table:

	Year 0	Year 10	Year 20
GDP	100	200	400
National consumption	90	157	285
Public receipts	20	35	64
Public expenditure:			
Current expenditure	10	15	24
Investments	10	20	40

It is clear that things cannot go on like this. While the exports of a particular product or of a particular country may increase at a very high rate for a certain period, for the periphery as a whole, exports that are destined for the center cannot grow faster than demand at the center — that is, approximately at the rate of growth of the center: it is impossible for a country to catch up on its historical handicap while sticking to the basis of international specialization. But, above all, on this basis the imports into the periphery must increase faster than the gross domestic product. This tendency, observed historically, is easy to explain by two fundamental causes. First, international specialization means for a country of the periphery a relative narrowing of its range of productive activities, whereas the increased income that reflects growth means an expansion in the range of demand. Second, the disarticulation that is characteristic of international specialization implies a more rapid growth of intermediate imports. Added to this is the very high import-content, both direct and indirect, of capital formation and public expenditure.

From a different aspect, current public expenditure must grow faster than income. There are several reasons, too, for this requirement. The public investments in the infrastructure called for by international specialization involve recurrent operational expenditures that will increase like the accumulated investments, namely, much faster than the product. The balance available to ensure the social services essential to growth (education, health, not to mention the classical administrative needs) cannot be reduced, in relative terms, in such a drastic way: the spontaneous tendency is here, on the contrary, for the share taken by this kind of expenditure to increase. And the burden of taxation has its limits.

The twofold crisis of public and external finances is thus inevitable, and thenceforth growth will be blocked. The mechanism of this dynamic will not be able to function unless a start is made from a low level of international integration, unless a resource of interest to the center is suddenly opened up (making possible a big increase in exports), unless the prosperity that results from this attracts a large influx of foreign capital, and unless the tax burden, low to begin with, can be increasingly lightened. Growth will then necessarily be very strong: there will be a "miracle." But this eventually comes to an end: there is no "take-off," whatever the level of income per head that may have been attained. This is why no underdeveloped country has so far taken off, either from among those whose income per head is of the order of $200 or from among those where it is higher than $1,000 or $2,000. Autocentric and autodynamic development never becomes possible there, whereas at the center it was possible from the start, even with very low income levels.

None of the features that define the structure of the periphery is thus weakened as economic growth proceeds: on the contrary, these features are accentuated. Whereas at the center growth means development, making the economy more integral, in the periphery growth does not mean development, for it disarticulates the economy — it is only a "development of underdevelopment."

We see how mistaken it is to identify underdevelopment with a low level of product per head. After all, in Kuwait the product per head in 1960 ($3,290) was greater than in the United States ($3,020), and in Venezuela it was higher than in Romania or Japan ($780, against $710 and $660, respectively), while in Portugal it was hardly bigger than in several African countries ($349, as against $230 for Ghana). As for Gabon, its product per head is today approximately the same as that of the France of 1900.

5

The Contemporary
Social Formations
of the Periphery

1. THE HISTORICAL FORMATION OF THE CONTEMPORARY PERIPHERY

The tendency of the capitalist mode of production to become exclusive when based on expansion and deepening of the home market is accompanied by a tendency for the social structure at the center to come close to the pure model of *Capital*, characterized by polarization of social classes into two basic classes: the bourgeoisie and the proletariat. The social classes formed on the basis of former modes of production (landowners, craftsmen, merchants, etc.) either disappear or are transformed (e.g., into an agrarian bourgeoisie). True, the social system gives rise to new stratifications at the same time as it becomes simpler: "white collars" and "blue collars," cadres and unskilled workers, native and foreign workers, etc. But these new stratifications are all situated within the framework of the essential division between bourgeoisie and proletariat, for all the new developing social strata are made up of wage-earning employees of the capitalist enterprises. The relevance of the new stratifications is therefore not economic — since from this standpoint the positions of the new strata are identical, being all sellers of their labor power — but political or ideological. Moreover, the concentration of enterprises by the formation of monopolies modifies the forms in which the bourgeoisie manifests itself. But the alleged dichotomy established between dispersed ownership and control (said to have passed into the hands of the "technostructure," to use the word coined by J. K. Galbraith) is only an illusion. For the "technocrats" who take decisions take them in accordance with the logic and in the interest of capital, which exercises a more and more concentrated control. Nevertheless, the fact that the social structure is thus directly molded by the movement of the economy itself leads to the ideologization of economics, that is, to economism. The illusion is created that the economy is a force above society, which the latter cannot control. This is the source of modern alienation and the reason why economics claims to fill the entire field of social science.

If, however, the capitalist mode of production, introduced from outside — that is, based on the external market — does not tend to become exclusive, but only dominant, it follows that the formations of the periphery will not tend toward this essential polarization. Contrasting with the growing homogeneity of the social formations of the center will be the persisting heterogeneity of those of the periphery, a heterogeneity that does not mean mere juxtaposition. For, just as the precapitalist modes of production are here integrated into a system subjected to the distinctive purposes of dominant capital (the peasant goes on producing within the setting of his former mode of production, but henceforth produces commodities that are exported to the center), so the new social structures form a structured, hierarchical totality, dominated by the "great absentee" of colonial society: the dominant metropolitan bourgeoisie. The economic system of the periphery cannot be understood in itself, for its relations with the center are crucial; similarly, the social structure of the periphery is a truncated structure that can only be understood when it is situated as an element in a *world* social structure.

The form assumed by peripheral formations will ultimately depend on the nature of the precapitalist formations subjected to attack, on the one hand, and, on the other, on the forms taken by this external attack.

The precapitalist formations that were attacked fall into two main types: on the one hand, we have the Oriental and African formations, and, on the other, the American formations. The former were combinations structured, on the one hand, by the various modes of production, the dominant mode being the tribute-paying mode — either in its early form (based, that is, on a surviving village community) or in its developed form (and in this case being gradually transformed into a feudal mode of production), with the simple commodity mode and the slaveowning mode being, so to speak, in the service of this dominant mode — and, on the other hand, by relations of long-distance trade with other formations. The simple, early variety was the African type, while the developed one was the Asian and Arab type. The American formations were different. The New World was not uninhabited when the Europeans discovered it, but it was quickly peopled with immigrants who mostly arrived before the final triumph of the capitalist mode of production at the center (that is, before the Industrial Revolution). The native inhabitants were either driven back or exterminated (North America, the West Indies, Argentina, Brazil), or else entirely subjected to the requirements of European merchant capital (the Andean areas of South America). The attack also took various forms. The Americas, Asia and the Arab world, and Black Africa were not all transformed in the same way, because they were not integrated at the same stage of capitalist development at the center and therefore did not fulfil the same functions in this development.

As there are already systematic studies concerning America, it will not be necessary to dwell much on this continent. More space will be devoted to the Arab world and to Black Africa.

The American Peripheral Formations

The Americas played an essential role in the mercantile period of the formation of the contemporary world system. At the outset the pre-Columbian formations were either destroyed or subjected to the merchant capital of the rising European center. Merchant capital, ancestor of fully developed capital, established annexes in America, in the form of enterprises for the exploitation of precious metals (mainly silver) and producing some exotic commodities (sugar, later cotton, etc.). European merchant capitalists, who held the monopoly of this exploitation, thus accumulated the money-capital needed for the subsequent complete development of capital. Exploitation took various forms: "pseudo-feudal" (the *encomienda* of Latin America) or "pseudo-slaveowning" (mines) or slaveowning (plantations in Brazil, the West Indies, and in the British colonies in the southern part of North America). They were all none the less in the service of nascent European capitalism: they produced for the market, and so must not be confused with the true feudal or slaveowning modes of production. Moreover, these annexes themselves developed annexes of their own: enterprises supplying them with foodstuffs for their manpower and the materials for use in their exploitation. These subsidiary enterprises sometimes had a "feudal" look about them, especially in Latin America, where stockbreeding took place on a large scale; but they did not in any way become really feudal, being functionally intended to produce for the capitalist market. They belonged in most cases to the simple petty-commodity mode of production, being formed by European immigrants, particularly the British in North America, on free land and in free towns, where farmers and craftsmen also produced for the market constituted by the plantation areas belonging to merchant capital.

It was during this mercantilist period that Latin America acquired the main structures that characterize it to this day. These were based on agrarian capitalism of the latifundia type, the labor force of which was supplied by peasants of degraded status (peons and former slaves). To this was added a local merchant bourgeoisie of the comprador type, when the monopoly of the mother country became overstretched. Along with this, a petty urban community of artisans, small traders, officials, domestic servants, etc., in the image of that existing in the Europe of the time, came into being.

At the beginning of the nineteenth century, independence meant transfer of power to the landowners and the Creole comprador bourgeoisie. The structures described were to persist and become reinforced throughout the century, as trade was intensified with Great Britain, the new metropolis, which established all over the continent a network of import-export firms and banks, and drew additional profits from financing the public debt of the new states.

The installation of oil and mining capital in the twentieth century (mostly from the United States), and then the establishment of import-substitution industries, engendered a limited proletariat, the higher categories of which were to appear all the more privileged, comparatively speaking, as the agrarian crisis brought about a steady impoverishment of the poor peasantry and an increase in rural and urban unemployment. Sometimes, and right from the beginning in association with foreign capital, the oligarchy of landlords and comprador merchants invested capital amassed in agriculture and trade in developing the new light industry or in highly profitable activities connected with expanding urban areas (investments in house property, in the "tertiary" sector, etc.).

Historians of Latin America — among others, Andre Gunder Frank, Celso Furtado, Fernando Cardoso, Enzo Falleto, Darcy Ribeiro—have shown how the latifundia-owning and Creole comprador bourgeoisie served as a transmission belt for rising dominant European capitalism. While in Europe liberal thought was the banner of the industrial bourgeoisie, in Latin America it was the banner of landowners and traders. The nineteenth century witnessed, from 1810 to 1860-1880, a long series of civil wars between the "European party," in favor of free trade, and the "American party," representing the interests of national development and advocating protectionism. The final victory of the former at the end of the century, when capitalism at the center entered its imperialist phase, was to blight every hope of industrial development and assert the dependence of Latin America. Porfirio Diaz in Mexico was a symbol of this national surrender. The taking over by foreign capital of industrial and mining enterprises until then belonging to Latin Americans that followed, especially in Chile after 1880, paved the way for imperialist capital.

Nevertheless, a new industrial bourgeoisie was constituted in the wake of the dominant foreign capital, particularly during the First World War, during the 1930s, and especially during the Second World War. Limited in its development by the submission of Latin America to the requirements of free trade, this new industrial bourgeoisie attempted to challenge, partially at least, the power of the landowners and traders. To achieve this, it tried to win the support of the masses, and this gave Vargas' regime in Brazil, that of Peron in Argentina, and that of Cárdenas in Mexico their populist character. But this bourgeoisie also tried to ensure that this popular support could not turn against it; hence, it forbade the popular classes to organize freely outside its control. After the Second World War, *desarrollismo*, a nonpopulist, technocratic ideology took over, marking also a step backward toward a compromise characterized by an appeal for external aid and association with foreign (now U.S.) capital. The new bourgeoisie often came from the same families of great landowners and traders who were formerly dominant, in association with foreign capital. The steady progress of the dominant foreign capital and its ever growing technological monopoly indicate the submission of these national bourgeoisies. The failure of this development-model, shown in the exhaustion of the possibilities of industrialization by import-substitution and the economic stagnation of the 1950s and 1960s, was to lead to the first breaks in the system in the direction of socialism, in Cuba and in Chile.

The Arab and Asian Peripheral Formations

The start came much later in Asia and in the Arab world. It was only in the second half of the nineteenth century that the former feudal classes turned into big capitalist landowners producing for the world market. Developments of this type were, moreover, very uneven, affecting only a fringe, sometimes a very narrow one, of the vast continent. The extreme case is that of Egypt, entirely transformed into a cotton farm for the mills of Lancashire by its few thousand big landowners. For a long time, the power of survival of the village community was to resist, in a number of regions, the development of agrarian capitalism — less so in India, where the British rulers gave the *zamindars* ownership of the land, forcibly breaking up the village communities; more so in China and in many areas of the Persian and Ottoman empires, which escaped direct colonial subjection. It was only recently, often not until the period since the Second World War, that small-scale agrarian capitalism (with rich peasants of the kulak type) made its appearance, particularly where agrarian reforms liquidated or limited the large estates. The belated and limited character of the development of agrarian capitalism, and the phenomena characteristic of the structures of the urban community and of the ideology and culture of the new dominant classes that emerged from the transformation of the old ones, or the phenomena characteristic of the forms of colonial subjection, restricted to a greater or lesser degree the expansion of the comprador trade sector, either to the advantage of European firms or to that of a partly Europeanized bourgeoisie of cosmopolitan background (Levantines, for instance). Later on, as in Latin America, sporadic industries founded by foreign capital made it possible for local oligarchies to associate themselves with the new activities. The structure of these new formations then tended to be similar to that of Latin America, with the lag being made up for all the faster because the penetration of modern forms of foreign capital was more powerful.

The case of British India has been studied by R. C. Dutt, Palme Dutt, and Frederick Clairmonte. From the beginning of the nineteenth century, the British systematically destroyed the Indian textile industry by economic means (prohibition of imports into England) and also extraeconomic means (destruction of the industrial towns of Surat, Dacca, Murshidabad, and others). They imposed agricultural specialization, by creating from scratch a pattern of large landed property, reinforced by the exemption of cotton fields from the land tax. Independent India and Pakistan inherited this structure. Since independence, partial agrarian reforms have opened the way to a more thorough development of kulak-type agrarian capitalism. Along with this, there is a tendency for the center of gravity of urban capitalism to move from comprador commercial capital to state capital as progress is made in industrialization by import-substitution.

Dutch colonialism in Indonesia created directly for its own benefit industrial plantations producing for export. The relative weakness of local large landownership that resulted from this policy explains the greater specific weight possessed by the petty-bourgeoisie and accounts for the particular nature of Sukarno's subsequent regime. The same thing happened, to some extent, in Malaya, in Indochina, and in the Philippines. Special circumstances, notably conflict between different imperialist interests, enabled Thailand to escape colonial subjection.

For these reasons, the history of the contemporary Thai social formation is particularly interesting. The manifestations of chaos and alienation that dependence entailed elsewhere are less noticeable here. Because it escaped direct shaping by colonialism, Thailand, for a long time a backward but not underdeveloped country, was able to recover and, by means of "enlightened despotism," to achieve a national unity and a state modernization more coherent and more solid than elsewhere. It was only after the Second World War that the country's process of underdevelopment accelerated, with its integration into the world system. The same applied to Afghanistan. Iran resisted for a shorter time, the Anglo-Russian agreement of 1907 and the exploitation of the oil of Abadan having entailed its integration into the world system as a semicolony.

The history of the formations of the contemporary Arab world covers a period that can be clearly divided into three parts. The first was marked by awareness of the European danger, and sometimes by an attempt to imitate Europe in order to offer a better resistance to it. The failure of this attempt was followed by the stage of colonial subjection during which the Arab formations acquired their final dependent peripheral character. The third stage, during which this dependence was challenged, began during the 1950s.

The Arab formations had been based on long-distance trade. The shifting of the center of gravity of world trade from the Mediterranean to the Atlantic Ocean, with the rise of European mercantilist capitalism, entailed the decline of the Arab world. Consequently, at the dawn of imperialist aggression, in the nineteenth century, the Arab world had lost real unity, and henceforth was only a heterogeneous conglomerate, subject moreover to a foreign power: the Ottoman Empire. Imperialism was both to accentuate the division of this world and to revive its unity.

The limits of Arab civilization coincided with those of the mercantile formations allied with the nomads. When they penetrated peasant countries, the Arabs failed to set their mark on the peoples concerned, except in Egypt. This explains their failure in Spain, where the Arab merchant class remained urban, amid a Christian countryside. When they were driven out of Spain, the Arabs left only monuments behind them. Similarly, the Turks failed in the Balkans. The failure of Arabization in Iran, Anatolia, and beyond, and that of Islamization in Abyssinia, reflect the same limitation.

The Arab world felt very early on the reality of the danger from European imperialism. Already in the sixteenth century, in the age of mercantilism, European merchants obtained from the Ottoman state the trading privileges conferred on them by the "Capitulations." The Arab merchant class was thus already defeated; Europe had won the battle. The next three centuries were a prolonged slumber during which the East was unaware of what was happening in the West. For the commercial development of mercantilist Europe had its corollary in the decline of the mercantile world of the Arabs. The Arab cities wilted, and the country districts became dominant, with all their heterogeneity; and the very centers where the causes of the decay of the Eastern world might have been reflected upon ceased to exist. The awakening, a rough one, came at the beginning of the nineteenth century, with Bonaparte's Egyptian campaign.

The long effort of resistance made by the Arab world was to culminate in defeat, and dates can be given for this defeat: 1882 in the case of Egypt, the period 1830-1911 in the Maghreb, 1919 in the Arab East. Then came the period of Arab revival, the period of the anti-imperialist struggle. All through this century of history, two characteristic features appeared and developed everywhere in the Arab world, with a greater or lesser degree of clarity or of delay in appearance in different parts of it. First, the revival was marked by the rise of a new class, the modern petty-bourgeoisie of the towns, brought into being by the very process of integration of the Arab world into the imperialist sphere. This petty-bourgeoisie took over from the old ruling classes, which were rapidly collapsing, and even from the new bourgeois classes engendered by integration into the world capitalist system. Secondly, this revival expressed itself in a growing sense of Arab unity. Since the Arab world had never, except in Egypt, been a peasant world, the revival could not base itself on genuine national peasant cultures; it therefore fell to the bourgeoisie of the towns to revive the former unity of the Arabs in language and culture. Where, as in Egypt, the revival *could* base itself on national peasant unity, there was a delay in the appearance of the sense of Arab unity, with, instead, a revival of (Egyptian) national feeling.

Egypt was the first province of the Arab world to react against the threat from without. But it was the danger from Israel that made Egypt realize that its fate was bound up with that of the Arab world as a whole. The Arab East did not really wake up until imperialism installed itself in the heart of the region by creating the state of Israel. From the start, therefore, the anti-imperialist struggle here was identified with the struggle against Zionism. The Maghreb, geographically remote, and colonized moreover by another power, France, was not to wake up to the problems of Arab unity until 1967. Gradually, the Palestine problem became the pivot of the "Arab question," the test of capacity for the various social classes that aspired to lead the anti-imperialist national movement. It was on this test that there came to grief both the comprador, latifundia-owning bourgeois generation and then the petty-bourgeoisie.

The Arab "renaissance" of the nineteenth century (the Nahda) was centered mainly in Egypt and Syria. In Egypt there had already been in the eighteenth century, with Ali Bey, a first attempt at modernizing the Egyptian state, something that required its emancipation from the Ottoman yoke. The circumstances following the adventure of Bonaparte's armies led to a second attempt being made, by Mehemet Ali Pasha. The Egyptian ruling class — of foreign origin (Turkish, Albanian, Circassian) — was the Pasha's military bureaucracy, which levied tribute from the peasantry, made up of families of small holders. Their surplus was used by the Egyptian state to finance modernization in the form of irrigation works and the establishment of a national army and of industry. The Anglo-Turkish alliance in 1840 dealt a blow to this attempt at modernization. Europe, hastening to the rescue of the Ottoman Sultan, whose armies had been beaten by the Egyptian Pasha's forces, compelled Mehemet Ali to submit to the Capitulations, thus putting an end to the effort to develop industry. The Pasha's successors, from 1848 to 1882, gave up this independent policy, in the hope (in the case of the Khedive Ismail) of Europeanizing and modernizing Egypt with the aid of European capital, integrating the country into the world market (by developing the growing of cotton), and appealing to the financial houses of Europe to find the capital for this outward-oriented development. This was the setting in which the ruling class of Egypt was to undergo a change of structure, taking possession of the land, with the help of the state, and transforming themselves from a mandarin-type bureaucracy into a class of latifundia-owners. This did not mean "feudalists," as has often been said, but agrarian capitalists, whose prosperity depended on the world market. Egypt having thus been made into a cotton plantation for Lancashire, when the British threat to Egypt's independence materialized, the Egyptian ruling class quickly agreed to submit, on being guaranteed the maintenance of its privileges. It was well repaid by the British and became the biggest beneficiary of the opening up of the Nile valley.

The urban Third Estate, made up of clerks and craftsmen, vestiges of the mercantile world of former times, with their rural equivalent, the village notables, reacted in a different way. As the heirs of the traditional culture they felt the danger of colonialism as the destroyer of the values of Arab and Egyptian civilization. They also experienced very soon the harmful effects of competition by imported goods. Rejecting European domination for these reasons, disappointed in the Khedive and the Turco-Circassian aristocracy, they were brought to rethink seriously the problem of national survival. It was this Third Estate that began the "renaissance" in Egypt from 1860 onward. This attempt nevertheless ended in defeat, despite some successes: revival of the language, remarkable adaptation of the language to the needs of cultural and technical renewal, awakening of the critical spirit. Hassan Riad remarks: "In face of the (imperialist) danger . . . the aristocrats had thrown over all the country's traditions, through selfish interest and also owing to their Turkish origin, without, however, really assimilating European culture. The Third Estate clung desperately to tradition in order to safeguard their personality. At one and the same time the power of the foreigners threatened them, fascinated them, and led them to examine their country's traditions with a critical eye. In the brief interval that history allowed them between the moment when the danger from without was felt (1840) and the moment when it materialized in the occupation of Egypt (1882), the thinkers of the Third Estate failed to overcome this contradiction between their will to defend their personality and their will to catch up on their backwardness. . . . Eventually they found themselves in a dead end, the empty assertion of their personality which was gradually to lead to that neurotic loyalty to tradition which paralyzes movement."

Syria provided the second pole of this nineteenth-century Arab revival. Syria's traditional orientation toward the Mediterranean explains the country's early awareness of the imperialist danger. Held fast in the Ottoman grip, however, the economy of the countries of the Mashraq was stagnant in those days: away from the trade routes of former times and also from the new colonial development to which Egypt was exposed, the Syrian towns were without their brilliant elites of an earlier age. As in Egypt, therefore, the "renaissance" was fostered by the semipopular elements of the Third Estate (craftsmen, clerks, religious leaders).

The Egypto-Syrian Nahda thus failed to formulate a coherent and effective program for the social changes that were needed in order to resist imperialist aggression. It was nonetheless a decisive moment in the shaping of modern Arab feeling, for it renewed the circulation of ideas between the "provinces" of the Arab world, and it remodeled the language on a uniform basis, while adapting it to the common requirements of modernization — thus, in short, giving new life to the principal instrument of Arab unity.

Mehemet Ali's attempt in Egypt was, with that of Japan, the only attempt at modernization made in the nineteenth century outside the European world. The Pasha's failure was due to two sets of causes: the proximity of Europe, which did not leave him time to reform the state and industrialize the country, and the fact that the local social conditions were insufficiently mature. The social formations of the Arab world were not preparing the birth of capitalism from within. Hence the Pasha's attempt to institute a state mercantilism to remedy the nonexistence of an indigenous bourgeoisie rested on a fragile social basis. Japan, on the other hand, which did not suffer from Egypt's strategic geographical position, was not the object of early European covetousness. Moreover, Japan's feudal social formation predisposed it to the birth of an indigenous capitalism.

After the defeat of the Nahda came a dark period marked by

self-absorption on the part of each separate province that lasted, broadly speaking, until the Second World War. This was the *belle époque* of triumphant imperialism. It was also that of the failure of the bourgeois nationalist movement that had withdrawn into the separate provinces of the Arab world. Finally, this was the period when the Zionists installed themselves in Palestine. The political history of Egypt in this period was analyzed for the first time in Hassan Riad's book, *L'Egypte nassérienne*. I am here following the essential thread of his account.

The military defeat suffered by Arabi in 1882 marked the end of the hopes that had been placed in the Nahda. The Third Estate was swept away, first politically and then economically. "The generation of petty officials, narrow-minded and submissive, who were their successors quickly accepted foreign rule and took refuge in rejection of the values of the modern world, in an opposition that was reactionary and that involved no risks." At the same time, in the setting of colonial development, an Egyptian bourgeoisie was formed, at first merely agrarian but later partly agrarian and partly mercantile, and even industrial. The highly concentrated aristocracy of large-scale capitalist landowners ventured after 1919 into commercial and industrial undertakings, with the formation of the Misr group in association with foreign capital, that of the Levantine bourgeoisie of Egypt (Greeks, Europeanized Jews, Europeanized Eastern Christians), and also British, French, and Belgian big capital. This class became the ruling class of Egypt, the transmission belt for imperialist domination right down to 1952. As Riad writes: "After the miscarriage of nineteenth-century renaissance, Egyptian society stopped thinking. The aristocracy, and the bourgeoisie that emerged from it, were thenceforth satisfied with a European veneer, and the petty-bourgeoisie with café chatter. There was practically no proletariat, and the deprived masses of the people, increasingly numerous, were dehumanized, reduced to the daily striving for the piastre that would enable them to go on living. . . . All the conditions were thus present in colonial Egypt for the forming, by reaction to them, so to speak, of an intelligentsia, that is, of a group of men in search of the truth beyond the limits of a crude society into which they could not integrate themselves, even materially, because of its inadequate development. . . . This is the setting in which we must see the first

Egyptian nationalist party, that of Mustafa Kamil and Mohammed Farid, the history of which extends from 1900 to the First World War. Established by men who belonged to the first generation of the intelligentsia . . . this first nationalist party cannot be regarded as the party of the Egyptian bourgeoisie: The Egyptian big bourgeoisie of that time was a bourgeoisified aristocracy reconciled to the foreign yoke. Nor was it the party of the rural bourgeoisie . . . which had its own organization, the Umma party, jealously conservative on ideological and social questions and a faithful supporter of the efficient British administration — which shows that already at that time the middle classes of the countryside felt solidarity with the aristocracy in face of the danger represented by the growing masses of landless peasants. . . . It was nevertheless a bourgeois party in the quite precise sense that its modern ideology was derived from the European bourgeois tradition. . . . Despite the wretched state of Egyptian society, the apathy of the impoverished masses, the instability of the petty-bourgeoisie, the reactionary attitude of the rural middle classes, and the open treason of the aristocracy and the bourgeoisie that had emerged from it, the nationalist party's call found many echoes. In critical moments the party became the nation, whose potentialities it symbolized. . . . But the history of the nationalist party was to be a brief one. . . . At the very moment when the entire nation rose up, in 1919, it vanished from the scene, yielding place to a party that represented more accurately the Egyptian society of that time: the Wafd."

This Wafd, whose history is the history of Egypt between 1919 and 1952, was not the party of the Egyptian bourgeoisie either. That bourgeoisie continued to be basically pro-king and pro-British. The inconsistency of the Wafd was to be on the scale of that of the petty-bourgeoisie: "This is why the Wafd showed itself in the end to be as conservative, where the main problems were concerned, as the parties of the monarchy, and why it never gave any thought, for example, to land reform. This is also why the British were never deceived by its nationalist demagogy. . . . The Wafd never contemplated for a moment Egypt's ceasing to be a client-state of Great Britain. . . . Doubtless, the British side in the negotiations showed cleverness in exploiting the existence of a monarchy ready to accept frankly the foreign presence in Egypt so as not to have to make more than the minimum of concessions to the Wafd, even purely formal ones. When, however, a serious danger threatened the entire edifice of British power, Britain quickly found a basis for compromise. This happened in 1936 and 1942, in face of the Fascist menace (the Anglo-Egyptian treaty of 1936 was to govern for twenty years the interests reserved by Britain in Egypt. The negotiating of it, which had dragged on since 1924, was suddenly speeded up by the threat to Egypt from Italy, which had installed itself the year before in Ethiopia). . . . The successive concessions made by Britain, along with the rapid development of light industry between 1920 and 1945 . . . facilitated compromise. . . . Thanks to this cohesion the system continued to function in spite of crises: for twenty-five years the alternation between Wafdist parliaments and royal dictatorships was adequate to ensure the survival of both the foreign interests and those of the aristocracy. . . . The breath-less pace of economic development — that is, ultimately, the gal-loping increase in the numbers of the deprived masses, which even-tually made up 40 percent of the urban and 80 percent of the rural population — with the impoverishment of the middle strata, on the one hand, and the appearance of communism on the political scene and the crisis of the colonial system in Asia, on the other, were responsible for the clashes of the second postwar period."

Throughout this long period of Egypt's provincial turning inward upon itself, during which imperialist domination was not fundamentally challenged but only criticized for the forms it took, and arrangements were being sought whereby it could be made "bearable," national feeling was strictly Egyptian. There was no attempt to set Egypt's anti-imperialist struggle in the wider context of the Arab world. True, the Palestinian revolt in 1936 called forth some echoes in Egypt, especially among the masses of the people, where there was a feeling that the region as a whole was oppressed by the same imperialism, with Zionism seen as the agent of this imperialism. However, this feeling remained diffused among the masses, who had no party or organization of their own through which to express themselves. The movements that found expression were those of the collaborating bourgeoisie and of the erratic and unstable petty-bourgeoisie. These, moreover, were no longer rooted in the history of Egypt, for they were products of colonialism. This rootlessness was clearly voiced by Taha Husayn when he declared that Egypt owes nothing to the East, being the child of Greece and of Europe. Hassan Riad spoke of "a superficial Westernism under which lies henceforth a real cultural vacuum. An easy position in which to give oneself satisfaction very cheaply: since we have never been 'Orientals' we have always been the equals of the 'Westerners,' from whom we have nothing to learn."

The same provincialism was characteristic of the political life of the Mashraq during this period. Here, however, because the imperialists divided the region artificially between the British and French Mandates, and because the installation of the Zionists offered a direct threat to the life of the region, the national reaction was more unitary and Arab in character.

Ottoman rule over the Fertile Crescent preserved the unity of this region until 1919. True, this rule did not form an effective safeguard against imperialist penetration, for the entire Ottoman Empire had been in a condition of underdevelopment and indirect colonial subjection ever since the Capitulations had given unequal privileges to European capital and European goods. The destruction of maritime Syria, which occurred as far back as the Crusades, had given the Europeans (especially the Italian cities) pre-eminence in the seaborne trade of the Mediterranean area. The opening up of the routes across the Atlantic and around the Cape had deprived the Fertile Crescent of most of its commercial role. From the nineteenth century onward the development of European capitalism hastened the process of degradation of the Arab East. The ruin of the crafts in Syria dates from the first half of the nineteenth century and resulted from the influx of British cotton goods. Later, the penetration of European finance capital was to take place by way of the Ottoman state debt. This debt absorbed, in 1874, four-fifths of the Ottoman government revenues. In order to meet these exactions, Istanbul intensified its exaction of tribute from the subject territories: at the end of the nineteenth century over 80 percent of the revenue collected in the vilayets of Syria and Mesopotamia was paid to the central government as tribute, less than 20 percent being thus devoted to the expenses of the local administration. To this was added direct penetration by European capital. Before 1919, however, this did not amount to much: a few industrial enterprises in Syria, the management of the railways and the ports, and the establishment of some public services (electricity, water supply). The big schemes were still in the planning stage (the Berlin-Baghdad railway, the exploitation of oil in the Mosul region) when the First World War broke out.

The integration of the Fertile Crescent into the world capitalist system thus did not begin on a large scale until the period of the Mandates. In Syria this integration remained very slight until the second postwar period, for the possibilities of developing commercial agriculture are limited by the poor agricultural resources of this region. Nevertheless, in the 1950s the Jezirah (the semiarid steppe situated between the Tigris and the Euphrates, which until then had been occupied only by nomad herdsmen) began to be opened up. This piece of colonial development was carried out by the Syrian town bourgeoisie, using modern capitalist methods: tractors, a small wage-earning labor force, large tracts of land leased from the state or from the nomad chieftains. It was to make possible a big growth in agricultural exports: cotton, wheat, and barley. In the traditionally rural West, progress was hindered by the social organization of the peasantry. For Syria, having lost its former trading role, had undergone a real process of social regression. The country's population had fallen from about 5 million in the best periods of the past (Antiquity and the Abbasid caliphate) to less than 1.5 million on the eve of the First World War. This population was still highly urban in character: in 1913 the towns held a third of the country's inhabitants, the nomads accounted for a quarter, and the agricultural districts had hardly 40 percent. The trading role of the Syrian towns was thenceforth trivial, since they served only the Mesopotamian and Arabian hinterland. The ruining of the crafts through competition by European imports aggravated the crisis. It was then that, in order to survive, the urban ruling classes of Syria "feudalized" themselves, that is, endeavored to obtain from the peasants of western Syria the surplus that they could no longer obtain from trade. The formation of the latifundia goes back to the nineteenth century, when the mercantile bourgeoisie, which had lost its function, began to turn toward the countryside. Between the two world wars, within the framework of the Mandate, this feudalization process speeded up, thanks to the

"French peace," which made it possible to subject the peasants who until then had been able to resist oppression. Since the path of industrialization was practically closed by the domination of French capital, the urban bourgeoisie had no other outlet. After Syria became independent, it got its second wind by establishing light industries (textiles, food processing) and by the agricultural conquest of the Jezirah: "The growth of agriculture was a victory for the townsmen," as Rizkalla Hilan says. Only after 1955 did this process draw to a close, losing momentum and compelling Syria to take a new road, that of state capitalism.

We see very well, in the case of Syria, how, between 1920 and 1955, integration into the world capitalist system enabled the local bourgeoisie to develop, and how this integration shaped a national bourgeoisie of the client-dependent type. It is thus easier to understand why, with its bourgeoisie satisfied in this way, Syria, which had been the lively center of Arabism in 1919, could doze for thirty-five years in a condition of dull provincialism.

The same thing happened in Iraq. The British established themselves there in 1920, in a semidesert region even lacking any towns worthy of the name: there was nothing comparable to Syria, even in that country's decadent state. However, the natural potentialities of the country were great. The British set about reviving an agricultural life that had disappeared centuries before: the irrigation works undertaken in the period of the Mandate were to play a decisive part in forming a new agrarian bourgeoisie, owners of latifundia. The British distributed 90 percent of the land to a thousand sheikhs, the chieftains of seminomadic tribes. The oilfields developed by the Iraq Petroleum Company were to do the rest. This process of development created, out of an Iraq that had been nationalist, Pan-Arabist, and turbulent in 1920, an Iraq that remained until 1958 a loyal client-state of Great Britain.

The urban world of the Fertile Crescent, however wretched it had been at the end of the Ottoman period, had been resolutely nationalist and in favor of Arab unity. In face of the imperialist threat it had long been pro-Ottoman, its "nationalism" wavering between "Moslem nationalism" in an "Ottoman" or an "Arab" form. Disappointed by the inadequacy of the Ottoman reforms (especially the Tanzimat of 1839), and still further disappointed when the Young Turk reform movement firmly took the road, after 1908, of Turkish nationalism, with even an antireligious aspect, the Arab townspeople of the region turned toward Arab nationalism, and looked around for the external alliance that would enable them to free themselves from the Ottoman yoke. British diplomacy was able to make use of Arab nationalism and to cheat it. At the end of the First World War, the urban bourgeoisie had thought it astute to give themselves "kings," chosen among the "desert grandees," thus reviving the traditional alliance between the trading towns and the nomads. In fact, the "desert grandees," the Hashemite family, accepted the partition of the region between the British and the French and were rewarded by being made kinglets of the British Mandates: Faisal I was given Iraq, and his brother Abdullah got Transjordan.

The drift into provincialism in Iraq was facilitated by the potential wealth of the country and its development, as well as by the intelligent policy followed by the British. It is true that the political history of Iraq from 1920 to 1958 was highly unstable, but this was only at the level of changing alliances between government cliques, for down to 1958 the dual *status quo* — social (the domination of the new latifundia-owning class) and external (Iraq's position as a client-state) — was not questioned by any regime. During the 1920s the old Arab nationalism of the Ottoman period disappeared, as the new collaborating latifundia-owning bourgeoisie took shape. The new opposition that began to arise during the 1930s did not go beyond the intellectual grouping of the Ahali club. This club was not "the party of the bourgeoisie," any more than the Wafd was in Egypt, for in Iraq as in Egypt the bourgeoisie was collaborationist. The club was thus merely a rather isolated group of the "intelligentsia" type. But from this group there emerged the principal political forces of the future, which were to take over in 1958: from petty-bourgeois populism, ancestor of the Baath, to the more radical elements of Iraqi communism.

French imperialism had a much harder task in Syria than faced the British in Iraq. In Syria there was neither oil nor potentialities for agricultural development, making it possible to rally the bourgeoisie around the mandatory regime. The Syrian bourgeoisie was, moreover, much more lively at the end of the Ottoman period than that of Iraq, to such an extent that it set the tone of the region, giving Syria its "Levantine" character, open to influences from the Mediterranean and so from the West. Under these conditions French imperialism had nothing more to offer the bourgeoisie of its Syrian cities than the indifferent "outlet" provided by intensified exploitation of the peasants of the western parts of the country. And it tried to make use of religious differences among the people. But Syria felt even more keenly than Iraq about the establishment of the Zionists in Palestine, for Syria and Palestine had always formed a single region of the Arab East. The bourgeoisie of Jerusalem, Damascus, Haifa, and Beirut belonged to the same families. The region was partitioned artificially in 1919 between France and Britain, and its southern section, Palestine, turned over to the Zionists in accordance with the Balfour Declaration of 1917. The Syrian people felt this alienation of Arab territory almost as bitterly as the people of Palestine itself. The fall of France in 1940 created the conditions for eliminating French imperialism from this region. First Great Britain, from 1941 to 1949, and then the United States, with the series of three coups d'état in 1949, took over control, without changing the basic social alliance between the new bourgeoisie and imperialism.

From 1920 until 1948, then, imperialism was master of the entire region. In Egypt, as in Iraq and Syria, the national bourgeoisie, essentially agrarian and latifundia-owning, enriched and strengthened by following in the wake of the imperialists, accepted a narrow provincial existence in the service of its foreign lords. Imperialist domination through this class did not seem to be seriously threatened, since the "opposition" remained very weak, lacking any real class backing — an intelligentsia-type opposition torn between its dissatisfaction, especially on national grounds, and the attraction it felt for the proimperialist national bourgeoisie.

The betrayal by the Arab latifundia-owning bourgeoisie had as corollary the abandonment of the Palestinian people to the mercy of Zionist colonization. Thus the year 1948 marked, with the creation of the State of Israel, the end of an era and the beginning of a challenge to the imperialist system throughout the region.

The twenty years from 1947 to 1967 were marked by three fundamental features. First, the bankruptcy of the Arab national bourgeoisie and the rise of the nationalist petty-bourgeoisie. Second, the elimination of Britain from the region in favor of the two superpowers, the United States and the Soviet Union, and the working out of a *modus vivendi* dividing the region between these two. Third, the affirmation in deeds of the expansionist nature of Zionist colonialism.

The social equilibrium that had been the basis for the dreary provincialism of the 1920-1947 period had been conditioned by the class alliance between the predominant imperialism of the region, that of Britain — with France playing an accessory role — and the latifundia-owning bourgeoisie of the various "states." This system was capable of functioning so long as colonial development could guarantee some "crumbs" for the petty-bourgeoisie. However, the internal contradictions of the regime of imperialist domination set limits to this system. Hassan Riad has analyzed, so far as Egypt is concerned, the increasing economic and social contradictions that were expressed in the tremendous growth in the masses of proletarians and semiproletarians after the Second World War, the increasing misery of these masses, the rise in unemployment, the growth of the dissatisfied petty-bourgeoisie, and, in the political sphere, the emergence of new forces, mainly the communist movement and the Moslem Brotherhood. In Syria and Iraq, the same phenomena expressed the same fundamental contradictions, although the still recent character of colonial development put off the moment of collapse longer than in Egypt.

It was Egypt, therefore, that opened the new period, with the military coup d'état of 1952. Hassan Riad and Mahmoud Hussein have analyzed the stages of the shift from the former social relations, based on the alliance between British imperialism and the latifundia-owning and comprador bourgeoisie, to the new alliance between the Soviet Union and Egyptian state capitalism. This shift began with the land reform of 1952, which, abolishing the power of the latifundia-owners, gave the leading position in the countryside to the kulaks, and continued with the nationalizations of 1957 and then of 1961, which transferred to the state the ownership of undertakings belonging to Western capital and its partner, the Egyptian bourgeoisie. It had as corollary the gradual affirmation of a new ideology, that of Nasserism. The new Egyptian ruling class being formed, timid at first, continued the old bourgeoisie's policy of withdrawal into provincialism. It was the imperialist-Zionist aggression of 1956 which forced it to react and declare for a Pan-Arab policy. In the same timid way, the new regime for a long time sought an internal compromise with the national bourgeoisie, just as it attempted to preserve the traditional foreign alliances. The refusal of the IBRD to finance the Aswan High Dam, Egypt's retort by nationalizing the Suez Canal in July 1956, the tripartite Anglo-Franco-Israeli aggression in October, and the halting of the aggressors by the Americans and the Russians ensured the regime's drift toward state capitalism in 1957.

The Egyptian example was to exert a very great force of attraction elsewhere in the Arab East. In Syria, the fall of the Shishakli dictatorship in 1954 brought to power a heterogeneous coalition composed of the new petty-bourgeois social forces of the Baath Party and the forces of the traditional bourgeoisie of the National Bloc. The coup d'état of 1963 put the Syrian Baath in power, alone this time, and the movement toward a new state capitalism was resumed. Between the first plan of 1960-1965, still based on illusions about active participation by Syrian and Western private capital, and the plan of 1965-1970, in which nationalization measures and Soviet aid were given pride of place, we note the same evolution as in Egypt, between the period before 1957 and that of the 1960-1965 plan.

In Iraq the outcome of events was the same. The front formed in 1957 put an end to the power of the Hashemite dynasty and the latifundia-owning bourgeoisie by the coup d'état of July 1958. Between 1958 and 1963 the new regime wavered between a Nasser-type line and a "left-wing" line. This was because matters had not proceeded in Iraq as in Egypt or Syria. The Anglo-Hashemite domination had been complete and had gone on for a long time: also the masses intervened with great violence; the forces of popular resistance (the militia) settled accounts with their enemies, liquidating the latifundia-owning bourgeoisie. The continual hesitations of the Kassem government led to its fall in 1963, giving place to a right-wing Baathist regime.

Thus, both in 1948 and 1956 it was Israeli expansionism which unmasked the nature of the latifundia-owning comprador bourgeoisie of the Arab states, exposing its submission to imperialism and the demagogic nature of its intermittent and purely verbal "Pan-Arabism." It also forced each Arab state to emerge from its isolation. For Israel by its very nature threatens the existence of these states, additional regions of which it must necessarily annex in order to attain its objective of creating a state to include the majority of Jews of the world. Twice therefore, in 1948 and 1956, the Israeli aggression had as its consequence the revolt of the Arab masses against their governments and the transfer of local power from the hands of the latifundia-owning comprador bourgeoisie to the petty-bourgeoisie. The third Palestinian war, initiated by Israel in 1967, culminated in a new and profound crisis of the Arab world, demonstrating the failure of the nationalist petty-bourgeoisie, which did not manage to do any better than the latifundia-owning comprador bourgeoisie that it replaced.

For a long time the Maghreb was kept untouched by the currents affecting the Arab East, because of French colonial rule, its specific forms of oppression, and the local problems to which it gave rise, as also through its geographical remoteness and its specific features — particularly its Berber character. French colonization in Algeria, probably because it began long before the age of imperialism, and because of the late development of French capitalism, took the form, in part, of a settlement of "poor whites." This aim of agricultural colonization applied, too, in relation to Tunisia and Morocco. Only later on were more advanced forms of colonization developed in the Maghreb, and particularly in Morocco, characterized by investment in mining and even in industrial enterprises by French financial capital. Analyzing the differences in social structure brought about by colonialism in each of these three countries, I wrote, in *The Maghreb in the Modern World* (p. 104): "The Algerian landed aristocracy had long disappeared — indeed Abdel Kader (1830-1848) himself did more to destroy it than did colonization — while in Morocco this class was actually reinforced by colonization. The situation in Tunisia lay somewhere between these two extremes. Even though these structures are today gradually losing their importance in the face of the rapidly rising tide of the petty-bourgeoisie — a phenomenon common to all three countries — they did for a long time condition the nature of the national movement." The war of extermination undertaken during the conquest of Algeria, down to 1848, gave a popular peasant character to Algerian resistance, while it led to the destruction or large-scale emigration of the urban elites. The new urban strata created by colonialism had no ties either with the countryside or with the former urban ruling classes. That is why their "nationalism" was for so long of a superficial sort and their demands "assimilationist" in character, as Ferhat Abbas defined them even after the Second World War. Opposition from the "pieds noirs," the French settlers, made this prospect impossible, however. The resistance movement gradually shifted its basis to the popular elements in the towns and the Algerian workers in France. From this movement came the armed insurrection of 1954. And it was during the Algerian war (1954-1962) that Algerian nationalism was truly reborn. This long gap, from 1850 to 1945, between the early period of Algerian nationalism and its rebirth in our own time, is without parallel in Tunisia and Morocco, which were colonized later. That is why the modern national movement there did not have popular antecedents such as it had in Algeria. In Tunisia the national movement, which began in the thirties among bourgeois and petty-bourgeois circles, never cherished the "assimilationist" illusion. But it was always "bourgeois" and "moderate," as symbolized by the man with whose name it has been linked from the beginning: Bourguiba. When this movement was overwhelmed by the revolt of the peasant masses in 1954, the situation was brought under control thanks to the policy of concessions followed by France which culminated in Tunisian independence in 1956. In Morocco, brought under colonial rule still more recently, continuity is still more marked. That is why the modern urban nationalist movement had to line up behind the country's traditional elites, who remained in unchallenged control until independence was achieved.

On emerging from the long night of French colonialism, the Maghreb had difficulty in rediscovering its personality, isolated as it was from the Arab East. Its nationalism was then purely local, although the feeling of belonging to the Arab world was not absent. I wrote of the period after independence (p. 188): "The political development of the Maghreb states over the last decade (1960-1970) has to some extent demonstrated that fundamental social realities must eventually break through the veneer of apparent political reality, itself produced by the arbitrary consequences of colonialism. The national movement in Algeria, after reaching its peak of radicalism during the first years of the war, was finally captured by petty-bourgeois social elements, representatives of the class which . . . was to be the principal beneficiary of independence. In Tunisia . . . under the growing influence of the petty-bourgeoisie, whose rise paralleled that of its counterpart in Algeria, the Néo-Destour, gradually slid away from the free-enterprise capitalism toward 'nationalist socialism.' . . . Algeria evolved from left to right, and Tunisia in the opposite direction. In Morocco, the regime has not yet found a comfortable resting place; petty-bourgeois pressure almost succeeded for a time in 1960, but ultimately failed, its failure marking the return to power of the conservative traditional ruling class. Algeria and Tunisia have practically completed their current evolutionary cycle: from 'moderate' nationalism in Tunisia, and from revolutionary peasant radicalism in Algeria, to petty-bourgeois nationalist 'socialism.' Morocco has not yet completed this chapter of her history, but the political and social elements behind petty-bourgeois socialism are already massing their forces."

The petty-bourgeois nationalism on which imperialist domination rests in our time, through the perpetuation of underdevelopment, is the same everywhere, whatever its foreign-policy orientations may be. At the same time, because the Palestinian theater is far from the Maghreb and the threat from Israel is not felt there, awareness of the necessary unity of the anti-imperialist struggle is more confined than in the Arab East to circles lacking mass influence.

The African Peripheral Formations

Leaving aside the question of "race" — in Africa the people are neither more homogeneous nor less mixed, since prehistoric times, than are the other "races" — a common, or kindred, cultural background and a social organization that still presents many similarities from one area to another make Black Africa a single entity. This living entity, vast and rich, did not wait for colonial conquest either to borrow from or to give of itself to the other great regions of the Old World. But these exchanges did not break up the unity of Africa's personality; on the contrary, they helped to assert and enrich it. And the colonial conquest strengthened this still further.

Looked at from within, however, Black Africa seems extremely variegated. It is true that hardly a single one of the present states, which are the result of an artificial carve-up, constitutes the sole or even the main basis of this diversity. One would be wrong, though, to think that this pattern, recent as it is, has not already left its mark on Africa and is not likely to consolidate itself, at least as far as the near future is concerned. Of even greater significance are some 100 or 200 regions, varying in extent, which often overlap the frontiers of the present states. They do not derive their definition from their geographical position alone, but also and above all from the homogeneous nature of their social, cultural, economic, and even political conditions.

Over and above this unity and this diversity the continent is divisible into three macroregions, based upon the effects of the most recent period of Africa's history, the period of colonialism.

Traditional West Africa (Ghana, Nigeria, Sierra Leone, Gambia, Liberia, Guinea-Bissau, Togo, former French West Africa), Cameroon, Chad, and the Sudan together constitute "the Africa of the old colonial economy, the *économie de traite.*" This whole is divisible into three subregions: (1) the coastal zone, which is easily accessible from the outside world and which constitutes the rich area; (2) the hinterland, which mostly serves as a pool of labor for the coast and as a market for the industries established there; and (3) the Sudan. The traditional Congo River basin (Zaïre, Congo-Brazzaville, Gabon, and the Central African Republic) form a second macroregion: "the Africa of the concession-owning companies." The eastern and southern parts of the continent (Kenya, Uganda, Tanzania, Rwanda, Burundi, Zambia, Malawi, Angola, Mozambique, Zimbabwe, Botswana, Lesotho, Swaziland, and South Africa) constitute the third macroregion, "the Africa of the labor reserves."

Ethiopia, Somalia, Madagascar, Réunion, and Mauritius, like the Cape Verde islands on the opposite side of the continent, do not form part of any of these three macroregions, even though here and there in them are to be found some aspects of each — combined, however, with features of other systems that have played an important part in their development: the slaveowning mercantilist system of the Cape Verde islands, Réunion, and Mauritius, and the pseudo-feudal systems of Ethiopia and Madagascar.

The mercantilist period extended from the seventeenth century to the early 1800s, and was characterized by the slave trade. It was not only the coastal zone that was affected by this trade: through its effects a decline in productive forces occurred throughout the continent. There were two distinct slave-trading areas: the area dependent on the Atlantic trade (by far the most harmful, owing to the great numbers involved), which extended along the coast of the continent from St. Louis in Senegal to Quelimane in Mozambique; and the area dependent on the Eastern trade, operating from Egypt, the Red Sea, and Zanzibar toward the Sudan and East Africa. This type of mercantilist activity was carried on after 1800 in the Eastern area, because the Industrial Revolution that shook the foundations of society in Europe and North America did not reach the Turco-Arabian East.

The period between 1800 and 1880-1890 was characterized by an attempt — at least in certain regions within the influence of Atlantic mercantilism — to establish a new form of dependence between these regions and that part of the world where capitalism had assumed its fully developed industrial form. The zone of influence of Oriental mercantilism was not affected by this process.

The next period, that of colonization, completed the work of the previous period in West Africa, took over from Oriental mercantilism in East Africa, and developed with tenfold vigor the present forms of dependence.

The premercantilist African formations, the only ones that really deserve to be called traditional, were independent formations but were not isolated from the rest of the world; on the contrary, they maintained with the Arab formations of North Africa relationships of long-distance trade that fulfilled essential functions for both groups of formations.

The mercantilist period saw the emergence of the two poles of the capitalist mode of production: the creation of a proletariat and the accumulation of wealth in the form of money. During the Industrial Revolution, the two were brought together: money-wealth turned into capital, and the capitalist mode of production reached its completed stage. During this period of incubation covering three centuries, the American periphery of the Western European mercantilist center played a decisive role in the accumulation of money-wealth by the merchant bourgeoisie of the Atlantic countries. Black Africa played a no less important role as the "periphery of the periphery." Reduced to the function of supplying slave labor for the plantations of America, Africa lost its independence. It began to be shaped according to external requirements, namely, those of mercantilism.

The devastating effects that the mercantilist slave trade had in Africa are now better known, thanks to such works as those of Boubacar Barry on the Waalo (Wolof), from which the following main points emerge.

While the premercantilist trans-Sahara trade, in which the Waalo participated, had strengthened state centralization and stimulated progress in that independent Senegalese kingdom, the Atlantic trade that replaced it (after the French settled in 1659 at St. Louis) did not give rise to any productive forces but on the contrary caused these to regress and brought about disintegration of the society and state of the Waalo-waalo. This was why force had to be used by the French to cut off the former trans-Sahara links, to subjugate that region of Africa, and to alter the direction of its external relations so as to suit the requirements of the French trading post of St. Louis. African society had tried to react against this, and Islam had provided the framework for this resistance. The traders of St. Louis paid with weapons for the slaves they bought. This upset the former balance of power between (1) the king, who maintained a permanent army of captives under crown control; (2) the assembly of grandees that nominated him and possessed a system of appanages juxtaposed with and superimposed upon the collective clan-ownership (*lamanat*) of lands by the village communities; and (3) the village communities themselves, based on the *lamanat*. The customs dues paid to the king by the traders of St. Louis encouraged a permanent civil war that involved the leading notables, who engaged in raiding the communities in order to obtain slaves. The Moslem priests (*marabouts*) tried to organize a resistance movement of the communities; their aim was to stop the slave trade, i.e., the export of the labor force (but not to end internal slavery). Henceforth, Islam changed its character: from being a religion of a minority caste of traders it became a popular movement of resistance. The first war led by the *marabouts*, in 1673-1677, failed in its attempt to convert the people of the river region and to stop the slave trade. A century later, in 1776, the Toorodo revolution in the Toucouleur country overthrew the military aristocracy and ended the slave trade. But in the Waalo kingdom, being too near to St. Louis, the attempt made by the Prophet Diile in 1830 failed in the face of French military intervention in support of the king.

Secondly, study of the Waalo case is of special interest because the slave trade took place alongside the trade in gum. However, the latter did not have the same impact on African society. The export of goods (instead of labor) does not necessarily have a negative effect, but may, on the contrary, lead to progress. This type of export was not characteristic of the mercantilist period for Africa as a whole, which almost exclusively supplied slaves. But here, exceptionally, it played an important role, because the slaves, like the gold of Galam, mainly followed the Gambia route. Now, the gum was supplied by the Waalo, but also and especially by the Trarza Moors. The latter could export it either via St. Louis, to the French alone, or else via Portendic, which was open to competition by the English and the Dutch. To cut off the Portendic route, the French helped the Trarza to settle on the river, and to cross it during the "Gum War" in the first quarter of the eighteenth century. These circumstances thus introduced into the region a specific secondary contradiction between the Waalo and the Trarza. It is this contradiction that explains the failure of the "war of the *marabouts*" in the seventeenth century, led simultaneously by the *marabouts* who were hostile to the slave trade, and by the Moors, who were putting increasing pressure on the Waalo in order to monopolize the gum trade.

Along the coast, from St. Louis to Quelimane, the slave trade affected almost the whole of the continent, except the northeastern area (the Sudan, Ethiopia, Somalia, and East Africa). There were wars and anarchy everywhere, with the flight of peoples toward regions of refuge that were difficult to reach but also, for that same reason, very often poor — such as those of the paleonegritic peoples in the overpopulated mountains of West Africa. All this resulted in an alarming decrease in the population. The processes of integration of peoples were stopped, along with those of the construction of large entities that had begun in the premercantilist period. Instead there took place a fragmentation, isolation, and tangling-up of peoples, which is the root cause of one of the most serious handicaps of contemporary Africa.

It is impossible to conclude this chapter without touching on the question of the Oriental mercantilist period — if one can define in this way the relations of Egypt and Arabia with the Africa of the Nile and the East coast, along the Red Sea and the Indian Ocean as far as Mozambique. Neither the Ottoman Empire, nor Egypt under Mehemet Ali, and still less the southern Arabian sultanates, were mercantilist societies similar to those of Europe from the Renaissance to the Industrial Revolution. The disintegration of precapitalist relations — the necessary condition for the formation of a proletariat — was almost nonexistent. All that I wish to bring out here are the main trends in the evolution of the Sudan, which Mehemet Ali was to conquer in the second half of the nineteenth century. It was during the premercantilist period that two sultanates were established there, based on long-distance trade with Egypt and the East: the Sultanate of Darfur, still powerful at the time of the Egyptian conquest, and the Sultanate of Fung, between the two Niles, which was weakened as a result of the wars waged against it by Ethiopia. Mehemet Ali's aim was simple: to loot the Sudan of gold, slaves, and ivory, and to export these in order to intensify the industrialization of Egypt. This was a process of primitive accumulation similar to that of the European mercantilist period, and this is the justification for our speaking of Oriental mercantilism. The Industrial Revolution had, however, already occurred, and this was known to the Pasha; consequently the premercantilist period and that of the developed capitalist system were here mixed up together in an attempt to industrialize Egypt by raising funds through state taxation of the peasants, the monopoly of foreign trade, and, whenever possible, the looting of colonies.

Down to 1850 it was the Egyptian army itself that hunted for slaves and robbed the Sudan of local products. After that date, the soldiers handed over their task to Sudanese nomads, particularly the Baqqara, who sold the slaves they seized to Turkish, Coptic, Syrian, and European merchants established under the aegis of the Khedive. These operations soon resulted in changes in the social system of the nomads concerned; their clan organization was replaced by "nomad feudalism," a quasi-state organization founded on a territorial basis and dominated by warrior nobles. In the zones of secondary agriculture that had been conquered, the Egyptian army destroyed the old chiefdoms and subjected the villagers to a tax in kind (livestock and grain) for the purpose of feeding the officials and the army of the conquerors. Sheikhs were appointed by the Egyptians and made responsible for the collection of taxes; they rapidly became rich by this means. Moreover, the best lands were taken from the communities and given to Egyptian beys and to some of these Sudanese sheikhs. Peasants were taken from their villages and attached to these lands, half as slaves and half as serfs; the proceeds of the (largely commercial) farming of these lands went to swell the Egyptian treasury. Other peasants, hunted by the nomads and impoverished by the sheikhs, flocked into the market towns established by the army at crossroads and on the borders of the slave-raiding areas. A craft industry grew up, distinct from agriculture, while on the lands given to the beys and sheikhs Egyptian farming methods were introduced, with higher productivity. By 1870 it was feasible to replace the tax in kind with a money tax, because of the increased marketed surplus. The Sudan was becoming unified, Islamized, and Arabized.

The Mahdist revolt, 1881-1898, was a rebellion of those who were oppressed by this system: the people of the village communities, the slave-peasants of the estates, and the craftsmen, slaves, and beggars of the market towns. The successful revolt drove out the Egyptian army, the beys, and the sheikhs. But after the Mahdi's death, the state organized around the Caliph Abdullah changed in content. The military leaders of the revolt, who had sprung from the people, together with the Baqqara warrior chiefs who joined it, organized for their own advantage a state similar to that of the Egyptians; they seized the estates and levied taxes on their own account. It is true that the export of slaves was prohibited by the Mahdist state, but this traffic had largely lost its old importance, because the labor force was not used on the spot. The new state intended to continue exploiting the masses for its benefit and to that end destroyed the popular elements grouped around the Mahdi's family. They were imprisoned, and the most important of the people's military leaders were executed. Furthermore, the Mahdist state gradually resumed the export of slaves, but this time for its own benefit: the caliph organized slave raiding among the neighboring peoples of the Upper Nile, outside his own territory, in Darfur, and in Ethiopia; he kept a large number to strengthen his army and his economy, but authorized Sudanese merchants to export some of them. The caliph's army, which had lost the popular character that constituted its strength at the time of the revolt, was unable to withstand the British colonial expedition at the end of the century.

The slave trade organized from Zanzibar in the nineteenth century certainly falls within a mercantilist framework. For centuries, Arab trade on the coast, premercantilist in type, had brought these regions of Black Africa into contact with India, Indonesia, and even China. Here products were more important than slaves, as is shown by the very small black population of southern Arabia and the countries bordering the Indian Ocean. There was, though, one exception, at the time when the Abbasid caliphate was organizing sugar-cane plantations in Lower Iraq for which it imported black slaves. This experiment was quickly ended by the revolt of these slaves (the Qarmathian rebellion). In the nineteenth century the slave trade suddenly became much more important. There were in fact two new markets: the island of Réunion, which was supplied in this way — although the slaves were disguised as "contract labor" since the British had abolished the slave trade — and the island of Zanzibar itself. In 1840 the Sultan had transferred his capital there from Oman and gradually established a slave-plantation economy producing the cloves for which European trade now offered a market. Zanzibar, hitherto an entrepot, now became a plantation, on a model very similar to that of the West Indies, Réunion, or Mauritius — an Arab West Indies. Thus we once again see that integration into the world capitalist system was responsible for a devastating slave trade that had nothing in common with the long-distance trade of the precapitalist period.

The slave trade disappeared with the end of mercantilism. Capitalism at the center then took on its complete form; the function of mercantilism — the primitive accumulation of wealth — lost its importance, and capital's center of gravity shifted from the commercial sector to industry. The old periphery of the plantations of America — and that periphery's own periphery, the Africa of the slave trade — had now to give way to a new periphery whose function was to provide *products* that would help to reduce the value of both the constant and the variable capital used at the center: raw materials and agricultural produce. The condition ensuring that these products were supplied on terms advantageous to the center has been revealed by the theory of unequal exchange.

However, central capital had only very limited means of achieving that goal, until the end of the nineteenth century. It was only when monopolies appeared at the center that large-scale exports of capital became possible, and that central capital had the means of organizing directly in the periphery, by modern methods, the production that suited it, under conditions that were convenient to it. Until then the center could only rely on the ability of local social formations to adjust themselves to the system's new requirements.

The project of agricultural colonization in Waalo, turning it into a country of plantations for cotton, sugar cane, tobacco, etc., first formulated by the British governor of St. Louis, O'Hara, in the latter part of the eighteenth century, was put on the agenda again during the French Revolution and the First Empire as a consequence of the slave revolt in Santo Domingo. When Waalo was "bought" in 1819 by Governor Schmaltz, the experiment began. Barry analyzes the causes of its failure: the resistance of the village communities to their dispossession in favor of European planters, which had been agreed to by the aristocracy in return for extra "customs," was the main cause. Another cause was the lack of manpower, since there was no reason why the peasants should leave their communities and become proletarians on the plantations. The king provided some warriors who to all intents and purposes were slaves — long-term recruits. But the scheme could only use makeshift methods. It was not until the colonial conquest that a proletariat could be created: by taxation, by pure and simple dispossession, and by forced labor. The fact remains that the Waalo agricultural colonization scheme ended in failure in 1831. But the attempt had accentuated the people's hatred of their own aristocracy and had prepared the way for their conversion to Islam: outside the range of the official authority, Muslim communities organized themselves. When Faidherbe conquered the Waalo between 1855 and 1859, with the intention of restarting the agricultural colonization scheme, and at last procuring for French industry the cotton it needed, the vanquished aristocracy embraced Islam, which thus changed its content a second time: instead of being a resistance ideology, it was now to become a means of integrating the new periphery.

Other African societies made an effort to adjust themselves spontaneously to this process, even before they were conquered. Walter Rodney points out that, all along the Benin coast, the slaves who were still being raided for, but who could no longer be exported, were put to work inside the local society, to produce among other things the exports that Europe demanded. Catherine Coquery has analyzed in these terms the prodigious development of palm groves in Dahomey. Onwuka Dike has shown how another society, that of the Ibo, unable to make use of slaves, nevertheless adapted itself to the production of palm oil for export.

The collection of products for export and the conveyance of imports received in exchange strengthened the position of the Dioula Muslims, a minority inherited from remote premercantilist days. The "Dioula revolution" enabled them to establish a state under their own control. But this belated episode occurred when the colonial period had already begun. The state had scarcely been founded by Samory when it had to face the conquerors who destroyed it; they reorganized the channels of trade in the direction that suited them and reduced the Dioula to the subordinate functions of colonial trade.

The partitioning of the continent, which was completed by the end of the nineteenth century, multiplied the means available to the colonialists to attain the purpose of capital at the center, namely, to obtain cheap exports. To achieve this end, central capital — which had now reached the monopoly stage — could organize production directly on the spot, and there exploit both the cheap labor and the natural resources (by paying a price for the latter that did not enable alternative activities to replace them when they were exhausted). Moreover, through direct and brutal political domination, incidental expenses could be kept down by maintaining the local social classes as transmission belts and using direct political methods of coercion. Hence the late development in Africa of the peripheral model of industrialization by import-substitution. It was not until independence that the local strata who took over from the colonial administration constituted the first element of a domestic market for luxury goods.

However, although the target was the same everywhere, different variants of the system of colonial exploitation were developed. These did not depend, or only slightly, on the nationality of the colonizer. The classical contrast between French direct and British indirect rule is not very noticeable in Africa. It is true that a few differences are attributable to the nationality of the masters. British capital, being richer and more developed, and having, moreover, acquired the "best bits," carried out an earlier and more thorough development than French capital. Thus, the structures established in the Gold Coast from 1890 onward, and still characteristic of Ghana, did not appear in the Ivory Coast until after the abolition of forced labor. Belgium, a small power that had been forced to come to terms with the "great powers," did not possess the direct colonial monopolies that France used to advantage. Portugal similarly agreed to share colonies with big Anglo-American capital.

In the region I have called "Africa of the labor reserves," central capital needed to have a large proletariat immediately available. This was because there was great mineral wealth to be exploited (gold and diamonds in South Africa, and copper in Northern Rhodesia), and a settler agriculture that was exceptional in Tropical Africa (the old Boer colonies in South Africa, and the new British ones in Southern Rhodesia and, in the extreme north of the region, in Kenya, separated until 1919 from the southern part of the Africa of labor reserves by German Tanganyika). In order to obtain this proletariat quickly, the colonialists dispossessed the African rural communities by force and deliberately drove them back into confined, poor regions, with no means of modernizing and intensifying their farming. They thus compelled the traditional society to become a supplier of temporary or permanent migrants, so providing a cheap proletariat for the European mines and farms, and later for the manufacturing industries of South Africa, Rhodesia, and Kenya. Henceforth we can no longer speak of a traditional society in this part of the continent, since the society of the labor reserves had acquired a wholly new function. The African social formations of this region, distorted and impoverished, lost even the semblance of independence: the unhappy Africa of apartheid and Bantustans was born, and was to supply the greatest return to central capital.

Until recently there was no known large-scale mineral wealth in West Africa likely to attract foreign capital, nor was there any settler colonization. On the other hand, the slave trade was very active on this coast and caused the development of complex social structures that made possible the large-scale production of tropical agricultural products for export.

The net result of these methods, and the structures to which they gave rise, constituted the *économie de traite*. The principal methods were these: (1) the organization of a dominant trade monopoly, that of the colonial import-export houses and the pyramidal structuring of the trade network they dominated, in which the Lebanese occupied the intermediate positions while the former African traders were crushed and had to be content with subordinate positions; (2) the taxation of the peasants in money terms, which forced them to produce whatever the monopolists offered to buy; (3) political support to the social strata and classes that were allowed to appropriate *de facto* some of the tribal lands, and organization of internal migrations from regions that were deliberately left poor so as to be used as labor reserves for the plantation zones; (4) political alliance with social groups which, in the theocratic framework of the Muslim confraternities, were interested in putting to commercial use the tribute they levied from the peasants; and (5) when the foregoing procedures proved ineffective, recourse pure and simple to administrative coercion: forced labor.

Traditional society was distorted to the point of being unrecognizable; it lost its independence, and its main function was now to produce for the world market under conditions which, because they impoverished it, deprived this society of any prospect of radical modernization. This traditional society was not, therefore, in transition to modernity; as a dependent, peripheral society it was complete, and hence a dead end; its progress blocked. It consequently retained certain traditional appearances, which constituted its only means of survival. The *économie de traite* defined all the subordination-domination relationships between this pseudo-traditional society integrated into the world system, and the central capitalist economy that shaped and dominated it. The concept of the *économie de traite* has often been used as a mere description of the exchange of agricultural products for imported manufactured goods: actually, it describes analytically the exchange of agricultural commodities provided by a peripheral society, shaped in this way, for the products of a central capitalist industry, either imported or produced on the spot by European enterprises.

The results of this economy have varied in different regions. When, at the beginning of colonization, Lever Brothers asked the governor of the Gold Coast to grant concessions that would enable them to develop modern plantations, he refused because "this was not necessary." It would be enough, the governor explained, to help the "traditional" chiefs to appropriate the best lands so that these export products could be obtained without extra investment costs. The complete model of the *économie de traite* was achieved in the Gold Coast and German Togo by the end of the nineteenth century and was reproduced much later in French West Africa and then in French Equatorial Africa. This lateness, which reflects that of French capitalism, explains the attempts to form quasi-settler colonies even in not very favorable conditions (French planters in the Ivory Coast and Equatorial Africa), and the corresponding maintenance of forced labor right down to our own time, after the Second World War.

The *économie de traite* takes two main forms. Kulakization, i.e., the constitution of a class of native planters of rural origin; the quasi-exclusive appropriation of the soil by these planters and the employment of wage labor is the dominant form on the Gulf of Guinea, where conditions made possible the development of the *économie de traite*. But in the savannah country, extending from Senegal to the Sudan through northern Nigeria, the Moslem confraternities facilitated a different type of economy: the organization of export production (groundnuts and cotton) in the context of vast areas subject to a theocratic-political authority — that of the Murid confraternities of Senegal, the sultanates of Nigeria, the

Ansar and Ashiqqa in the Sudan — which kept the form of a tribute-paying social formation, but one that was integrated into the international system, since the surplus appropriated in the form of tribute exacted from the village communities was itself marketed. It was the Egyptian colonization of the Sudan that created the most advanced conditions for the development of this type of organization, which in that country tends to become a latifundium, pure and simple. The British merely reaped the fruits of this evolution. The new latifundia-owners who rallied after 1898 to the colonial administration cultivated cotton for the benefit of British industry, and powerful modern technical facilities were made available to them.

But the second mutation of Islam in West Africa, after the colonial conquest, opened the way to an evolution of the same kind, though slower and less overt. "Taken over" by the aristocracy and the colonizers, Islam became the ideology of those controlling the peasants in order to organize the export production desired by the colonizers. The Murid phenomenon in Senegal is the most striking example of this second mutation. Small matter that the initiators of the confraternity and some narrow-minded colonial administrators thought themselves hostile to each other. In fact, the confraternity was the most important vector of expansion of the groundnut economy, by getting the peasants to submit to the aim of that economy: to produce a great deal and to accept a very low and stagnant reward for this work, despite progress in productivity.

To organize the *économie de traite* it was necessary to destroy the precolonial trade and to reshape the circuits in the direction required by the outward orientation of the economy. For before the conquest there had existed regional complementarities with an important natural basis (forest and savannah) and strengthened by the history of the relations between the different societies of West Africa. The internal trade in cola and salt, the exchanges between livestock breeders and farmers, the disposal of exported commodities and the dissemination of imported commodities, constituted a dense and integrated network, dominated by African merchants. The colonial trading houses had to capture all those flows and guide them all toward the coast, and for this reason colonialism destroyed the internal African trade and then reduced the African traders to the role of subordinate primary collectors, when it did not purely and simply do away with them altogether. The destruction of Samory's trade, like that of the trade of the half-breeds of St. Louis, Goree, and Freetown, the destruction of the Hausa and Ashanti trade of Salaga and that of the Ibo of the Niger delta bear witness to this devastating socioeconomic effect of the *économie de traite*.

At regional level, then, the colonial economy necessarily engendered a polarization of dependent peripheral development. The wealth of the coast had as a necessary corollary the impoverishment of the hinterland. Africa, whose geography and history dictated a continental development — organized around the major river arteries of the interior, facilitating transport, irrigation, and the supply of power — was doomed to be developed only in its narrow coastal zone. The exclusive allocation of resources to the latter zone — (a planned policy of the *économie de traite*) — accentuated the regional imbalance. The massive emigration from the hinterland to the coast is part of the logic of the system: it makes cheap labor available to capital where capital requires it, and it is only the ideology of "universal harmonies" that sees in these migrations anything but movements that impoverish the zones of origin of the migrants. The *économie de traite* culminated, moreover, in balkanization, since the "gaining" microregions had no interest in sharing with their reserves in the hinterland the crumbs of the colonial cake that they secured for themselves.

It was not possible to establish this system in the third macroregion of the continent, Central Africa. Here the ecological conditions had protected the peoples, who had taken refuge in areas difficult to penetrate from the coast, from the ravages of the slave trade. The low population density and the absence of adequate hierarchical structures made the *économie de traite* model impossible. Discouraged, the colonizers abandoned the country to adventurers who were willing to try "to get something out of it" without big resources, since the undertaking did not attract capital. The concessionary companies that, from 1890 to 1930, ravaged French Equatorial Africa with no result other than a paltry profit, and King Leopold's policy in the Congo, have been duly denounced. In the Belgian Congo, where the alternative of industrial plantations established directly by big capital was adopted (Lever Brothers, who were refused permission to establish themselves in the Gold Coast, were welcomed by the Belgians), it was only after the First World War that, as an extension of these plantation zones controlled by foreign capital, a small-scale *économie de traite* emerged. As to French Equatorial Africa, it was not until 1950 that the first symptoms of the *économie de traite* appeared. But the imprint left by the concessionary-company period, still omnipresent, justified the title of "Africa of the concessionary companies" that we give to this region.

In all three cases the colonial system organized society so as to produce, under the best possible conditions from the point of view of the metropolitan country, export commodities that provided only a very low and stagnant reward of labor. Once this aim was achieved, there were no longer any traditional societies in contemporary Africa, but only dependent peripheral societies.

The original history of Ethiopia must be seen as a contrast to the wretched dependent societies established by colonialism in Africa. The current prejudice is to consider colonialism as a stage in modernization. In fact Ethiopia was fortunate not to have been colonized. The ancient state of Axum belonged to that group of trading centers of Antiquity in which the brilliant civilization of the court derived its resources from the taxation of long-distance trade. Abyssinia, isolated by the Moslem establishments along the coast, became feudalized from the ninth century onward: the scattered ruling class tried to survive by taxing its peasantry. In the ninth century the Negus Menelik, aware of the imperialist danger, took the initiative and conquered the southern half of present-day Ethiopia (including the Galla and Sidamo countries) before the arrival of the Europeans. He subsequently modernized his state, without alienating it, by the methods of "enlightened despotism." The exploitation of his own Abyssinian peasantry and that of the conquered regions enabled him to mobilize a large surplus for the state and thus to strengthen the administrative apparatus. Preserving control of the system, the empire obtained from abroad the means necessary to achieve its goal, particularly firearms. The historic significance of this effort can be judged if it is recalled that the Galla and Sidamo peasants were at that time ignorant of the use of the plough and, like those of the other regions of Black Africa, cultivated by means of the hoe. The Ethiopian administration and feudal lords introduced the use of the plough between 1880 and 1935. The British, French, and Belgian colonial administrations had aimed at the same goal and failed. There can be no doubt that, between 1880 and 1935, the modernization of Ethiopian agriculture, and the rates of growth of its productivity, were far more marked than elsewhere in Africa. Indeed, it was this progress that gave rise to a population growth that was also higher than in colonial Africa. Ethiopia, isolated from the world market, did not suffer from the competition of imported products. The surplus, necessarily formed of foodstuffs, was destined for the home market; hence the development of this period was autocentric. The result was a more cohesive national state, with less alienated elites, despite the persistence of problems of regionalism that showed there were limits to the methods of enlightened despotism, which were inadequate to assimilate the variegated peasant masses and fuse them into a single nation. It was only after the Italian conquest of 1935 and, above all, after the Second World War that Ethiopia really entered the world system. It is also since then that the phenomena of underdevelopment have begun to appear.

2. THE GENERAL CHARACTERISTICS OF PERIPHERAL FORMATIONS

Despite their different origins, the peripheral formations tend to converge toward a pattern that is essentially the same. This phenomenon reflects, on the world scale, the increasing power of capitalism to unify. All peripheral formations have four main characteristics in common: (1) the predominance of agrarian capitalism in the national sector; (2) the creation of a local, mainly merchant, bourgeoisie in the wake of dominant foreign capital; (3) a tendency toward a peculiar bureaucratic development, specific to the contemporary periphery; and (4) the incomplete, specific character of the phenomena of proletarianization.

The Predominance of Agrarian Capitalism

The predominance of agrarian capitalism is the most striking and obvious of the classical features of the underdeveloped societies. The classical image of the dominant class in the underdeveloped world is that of the large landowner — not the feudalist, but the planter, producing for the export market. Its most characteristic form is the Latin American latifundia-owner. Cuba was the most complete example, because the system was established there from the beginning to serve this function, without the existence of any process of internal change or transformation of precapitalist formations. The fact that this latifundiary form used servile labor (slaves and peons) for a long time before evolving toward the systematic use of wage labor shows that, when capital finds that it lacks labor, it does not hesitate to use political means to obtain what it needs.

When the formation of the capitalist latifundium proceeds by way of transformation of precapitalist formations, it encounters resistance from internal social forces, which are all the livelier because the village community forms the basis of these precapitalist formations. In some cases when these forces are completely overcome, the finished pattern is realized, as in Egypt. Often, however, evolution proves unable to reach this point. When this is the case, the result is the constitution of agrarian capitalist formations that are integrated into the world market because of their primary function but are none the less clothed in feudal-type forms. The systems of groundnut cultivation in the Murid region of Senegal and the sultanates of northern Nigeria, and the economic system of the Sudan, exemplify this process of incomplete transformation. The new ruling classes take directly for themselves only a part, often a small part, of the land. They continue to benefit from the tribute-paying system on which their position was originally based. In the above-mentioned African countries this tribute is levied in the name of new religious functions, since the peasant society is integrated into a system of confraternities. Isolated from the world market, the local ruling class can only levy a tribute in the form of subsistence goods, to provide for its own consumption and that of its hangers-on and its machinery of government. Once integrated into the market system, it can sell the tribute products and adopt European patterns of consumption. But it can obtain increasing tribute only if the peasants agree as a result of a new force; in this case, religion.

Paradoxically, where the road is closed because the original precapitalist formations are not sufficiently well-developed, it is the most dynamic and modern form of agrarian capitalism that clears a way for itself. This is the case with the formations in the native plantation zones of Black Africa where the rich peasant has at once become the central figure of the new formations, whereas elsewhere agrarian reforms have not been able to favor kulakization until the internal contradictions of a latifundiary system integrated into the world market have developed (e.g., in Egypt, India, Mexico). Even where the conditions for transforming precapitalist formations integrated into the world market into formations of kulak-type agrarian capitalism are not favorable, it is in this direction that the tendency runs. We then see meager forms of sporadic agrarian microcapitalism, as in the savannah country of Niger. The concentration of modern means of production (animal-drawn equipment) through cooperatives, and the hiring out of these means, which is often found in Africa, reflects the power of this tendency toward capitalism.

In the East and in Latin America the new dependent national bourgeoisie generally grew out of the classes of large landowners and higher civil servants, and in some cases also out of the merchant class. The large landowners, often merging with the political ruling groups, by adapting to the requirements of export agriculture, grew stronger and changed into bourgeois-type land-owners. This large land-holding class was missing in Black Africa. Export agriculture was often carried on in large European plantations, as in the Belgian Congo and French Equatorial Africa. In other regions the *économie de traite* resulted from the work of millions of small peasants gathered in village communities. The survival of these community relations slowed down the process of differentiation that goes with the commercialization of agriculture. Nevertheless, under certain conditions, a rural bourgeoisie could most easily be formed within this type of small peasant economy.

For this to happen, four conditions had to be present. The first of these conditions seems to be the existence of a traditional society that is sufficiently hierarchical, so that certain strata of the traditional chiefdom have enough social authority to be able to appropriate large tracts of tribal land for themselves. This is how the traditional chiefdoms in Ghana, southern Nigeria, the Ivory Coast, Uganda, and the Kilimanjaro region were able to set up a plantation economy for their own benefit; anything of this kind was practically nonexistent among the Bantu peoples, who did not have such a hierarchy. It should be noted, however, that those (semifeudal) hierarchies that were too pronounced and well-developed, as in the Islamic savannah regions, did not foster the development of a rural bourgeoisie.

The second condition is the existence of an average population density of between ten and thirty persons per square kilometer. If the density is less, exclusive appropriation of the land becomes ineffective and the potential supply of wage labor inadequate. The mechanics of proletarianization are much easier when labor can be enrolled from outside the local ethnic group, as happened with the Volta people in the Ivory Coast. During a second phase, the junior members and dependents of original planter families may in turn join the proletariat. If the population densities are too high, as in Rwanda and on the Bamileke Plateau in Cameroon, the tribal chiefs have difficulty in appropriating sufficient lands.

The third condition is the existence of rich crops, so that there is adequate surplus produced per worker and per hectare from the earliest stage of development, when mechanization is very slight and therefore the productivity of agriculture, which is still largely extensive, is only mediocre. This is why it was not possible to do with cotton in Uganda, groundnuts in the Serer region, or in general other food crops that are too poor, what could be done with coffee and cocoa in other places.

The fourth and last condition is that the political authority does not oppose this type of spontaneous development. Facilities offered for private appropriation of land, freedom of labor, individual agricultural credit have everywhere played an important role in the formation of this rural bourgeoisie. The role played by the abolition of forced labor in the French colonies in 1950 was characteristic in this connection. The typical bourgeois demand for freedom of labor made it possible for the planters in the Ivory Coast to use for their own benefit a flow of immigrants whose numbers were incomparably greater than those provided by forced labor — which, moreover, had only been assigned to the *French* planters. It also became possible to organize a large-scale political battle in the countryside by obtaining support for the planters from the peasants who had been the victims of forced labor. On the other hand, the paternalism of the Belgian *paysannats* unquestionably played a negative role and held back trends toward bourgeois development in certain regions such as Lower Congo. Only after this policy had been abandoned, with the coming of independence, could a bourgeois development of this sort make headway there, accelerated by the possibility of using foreign labor, thanks to the refugees from Angola. The policies of apartheid and "defense of African traditions" practiced in South Africa and in Rhodesia also obstruct the progress of a rural bourgeoisie.

Does the same apply to policies of "rural guidance," "rural action," and "cooperative" development? These policies are implemented according to the same rather naïve, paternalistic formulas everywhere, reflecting the utopian wish to see progress in the countryside take place everywhere at the same sustained pace. They have not prevented the development of a plantation system in places where this was possible, nor have they brought about appreciable qualitative changes elsewhere.

There are still enormous areas that are not affected by the movement because the prevailing conditions do not allow of change; the part of Africa "that has not taken off" and that "cannot take off," as Albert Meister puts it. This is also "problem-free" rural Africa, in so far as it can absorb population growth by merely extending the traditional subsistence economy without changing its structures. The incorporation of this Africa into the colonial world gave rise to a very limited development of export crops, often imposed by the government in order to ensure the payment of taxes. In some cases, when the terms of trade between these export products and the manufactured products that could be obtained in exchange for them deteriorated, or simply when the power of the government imposing them grew weaker, these crops were replaced by subsistence crops. The development of a parasitic urban economy and resultant inflation often underlie the deterioration in the terms of trade: e.g., the decline of the cotton economy in Zaïre, which is the most spectacular example of this process. Similar phenomena can be found in Mali, Guinea, Chad, the Central African Republic, Senegal, etc.

The predominance of agrarian capitalism brings about agrarian crisis, which is also a general phenomenon in the Third World. Since the natural population growth cannot find a normal outlet in industrialization, pressure on the land increases. Also, agrarian capitalist forms result in the eviction of overabundant farm labor from the production circuits. In the precapitalist systems, however large the theoretical surplus of labor, all the people had the right of access to the land. As capitalist forms develop, this right is lost. The consequences of this process are an increase in the proportion of landless peasants and the elimination of a growing fraction of these peasants from the production circuit. At the same time the mechanisms of unequal exchange cause the rural population to grow poorer in spite of improvement in the productivity of their labor. These are the profound reasons for the exodus from the rural areas, and the increasing speed of this exodus, despite the lack of sufficient jobs in the towns.

The Limits Imposed by Foreign Capital

The predominance of the commercial capitalism that accompanies export agriculture is the second aspect of the problem. The comprador trade that arises assumes mainly two forms. This function can be carried out by a new urban bourgeoisie originating in the landed oligarchy, which was generally the case in Latin America and in many countries of the East. But it can also be carried out directly by colonial capital, as happened in Black Africa. When this has occurred, the room left for the formation of a local merchant bourgeoisie is extremely limited.

In the Eastern world the urban bourgeoisie generally appeared much earlier than the rural bourgeoisie, whose development was obstructed by the semifeudal relations existing in the rural areas. On the other hand, the fact that the urban civilization was very old made it easy for the old-type merchants to change into that modern type of bourgeoisie that the Chinese Marxists have dubbed "comprador" — middlemen between the dominant capitalist world and the rural hinterland. More often than not, this bourgeoisie of traders, together with the large landowners and the senior levels of administration, cooperated with foreign capital in setting up industries. The main nucleus of the national bourgeoisie came from these higher strata of society and not from the rural bourgeoisie or the Third Estate. As for the various strata of the Third Estate, especially the craftsmen, competition from foreign and local industry either proletarianized them or plunged them into irreversible regression. The large-scale underemployment in the major cities of the East is due mainly to this phenomenon.

This model for the constitution of a national bourgeoisie is different both from the European model and from that of contemporary Black Africa. In Europe the bourgeois classes of the *Ancien Régime* did not often play the chief part in the formation of the new industrial bourgeoisie. They frequently became feudalized through the purchase of lands, while the new rural bourgeoisie and the craftsmen provided most of the entrepreneurial elite of the nineteenth century. In the East the weakness of the rural bourgeoisie and the inability of the craftsmen to progress because of international competition caused the national bourgeoisie to be highly concentrated from the very beginning. The concentration of landownership, of which India and Egypt provide the best examples, and the constant transfer of urban fortunes to the countryside for the purchase of land, enhanced the concentration of wealth and the merging of the large landowners with the new urban bourgeoisie.

In Black Africa, where urbanization developed only in the colonial period and large landownership hardly exists, the constitution of an urban bourgeoisie was long delayed. The traditional merchants had little ability to modernize their methods and enter into the modern trade circuits, for lack of financial resources. Their development remained limited, and their field of operation often restricted to traditional trade (e.g., cola, dried fish). Some of their activities, such as trade in salt and metals, even disappeared altogether. Certain sectors became quite profitable, however, as the volume of trade increased. This happened with the cattle trade in the Niger Bend, Nigeria, and the Sudan, and with the dried fish trade in

Mali, Chad, and the Gulf of Benin. Some of these traders ventured into trade in modern items such as cloth and hardware but generally met with very limited success. The spirit of enterprise, however, was not lacking, as was evidenced by the migration of the Sarakole and Hausa to the far-off Congo, attracted by the diamond traffic. But numbers remained small, financial resources poor, and technical knowledge scanty.

For several centuries before the colonial conquest trade was carried on in coastal establishments where a merchant bourgeoisie, European in origin on the west coast and Arab in origin on the east coast, quickly became a community of mixed blood. This might have been the starting point for a national bourgeoisie of traders. Actually, although these traders followed the colonial conquest, they did not set themselves up in the new inland towns in the heart of the regions where agriculture was becoming commercial. Their development, which had begun too late, was suddenly halted by the victorious competition of the big monopolies of colonial trade at the beginning of the twentieth century. This was the cause of the bankruptcy of the merchants of St. Louis and Goree at the end of the nineteenth century, ruined by competition from firms based in Bordeaux and Marseilles. Their children all became civil servants.

The development of commercial relations in the countryside was also bound to give rise to a bourgeoisie of small merchants. Here, again, however, the power of the big commercial monopolies barred their advance beyond the level of retail trade, and wholesale trade in small quantities, to that of large-scale wholesale and import-export trade. The one field left to the local merchant bourgeoisie was trade in local food products, which to this day has remained very fragmented, and is often reserved for the women. In certain places there seem, nevertheless, to be some tendencies toward concentration.

All these strata that might have become bourgeois suffered from the absence of a rich landowning aristocracy in association with whom they might have been able to accelerate the rate of their accumulation. The fact that the African markets were very small also played a negative role. The needs of commerce were met by a very small number of agencies of the big firms located in the ports of call, and by petty immigrant traders (Greek, Lebanese, and

Indian). Only exceptional recent circumstances — when European business withdrew after independence, or when the state intervened actively on behalf of national traders — have enabled the latter to enter the worlds of large-scale wholesale and import-export business.

In general, control by foreign capital over national enterprises is more effective or less depending on whether or not these enterprises form part of trade circuits including external exchanges and, consequently, dominated by foreign capital. In Senegal, for instance, the margin from which accumulation for the benefit of the local bourgeoisie can be taken is completely determined by the hierarchical relations between the bourgeoisie at the center and the bourgeoisie at the periphery. Left to spontaneous economic laws alone, this margin always tends to be reduced to zero, because changes in relative prices cause profits to be transferred from the national bourgeoisie to the bourgeoisie at the center. These mechanisms explain the downfall of the Senegalese bourgeoisie between 1900 and 1930, and the poor results obtained in the modern sectors that are grafted onto the world market, e.g., truckers.

Arrighi used the term "lumpen-bourgeoisie" for this micro-bourgeoisie formed in the wake of foreign capital, which can only develop within the strict bounds assigned to it by the policy of the dominant capital. This wretched form of national capitalism is often found in Africa, where the bourgeoisie is mainly recruited from ethnic groups that have traditionally been traders (Dioula, Hausa, Bamileke, Baluba, Bakongo, etc.), or in certain countries consists of "market-women." Although strictly limited by the degree of toleration shown by the dominant capital, this bourgeoisie can, amid the general poverty, constitute a local social force of decisive importance, as is the case in southern Nigeria, where this type of "African enterprise" is often cited as an example of the success of a policy of promoting indigenous private enterprise.

Where the main aspect of colonial economic dependence was to be found in the field of trade relations, and where the main form of foreign capital was old-style colonial merchant capital, even this limited type of national capitalism had no possibility of developing. In the French colonies, especially, the mediocre dynamism of the metropolitan capitalism itself gave disproportionate specific weight to this old-style merchant capital of Bordeaux and Marseilles, a survival from the olden days of monopolistic companies and the slave trade. In our time, however, since the center of gravity of the dominant foreign capital has shifted from the trading houses to the large interterritorial mining and industrial concerns, this sector has lost its importance and is having to be relinquished to local capital.

The change in relations as a result of political independence has also had a decisive influence. The national bourgeoisie has blossomed all the more remarkably because of the many links with the state apparatus — family ties, corruption, etc. — which have favored its constitution. In the most extreme cases of concentration of local power, it has been the higher strata of the bureaucracy — merged with the landed oligarchy, where this exists — that have, either openly or through intermediaries, formed the comprador neobourgeoisie. Thus they have not only been able to take over the functions of colonial trade but have even managed to secure association with foreign capital in the modern sectors such as mining, industry, and banking.

After the First World War the latifundia-owning and comprador oligarchy went over, in Latin America and the East, to sporadic industrialization through import-substitution. As a rule, it joined forces with the foreign capital that dominated this new light industry.

There are striking differences between the industrialization movement in Black Africa today and the pattern this has assumed in the East and Latin America. In the first place, the movement in Black Africa was launched much later. The *pacte colonial* and the smallness of the markets were certainly the reason for this lag. But even after independence, wherever industrialization took place, it was carried out almost exclusively by foreign capital. Modern industry, even light industry, requires too much capital for participation by local national capital to be possible, deprived as it is of the source of accumulation constituted in the East by the large landowners. The result is that there is practically no small-scale African industry. Those industries classified as such in statistical data are usually in fact urban craft enterprises (e.g., bakeries, carpenters' shops) with very slight chances of accumulating capital. European enterprise penetrates very far down the scale of business activity.

The African rural bourgeoisie cannot itself create a modern industry because it does not have the financial resources. Those of its members who have gone into state service invest the money of their relatives who have remained on the plantations, in sectors that do not need too large amounts of capital, such as road transport, taxis, services, building. Conversely, civil servants buy plantations or lands cultivated as market gardens; but the meagerness of private urban fortunes limits the size of such transfers.

Whereas in the East capitalism started in the cities and spread later, and with difficulty, to the countryside, the opposite process is more usual in Black Africa, where, from the beginning, rural capitalist activity was divided among tens of thousands of planters. On the other hand, the highly concentrated big bourgeoisie of the towns, often allied to the class of large landowners, which is common in the East and in Latin America, does not exist in Black Africa.

Contemporary Tendencies Toward the Development of National Bureaucracies

The contemporary world sees bureaucratic machinery developing in all fields of social life (state and business administration, trade union and political life, etc.) that in its scope and efficiency is on a completely different level from anything that existed in the past, at least in the capitalist formations at the center. Some say that it has been made necessary by the development of "technology," sometimes adding (Burnham and Galbraith) that this phenomenon represents a transfer of political power from parliamentary democracy to state technocracy. The proof that it is required by modern technology is said to be found in the development going on in Russia and in Eastern Europe, the convergence of the systems that is taking place despite the fact that the means of production are publicly owned in one part of the world and privately owned in the other. The requirements of accelerated development in the Third World, it is said, only strengthen this general trend.

This theory does not stand up well to analysis. The capitalist mode of production at the center implies polarization of society into two classes, the bourgeoisie and the proletariat (even if increasingly large sections of the latter — cadres of every type — though wage earning, deny that they are members of the proletariat). When the bourgeoisie exercises political power and administers the economy, it cannot carry out all the functions of management and execution itself. As society progresses, these mechanisms become ever more complicated, and this phenomenon becomes more marked. That is why social bodies responsible for these duties are set up: higher administration, police, army, technostructures of large firms, groups of professional politicians, etc. Some of these bodies have lost their traditional function — e.g., the professional politicians who, in the context of parliamentary democracy, served as negotiators on behalf of different interests when capital was still dispersed and competitive. With the rise of monopolies, these men have been replaced in their functions by the technocrats of the large firms or the state, and this has led to the decline of parliamentary government in the West. It is only during periods of serious crisis, such as the one that gave rise to Nazism, that the bourgeoisie loses control of these bodies, which then seem to constitute an independent social force. In the countries of the Soviet bloc, the strengthening of the technocratic machinery and its demand for democracy (limited to the technocrats) reflect an evolution toward a new form of generalized state capitalism, mainly characterized by the re-establishment of the market mechanisms and the ideology that goes with this: economism.

But nothing justifies transposing these analyses to the periphery. In the East and in Latin America the domination of central capital engendered, as we have seen, social formations comprising local ruling classes (large landowners and comprador bourgeoisie) on whom the local political power devolved. These classes exercised this power within the framework of the world system, that is, to the benefit of the center and of themselves. This did not happen in certain other regions of the periphery. In the Maghreb, for instance, because of direct colonization and the settlement of "poor whites," the possibility for social classes similar to those in the East to be formed was extremely limited. In Black Africa, generalized direct colonization, which was especially crude and brutal, for a long time reduced the local population of vast areas to the condition of an undifferentiated mass, since the traditional hierarchical structures had largely lost their significance, all the new economic functions having been taken over by foreigners.

With the coming of political independence and the formation of national states, the connection between the new bureaucracies and the social structures took on very different forms. In places where the peripheral formations were advanced, the national bureaucracy found itself, in relation to the social structure, in a position apparently similar to that of the national bureaucracy at the center. This was only apparent, however. Since the peripheral economy exists only as an appendage of the central economy, peripheral society is incomplete; what is missing from it is the metropolitan bourgeoisie, whose capital operates as the essential dominating force. Because of the weaker and unbalanced development of the local bourgeoisie, the bureaucracy appears to have much more weight. Where the peripheral formations are not very highly developed, the local bureaucracy is even the only actor on the stage. Elsewhere, however, a specific contradiction may develop. The state either fulfils its function within the system — that is, at best, helps to promote a local peripheral bourgeoisie — or it seeks to free the nation from domination by the center through promoting national industry, which then must be publicly owned, and so may come into conflict with the social groups from which it has arisen.

The trends for state capitalism to develop, found throughout the Third World, thus originate in the dominant place held by foreign capital and the weakness of its counterpart, the urban national bourgeoisie. Often, especially in Africa, this national movement was led by the urban petty-bourgeoisie (civil servants and office workers), together with a bourgeoisie of small entrepreneurs and planters, where there were any. The traditional elites in the countryside generally backed the colonial order which they felt safeguarded tradition, threatened by cultural modernization in the cities. The urban bourgeoisie was overwhelmed by the petty-bourgeois nationalist movement.

Independence suddenly increases the specific weight of the new state bureaucracy in the national society — all the more so because the rural bourgeoisie (where it exists) is still dispersed and limited in its horizon. The bureaucracy inherits that prestige of state power that is traditional in non-European societies and is strengthened by the experience of the colonial administration's power, which seemed absolute, and by the fact that the petty-bourgeoisie from which this bureaucracy stems has a monopoly of modern education and technical skill.

The new bureaucracy tends to become the main social driving force. What will most probably be the form of development of national capitalism? Private capitalism or state capitalism? Actually, these two forms combine in different ways, depending on the stage of development attained at the end of colonization.

The development of capitalism under colonial rule was first based on the transformation of subsistence agriculture into export agriculture, and on mining. The rate of growth of colonial capitalism was thus determined by the growth rate of the developed countries' demand for basic products from the colonies. At a later stage, the local market created by the commercialization of agriculture and related urban development made it possible for units of light industry — almost exclusively financed by colonial capital — to be set up. In certain cases foreign capital had not exhausted potential development of this type when independence came, and so the new local administration has had to leave untouched the economic structures inherited from the colonial period. But in other cases the new administration has been impelled to covet the foreign-owned sector, which constitutes its only means to expand rapidly by acquiring an economic basis. It then tends to change from a classical administrative bureaucracy into a state bourgeoisie.

In the first case, as the foreign sector develops, a certain place may be found for national capital through the state's efforts to promote this type of development. But this place is necessarily very limited. In the other case, the development of national capitalism at the expense of the foreign sector offers greater possibilities and can take various forms, benefiting either private or state-owned national capital. The transfer of foreign-owned plantations to the well-to-do classes of urban society, and acquisition of shares in new foreign-owned industries, are examples of this type of process. In all cases, however, the state's role is essential, because the process would be impossible through the operation of economic forces alone. The local bourgeoisie of planters and traders does not possess the financial resources to buy up the investments of foreign capital. In order to do this, public funds must be made available. This drift toward state capitalism constitutes the essence of what is called "Third World socialism."

Some circumstances have favored making the ongoing evolution more radical and bending it toward what is called the socialist type of organization (in the sense that it is inspired by the Soviet state model); others, on the contrary, favor what are called liberal forms (in the sense that they draw inspiration from the Western mode of economic organization). When advanced colonial-style development had been arrested for a long time, so that problems became more critical, pressure from the masses in town and country led, after independence, to the adoption of a more severe attitude toward the private bourgeoisie. Similarly, and paradoxically, when there is *no* private bourgeoisie, because of backwardness caused by colonial development, the administration's influence over the life of the country can enhance trends toward state control. On the other hand, an ongoing colonial style of development, as in the Ivory Coast, can strengthen liberal tendencies and change the relations between the private bourgeoisie and the administration. In general, however, state bourgeoisies have never eliminated private bourgeoisies but have been satisfied with absorbing them or merging with them. The rural bourgeoisie of planters in particular has always maintained a dynamic economic role and an important political position.

Phenomena such as the role of the privileged strata and classes in the Third World cannot be understood without prior analysis of the structure as a whole. Colonialism, especially in Black Africa, was led to favor, during the preindependence phase, certain differentiations in the reward of labor. Direct colonial rule became less and less bearable. Urban growth and the creation of industries made it essential for the city wage earners, brought into contact with European modes of consumption, to receive higher pay. Moreover, the solidity of traditional social relations in the countryside, which were slow in disintegrating, limited the inflow of labor into the towns. Revision of wage levels was made possible by the shifting of the center of gravity of foreign capital from old-style merchant capital to that of the big firms with a high level of productivity. In the Belgian Congo, the most highly industrialized country in Africa, between 1950 and 1958 real wages in industry doubled, without this increase hindering the progress of new industry; on the contrary, it stimulated modernization and expansion. Instead of relying on a dependent, peripheral local bourgeoisie, colonialism sought to make concessions in this way only to social strata with a low level of skill, avoiding the constitution of more demanding elites.

The scope and distribution of these petty privileges were changed after independence. Inflation in the ex-Belgian Congo between 1960 and 1968 ended in a considerable change in the distribution of native income, but with the share taken by foreign capital remaining unchanged. The setting up of a local bureaucratic machine (and simultaneous creation of a bureaucracy whose upper levels today constitute by far the most privileged strata of the Congolese community) was financed, on the one hand, by a drastic reduction in the real income of the peasants producing for export (a deterioration of the internal terms of trade for them that was much worse than the deterioration of the external terms of trade), and, on the other, by a no less drastic reduction in the real wages paid to workers in industry and commerce, which fell back to the 1950 level. Ryelandt showed the regressive nature of these changes: the larger import-content of the new income distribution, which involved greater consumption; the twofold, potentially permanent, structural crisis of the public finances and of the balance of payments that was entailed; and the increased dependence on the outside world implied. With inflation absent, similar phenomena are characteristic of the development of the countries in the franc area, as well as in other countries such as Ghana, where there was only moderate inflation. The mechanism worked as follows: freezing of wages and of prices paid to the producer for agricultural products; increased indirect taxes to balance public finances; leading to an internal increase in prices and a drop in the incomes of peasant farmers and wage earners. The peasant classes everywhere react to this deteriorated situation by withdrawing from the market and going back to a subsistence economy, thus diminishing the tax base available to the state for raising revenue.

Despite this, there is a deep-rooted tendency throughout the Third World today for political and social changes that go in the

same direction, namely, overthrow of the local political power of
the large landowners and the comprador bourgeoisie wherever
these exist, direct exercising of authority by the bureaucracies, civil
or military (the army often appearing as the vehicle for the new
regimes, since it is the best-organized and sometimes the *only*
organized body), and the creation and subsequent development of
a public economic sector. A similar evolution takes place, through
a continuous internal movement, even when there is no old authority
to be overthrown. This phenomenon can be explained by the contradictions specific to peripheral formations. Because of inadequate
industrialization and the absence of the foreign bourgeoisie, petty-
bourgeois-style strata (civil servants, office workers, sometimes
survivors from the crafts, small traders, middle peasants, etc.)
acquire great importance. The expansion of the educational system
and increasing unemployment give rise to a crisis of the system.
The very requirements of accelerated industrialization in order to
overcome the crisis lead to the development of a public sector,
since the rules of profitability (which determine the flow of foreign
capital) and the insufficiency of private local capital hold back the
necessary rate of industrialization. The subsequent strengthening
of the state bureaucracy can lead to a general application of state
capitalism. This development is more radical or less so depending
on whether or not it nationalizes foreign capital and on whether
state capitalism tolerates to a greater or lesser extent a local private
sector, and associates itself with it. Even in extreme cases, however,
state capitalism tolerates, and even encourages, the development of
private capitalism in rural areas (kulakization subsequent to agrarian reforms is an example) — even if it tries to organize this development by controlling it, through cooperative systems, for example.
If it does not call in question the country's integration into the
international market, this state capitalism must remain fundamentally peripheral, like its predecessor, private capitalism, and merely
reflect the new lines of development of capitalism at the periphery
— the transition from the old forms into the future forms of international specialization.

The national bourgeoisie continues with differing degrees of
success the work started by foreign capital, namely, the development

of plantation economy and light industry. For a certain time it has even been able to expand by gradually taking over foreign enterprises. In order to go further it would be necessary to overcome serious handicaps in food cropping and to create those large economic spaces that are the necessary condition for further development.

Meanwhile, peripheral capitalism is engendering a special structure, mainly based on a development of agrarian capitalism in which the kulak form tends to become predominant. This structure is dominated by the industrial and financial capital of the center, and the main transmission belts tend to be represented either by the bureaucracies or by the local state bourgeoisies.

The first of these two models is undoubtedly the poorest. It corresponds to the situation in those Third World countries in which import-substitution industries are still directly dominated by foreign capital, and where a local business bourgeoisie cannot be formed. This is typical of Africa as a whole. Herein lies the fundamental failure of capitalist development policies in Africa. In the Ivory Coast, for example, after fifteen years of exceptional economic growth, there is no national bourgeoisie, apart from a few artificial enterprises that have been set up in between the state and foreign capital, and somewhere along the way collect a commission that is due merely to bureaucratic collusion.

In these formations, the basic national problems remain unsolved. Africanization of appointments corresponds to the aspirations of the petty-bourgeoisie, which seeks not to transform the colonial system but to take over the jobs held by its predecessors. The administrative bureaucracy serves it as a model here.

The second model appears when the bureaucracy seeks to play a role in the process of production. It then becomes a state bourgeoisie: that is, it takes over, by controlling the economy, part of the surplus generated in the country. This bureaucracy nonetheless remains dependent in so far as the economy itself is dependent and as domination by the center makes it possible for the latter to appropriate the main part of the surplus for itself.

Proletarianization and Marginalization:
The World Dimension of the Class Struggle

Current writing on employment, unemployment, and the social distribution of income in the Third World countries has recently uncovered a number of facts that have begun to worry the conventional theorists of underdevelopment.

Firstly, there is the inequality in the social distribution of income, which is not only very marked but also increasing. A comparison between the various countries of the Third World shows that the higher the average income is per head, the more marked is the inequality in income distribution. Thus, for the whole of Latin America, the 20 percent of the population that is richest receives 65 percent of the national income (as against 45 percent in the United States), with 5 percent taking 33 percent and 1 percent taking 17 percent; while, at the other end of society, the poor half of the population receives barely 13 percent of the income.

In Black Africa, for the coastal countries that are regarded as relatively developed and where income per head is around $200, 93 percent of the population — made up of the urban (20 percent) and rural (73 percent) masses — receives only 55 percent of the national income. Although the average monetary income for the urban popular masses is about twice that of the rural masses, in terms of standard of living, and allowing for the differences in the way of life and cost of living between town and country, these averages in fact indicate comparable degrees of poverty. The privileged stratum is therefore very small (7 percent of the population). It is smaller still in the less-developed savannah countries of the interior where average income is around $100, and the privileged stratum makes up not more than 2 percent of the population (although it takes a relatively smaller proportion — less than 10 percent — of the total income). In other words, when we pass from the present stage of some of the countries still underexploited to that of the ones that have been more fully opened up, we observe no change at all in the situation of the bulk of the population, whose average income remains at $70-80 per head per year; on the other hand, a small minority is being built up whose income is gradually approaching the average income of the developed countries ($1,500 per head).

This increasing inequality in the social distribution of income is a cause for concern for at least two reasons. The first is that the evolution of the system in no way suggests that, by gradual expansion, this privileged stratum will extend to embrace the whole population. Even when the rate of growth of overall income is very high (between 7 and 10 percent per annum, for example), the numerical growth of the privileged stratum remains small (increasing at the rate of 3-4 percent a year at most). In other words, the privileged stratum reaches a ceiling of some 20-25 percent of the population irrespective of the time-prospect, even if this be a century. The second reason is that this evolution is radically different from that which characterized the development of the countries of the center. All studies done in this field show that, at the center, the pattern of income distribution — in particular, between wages and profits — is relatively rigid, however far back we go into the nineteenth century. On a first estimate, the rate of surplus value has fluctuated only a little around its average of 100 percent since 1850 (although there have been a number of waves several decades in length and, along these waves, some more or less severe conjunctural fluctuations, depending on the particular period). This difference in situation means that the argument according to which inequality is the price that has to be paid for growth in the Third World is false.

In reality, increasing social inequality is the mode of reproduction of the conditions of externally oriented development. It opens up a much bigger market for luxury consumer goods, in particular for consumer durables, than would have existed if the distribution of income had been more even. When the privileged elite reaches 20-25 percent of the population, this means that durable luxury goods make up approximately the same proportion of total demand. At this level, and taking into account requirements in capital, technicians, ancillary infrastructure, etc., for the production and consumption of these luxury goods, the process of resource allocation is distorted to such an extent as to undermine all possibility of decisive progress in the sectors producing mass consumer goods.

Inequality in the distribution of income is increased owing to the constant spread of unemployment and underemployment. With rates of urban growth of between 4 and 10 percent per annum, according to country and period, in the Third World of today, the rates of growth of wage-paid employment are between 30 and 50 percent lower, that is, they range between 2 and 7 percent. At these rates, the population of all the towns of the Third World would rise from 300 million in 1970 to 2 billion in the year 2000, while the mass of unemployed would increase by 200 million adults.

It is everywhere observed that the ratio of wage earners to total urban population is falling; and this general tendency is even more marked if we consider only the wage earners of the modern productive sector, industry in particular. On the other hand, with capitalist development in the periphery, other categories of employment appear and increase at high rates. Some of them are the counterpart of the increasing inequality in income distribution (domestic servants, persons employed in services, etc.). Others are attempts to cover up disguised unemployment (hawkers, etc.). Under these conditions, the border zone between unemployment and employment is widening to the extent of removing all meaning from the official statistics on unemployment — as official organizations such as the ILO have now found out.

It is very tempting for the ideologists who avoid studying the functioning of the socioeconomic system, in order to attribute changes to natural phenomena independent of the system, to have recourse to the theory of Malthus. The most glaring example of this type of aberration was provided by McNamara, president of the World Bank, when he compared the "cost" of a child in the Third World (around $600) to the cost of the means of avoiding it ($6). This comparison clearly has no scientific value whatsoever, since the "cost" must be compared with the "benefit" in terms of the value of the labor that the child in question will provide throughout his adult working life. In reality, the ultimate motive of the Malthusian campaign lies elsewhere, and McNamara's formula is put forward only to mislead.

The predominant "neo-Malthusian" trend can in fact be summed up in the two following propositions. First, our planet is experiencing an unprecedented population explosion. Projections over thirty or fifty years or more, based on present rates of population growth, show that astronomical figures of population will be reached that make one feel giddy, and spell a danger of absolute overpopulation in relation to natural resources, and in particular to land. The exploitation of these resources will take place, it is said, under conditions of diminishing returns that will therefore require proportionately higher investments to obtain a given rate of growth. Second, a high rate of population growth increases the non-working proportion of the population (the young), who have to be cared for by that proportion responsible for production. This distortion lowers society's capacity to save and consequently slows down its potential economic growth. It shuts the underdeveloped countries still more firmly in "a vicious circle of poverty."

The facts as they appear at first sight may tend to confirm these two propositions. Stagnation in agriculture in many regions of the Third World, or at least stagnation in agricultural output per head, limits the possibilities of financing accelerated industrialization. It brings us to the paradox that the countries of the Third World, which are agricultural countries, are finding it harder and harder to feed themselves and that the increasing imports of food products they need in order to feed their town populations reduces their capacity to import equipment. Now, this stagnation is often due to the shortage of arable lands, or to the high cost involved in increasing the area of such lands (irrigation, etc.). The exodus from the countryside caused by the overpopulation of certain regions leads to a high rate of urban growth. Even rapid industrialization is unable to cope with such a growth; therefore unemployment results and assumes alarming proportions. The cost of installing a social infrastructure (investment costs and running expenses, in particular as regards education) being very high under conditions of a high rate of population growth, this lessens the capacity of a society to keep up with the growth of its population.

This reasoning leads to an obvious conclusion: a decrease in population growth would not only make it possible, with a given rate of growth of the economy, to increase income per head, but it would also ensure a higher rate of overall economic growth, since an allocation of resources would become possible that is relatively more favorable to accumulation. Hence the world campaign for birth control.

This very broad reasoning is, at all events, not valid for the Third World as a whole, which is highly heterogeneous as regards the ratio between population and natural resources. Many regions of the African continent, for example, were more densely populated in the past than they are today. The flourishing kingdom of Kongo had two million inhabitants in the sixteenth century, when the Portuguese visited it. At the time of the colonial conquest, after three centuries of slave trading, the region did not contain even a third that many people. Even now, it has hardly got back to the figure of the sixteenth century. The depopulation resulting from slave trading often led to a regression of agricultural techniques and productivity. But the devastation of Africa did not stop with the end of the slave trade: colonial rule continued this work. Forced labor (porterage in Central Africa, road and railway construction, etc.), compulsory military service, the herding of the population into cramped "reserves" intended to provide cheap migrant labor, all contributed to the depopulation of the rural areas, taking away a large proportion of their labor force. These phenomena led to a deterioration in the food and health conditions of the population, and sometimes to famines; they were instrumental in the spread of serious endemic diseases (such as sleeping sickness). The same is true for the American Indian territories.

Today, everywhere in Tropical Africa, there are large areas of potential arable lands that have yet to be cultivated. But the low population density of the rural areas is a serious handicap to the raising of agricultural productivity. The capital outlay needed for the development of these lands is so high that the reduction of this cost per head that can be obtained through an increase in population density will outweigh the additional cost (in particular for education) that a high population growth would require, in order to get this better density. As an example, let us consider two agricultural regions, A and B, of 100 square kilometers each, with different population densities: 10 inhabitants per km^2 in A (which has 1,000 inhabitants) and 30 in B (with 3,000 inhabitants). The cost of the transport network to be set up in the region in the course of the year is independent of the population density: 200 kms. of road, costing 1 billion CFA francs. The relative advantage of B over A can therefore be estimated at 666 million, this being the marginal benefit to community B, with a population three times that of A. What would be the discounted cost of education if the population were to rise from 1,000 to 3,000 in thirty-five years (assuming a high population growth rate of 3 percent per annum)? The community with a fixed population of 1,000 inhabitants needs 8 classes at an annual cost (investment and running costs) of about 20 million. Community B will require 24 classes (annual cost: 60 million). The transition from situation A to situation B over thirty-five years would therefore involve, in discounted terms, an additional (marginal) cost that will depend on the discount rate. At a rate of 5 percent the cost of education is equivalent to only half the benefit to be gained from a trebled density of population; at a rate of 10 percent, it would be one-third. In this case, the cost of population growth is much less than the benefit to be derived from a higher density of population.

But the argument in cost-benefit terms is not the main one. Ester Boserup has shown that population pressure has, in the course of history, been a favorable and decisive factor in the intensification of agriculture, a precondition for raising productivity. A number of modernization programs in Tropical Africa have failed because, among other things, they ignored the fact that under conditions of a weak pressure of population on the land, extensive cultivation with low productivity can successfully combat the proposed change. The forms of social organization related to the type of extensive agriculture constitute a serious handicap. It is noted that the areas of high population density (such as the Ibo or Bamileke regions) have experienced a greater degree of development than the vast underpopulated areas. Again, the development of export crops requires a relatively high population density. The reason why these regions of potential growth have failed to give the results that might have been expected from them lies in the general policy adopted by peripheral capitalism, which confines them to the role of suppliers of export crops, or of a pool of cheap labor for the modern economy of the plantation zones or of the towns. In Japan, however, important progress was made in rice production and this made it possible to feed a very large town population, since the entire (autocentric) economic policy contributed to this progress: intensified agronomic research made possible improved cultivation of food crops for the home market, improvement of this sector of agriculture being necessary as part of the overall strategy.

The same applies in Latin America and in some regions of western Asia, the southern part of the Indian subcontinent and Southeast Asia (Thailand, Indonesia excluding Java, etc.). There are only a few regions of the Third World (the Caribbean, the Egyptian Nile valley, the delta areas of Asia, Java) that are *not* underpopulated in the sense in which I have defined this phenomenon.

Although it does not stand up to the facts as regards agriculture, is the neo-Malthusian argument of some validity in explaining urban unemployment? The argument that, if urban growth can be slowed down, the increase in both employment (in relative terms) and urban income per head will be higher overlooks two facts. The first is that industrialization at the center of the system absorbed an urban population increasing at very high rates (rates of 3 percent in the nineteenth century were as costly as rates of 7 percent today) because this industrialization was autocentric. The second is that externally oriented development gives rise to a distortion in resource allocation which, coupled with technological dependence, is the source of increasing underemployment, whatever may be the demographic characteristics of urban growth. Thus, when population growth is lower, we find that the overall rate of growth of output is also lower.

The important phenomenon of marginalization, which is entirely independent of demography, manifests itself as the increasing gap between economic dynamics and population dynamics. It may therefore give the impression that the population explosion constitutes a barrier to development. In fact, overpopulation is only the appearance outwardly revealing the functioning of a certain socio-economic system, that of peripheral capitalism.

The failure of birth control campaigns is often attributed to the inadequacy of the means utilized, to the ignorance of the peoples involved, and to the irresponsibility of the agencies responsible for the implementation of these campaigns. The question ought rather to be asked whether, at the level of the families addressed, the aim of reducing the number of children is justified. In the context of marginalization — that is, of increasing underemployment and poverty — a large family constitutes, in reality, the only form of social security. A strategy for development may well include measures with respect to population, either to slow down or to speed up its growth. But these measures will bring results only if there is compatibility between the motivations of the individual families and the objectives of the nation. This presupposes that the strategy followed aims at autocentric, independent development. The independent precapitalist societies already knew how to influence the population variable, using the means then available to them. And if today China has succeeded in controlling this variable, it is because other, more fundamental problems in defining an independent development strategy have been solved.

All the computations in "cost-benefit" terms disregard the vital psychosocial aspect of population phenomena. The history of all known civilizations shows that every period of intensive change and development has been characterized by a population explosion. No civilization with a stagnant population has ever been progressive. The population challenge, the stimulating conflict that it gives rise to between generations, the readiness to absorb new ideas and the active search for new solutions, explain why this is so.

The world campaign for birth control in the Third World expresses, in fact, the fears of the developed countries faced with the danger of a radical challenge to the international order by the peoples who have been its first victims. Taken to the limit, a development of the spontaneous trends in the present system would require a reduction in the population of the periphery. The contemporary technical and scientific revolution within this system in fact rules out the possibility of productive employment of the marginalized masses of the periphery. The literature on the "environment" has made Westerners aware of the rate at which they are exploiting the natural resources not only of their own countries but of the entire planet. If the masses of the Third World could divert these resources and exploit them for their own benefit, the conditions under which the capitalist system functions at the center would be upset.

The center and the periphery both belong to the same system. To understand this set of related phenomena, one should therefore not reason in terms of nations, as if the latter constituted independent entities, but in terms of a world system (a world context for the class struggle), possessing strong links and weak links, which are the points of maximum contradiction.

The controversy relating to the question of unequal exchange concerns the main problem of our day. Since the relations between the center and the periphery of the system are relations of domination, unequal relations resulting in a transfer of value from the periphery to the center, should not the world system be analyzed in terms of bourgeois nations and proletarian nations, to use expressions that have become common? If this transfer of value from the periphery to the center leads to a larger increase in the reward of labor at the center than would otherwise be the case, ought not the proletariat at the center to side with its own bourgeoisie in order to maintain the *status quo* in the world? If this transfer lowers both the reward of labor and the profit margin of domestic capital at the periphery, is there not reason for national solidarity between the bourgeoisie and the proletariat of the periphery in their struggle for national economic liberation?

This argument remains confined to a "classical" context, that is, it is *pre-Leninist*. By this, we mean that it deals with the question as if the world system were simply the juxtaposition of national capitalist systems. In reality, the class struggle takes place not within the context of the nation but within that of the world system.

The main contradiction of the capitalist mode of production is that which exists between production relations that are based on private ownership of the principal means of production (which become capital), and are therefore restrictive, and productive forces that, as they develop, reflect the necessarily social nature of the organization of production. The monopolies carry this contradiction to its highest degree: the time is ripe for socializing the ownership of the means of production. This maturity is reflected in the monopolists' increasing recourse to state intervention, needed to coordinate the monopolies' activities and to support them. Hence national economic policy takes over from *laissez-faire*, which was possible only so long as the spontaneous market mechanisms made it possible to increase accumulation, only so long as the capitalist mode of production was progressive. But recourse to the state does not cause the contradiction to disappear. For the state is the monopolies' state, and the rationality of the system remains capitalistic.

The main contradiction, between productive forces and production relations, is expressed, on the social level, in the contradiction between the two opposing classes of the system: the bourgeoisie and the proletariat. So long as we confine ourselves to the frame of reasoning of the capitalist mode of production, matters remain quite simple. But capitalism has become a world system. The contradiction is not between the bourgeoisie and the proletariat of each country considered in isolation, but between the world bourgeoisie and the world proletariat. But this world bourgeoisie and this world proletariat do not fit into the framework of the capitalist mode of production — they belong to a system of capitalist formations, central and peripheral. Therefore the problem is: what constitutes the world bourgeoisie and the world proletariat, respectively?

As regards the world bourgeoisie, this consists principally of the bourgeoisie at the center and, secondarily, of the bourgeoisie that has been constituted in its wake at the periphery. But where is the world proletariat situated? What is its structure? For Marx, there was not the least doubt: in his time, the main nucleus of the proletariat was to be found at the center. At that stage of the development of capitalism, it was impossible to understand the full implication of what was later to become the colonial problem. Since the socialist revolution did not take place at that time at the center, and since capitalism continued to develop and became monopolistic, the world conditions of the class struggle altered. This was clearly expressed by Lenin in a line that has now been taken over by Maoism, namely, that, "in the last analysis, the outcome of the struggle will be determined by the fact that Russia, India, China, etc., account for the overwhelming majority of the population of the globe." This meant that the central nucleus of the proletariat henceforth lay at the periphery and not at the center.

The main increasing contradiction of the system is expressed in the tendency of the rate of profit to fall. There is only one way to combat this on the world scale: raise the level of the rate of surplus value. The nature of the formations at the periphery makes it possible to raise this rate to a much higher degree there than at the center. Consequently the proletariat at the periphery is being more severely exploited than the proletariat at the center.

But the proletariat at the periphery takes different forms. It does not consist solely or even mainly of the wage earners in the large modern enterprises. It also includes the mass of peasants who are integrated into the world trade system and who, like the urban working class, pay the price of unequal exchange. Although various types of social organization (very precapitalist in appearance) form the setting in which this mass of peasants live, they have eventually become proletarianized, or are on their way to suffering this fate, through their integration into the world market system. The peripheral structure — the condition for a higher rate of surplus value — also gives rise to an increasing mass of urban unemployed. These are the masses, in our contemporary world, "who have nothing to lose but their chains." Clearly, they are also forms of incomplete proletarianization at the periphery. Their revolt, the most important one, leads to a worsening of the conditions of exploitation at the center, since this is the only means available to capitalism to compensate itself for the shrinking of its area of influence.

We must try to transcend a sterile controversy. The contention of some that the proletariat at the center remains the principal nucleus of the world proletariat, is not Leninist: it denies the worldwide character of the system. The thesis that suggests an opposition between proletarian nations and bourgeois nations also denies the worldwide character of the system, the effect that the revolt at the periphery must have on conditions at the center, and implies that the bourgeoisie of the periphery, equally "exploited" (the term is inaccurate: only its scope for expansion is limited), can oppose its counterpart at the center. But the violence of the main revolt means precisely the opposite; for the bourgeoisie of the periphery is obliged to make its own proletariat pay for the plundering from which it suffers.

Furthermore, the picture that represents the proletariat at the center as being collectively privileged, and therefore necessarily in league with its own bourgeoisie in the exploitation of the Third World, is only an oversimplification of the facts. It is true that, with equal productivity, the proletariat at the center receives, on average, a better reward than the workers at the periphery. But in order to counteract the law of the tendency of the rate of profit to fall at the center itself, capital imports labor from the periphery at a lower wage (reserving for this labor the most thankless tasks), in order to depress the labor market of the metropolitan countries. This import is assuming considerable proportions: in Western Europe and in North America, immigration from the periphery has been increasing since 1960 at rates of between 0.7 percent and 1.9 percent per annum, depending on the country and the year; in other words, at levels far higher on the average than the rate of growth of the national labor force. This additional immigrant labor force constitutes also a disguised transfer of value from the periphery to the center, since the periphery has borne the cost of training this labor force.

Similarly, there is the mobilization of the internal colonial reserves: thus we have the proletarianization of the blacks in the United States, now forming the bulk of the proletariat of many large industrial towns in North America. The extreme form of this system is to be found in the racist countries: South Africa, Rhodesia, Israel. Thus the world system increasingly mingles together the masses it exploits, raising the need for internationalism to an even higher degree than before. At the same time, it uses this process of mingling to develop racist and chauvinist tendencies among the "white" workers for its own benefit. Capital, through its development at the center itself, continually gives rise to unification and differentiation. The mechanisms of centralization for the benefit of the dominant capital also operate between the various regions of the center: the development of capitalism everywhere means developing regional inequalities. Thus each developed country has created within itself its own underdeveloped country: the southern half of Italy is one example. The resurgence of regionalist movements in our time would be difficult to understand without this analysis. It follows that even if the concept of the labor aristocracy, in the Leninist sense, has now been overtaken in reality by more complex differentiations, the concept of aristocratic nations *conceals* these complex differentiations.

In putting forward the existence of the theoretical concept of marginalization, José Nun denies that Marx's analysis of the capitalist mode of production can explain this new and specific set of facts. For, he says, Marx's *Capital* is an analysis of the *pure* capitalist mode of production, whereas marginalization, peculiar to the periphery, belongs to the analysis of formations, the theory of which (historical materialism), merely outlined in the works of Marx, is yet to be perfected.

Capital is, to be sure, not the theory of the world capitalist system. It is clear that Marx proposed first to clarify the main point: the theory of the capitalist mode of production. He also did not fail to analyze the relations between the center and the periphery in the *genesis* of this mode, in his chapter on primitive accumulation. But he could not possibly set out the theory of the future world system.

How can this necessary theory be constructed? Two ways are open. One, outlined by José Nun, attempts to propound this theory of the world system without basing it on the theory of the capitalist mode. This is clear in Nun's repeated contrast between the plane of the theory of the capitalist mode and that of the theory of formations. But here, as Fernando Henrique Cardoso observes, historical materialism turns into metaphysics if it attempts to derive general laws of history over and above those governed by the modes of production. There is no possible general theory of formations, but only the theory of particular formations or groups of interconnected formations. There are no general laws of social formations, but only a set of scientific concepts that make it possible to formulate laws for particular formations. These concepts are those of mode of production, interconnection between different modes, dominance, instance, and articulation of instances.

How then do we proceed to deduce the laws of the capitalist system, conceived as a structured group of capitalist formations that, central and peripheral alike, are all dominated by the capitalist mode of production? Not by looking for specific social laws situated at a level other than that defined by the above-mentioned concepts — for example, by looking for a specific "law of population," as suggested by Nun — but simply by making a concrete analysis of the functioning of the system, using the concepts in question. We then notice that the phenomena of marginalization are no more than an expression of the fundamental law of the capitalist mode of production under the concrete conditions of the world capitalist system.

As Cardoso says, the general law of accumulation and of impoverishment expresses the tendency inherent in the capitalist mode of production, the contradiction between productive forces and production relations, between capital and labor. This contradiction rules out an analysis of the capitalist mode of production in terms of harmony, and leads us to understand that the quest for an ever increasing rate of surplus value in order to compensate for the downward trend in the rate of profit makes a harmonious development impossible. This law operates within a concrete historical framework. In Marx's time, England provided this framework, because the world system was not yet established. Today, this framework has been enlarged to include the capitalist world as a whole. Hence the "harmony" achieved here, at the center, where the rate of surplus value cannot be raised, must be counterbalanced by an increasing "disharmony" elsewhere, at the periphery, which is made to pay for the fundamental contradiction of the mode. This disharmony is revealed in the "marginalization" group of phenomena, which are the way in which the general law of capitalist accumulation finds expression today.

One final problem is — whether marginalization constitutes a concept. In fact, it is only a convenient way of describing a group of phenomena resulting from a law (that of capitalist accumulation) that operates within a concrete framework (that of the present-day capitalist system), just as the expression "industrial reserve army" corresponds to a realistic description of the effects of the same law within a different context (that of England at the time of Marx). There is therefore no need to raise the question of the meaning of marginalization in functionalist terms. The marginalization of today and the industrial reserve army of yesterday are results of the system. Their function, which is the same, is to enable the rate of surplus value to be raised. Social disharmony is necessary for the functioning of the system.

New Central and Peripheral Formations

The most popular theory regarding the origins of the development of English-speaking North America and the "White" Dominions is that of Max Weber, according to which these countries owe the dynamism they have shown to the Protestant ideology of their population, which is contrasted with Latin Catholicism.

Colonization by European settlers formed, as a whole, part of the gradual formation of a periphery. In Latin America, its function was to set up, from the start, the peripheral structure toward which tended later on the national societies of the other regions that were to form the Third World. The settlement of the "poor whites," as in the Maghreb and in Kenya, performed the same functions of peripheral agrarian and commercial capitalism. It was only in the extreme and exceptional cases of North America, Australia, and New Zealand — and also, with some special characteristics, of South Africa, Rhodesia, and Israel — that colonization by European settlers ended in the creation of new central formations.

The British colonies of North America, taken as a whole, were no exception to the rule. The West Indies and the slave colonies of the southern part of North America were no different from the Spanish and Portuguese colonies. They fulfilled the same peripheral functions within the framework of the same mercantilist system. The exception was constituted not by the British colonies in North America as a whole, but by New England alone. This was not formed as a periphery of the mercantilist system: from the start, it was special, and not shaped by the metropolis as a dependency. New England was a by-product of the proletarianization process in England. The destitute emigrants who were to form the population of New England were of no interest to mercantilism in the metropolitan country, which allowed them freedom to organize themselves for their own survival. The petty-commodity economy of farmers and craftsmen that they organized was poor but autocentric. This type of society based primarily on the simple commodity mode of production — only seldom realized throughout history — has the capacity to give rise to capitalism. Thus, gradually, New England acquired the function of metropolis in the American system. It replaced Britain as the new center dominating the British slave colonies. This substitution was only partial, until the war of independence, but it then became total. Freed from the monopolistic control of metropolitan merchant capital, the United States became a full-fledged center before reaching the position of world metropolis.

There is a widespread trend in current American literature that seeks to "rehabilitate" the South by attributing to it a decisive role in the development of the United States. Among others, Douglass North has shown the strategic role of cotton exports from the South in financing the United States's "take-off" in the nineteenth century. The ideologists of the system have concluded from this that development is possible with an externally orientated economy based on the export of raw materials. This view disregards the decisive fact that it was the North that animated the life of the United States from the end of the eighteenth century onward, and that the South remained its domestic colony, as was shown by the Civil War.

The history of Canada was no different. Here also, from both the French and British standpoints, what was involved was not a periphery but a distinct by-product of social changes in Europe. When, by the Treaty of Paris of 1783, France preferred to retrieve Martinique rather than Canada, which she had lost twenty years earlier, Voltaire declared the choice to be an intelligent one: 30,000 Negro slaves were worth more to French mercantilism than a few "thousands of acres of snow" inhabited by poor devils who had nothing to export.

In much the same way took place the original formation of a white Oceania based on petty-commodity production. But for a long time this remained predominantly agricultural, exporting to Europe rather than to the periphery, as in the case of North America. For that reason, it experienced greater difficulties in passing over to the industrial stage. But again the dynamism of the simple commodity mode of production, unhampered by precapitalist modes, showed its ability to move forward to that stage. Here, it is worth comparing Australia and Argentina. At the end of the nineteenth century, the two countries were in an identical situation: exporters of agricultural products (meat and wool) supplied by a commodity economy of independent producers. But, in Australia, the discovery of gold led to the creation of a working-class nucleus. It was the latter that insisted on a protectionist policy to maintain its level of employment. This protectionism altered the center of gravity of the economy and of the society from the externally oriented sector to the autocentric sector, and so made possible the entire subsequent development. The compradors of Buenos Aires and the cattle breeders of La Plata imposed free trade on Argentina; and that country, which in 1900 enjoyed the highest standard of living in the world, then began to slip down the slope of under-development.

Much the same can be said about white South Africa. The patriarchal Boer economy was at first a simple commodity economy linked with the maritime navigation system of the seventeenth to the nineteenth centuries: the Boers supplied ships with dried meat, under conditions similar to those which characterized the nascent capitalist agriculture of the European metropolises. At that stage, white society was still isolated from the black world that surrounded it, but which it did not exploit: it drove this black world back, in the same way as had happened with the North American Indians earlier. At the end of the nineteenth century, the British conquered the country, not for any attraction the Boer economy might have had for them but in order to work the gold and diamond mines that had recently been discovered. For that purpose, they required a proletariat, and this was derived from the black population. It was the British colonial administration that created the system of reserves: the British were the originators of apartheid. The Boers were then of no importance; they lived in an autocentric economy that made it impossible to proletarianize them for the benefit of the new British capital dominating the externally oriented mining sectors.

Gradually, however, the Boers' petty-commodity economy gave birth to a local capitalism, which was autocentric even though partly grafted onto the externally oriented colonial economy. This later took over economic and political control from British capital, relying on its state power and exploiting for its own benefit the internal colony constituted by the reserves.

In the analysis of this particular formation made by Ralph Horwitz and Serge Thion, among others, South African racism no longer appears as an epiphenomenon inherited from the past that the present economic system could do without if it chose. The reserves play an essential role in the service of the modern sector: the supplying of cheap labor. Henceforth, the economy must necessarily remain essentially externally oriented. The reason is that the internal market is restricted by the low wages of the Africans, while the export sector takes advantage of these wages which, combined with the use of modern techniques, produce particularly high profits. The mining economy set up by British capital was the first to benefit from the system of reserves and apartheid. The patriarchal Boer agrarian economy, which appeared to be threatened by modernization and concentration, managed to survive despite its backward techniques, thanks to the cheap labor available. It is also because of the limited internal market that the state has had to take the initiative in creating autocentric industries. The system, which is perfectly coherent, is not likely to collapse by itself, as a result of an alleged contradiction between the economic structure (which is said to be interested in improving wages) and the politico-ideological structure. The natural solution for the system is expansionism, that is, the extension of the dominated area in order to make up for the narrowness of the domestic market. The link with Rhodesia, South Africa's designs upon Angola and Mozambique, the economic annexation of Malawi, the threat that hangs over Zambia, Madagascar, and Tanzania, show that fifteen years of growth have brought South Africa to this conclusion. To the optimists who think that economic wealth must necessarily lead to a reduction in social distortions, South Africa provides a hard refutation.

In Israel the Zionist colonies are also the by-product of proletarianization in Central and Eastern Europe. They also are organized in a petty-commodity production economy that has given rise to a local capitalism. Here also the state plays an important role in this process: it is the Zionist bureaucracy of the Histadrut that organizes and exploits this capitalism for its own benefit. Machover has shown that there is nothing here of a "socialist" nature and that the Histadrut is not a social-democratic trade union. Backed by imperialism — at first British, then American — and with international Zionism as its tool, the Histadrut, having benefited from a capital inflow that is totally out of proportion with what is known as "aid" to the underdeveloped countries, maintains a tight control over this inflow. As regards the Israeli working class, this consists of immigrants who are ranked on the basis of a racial hierarchy (Jews from Central and Eastern Europe on top, Jews from the Arab countries underneath) and still retain petty-bourgeois aspirations of climbing the social ladder out of the working class. This autocentric society had no room for the Arabs that formed the population of Palestine. They had to be exterminated or driven out. Today, Israel has reached the crossroads. One way forward is to consolidate this autocentric economy, giving it the status of an independent imperialist capitalism (even if it has to be small-scale and hence necessarily allied to other imperialisms, as a minor partner but not as a vassal) and opening up the markets of the Arab world to its products — in other words, carving out a share of periphery for itself from the Arab world. The alternative is to set up an *internal* colony by extending its frontiers so as to acquire an Arab proletariat. In both cases, expansionism, either by peaceful or warlike means, is the law of the system.

We must take care not to confuse these models of the genesis of new capitalist centers based on petty-commodity formations with that of Japan. The Japanese model is no different from that of Europe. The social formation of precapitalist Japan, at the periphery of the tribute-paying system of eastern Asia, was similar to that of Europe at the periphery of the tribute-paying systems of the ancient East. From the start, therefore, Japan gave birth to its own autocentric capitalism. The fact that it came later, so that it was able to draw inspiration from the European development, did not do it any harm, as would have been the case had the country been colonized. Fortunately for Japan, since it was lacking in resources, it was of no interest to the Europeans and Americans, who looked instead toward China.

A few other precapitalist societies also escaped the world capitalist system for more or less prolonged periods (Ethiopia, Yemen, Afghanistan, Thailand). Precapitalist but not underdeveloped (peripheral capitalist), these societies did not, however, give rise to an independent autocentric capitalism, because their original formations (of the central tribute-paying type) did not permit it. This explains why, sooner or later, they gave in and started, in the aftermath of the Second World War, along the road of underdevelopment.

3. FOR A STRATEGY OF TRANSITION

The Soviet Mode of Production

What is the present position of socialism? If we start from the principle that the socialist mode of production is not a commodity mode, that products and labor power are not commodities in this mode, then the Soviet mode cannot be considered as socialist. It is not capitalist either, of course. The capitalist mode is not only characterized by the generalization of the commodity form of the product and the commodity nature of capital but also by distribution of surplus value in proportion to capital invested, that is, surplus value is converted into profits and value into price. This feature is not present in the Soviet mode, because capital is entirely owned by the state instead of being in private ownership, which is necessarily *divided*.

This difference is the justification given for qualifying the Soviet system as socialist. What this means, however, is reducing the concept of production relations to that of ownership relations, that is, reducing society to its economic infrastructure and eliminating the question of relations between the economic instance and the political and ideological instances. The attempt to see matters in this way accounts for the disappearance of study of the tribute-paying ("Asiatic") mode of production from Soviet writing. In that mode, production relations *cannot* be reduced to ownership relations, since there is no appropriation of the land, and we can only speak of control over the means of production, a collective control, that is, a class control exercised by the state. Can the Soviet mode of production be regarded, then, as a tribute-paying mode? Certainly not: the tribute-paying mode does not know the commodity form of the product and of labor power; the surplus is extracted in kind and according to laws unrelated to the market.

However, to describe the Soviet mode as state capitalism is also unsatisfactory. This epithet describes a variety of situations: advanced capitalism in which the centralization of capital leads to monopolies and to specific forms of interpenetration between the state and the monopolies; the forms, contrasting directly with nascent capitalism, in which the state plays a decisive role in setting up new enterprises of a capitalist nature; those which are peculiar to some underdeveloped countries in which the state takes over from inadequate private enterprise; and, lastly, those peculiar to the period of transition, as in Russia under the NEP (New Economic Policy).

I shall therefore speak of the Soviet mode of production as a specific mode. Its characteristics are: (1) the main means of production — here, equipment produced by social labor — are owned by the state; (2) labor power is a commodity; (3) products for consumption are also commodities; and (4) capital goods are not commodities, at least at the beginning, though they soon tend to become so.

Over a long period of time, not yet in fact ended in Russia, the allocation of investments was controlled by the Plan, irrespective of the market and the equalization of profit that it presupposes. This enabled the rate of accumulation to be increased through priority allocation of resources for the production of capital goods intended for the production of other capital goods, and not to satisfy immediately the ultimate demand for consumer goods. This procedure removed the need to maintain a certain ratio between the two sections of social production, as required by the market; or, more precisely, made it possible to postpone the point in time when adjustment between them became necessary. The purpose of this procedure was clearly transitory.

Hence, as soon as the main objectives of accumulation had been attained, the system began to evolve toward the adoption of resource allocation rules that were closer to those of the capitalist mode. The completed model of this type of mode of production was formulated as early as 1908 by Barone: he considered that the task of the planning ministry of a socialist country was to take the place of the market by making an *ex ante* calculation that should lead to results similar to those achieved *ex post* in an economy of pure and perfect competition. The discussion in Soviet economic writings falls entirely within this framework. Two questions are raised: (1) Is the allocation of resources to Department I during a transition period an efficient means of speeding up accumulation, and how far should this deliberate distortion be pursued? (2) What is the most effective method for achieving an allocation of resources that conforms to the laws of the market (that is, to equal rewarding of capital): decentralization of management, or (on the contrary) complete centralization accompanied by strict adherence to the calculation regarding the pseudo-market made by the central planning department?

However, neither the one nor the other of the two questions belongs to the problematic of socialism. Socialism is not "capitalism without capitalists." Marx and Engels had already foreseen the danger of an interpretation of this kind, which they attributed to the persistence of capitalist ideology in the workers' movement. To prove his thesis, Barone had to separate the problem of production from that of distribution, and also the problem of infrastructure (the economic instance) from that of the superstructure (the ideology). Following this line of thought, Russia has created a mode of production *sui generis*. The persistence and strengthening of the state reveal the class nature of the mode of production and the specific nature of the articulation of instances that this mode calls for.

The Soviet mode of production implies the dominance of the ideological instance. In this respect, it signifies a break with the capitalist mode and a return to the type of articulation characteristic of the precapitalist modes. The control and appropriation of the surplus by a state-class are apparent as soon as one abandons the capitalist ideology according to which the objective rewarding of capital is associated with a social-class distribution of income. The system only works if the control over the surplus exercised by a state-class is accepted by society. The ideology then becomes the instrument for reproducing the conditions for the functioning of society, as in precapitalist modes. Its two necessary foundations are elitism and nationalism. Elitism ensures that control of the surplus by a minority class is accepted. It dictates social reproduction procedures based on esoteric respect for "knowledge," "science," and "technique." At the same time, it fosters the myth of social mobility. The function of the elite that forms the state-class is to ensure the nation's cohesion and strength. It is to the extent that it achieves this objective that it can be accepted by the proletariat, which sells its labor power. External successes are therefore almost vitally essential to the system.

In the capitalist mode, democracy derives from two internal

requirements of the system: on the one hand, the competition between private capitalists, and, on the other, the dominance of the economic instance and the economistic nature of the ideology. The absence of democracy and freedom of debate in Russia is therefore not a reflection of "deviations" or "shortcomings," and still less "vestiges of the past." On the contrary, it is a necessary condition for the functioning of a system that cannot survive if its elitist and nationalist ideology is questioned.

The essential law of the capitalist mode is the law of accumulation. The capitalist mode "internalizes" economic progress, which in the noncapitalist modes is not an internal requirement for reproduction. Competition is at the root of this peculiarity of the capitalist mode, which is solely concerned with expanded reproduction, in contrast to precapitalist modes based on simple reproduction. The disappearance of competition, by renewing the "externalization" of economic progress, is the prerequisite for society's recovery of control over its own future; and this is the precondition for an end to alienation. In this respect, the socialist mode will recover the character of the precapitalist modes, which were not dominated by the economic instance. But while the precapitalist modes suffered from a lack of development of the productive forces, which confined them to simple reproduction, the socialist mode can opt for an expanded reproduction, which is nevertheless different from that of capitalism, in so far as it will be controlled.

The Soviet mode — at least so long as capital goods are not commodities — does not include competition. The aim of accelerated maximum accumulation for the purpose of "catching up" with the advanced capitalist countries is the chief motive of economic progress, directly reflected at the ideological and political level. This dominance of the political instance actually makes possible accelerated accumulation by partially freeing the economic instance from the constraints of the market. At this stage, the principal law of the Soviet mode is accelerated accumulation. The main, specific contradiction of this mode does not lie within the economic instance but between it and the politico-ideological instance. It brings the declared socialist objective into conflict with the methods and objectives of accelerated accumulation.

This contradiction has been gradually transcended by the decline of the socialist elements and the increasingly strong imposition of "capitalism without capitalists." This explains why the mode tends to evolve toward re-establishing the commodity nature of capital goods. This does not necessarily imply competition. When the latter is actually re-established through the medium of a real market (as in Yugoslavia), the unity of the given society is broken and the groups of competing workers become alienated in an economistic commodity ideology; the socialist objective recedes from view, and economic progress, again internalized in the economic mechanism, leads society to lose control of itself. But when competition is not re-established, the Plan being substituted for the market according to Barone's theses, economic progress remains independent of the economic mechanism and directly dependent on the political instance. But the ideology of this nonsocialist mode is also an ideology of economistic commodity alienation, prerequisite for the reproduction of a class society. This mode is governed by the law of uneven development of the sectors of activity: those of which the progress is essential for the strengthening of the dominant ideological instance will receive an allocation of resources that is systematically biased in their favor, at the expense of progress in the other sectors. This explains the impressive achievements in the military field (necessary for the success of nationalism) and in the sectors serving privileged consumption (necessary for the success of elitism), accompanied by a persistent inefficiency in the other sectors, in particular, those concerned with the production of goods needed for the reproduction of the labor force, which is itself treated as a commodity.

The Soviet phenomenon is sometimes explained as a "degeneration" due to the backward state of Russia. In fact, the spontaneous trends of the center are moving in the same direction, and it can be said that the economistic ideology that has been at the root of Soviet orientations right from the start is derived from the developed center.

At the beginning of this century, Russia was not a peripheral country but one of a backward central capitalism. Its structures were different from those of underdevelopment, that is, from those of dependent capitalism. Thus the Revolution of 1917, though intended to be socialist by the Bolsheviks who carried it out, made it possible to speed up the *process* of accumulation without basically altering the capitalist *model* of accumulation. The abolition of private ownership of the means of production in favor of state ownership was the condition of this acceleration. History has shown that it was possible, under Russian conditions, to achieve the task of accumulation as it would have been possible under capitalism, but with different forms of ownership. This possibility is reflected in the Soviet theory of socialist revolution seen as a change in the forms of ownership that allows the adaptation of the latter to the level of development of the productive forces (the potential productive forces, that is, corresponding to the industrialization target achieved). This theory leads to an economistic ideology of transition formulated in such terms as: priority of heavy industry over light industry and of industry over agriculture; copying of Western technologies and consumption patterns, etc., in order to "catch up" with the advanced countries.

Since England was where industrial capitalism began, all the other countries that are now developed were to a certain degree and at one time "backward" in relation to it. But none of these countries was ever a periphery. After a certain time lag, Continental Europe and North America overtook (and then surpassed, in the case of the United States and Germany) Great Britain, in forms similar to those of the English model. Japan eventually finished up with a first-class model of complete capitalism; but already in this case the forms of the transition period presented some interesting peculiarities, in particular the central role played by the state. Russia carried out the most recent experiment with this model of accumulation, original only in that state ownership was not just a transitory form.

In all these models, the transition period was characterized by submission on the part of the masses, reduced to the passive role of a pool of labor gradually transferred to the modern sector being set up and later enlarged, up to the point when the whole society had been absorbed by it. The kolkhoz and administrative oppression fulfilled this role, which in the English model was performed by the Enclosure Acts and the Poor Laws.

The quest for maximum growth at all costs is mirrored in the slogan of the Stalin era: "Overtake and then surpass the United

States in all fields of production." Formulated in this way, both at the theoretical and practical levels, the target deliberately ignores the content of this measurable economic growth. But the aggregates measured in national accounting include only magnitudes with commodity values, i.e., those of interest to the capitalist mode of production. The mind that focuses on the gross domestic product forgets that the growth of this magnitude is obtainable, in the last resort, through the destruction of productive forces: man and natural resources. The latter are, in fact, only *means* in the capitalist mode of production, the sole end being profit maximization. In economic jargon, "the cost-benefit analysis of the firm internalizes the external economies" — those external economies that arise precisely from the destruction of human forces and natural resources. This explains why the capitalist mode of production has an inherent capacity for growth — in the economistic sense — larger not only than all previous modes of production, but also, no doubt, than that of socialism, if the latter places man above the quest for profits.

In precapitalist modes, man is still alienated in nature, but social relations are obvious; hence the dominance of the ideological instance. Poverty confines men to a model of simple reproduction, but ideology provides a justification for this model through its "eternalist" vision of the world. This is why men build pyramids and cathedrals. The capitalist mode internalizes technical progress in the economic instance, and this makes possible rapid accumulation, and hence frees man from alienation in nature. But, at the same time, alienation is transferred to the social plane. For the price of this accumulation is the submission of society to the law of profit. This submission is expressed in terms of the degradation of man to mere labor power and disregard for the natural ecological environment. Capitalism has stopped building cathedrals without, for all that, liberating man. For the short time-prospect that it offers from the start is the root of the social problems over which it has no control.

By turning the prerequisite of capitalist accumulation into an absolute, economism denies the world system, in which it sees only a juxtaposition of national systems, unevenly developed but not arranged on a hierarchical basis and integrated into one whole.

So far as it is concerned, the periphery is condemned to degenerate even if, by chance, a political authority with socialist aims were to take over there. The miracle of the socialist revolution can only come from the center. The mechanistic pre-eminence of the productive forces in these views comes remarkably close to the most bourgeois "philosophies of history."

In fact, from the end of the nineteenth century, German social-democracy interpreted Marx in economistic terms. The linear mechanistic conception of a chain that, starting with technology, goes on to the productive forces, the production relations, and class consciousness, overcame the dialectical analyses made by Marx when he considered the relations between the infrastructure and the superstructure. Kautsky popularized this mechanistic ideology, which found fertile soil not in backward regions of the capitalist world but in its most developed centers: in Germany under a Marxist disguise; in Britain with the Labour Party, in an openly eclectic version; in the United States in forms that were even more alienated in the liberal ideology. The fact is that at the center the working class was steeped in bourgeois ideology; like the bourgeoisie, it accepted the fetishistic alienation of commodities and economism.

Kautsky's ideas regarding the organization of the working class were not unrelated to this economistic ideology. The idea of a party that represents the external consciousness of the proletariat, an elite versed in social science and applying it, is the product of the superficial adherence of the European working class to "Marxism" after 1870. The workers' alienation, henceforth accepted — whereas until 1870 the proletariat still clung to communist utopias — resulted in a separation, in the so-called Marxist parties, between theory and practice, in the liquidation of the philosophy of praxis in favor of economistic dogmatism. Nevertheless, the Bolsheviks were to base themselves on those forms of organization because centralization — which in Germany reflected the elitist economistic ideology — was a vital practical necessity in oppressive Russia, where the working class was a minority and the intelligentsia was in opposition. Hence the "dialogue of the deaf" between Lenin, who was surprised by Kautsky's "treason" in 1914, and Rosa Luxemburg, who understood it better.

The Bolsheviks therefore set out, as from 1917, on the road that led to present-day Russia. It is true that circumstances, like the devastating civil war, the breakup of the proletariat, etc., provided them with the necessary incentives. It is equally true that Lenin became concerned about this; but neither Trotsky nor Stalin, representing the two sides of the same economistic coin, had this worry. The former awaited the miracle of liberation from the West, and the latter was convinced that one had to imitate, to "overtake" before surpassing. It was the Chinese Cultural Revolution that was to reinstate Marx by giving its real meaning to the law of uneven development, and breaking with this line of adapting production relations to the spontaneous development of the productive forces.

The history of China is not the only proof that the Soviet mode is better suited to the advanced countries than to the backward ones. In Eastern Europe itself, the most convincing economic performances have occurred neither in backward Russia (in spite of centralization) nor in Yugoslavia, equally backward (in spite of decentralization), but in East Germany. The working class of the center, molded by decades of capitalist alienation, as reflected by its adherence to "economism," was prepared to overcome the contradiction of the capitalist mode without liberating itself from this alienation. This is why it accepted fascism and why it accepts trade-union bureaucracy, and the elitist party as candidate to the succession to the bourgeoisie, which is capable of bringing centralization to the level required to overcome the contradiction between the social character of production and the constricting forms of private ownership.

The Spontaneous Tendencies of the System

The historic experience of Soviet Russia reminds us that the spontaneous tendency of the capitalist system is not such as to give rise to socialism. In the absence of conscious action, the capitalist system overcomes the contradictions that are characteristic of it at a certain stage in its development, while at the same time it retains its essential determinant, that is, commodity alienation. We then move on to a new stage in capitalism, which is never "the highest" but only higher, and in which the fundamental contradiction of the capitalist mode is expressed in new forms.

In the central capitalist system, awareness of belonging to a social group (the proletariat for example) does not by itself define class consciousness. The latter may be a "reformist consciousness." At the periphery, however, a social awareness of this type is not possible since the objective functioning of the system does not integrate the masses. Consequently, awareness of the situation must lead to a rejection of the system. The only question then is whether in a given country and at a given time the popular masses that are proletarianized, or on the way to becoming so, attribute their fate to the objective functioning of the system or whether they see in it the effect of aberrant or even supernatural social forces, in which case their political action is doomed to remain at the stage of revolts without a strategy.

At the center, a social-democratic consciousness alienated in "economism," combined with the laws of increasing concentration of economic power, speed up the movement toward a sort of state capitalism. Already in the course of its historical development, successive solutions to the fundamental contradiction of the mode of production have been found, in the form of the limited company, then the trust, the holding company, and the conglomerate. The combination between social-democrats and technocrats renders possible a "convergence" of the systems of Western liberal capitalist origin and of Soviet origin. Orwell's *1984* and Marcuse's *One-Dimensional Man* remind us that this prospect, far from being impossible, forms on the contrary a feature of spontaneous evolution.

At the periphery, the tendency is for adaptation of the higher forms of dependence. Can a spontaneous development of this type create the conditions for its own transcendence within the framework of the system, in which case it would appear as a necessary stage? One would doubt this: the model on which it is based is in fact a model of reproduction of its own conditions. This deepening of dependent peripheral development follows paths that in the future will constitute the main forms of advanced underdevelopment. Technological domination manifests itself through the priority given to the development of sectors that must be competitive at the international level, whether this involves exports or luxury goods, the promotion of which reflects the adoption of Western consumption patterns.

In the early stages of the formation of the peripheral economies, the technological gap being as yet narrow, the dominant central capital must, in order to ensure the functioning of the system in its favor, directly control the modern sectors it promotes. Political means of control are also necessary at this stage, whence colonization. At a more advanced stage of peripheral development, technological domination based on an ever-widening gap, linked with the existence of local social strata and classes integrated through their consumption pattern and its attendant ideology, ensures the conditions for reproducing the system without control investments and without direct political interference. Such is the meaning of neocolonialism or neoimperialism. The investment burden can then be taken care of through local savings, private or (mostly) public. The development of a public sector, which can become very important and even dominant at the domestic level, therefore does not exclude the dependence of the system as a whole, including the public sector, *vis-à-vis* the developed world. This dependence is guaranteed through the interplay of local social forces, even if they are organized in a state capitalism that claims to be socialist. At a very advanced stage one can imagine the development of a heavy industry that serves as local backing for the overall dependent development while assuming the form of a public sector. A vehicle of the dependent local state capitalism, the petty-bourgeoisie becomes the transmission belt of imperialist domination, thus taking the place of the latifundiary comprador bourgeoisie that was the vehicle of the dependent private capitalism of the previous period.

Should the system be given a sufficiently long life, is there any chance that the countries of the periphery that are farthest advanced in this process may end by "freeing" themselves from dependence and acquiring a completely central character? Must we exclude the prospect of an autocentric capitalist development in the semi-industrialized countries, in particular Brazil, Mexico, and India, where size-effect operates? Cannot Mexico and Canada become fully developed provinces of the United States, in the sense that the marginality phenomena at present visible there would decrease until they finally disappear? Autocentric development would be ensured not by national capital but by that of the United States, with which the country would be associated in a minor capacity. In that case the contradiction would shift from the economic to the cultural and political domains.

We must remember that we have defined three symptoms of underdevelopment: sectorial inequality of productivities, disarticulation, and domination. Disarticulation does not appear in the same way in Brazil as it does in Tropical Africa. In the case of the semi-industrialized countries of Latin America (Brazil, Mexico, Argentina), an integrated industrial complex already exists. This complex itself tends to become autocentric, in a special way: it is not, in fact, based on a large internal market embracing the entire population, as in the developed countries, but on a partial market made up of the rich, integrated fraction of the population. Industry therefore leaves out of the market a marginal population that forms the major part of the rural population as well as of its extension, the urban shanty-towns. Agriculture, developed at an earlier stage of integration into the world system, remains externally oriented and therefore suffers from a very low and stagnating wage level for its workers. The disarticulation, which does not manifest itself at the industrial level, occurs between agriculture and industry at the national level. As is seen in the case of Brazil, foreign trade acquires a special structure as a result of this phenomenon. The pattern of exports is typically that of a classical underdeveloped country (predominance of primary products, especially agricultural ones) while imports are like those of a developed country (predominance of energy, semifinished goods, capital goods, and food products, and *not* manufactured consumer goods). We must ask ourselves, moreover, whether, in the event of a gradual disappearance of disarticulation through integration of the as yet marginalized sectors, underdevelopment will follow a course entirely different from its present one, as we generally know it.

The prospects in sight at the present time do not suggest a progressive narrowing of the center-periphery gap, within the context of capitalism. The transnational companies are actually taking advantage of this gap (and of its effect, the inequalities in the levels of remuneration of labor). In Taiwan, South Korea, Hong Kong, and Singapore, we can already perceive the results of the installation there of large numbers of transnational companies. The massive transfer of labor-intensive industries, whose products are intended for export to the United States and Japan, speeds up the creation of a new division of labor, which remains unequal. In this new division, the periphery inherits industries that have a limited scope for expansion, while the center keeps back for itself those with the highest potential for progress.

It is true that the widening gap between the center and the periphery leads to increasing migration from the underdeveloped to the developed countries. The "brain drain" started off this trend after the Second World War, as regards those persons possessing high qualifications. As usual, labor is made available to capital wherever the latter requires it. But even if these migrations were to become important, capital could still exploit the national cultural differences that exist, as is clearly revealed by the present unequal status of immigrant workers in the developed world. In the worst case, this massive transfer of labor can lead to an "internal colonialism" such as we see in South Africa.

Moreover, the concentration of the new activities of the transnational companies and the development of the public sector, in particular in the basic industries in some countries of the Third World, is already giving rise to a new type of hierarchic development inside the periphery. Some regions of the periphery "benefit" from the geographical concentration, within their territory, of luxury-goods or even capital-goods industries producing not only for their own national market but also for those of their neighbors, which are left mainly to serve as reserves of cheap labor. Such prospects are not only visible in a few big countries of the Third World (Brazil being the best example, but we must also examine in this light the role of this kind that India may acquire) but they also exist in smaller areas, in the Arab world or in Black Africa.

The Problematic of Transition

For the periphery the choice is in fact this: either dependent development, or autocentric development, necessarily original in form as opposed to that of present-day developed countries. Here the law of uneven development of civilizations reappears: the periphery cannot just overtake the capitalist model; it is obliged to surpass it.

In fact, it must radically revise the capitalist model of resource allocation and reject the rules of profitability. For choices made on the basis of profitability within the structure of relative prices prescribed by integration into the world system foster and reproduce the model of increasingly unequal distribution of income (and hence marginalization), restricting the country to the peripheral model of resource allocation. The action of righting the resource-allocation process must largely be undertaken independently of the rules of the market, by a direct assessment of needs: requirements in respect of food, housing, education and culture, etc.

It is not by accident that every serious attempt by the periphery to free itself from the political domination of the center has led to conflicts that suggest the need to consider a socialist way forward. It is true that, according to circumstances, realization of this prospect may be delayed or even distorted and reabsorbed. It remains no less a fact that Cuba started a socialist revolution without knowing it, that the Cuban peasantry accepted the collectivization that was opposed by that of Russia, and that the chances of socialism are today greater in Cuba than in the United States or Europe. It is also not mere chance that it is in China that Marx has been rediscovered.

The transition, envisaged on a world scale, must start with the liberation of the periphery. The latter is compelled to have in mind, from the beginning, an initial local model of accumulation. Under the present conditions of inequality between the nations, a development that is not merely development of underdevelopment will therefore be both national, popular-democratic, and socialist, by virtue of the world project of which it forms part.

With capitalism having already assumed a planetary dimension and having organized production relations on this scale, socialism can only come into existence on a world scale. Therefore the transition will include a series of specific contradictions between the socialist objective, of a necessarily universal nature, and the transitional framework, which remains national. But it is only in so far as the aim of maturing and developing socialist consciousness is not sacrificed at any stage to the aim of economic progress that a strategy can be described as a strategy of transition. Transition requires much more than the extension of public ownership, or the expansion of heavy industry. If it is not accompanied by a radical revision of economic choices, even if this means slowing down to some degree the maximum growth rate, such an extension contains the danger of perpetuating at the periphery the model of dependent development. The aim must be to combine the most modern installations with immediate improvements in the poor sector in which the bulk of the population is concentrated, to use modern techniques for immediate improvement in productivity and in the situation of the masses. This immediate improvement, and this alone, can free the productive forces and men's initiative and really mobilize the whole of the people. This combination between modern techniques and immediate improvement of the situation of the masses calls for a radical change in the direction of scientific and technological research. Copying the technology of the developed world is not likely to answer the problems of the underdeveloped world of today. But this specific dialectic of transition does not, however, imply a rejection of the modernistic prospect. The "protest" movement in the West has revealed through its critique of everyday life that the maximum rate of growth ought not to be sought at any price, and has attempted to reinstate labor-intensive techniques, in a combination of hippy ideology, a return to the myth of the noble savage, and a critique of the reality of the capitalist world. It is on such erroneous foundations that some people have wrongly felt entitled to interpret in their own way certain aspects of Chinese policy, isolated from the conception of the future to which they belong.

The socialist aim is not to be defined in economistic terms, but it integrates the economic instance. Complete socialism will necessarily be based on a modern economy with high productivity. To think otherwise is to believe that "what is wrong is due to technology" and not to the social system that provides the present framework for this technology. In fact, it is the capitalist mode of production that is in conflict with modernization and is distorting its potentialities. A great deal has been written on the destructive effect of the fragmentation and monotony of industrial work. This form of labor will, in time to come, appear as characteristic of the capitalist mode of production, which will have fulfilled a historical role, that of accumulation, and thus paved the way for its own disappearance. The contemporary technical revolution will replace the fragmented unskilled labor — which has been the main form of labor since the introduction of machine industry — by automation. It will both make more leisure time available and introduce new types of work requiring very high skill.

How does the present system react to this prospect? It sees in it not the dawn of mankind's liberation, but the threat of mass unemployment, with increasing marginalization of part of mankind (in the Third World especially) in relation to a system that integrates only a minority. This is the propensity natural to calculations of profitability based on profit as an end in itself, of the economistic alienation that sees men only as "manpower." In ridding society of the ideology that the capitalist mode of production imposes upon it, mankind will liberate its productive forces.

There can be no conflict between growth and the construction of a worldwide socialist civilization.

Bibliography

CHAPTER 1. THE PRECAPITALIST FORMATIONS

1. Modes of Production

Centre d'Etudes et de Recherches Marxistes. *Sur le mode de production asiatique.* Paris, 1969.
———. *Sur le féodalisme.* Paris, 1971.
Dhoquois, Guy. *Pour l'histoire.* Paris, 1971.
Hobsbawm, Eric. *Introduction to Karl Marx, Precapitalist Economic Formations.* London, 1964; New York, 1965.
Marx, Karl. *Grundrisse.* Harmondsworth, 1973; New York, 1974.
Meillassoux, Claude. "Essai d'interprétation du phénomène économique dans les sociétés traditionnelles d'auto-subsistance." *Cahiers d'études africaines,* no.1 (1960).
Melotti, Umberto. *Marx ed il Terzo Mondo.* Milan, 1971.
Rey, Pierre-Philippe. "Le Mode de production lignager." Office de Recherche Scientifique dans les Territoires d'Outre-Mer. Paris, 1968 (mimeo).
Sofri, Gianni. *Il Modo de produzione asiatico.* Turin, 1969.
Terray, Emmanuel. *Marxism and "Primitive" Socities.* New York, 1972.
Tokei, Ferenc. *Sur le mode de production asiatique.* Budapest, 1966.
Wittfogel, Karl A. *Oriental Despotism.* New Haven and London, 1963.

2. Social Formations

Coquery, Catherine. "Research on an African Mode of Production." In P. Gutkind and P. Waterman, eds., *African Social Studies*. London, 1976; New York, 1976.

Genovese, Eugene D. *The Political Economy of Slavery*. New York, 1965.

Leon, Abraham. *The Jewish Question: A Marxist Interpretation*. New York, 1971.

Pelletier, Antoine, and Goblot, Jean-Jacques. *Matérialisme historique et histoire des civilisations*. Paris, 1969.

Rey, Pierre-Phillipe. "Sur l'articulation des modes de production." *Problèmes de planification*, no. 13 (Paris: Ecole Pratique des Hautes Etudes, mimeo).

Silva Michelena, Héctor. "The Economic Formation: Notes on the Problem and Its Definition." Dakar: Institut Africain de Développement Economique et de Planification, 1971 (mimeo).

Vernant, Jean-Pierre. *Les Origines de la pensée grecque*. Paris, 1962. (To be published in English by Monthly Review Press.)

3. Social Classes: The Articulation of Instances

Althusser, Louis. *For Marx*. London, 1969; New York, 1970.

Althusser, Louis, and Balibar, Etienne. *Reading Capital*. London, 1970; New York, 1971.

Miliband, Ralph. *The State in Capitalist Society*. New York, 1969; London, 1969.

Poulantzas, Nicos. *Political Power and Social Classes*. London, 1973. New York, 1975.

Socialist Register. London and New York, 1965, 1967, 1968, 1969, 1970, 1971. Articles by Anthony Arblaster, Isaac Deutscher, Hal Draper, Donald Clark Hodges, Monty Johnstone, John Merrington, Istvan Meszaros, Ralph Miliband, Rossana Rossanda, J-P. Sartre.

4. Nations and Ethnic Groups

Stalin, Joseph. "Marxism and the National Question." In *Selected Works*, vol. 2. London, 1953; New York, 1971.

5. Long-Distance Trade and the Breakup of Feudal Relations

Bairoch, Paul. *Révolution industrielle et sous-développement*. Paris, 1965.

Balazs, Etienne. *La Bureaucratie céleste.* Paris, 1969.

Chesneaux, Jean, ed. *Popular Movements and Secret Societies in China, 1840-1950.* Stanford, California, 1972.

Dobb, Maurice. *Studies in the Development of Capitalism.* London, 1946; rev. ed., New York, 1964.

Lanternari, V. *The Religions of the Oppressed.* London, 1963.

Sweezy, P. M., Dobb, M., Hilton, R., Hill, C., and Takahashi, H. *The Transition from Feudalism to Capitalism.* London, 1954.

Weber, Max. *The Protestant Ethic and the Spirit of Capitalism.* New York, 1958.

6. The Blocking of the Development of the Trading Formations

Batuta, Ibn. *Travels in Asia and Africa.* 1929; reprint ed., New York, 1973.

Bekri, El. *Description de l'Afrique septentrionale.* Paris, 1965.

Bovill, Edward W. *Caravans of the Old Sahara.* London, 1933.

Braudel, Fernand. *The Mediterranean and the Mediterranean World in the Age of Philip II.* London, 1972; New York, 1972.

Cahen, Claude. *L'Islam des origines aux débuts de l'empire ottoman.* Paris, 1970.

Centre d'Etudes et de Recherches Marxistes. *Sur le féodalisme.* Paris, 1971.

Cook, M.A., ed. *Studies in the Economic History of the Middle East.* London, 1970; New York, 1970. Articles by Ashraf, Baer, Cahen, Chevallier, Davis, Ehrenkreutz, Labib, Lopez, Miskimin, Rodinson, Udovitch.

Coquery, Catherine. "Research on an African Mode of Production." In P. Gutkind and P. Waterman, eds., *African Social Studies.* London, 1976; New York, 1976.

Gray, John Richard, and Birmingham, David, eds. *Pre-Columbian African Trade.* London, 1970.

Hamdan, Jamal. *Shakhsiya Miçr, dirasat fi abqariya al makan.* Cairo, 1970.

Lacoste, Yves. *Ibn Khaldun.* Paris, 1965.

Laroui, Abdallah. *L'Historie du Maghreb.* Paris, 1970.

Meillassoux, Claude, ed. *The Development of Indigenous Trade and Markets in West Africa.* London, 1971. Articles by Arhin, Auge, Boutillier, Cohen, Coquery, Curtin, Daaku, Meillassoux, Wilks.

Miguel, Andre. *L'Islam et sa civilisation.* Paris, 1968.

Rodinson, Maxime. *Mohammed.* London, 1971; New York, 1971.

Valensi, Lucette. *Le Maghreb avant la prise d'Algier.* Paris, 1969.

Wahida, Çobhi. *Fi Ucul Al Masala al miçriya.* Cairo, 1950.

7. *The Blocking of the Development of the Tribute-Paying Formations*

Balazs, Etienne. *La Bureaucratie céleste.* Paris, 1969.

Chesneaux, Jean. *Le Viet-Nam.* Paris, 1968.

Chesneaux, Jean, ed. *Popular Movements and Secret Societies in China: 1840-1950.* Stanford, Cal., 1972.

Grousset, René, and Léonard, Emile, eds. *Encyclopédie de la Pléiade: Histoire Universelle,* vol. 3. Paris, 1958. Chapters on India (Pierre Meile), China (Roger Levy), Southeast Asia (Le Thành Khôi), Indonesia and Malaya (Jean Cuisinier).

CHAPTER 2. THE FUNDAMENTAL LAWS OF THE CAPITALIST MODE OF PRODUCTION

1. Productive Forces and Production Relations in the Central Capitalist Formations

Abdel Fadil, Mahmoud. "L'Ecole de Cambridge fait une critique radicale de la théorie économique officielle." *Le Monde.* November 30, 1971.

Bairoch, Paul. *Révolution industrielle et sous-développement.* Paris, 1965.

Bettelheim, Charles. *Economic Calculation and Forms of Property.* London, 1976; New York, 1976.

Braun, Oscar. *Comercio internacional e imperialismo.* Buenos Aires, 1972.

Denis, Henri, and Lavigne, M. *Le Problème des prix en Union soviétique.* Paris, 1965.

Engels, Friedrich. *Anti-Dühring.* Moscow, 1954.

———. Preface to Karl Marx, *Capital,* vol. 3. Moscow, 1959.

Godelier, Maurice. *Rationality and Irrationality in Economics.* London, 1972; New York, 1972.

Jakubowsky, F. *Les Superstructures idéologiques dans la conception matérialiste de l'histoire.* Paris, 1972.

Jobic, Bernard. "La Révolution culturelle et la critique de l'économisme." *Critiques de l'économie politique,* nos. 7-8 (1972).

Kantorovitch, Leonid V. *The Best Use of Economic Resources.* Oxford, 1965; Cambridge, Mass., 1965.

Marx, Karl. *Un Chapitre inédit du "Capital."* Paris, 1971.

Miliband, Ralph. *The State in Capitalist Society.* New York, 1969; London, 1969.

Mishan, E.J. *The Costs of Economic Growth.* London, 1969.

Rey, Pierre-Phillippe. *Colonialisme, néo-colonialisme et transition au capitalisme: L'expérience de la Comilog au Congo.* Paris, 1971.

———. "Sur l'articulation des modes de production." *Problèmes de planification,* no. 13 (Paris: Ecole Pratique des Hautes Etudes, mimeo).

Robinson, Joan. "The Measure of Capital: The End of the Controversy." *Economic Journal,* September 1971. Reprinted in *Collected Economic Papers,* vol. 4. Oxford, 1973; New York, 1972.

———. "The Relevance of Economic Theory." *Monthly Review,* January 1971.

Sraffa, Piero. *Production of Commodities by Means of Commodities.* Cambridge, 1960; New York, 1960.

Sweezy, Paul. *The Theory of Capitalist Development.* New York, 1942.

Tanzer, Michael. *The Political Economy of International Oil and the Underdeveloped Countries.* London, 1970; Boston, 1970.

Ward, Barbara, and Dubos, René. *Only One Earth.* New York, 1972.

2. The Accumulation of Capital in the Central Capitalist Formations

Baran, Paul, and Sweezy, Paul. *Monopoly Capital.* New York, 1966.

Critiques de l'économie politique, no. 3 (1971). Articles by Jean Bailly and Patrick Florian.

———. nos. 4-5 (1971). Articles by J. Valier and Roman Rosdolsky.

Denis, Henri. "Marchés nouveaux et accumulation du capital." *L'Homme et la Société,* no. 22 (1971).

———. "Le Rôle des débouchés préalables dans la croissance économique de l'Europe occidentale et des Etats-Unis." *Cahiers de l'Institut de Science Economique Appliquée,* no. 5 (1961).

Delilez, J.-P. *La Planification dans les pays d'économie capitaliste.* Paris, 1968.

Gruson, Claude. *Origines et espoirs de la planification française.* Paris, 1968.

Horowitz, David, ed. *Marx and Modern Economics.* London, 1968; New York, 1968.

Laulagnet, Anne-Marie. "Les schémas de la reproduction du capital chez Marx." *Problèmes de planification,* no. 9 (Paris: Ecole Pratique des Hautes Etudes, mimeo).

Lenin, V.I. "A Characterization of Economic Romanticism." In *Collected Works,* 4th ed., vol. 2. Moscow, 1960.

———. "On the So-called Market Question." In ibid., vol. 1.

Luxemburg, Rosa. *The Accumulation of Capital.* New York and London, 1968.

Nagels, Jacques. *Genèse, contenu et prolongements de la notion de reproduction du capital selon Marx.* Brussels, 1970.

Robinson, Joan. *An Essay on Marxian Economics.* London, 1947; 2nd ed., New York, 1966.

——. *The Rate of Interest and Other Essays.* London, 1952.

3. *The Conditions for Autocentric Accumulation: The Role of the Monetary System*

Amin, Samir. *Accumulation on a World Scale.* 2 vols. New York, 1975. *Critiques de l'économie politique,* no. 1 (1970).

Dallemagne, J.-L. *L'Inflation capitaliste.* Paris. 1972.

de Brunhoff, Suzanne. *L'Offre de monnaie.* Paris, 1971.

Denis, Henri. *La Monnaie.* Paris, 1950.

Friedman, Milton. *Studies in the Quantity Theory of Money.* Chicago, 1956.

Hicks, John R. *Value and Capital.* 2nd ed. Oxford, 1946; New York, 1946.

Laulagnet, A.-M. "Les schémas de la reproduction du capital chez Marx." *Problèmes de planification,* no. 9 (Paris: Ecole Pratique des Hautes Etudes, mimeo).

Lenin, V.I. "A Characterization of Economic Romanticism." In *Collected Works,* 4th ed., vol. 2. Moscow, 1960.

——. "On the So-called Market Question." In ibid., vol. 1.

Luxemburg, Rosa. *The Accumulation of Capital.* New York and London, 1968.

Mattick, Paul. *Marx and Keynes.* London, 1971; New York, 1973.

Modigliani, Franco. "Liquidity Preference and the Theory of Interest and Money." *Econometrica,* vol. 12, no. 1 (January 1944).

Nogaro, B. *A Short Treatise on Money and Monetary Systems.* London, 1949.

Patinkin, Don. "Price Flexibility and Full Employment." *American Economic Review,* September 1948.

Robertson, D.H. *Money.* Cambridge, 1948.

Schumpeter, Joseph. *The Theory of Economic Development.* Cambridge, Mass., 1934.

Von Mises, Ludwig. *Theory of Money and Credit.* New York, 1934.

Warburton, C. "The Misplaced Emphasis in Contemporary Business-Fluctuation Theory." In American Economic Association, *Readings in Monetary Theory.* London, 1952.

Wicksell, Knut. *Interest and Prices.* London, 1936; reprint ed., New York, 1965.

4. *The Form of Autocentric Accumulation: From Cycle to Conjuncture*

Aftalion, A. *Les Crises périodiques de surproduction.* Paris, 1913-1914.
Angell, James W. *Investment and the Business Cycle.* New York, 1941.
Baran, Paul, and Sweezy, Paul. *Monopoly Capital.* New York, 1966.
Dobb, Maurice. *Political Economy and Capitalism.* London, 1937; reprint ed., New York, 1972.
Harrod, Roy F. *Towards a Dynamic Economics.* London, 1948; New York, 1948.
Hicks, John R. *A Contribution to the Theory of the Trade Cycle.* London, 1950; New York, 1950.
Kaldor, N. "A Model of the Trade Cycle." *Economic Journal,* March 1940.
Kalecki, Michal. *Studies in Economic Dynamics.* London, 1943.
Mockers, J.-P. *Croissances économiques comparées: Allemagne, France, Royaume-Uni, 1950-1967.* Paris, 1967.
Néré, Jacques. *La Crise de 1929.* Paris, 1969.
Sartre, Léon. *Esquisse d'une théorie marxiste des crises périodiques.* Paris, 1937.
Sweezy, Paul. *The Theory of Capitalist Development.* New York, 1942.

5. *International Relations and the Interlinking of the National Formations*

Aftalion, A. *Monnaie, prix et change.* Paris, 1935.
Balogh, Thomas. *Unequal Partners.* 2 vols. Oxford, 1963; New York, 1963.
Bye, Maurice. *Les Relations entre les structures nationales et l'investissement international.* Lectures, 1950-51. Paris, Faculté de Droit.
———. *La Transmission internationale des fluctuations économiques.* Lectures, 1952-53. Paris, Faculté de Droit.
"Capitalism in the 1970s." Tilburg Conference, September 1970 (mimeo). Note especially the contribution by Victor Perlo.
Chang, T.C. *Cyclical Movements of the Balance of Payments.* Cambridge, 1951.
Clark, Colin, and Crawford, J. *The National Income of Australia.* London, 1936.
Critiques de l'économie politique, no. 2 (1971). See "La Crise du système monétaire international."

Graham, Frank D. "International Trade Under Depreciated Paper: The U.S.A. 1862-1879." *Quarterly Journal of Economics,* vol. 36, no. 2 (February 1922).

Haberler, Gottfried. *Prosperity and Depression.* 3rd ed. Geneva, 1941.

Hayter, Teresa. *Aid as Imperialism.* London, 1971; New York, 1971.

Hirschman, Albert O. "Devaluation and Trade Balance." *Review of Economics and Statistics,* November 1945.

"Imperialism." Elsinore Conference, Danish Institute for Peace and Conflict Research, April 1971 (mimeo).

Iversen, Carl. *Aspects of the Theory of International Capital Movements.* London, 1936; reprint ed., New York, 1967.

Kindleberger, Charles. *Balance of Payments Deficits and the International Market for Liquidity.* Princeton, 1965.

———. *International Short-Term Capital Movements.* New York, 1943.

L'Huillier, J. *Le Système monétaire international.* Paris, 1971.

Lobel, Eli. "Liquidités internationales et éléments d'une politique monétaire de l'Afrique." *Le Mois en Afrique,* May 1969.

Machlup, Fritz. *International Trade and the National Income Multiplier.* New York, 1943.

Meade, J.E. *The Theory of International Economic Policy. Vol. 1: The Balance of Payments.* London, 1951.

Metzler, Lloyd A. "The Transfer Problem Reconsidered." *Journal of Political Economy,* June 1942.

Mosak, J.L. *General Equilibrium Theory in International Trade.* Bloomington, Ill., 1944.

Nurske, R. *Essays on International Finance.* Geneva, 1945.

Ohlin, Bertil G. *Interregional and International Trade.* London, 1933; rev. ed., Cambridge, Mass., 1967.

Robinson, Joan. *Essays in the Theory of Employment.* 2nd ed. Oxford, 1947; New York, 1962.

Taussig, F.W. *International Trade.* 1927; reprint ed., New York, 1966.

Tinbergen, Jan. "Some Measurements of Elasticities of Substitution." *Review of Economic Statistics,* August 1946.

Triffin, Robert. *Gold and the Dollar Crisis.* Rev. ed., New Haven, 1961.

———. *Our International Monetary System.* New York, 1968.

Viner, Jacob. *International Trade and Economic Development.* Oxford, 1953.

———. *Studies in the Theory of International Trade.* London, 1937; reprint ed., New York, 1965.

Wallich, Henry C. *Monetary Problems of an Export Economy.* Cambridge, 1950.

Williams, John H. *Argentine International Trade Under Inconvertible Paper Money, 1880-1900.* Cambridge, Mass., 1920.

Wolff, Richard. "L'expansion à l'étranger des banques américaines." *Critiques de l'économie politique,* nos. 4-5 (1971).

Zakaria, Ismail. *Change, commerce extérieur et équilibre économique international.* Paris, 1953.

CHAPTER 3. FROM SPECIALIZATION TO DEPENDENCE

1. The Foundations of International Specialization

Amin, Samir. *Accumulation on a World Scale.* 2 vols. New York, 1975.

Balogh, Thomas. *Unequal Partners.* 2 vols. Oxford, 1973; New York, 1963.

Baran, Paul, and Sweezy, Paul. *Monopoly Capital.* New York, 1966.

Bastable, C.F. *The Theory of International Trade.* 4th ed. New York, 1928.

Bukharin, Nikolai. *Imperialism and World Economy.* New York, 1973.

Ellswoth, M. *International Economy.* New York, 1950.

Emmanuel, Arghiri. *Unequal Exchange.* New York and London, 1972.

Graham, Frank D. "Some Aspects of Protection Further Considered." *Quarterly Journal of Economics,* February 1923.

————. "The Theory of International Values Re-examined." *Quarterly Journal of Economics,* November 1923.

Haberler, Gottfried. *The Theory of International Trade.* London, 1936; reprint ed., New York, 1968.

Heckscher, Eli F. "The Effects of Foreign Trade on the Distribution of Income." *Ekonomisk Tidskrift,* vol. 21 (1919).

Lenin, V.I. *Collected Works.* 4th ed., vol. 2. Moscow, 1960.

Leontief, Wassily W. "The Use of Indifference Curves in the Analysis of Foreign Trade." *Quarterly Journal of Economics,* May 1933.

Lerner, A.P. "The Diagrammatical Representation of Cost Conditions in International Trade." *Economica,* August 1932.

Marshall, Alfred. *The Pure Theory of Foreign Trade.* 1897; London, 1930; New York, 1967.

Ohlin, Bertil G. *Interregional and International Trade.* London, 1933; rev. ed., Cambridge, Mass., 1967.

Palloix, Christian. *Problèmes de la croissance en économie ouverte.* Paris, 1969.

Preobrazhensky, Evgeny. *The New Economics.* Oxford, 1965; New York, 1965.

Rachmuth, I. *Problèmes de planification,* no. 84 (Paris: Ecole Pratique des Hautes Etudes, mimeo).

Samuelson, Paul A. "The Gains from International Trade." *Canadian Journal of Economics and Political Science,* May 1939.

Taussig, Frank W. *International Trade.* 1927; reprint ed., New York, 1966.

2. The Theory of Unequal Exchange

Brown, Michael Barratt. "Imperialism and Working-Class Interests in the Developed Countries." In *Essays on Imperialism.* Nottingham, 1972.

Critiques de l'économie politique, no. 3 (1971). Articles by E. Chatelain, P. Florian, J. Bailly.

L'Homme et la Société, nos. 12, 15, 18, 19 (1969-1971). Articles by A. Emmanuel and C. Palloix.

Marx, Karl. Letter to Engels, 8 October 1858. In S. Avineri, ed., *Karl Marx on Colonialism and Modernization.* New York, 1969.

Politique aujourd'hui (1969-1970). Articles by A. Emmanuel, H. Denis, A. Gramon, G. Dhoquois, and C. Bettelheim.

A Fundamental Contribution

Bettelheim, Charles. "Présentation et remarques théoriques dans l'ouvrage d'Emmanuel." *Le Monde,* November 11, 1969.

Braun, Oscar. *Comercio internacional e imperialismo.* Buenos Aires, 1972.

Emmanuel, Arghiri. *Unequal Exchange.* New York and London, 1972.

Van de Klundert, M. *Labour Values and International Trade: A Reformulation of the Theory of A. Emmanuel.* Tilburg Institute of Economics publication no. 26 (1970).

Is an Economic Theory of International Exchange Possible?

Arrighi, Giovanni. "Labor Supplies in a Historical Perspective: A Study of the Proletarianization of the African Peasantry in Rhodesia." In Giovanni Arrighi and John Saul, *Essays on the Political Economy of Africa.* New York, 1973.

———. "The Political Economy of Rhodesia." In ibid.

Bukharin, Nikolai. *Imperialism and World Economy.* 1930; reprint ed., New York, 1972.

Lewis, W. Arthur. "Economic Development with Unlimited Supplies of Labor." *The Manchester School,* May 1954.

Palloix, Christain. *Problèmes de la croissance en économie ouverte.* Paris, 1969.

Preobrazhensky, Evgeny. *The New Economics.* Oxford, 1965.

Other Formulations and Aspects of Unequal Exchange

Durand, Daniel. *La Politique pétrolière internationale.* Paris, 1962.

Owen, Geoffrey. *Industry in the U.S.A.* Harmondsworth, 1966; Santa Fe, N. Mex., 1966.

Peyret, Henri. *La Stratégie des trusts.* Paris, 1966.

Semonin, Paul. "Nationalization and Management in Zambia." Lusaka: University of Zambia, 1971 (mimeo).

3. The Expansionism of the Capitalist Mode of Production

Precapitalist and Mercantilist Foreign Trade

Cook, M.A., ed. *Studies in the Economic History of the Middle East.* London, 1970; New York, 1970.

Mauro, Frederic. *L'Expansion européene (1600-1870).* Paris, 1964.

Meillassoux, Claude, ed. *The Development of Indigenous Trade and Markets in West Africa.* London, 1971.

Williams, Eric. *Capitalism and Slavery.* 1944; London, 1964; New York, 1966.

The International Flow of Capital

Bairoch, Paul. *Evolution 1900-1967 et perspectives à court terme de l'économie du Tiers Monde.* Colloquium at Vienna Institute for Development and Cooperation, June 1968.

Bertin, Gilles-Y. *L'Investissment international.* Paris, 1967.

Cairncross, Alexander K. *Home and Foreign Investment, 1870-1913.* 1953; reprint ed., Clifton, N.J., n.d.

Clark, Colin. *The Conditions of Economic Progress.* London, 1940.

Feis, Herbert. *Europe, the World's Banker, 1870-1914.* 1930; reprint ed., Clifton, N.J., n.d.

General Agreement on Tariffs and Trade (Geneva). *Annual Reports on World Trade.*

Hobson, Charles K. *The Export of Capital.* 1914; reprint ed., New York, 1963.

Hobson, J.A. *Imperialism.* 1903; reprint ed., New York, n.d.

Imbert, Jean. *Histoire économique des origines à 1789.* Paris, 1965.

Jalée, Pierre. *Imperialism in the Seventies.* New York, 1973.

Kuznets, Simon. *National Income of the United States.* New York: National Bureau of Economic Research, 1946.

Lary, Hal B. *Imports of Manufactures from Less Developed Countries.* New York, 1968.

Layton, Christopher. *Trans-Atlantic Investments.* 2nd ed. Boulogne-sur-Seine, 1968.

League of Nations Secretariat, Economic Intelligence Section. *The Network of World Trade.* Geneva, 1942.

Lenin, V.I. "Imperialism, the Highest Stage of Capitalism." In *Collected Works.* 4th ed., vol. 22. Moscow and London, 1964.

Lewis, Cleona. *America's Stake in International Investments.* Washington, D.C., 1938.

Magdoff, Harry. *The Age of Imperialism.* New York, 1969.

Organization for Economic Cooperation and Development (Paris). *L'Aide au développement.*

United Nations Organization. *Les Flux internationaux de capitaux.* New York, 1952.

The Question of the Terms of Trade

Bairoch, Paul. *Diagnostic de l'évolution économique du Tiers Monde, 1900-1968.* 4th ed. Paris, 1970.

Imlah, Albert H. "The Terms of Trade of the United Kingdom, 1789-1913." *Journal of Economic History,* vol.10, no. 2 (November 1950).

Kindleberger, Charles P. "The Terms of Trade and Economic Development." *Review of Economics and Statistics,* vol. 50, no. 1, part 2 (February 1958).

Prebisch, Raul. *The Economic Development of Latin America and Its Principle Problems.* New York, 1950.

————. *Change and Development: Latin America's Great Task.* New York, 1971.

Richta, Radovan. *Civilization at the Crossroads: Social and Human Implications of the Scientific and Technological Revolution.* White Plains, N.Y., 1969.

Singer, Hans Wolfgang. "The Distribution of Gains Between Investing and Borrowing Countries Revisited." Brighton: University of Sussex Institute of Development Studies, 1971 (mimeo).

Van Haeverreke, André. *Rémunération du travail et commerce extérieur. Essor d'une économie paysanne exportatrice et termes de l'échange des producteurs d'arachides au Sénégal.* Louvain, 1970.

The Inherent Tendency of Capitalism to Expand Markets

Cox, Oliver C. *Capitalism as a System*. New York, 1964.

Denis, Henri. "Marchés nouveaux et accumulation du capital." *L'Homme et la Société*, no. 22 (1971).

Hecksher, E. "The Effects of Foreign Trade on the Distribution of Income." *Ekonomisk Tidskrift*, vol. 21 (1919).

Lenin, V.I. "A Characterization of Economic Romanticism." In *Collected Works*. 4th ed., vol. 2. Moscow, 1960.

————. "On the So-called Question of Markets." In ibid., vol.1.

Luxemburg, Rosa. *The Accumulation of Capital*. New York and London, 1968.

Samuelson, Paul A. "International Trade and the Equalization of Factor Prices." *Economic Journal*, June 1948; and "International Factor-price Equalization Once Again." *Economic Journal*, June 1949.

International Flows of Capital

Amin, Samir. *L'Afrique de l'Ouest bloquée*. Paris, 1971.

Baran, Paul, and Sweezy, Paul. *Monoply Capital*. New York, 1966.

Bertin, Gilles-Y. *L'Investissement international*. Paris, 1967.

Magdoff, Harry. *The Age of Imperialism*. New York, 1969.

The Functions of the Periphery

Alavi, Hamza. "Imperialism, Old and New." In Kathleen Gough and Hari P. Sharma, eds., *Imperialism and Revolution in South Asia*. New York and London, 1973.

Braun, Oscar. *Comercio internacional e imperialismo*. Buenos Aires, 1972.

Coquery, Catherine. "De l'impérialisme britannique à l'impérialisme contemporain: l'avatar colonial." *L'Homme et la Société*, no. 18 (1970).

Lee, George. "A Marxian Model of an Assimilating Imperialism." Tilburg Conference on Imperialism, 1969 (mimeo).

————. "Rosa Luxemburg and the Impact of Imperialism." *Economic Journal*, December 1971.

Magdoff, Harry. *The Age of Imperialism*. New York, 1969.

Palloix, Christian. *Problèmes de la croissance en économie ouverte*. Paris, 1969.

Schmidt, Alfred. *Imperialism and Economic Crisis of the Classical Epoch Before World War I in Theory and Practice*. Elsinore Conference on Imperialism, April 1971.

4. *Extraverted Accumulation and Dependence*

Bettelheim, Charles. "A propos du 'Marxisme de Mao': lettre à Rossana Rossanda." In R. Rossanda, ed., *Il Manifesto. Analyses et thèses de la nouvelle extrême-gauche Italienne.* Paris, 1971.

CHAPTER 4. ORIGIN AND DEVELOPMENT
OF UNDERDEVELOPMENT

1. *The Theory of the Transition to Peripheral Capitalism*

Arrighi, Giovanni. "The Relationship Between the Colonial and the Class Structure. A Critique of A.G. Frank's Theory of the Development of Underdevelopment." University of Dar-es-Salaam, 1969 (mimeo).
Avineri, Schlomo, ed. *Marx on Colonialism and Modernization.* New York, 1969.
Baran, Paul, and Hobsbawm, Eric. "The Stages of Economic Growth." *Kyklos,* no. 2 (1961).
Frank, Andre Gunder. "The Development of Underdevelopment." In *Latin America: Underdevelopment or Revolution.* New York and London, 1969.
———. "Towards a Theory of Underdevelopment." Centro de Estudios Economicas y Sociales, Santiago de Chile, 1970 (mimeo).
———. "W.W. Rostow: Ode to Underdevelopment." *Tricontinental* (English edition), no. 7 (1968).
Szentes, Tamás. *The Political Economy of Underdevelopment.* Budapest, 1971.

2. *The Extraversion of the Underdeveloped Economies*

The Historical Origin: Economic History

Amin, Samir. *The Maghreb in the Modern World.* London, 1970.
———. *L'Afrique de l'Ouest bloquée.* Paris, 1971.
Amin, Samir, and Coquery, Catherine. *Histoire économique du Congo, 1880-1968.* Paris, 1969.
Clairmonte, Frederick. *Economic Liberalism and Underdevelopment.* Bombay, 1960.
Dutt, Rajani Palme. *India Today.* London, 1940.
Frank, Andre Gunder. *Capitalism and Underdevelopment in Latin America.* New York, 1967.
Issawi, Charles, ed. *The Economic History of the Middle East.* Chicago, 1966.

Rey, Pierre-Philippe. *Colonialisme, néo-colonialisme et transition au capitalisme. L'expérience de la Comilog au Congo.* Paris, 1971.

Riad, Hassan. *L'Egypte nassérienne.* Paris, 1964.

The Historical Origin: Foreign Investment

Adam, György. "Multinational Corporations in the Early 1970s: New Trends in International Business, World-Wide Sourcing and Dedomiciling." Belfast: Queen's University, International Conference on Multinational Corporations, June 1971 (mimeo).

―――. "The World Corporation Problematics." In Hungarian Scientific Council for World Economy (Budapest), *Trends in World Economy,* no. 5 (1971).

Arrighi, Giovanni. "International Corporations, Labor Aristocracies and Economic Development in Tropical Africa." In Giovanni Arrighi and John Saul, *Essays on the Political Economy of Africa.* New York, 1973.

De Cecco, Marcello. "The Influence of Multinational Corporations on the Economic Policies of Underdeveloped Countries." Tilburg Conference on Capitalism in the 1970s, September 1970 (mimeo).

Hymer, Stephen. "The Efficiency (Contradictions) of Multinational Corporations." New Haven: Yale University, 1970-72 (mimeo).

―――. "Excerpt on Mercantilism III: The Age of the Multinational Corporation." New Haven: Yale University, 1970-72 (mimeo).

―――. "The Multinational Corporation and Its Aims." New Haven: Yale University, 1970-72 (mimeo).

―――. "The Multinational Corporation and the Law of Uneven Development." New Haven: Yale University, 1970-72 (mimeo).

Hymer, S. and Resnick, A. "International Trade and Uneven Development." New Haven: Yale University, 1970-72 (mimeo).

Hymer, S. and Rowthorn, R. "Multinational Corporations and International Oligopoly: The Non-American Challenge." New Haven: Yale University, 1970-72 (mimeo).

Jenkins, Robin. "Imperialism in Mozambique." Elsinore Conference on Imperialism, April 1971 (mimeo).

Martinelli, Alberto, and Somaini, Eugenio. "Les Etats nationaux et les firmes multinationales." Congrès des sociologues de langue française Hammamet (Tunisia), September 1970 (mimeo).

Miller, R.E., and Carter, P.R. "A Modern Dual Economy: A Cost-Benefit Analysis of Lamco Cy." Monrovia Conference on Planning in Liberia, April 1971. Dakar, Institut Africain de Développement Economique et de Planification, 1973 (mimeo).

Sunkel, Osvaldo. "Intégration capitaliste transnationale et désintégration nationale en Amérique latine." *Politique étrangère,* no. 6 (1970).

Szentes, Tamás. "Socio-Economic Effects and Patterns of Foreign Capital Investment." IDEP, Dar-es-Salaam Seminar on Foreign Capital, April 1972 (mimeo).

Tanzer, Michael. *The Political Economy of International Oil and the Underdeveloped Countries.* London, 1970; Boston, 1970.

The Historical Origin: Industrialization by Import-Substitution

Furtado, Celso. *Development and Stagnation in Latin America: A Structural Approach.* New Haven, 1965.

Tavares, Mario Conceição, et al. "The Growth and Decline of Import Substitution in Brazil." In United Nations Economic Commission for Latin America, *Economic Bulletin for Latin America,* vol. 9, no. 1 (March 1964).

The Historical Origin: Technological Dependence

Amin, Samir. *Le Développement du capitalisme en Côte d'Ivoire.* Paris, 1968.

———. *L'Economie du Maghreb.* Paris, 1966.

———. *Trois expériences africaines de développement: le Mali, la Guinée et le Ghana.* Paris, 1965.

Cooper, Charles. *The Transfer of Industrial Technology to the Underdeveloped Countries.* Brighton: University of Sussex, Institute of Development Studies, 1971 (mimeo).

International Bank for Reconstruction and Development (Washington, D.C.), *Public Finance Surveys.*

Issawi, Charles P. "Egypt Since 1800. A Study in Lopsided Development." *Journal of Economic History,* March 1961.

Meillassoux, Claude. *Anthropologie économique des Gouro de Côted'Ivoire.* Paris, 1965.

———. "Essai d'interprétation du phénomène économique dans les sociétés traditionelles d'auto-subsistance." *Cahiers d'études africaines,* no. 1 (1960).

Müller-Plantenberg, Urs. "Technologie et dépendance." *Critiques de l'économie politique,* no. 3 (1971).

Rey, Pierre-Philippe. *Colonialisme, néo-colonialisme et transition au capitalisme. L'expérience de la Comilog au Congo.* Paris, 1971.

Riad, Hassan. *L'Egypte nassérienne.* Paris, 1964.

Singer, Hans Wolfgang. *The Distribution of Gains Between Investing and Borrowing Countries Revisited.* Brighton: University of Sussex, Institute of Development Studies, 1971 (mimeo).

————. "The Foreign Company as an Exporter of Technology." Brighton: University of Sussex, Institute of Development Studies, 1971 (mimeo).

United Nations Committee for Trade and Development. *Guidelines for the Study of Transfer of Technology to Development Countries.* Geneva, 1972.

United Nations Organization. *La Dette publique 1914-1946.* New York, 1948.

Vaitsos, Constantine. *Bargaining and the Distribution of Returns in the Purchase of Technology by the Developing Countries.* United Nations Committee for Trade and Development, 1971.

Sectoral Unevenness in Productivity

Amin, S., Pinto, A., and Smith, A.D. *Les Problèmes de la politique des salaires dans le développement économique.* Paris, 1970.

Baran, Paul, and Sweezy, Paul. *Monopoly Capital.* New York, 1966.

Kalecki, Michal. *The Theory of Economic Dynamics.* London, 1954; 2nd ed., London, 1965, New York, 1968.

Robinson, Joan. *The Economics of Imperfect Competition.* London, 1933; New York, 1969.

Sraffa, Piero. *Production of Commodities by Means of Commodities.* Cambridge, 1960; New York, 1960.

The Choice of Production Techniques in the Periphery

Allais, M. *Economie et Intérêt.* Paris, 1947.

Balogh, Thomas. "A Note on Deliberate Industrialization for Higher Incomes." *Economic Journal,* June 1947.

Bettelheim, Charles. *Studies in the Theory of Planning.* Bombay, 1959; New York, 1968.

Chenery, Hollis B. "The Application of Investment Criteria." *Quarterly Journal of Economics,* February 1953.

Dobb, Maurice. *On Economic Theory and Socialism.* London, 1955; reprint ed., New York, 1965.

Galenson, W., and Leibenstein, H. "Investment Criteria, Productivity and Economic Development." *Quarterly Journal of Economics,* August 1955.

Harrod, Roy F. *Towards a Dynamic Economics.* London, 1948; New York, 1948.

Kahn, R.F. "Investment Criteria in Development Programs." *Quarterly Journal of Economics,* February 1951.

Massé, Pierre. "Pratique et philosophie de l'investissement." *Economie appliquée,* vol. 5, no. 4 (October-December 1952).

Polak, J.J. "Balance of Payments Problems of Countries Reconstructing with the Help of Foreign Loans." *Quarterly Journal of Economics,* February 1943.

Sen, Amartya K. *Choice of Techniques.* 3rd ed. London and New York, 1968.

Unequal International Specialization

Aftalion, A. *Les Crises périodiques de surproduction.* Paris, 1913-14.

Goodwin, *The New Economics.* New York, 1948.

Habèrler, Gottfried. *Prosperity and Depression.* 3rd ed. Geneva, 1941.

Hirschman, Albert O. *The Strategy of Economic Development.* New Haven, 1958.

Keynes, John M. *The General Theory of Employment, Interest and Money.* London, 1936; New York, 1965.

Klein, Lawrence R. "Theories of Effective Demand and Employment." *Journal of Political Economy,* April 1947.

Lange, Oskar. "On the Theory of the Multiplier." In *Papers in Economics and Sociology.* Oxford, 1970.

Mattick, Paul. *Marx and Keynes.* London, 1971; New York, 1973.

Perroux, François. *L'Economie des jeunes nations.* Paris, 1962.

————. *L'Economie du XXe siècle.* Paris, 1969.

Stolper, W.F. "A Note on the Multiplier." *Economia Internazionale,* vol. 3, no. 3 (August 1950).

3. Marginalization

Amin, Samir. *L'Economie du Maghreb.* Paris, 1966.

————. *Le Développement du capitalisme en Côte d'Ivoire.* Paris, 1968.

————. *L'Afrique de l'Ouest bloquée.* Paris, 1971.

Amin, Samir, and Coquery, Catherine. *Histoire économique du Congo, 1880-1968.* Paris, 1969.

Baran, Paul, and Sweezy, Paul. *Monopoly Capital.* New York, 1966.

Chamberlin, Edward H. *The Theory of Monopolistic Competition.* 1933; 8th ed., Cambridge, Mass., 1962.

Clark, Colin. *The Conditions of Economic Progress.* London, 1940.

Kuznets, Simon. *Les Aspects quantitatifs de la croissance économique des nations.* International Bank for Reconstruction and Development, 1963.

Mumford, Lewis. *Technics and Civilization.* London, 1934; New York, 1963.

Riad, Hassan. *L'Egypte nassérienne.* Paris, 1964.

4. Dependence

Commercial, Financial, and Technological Dependence

Pearson, Lester B. *Partners in Development. Report of the Commission on International Development.* New York, 1969.

Theoretical studies on Latin America:

Caputo, Orlando, and Pizarro, Roberto. "Imperialismo, dependencia y relaciones económicas internacionales." *Centro de Estudios Sociales* (Santiago de Chile), nos. 12-13 (1971).

Cardoso, F.H., and Corréa Weffort, F. *Sociológia de la dependencia.* Santiago de Chile, 1971.

Cardoso, F.H., and Faletto, E., *Dependencia y desarrollo en América latina.* Mexico, 1969.

Dos Santos, Theotonio. "Dependencia y cambio social." *Centro de Estudios Sociales* (Santiago de Chile), no. 11. (1970).

————. "The Structure of Dependence." *American Economic Review,* May 1970.

Furtado, Celso. "Dépendance externe et théorie économique." *L'Homme et la Société,* no. 22 (1971).

————. *Los Estados Unidos y el subdesarrollo de América Latina.* Lima, 1971.

Various Studies on Africa

Africa Research Group, *International Dependence in the 1970s.* Cambridge, Mass., 1970 (mimeo).

Clower, W., Dalton, G., Harwitz, M., Walters, A. *Liberia: Growth Without Development.* Evanston, Ill., 1965.

Ehrensaft, Philip. "Semi-Industrialized Capitalism in the Third World." University of Dar-es-Salaam, 1971 (mimeo).

Ghai, Dharam. "The Concept and Strategies of Economic Independence in African Countries." Committee of Directors of Economic and Social Research Institutes in Africa, Nairobi, February 1971 (mimeo).

Green, Reginald H. "The International Economic System and Development." New York: Columbia University, Conference on International Development, 1970 (mimeo).

―――. "Notes Toward a Strategy for Achieving Economic Independence." International Seminar on Imperialism, New Delhi, March 1972 (mimeo).

Guruli, Kassim. *On the Concept of Socialism and Self-Reliance in Tanzania.* University of Dar-es-Salaam, Economic Research Bureau, 1970.

Harvey, Charles. "Economic Independence: A View from Zambia." CODESRIA meeting, Nairobi, February 1971 (mimeo).

Saul, John. "The Political Aspects of Economic Independence." CODESRIA meeting, Nairobi, February 1971 (mimeo).

Sutcliffe, Robert Baldwin. "Outlook for Capitalism in the 1970s. The Peripheral Capitalist Countries." Tilburg Conference on Capitalism in the 1970s, September 1970 (mimeo).

The Tendency to Deficit in the External Balance of Payments

De Vries, Margaret G. "The Magnitudes of Exchange Devaluation." *Finance and Development,* vol. 5, no. 2 (June 1968).

Harrod, Roy. *The Dollar.* London, 1953; New York, 1963.

International Monetary Fund (Washington, D.C.). *Annual Reports.*

―――. *Balance of Payments Yearbook.*

Kindleberger, Charles P. "The Dollar Shortage." In *International Economics.* 1953; 5th ed., Homewood Ill., 1973.

Lambert, Denis. *Les Inflations sud-américaines.* Paris, 1959.

League of Nations. *Documents sélectionnés sur la distribution de l'or.* Geneva, 1939.

―――. *L'Expérience monétaire internationale.* Geneva, 1939.

Prebisch, Raul. *The Economic Development of Latin America and Its Principal Problems.* New York, 1950.

The Role of the Monetary Systems of the Periphery

Allen, George C. *A Short Economic History of Modern Japan, 1867-1970.* 3rd ed. London, 1972.

Amin, Samir. *L'Afrique de l'Ouest bloquée.* Paris, 1969.

―――. *Le Monde des affaires sénégalais.* Paris, 1969.

―――. "Pour un aménagement du système monétaire des pays africains de la zone franc." *Le Mois en Afrique,* no. 41 (1969).

Amin, Samir. *Trois expériences africaines de développement: le Mali, la Guinée et le Ghana.* Paris, 1965.

Bloch-Lainé, F., ed. *La Zone franc.* Paris, 1956.

Chabert, Alexandre. *Structure économique et théorie monétaire.* Paris, 1956.

de la Fournière, Xavier. *La Zone franc.* Paris, 1971.

Felix, David. "Structural Imbalances, Social Conflict and Inflation (in Chile)." *Economic Development and Cultural Change,* January 1960.

Greaves, Ida. *Colonial Monetary Conditions.* 1950; reprint ed., New York, n.d.

Lambert, D. *Les Inflations sud-américaines.* Paris, 1959.

Loxley, J. "The Monetary Systems of Tanzania Since 1967." Dar-es-Salaam, 1969 (mimeo).

Newlyn, Walter T., and Rowan, D.C. *Money and Banking in British Colonial Africa.* Oxford, 1954.

Ryelandt, Bernard. *L'Inflation au pays sous-développé (Congo, 1960-1969).* Kinshasa, 1970.

Schmidt, H.D. *Monetary Policy and Social Conflict in Indonesia.* Berkeley, 1969.

Seers, Dudley. "A Theory of Inflation and Growth in Underdeveloped Countries, Based on the Experience of Latin America." *Oxford Economic Papers,* vol. 14, no. 2 (1962).

Than Van Thuan. *Les Fondements socio-économiques de la révolution industrielle du Japon.* Lausanne, 1966.

Wallich, H.C. *Monetary Problems of an Export Economy.* Cambridge, 1950.

The Functions of the Periphery in the Movement of the World Conjuncture

Clark, Colin, and Crawford, J. *The National Income of Australia.* London, 1936.

Haberler, Gottfried. *Prosperity and Depression.* 3rd ed. Geneva, 1941.

5. The Blocking of Transition

Amin, Samir. *L'Afrique de l'Ouest bloquée.* Paris, 1971.

———. *The Maghreb in the Modern World.* London, 1970.

Amin, Samir, and Coquery, Catherine. *Histoire économique du Congo, 1880-1968.* Paris, 1969.

Riad, Hassan. *L'Egypte nassérienne.* Paris, 1964.

CHAPTER 5. THE CONTEMPORARY SOCIAL FORMATIONS OF THE PERIPHERY

1. The Historical Formation of the Contemporary Periphery.

Boeke, J.H. *Indische Economie*. Amsterdam, 1940.

Economic Development and Cultural Change. Chicago, Northwestern University.

Frank, Andre Gunder. "The Sociology of Development and Underdevelopment of Sociology." In *Latin America: Underdevelopment or Revolution*. New York and London, 1969.

The American Peripheral Formations

Braun, Oscar. *Desarrollo del capital monopolista en Argentine*. Buenos Aires, 1970.

Cardoso, F.H. *Capitalismo e escravidão no Brasil do Sur*. São Paulo, 1962.

———. *Politique et développement dans les sociétés dépendantes*. Paris, 1971.

———. *Sociologie du développement en Amérique latine*. Paris, 1971.

Cardoso, F.H., and Faletto, E. *Dependencia y desarrollo en América latina*. Mexico, 1969.

Chaunu, Pierre. *L'Amérique et les Amériques*. Paris, 1964.

Dominguez Noceto, José, et al. *El proceso económico del Uruguay*. Montevideo, 1969.

Ferrer, Aldo. *The Argentine Economy*. Berkeley, 1967.

Frank, Andre Gunder. "The Development of Underdevelopment." In *Latin America: Underdevelopment or Revolution*. New York and London, 1969.

Furtado, Celso. *L'Amérique latine*. Paris, 1970.

———. *Un Projeto para Brasil*. Rio de Janeiro, 1969.

Germani, Gino. *Política y sociedad en una época de transición*. Buenos Aires, 1968.

Gonzalez Casanove, Pablo. *Democracy in Mexico*. New York, 1970.

Ianni, Octavio. *Estado e capitalismo, estructura social e industrialização do Brasil*. Rio de Janeiro, 1965.

Instituto Latino-Americano de Planificación Económica y Social. *Dos polémicas sobre el desarrollo de América latina*. Mexico, 1970.

Laclau, Ernesto. "Feudalism and Capitalism in Latin America." *New Left Review*, no. 67 (1971).

Ortiz, Ricardo M. *Historia económica de la Argentina, 1850-1930.* Buenos Aires, 1964.

Roel, Virgilio. *Historia social y económica de la colonia.* Lima, 1970.

Silva Herzog, Jesus. *La Révolution mexicaine.* Paris, 1968.

Stavenhagen, Rodolfo. *Sept thèses erronées sur l'Amérique latine.* Paris, 1973.

Sunkel, Osvaldo, and Paz, Pedro. *El subdesarrollo latinoamericano y la teoría del desarrollo.* Mexico, 1970.

Vilela Luz, Nícia. *A Luta pela industrialização do Brasil, 1808-1930.* São Paulo, 1961.

Williams, Eric. *Capitalism and Slavery.* 1944; London, 1964; New York, 1966.

The Arab and Asian Peripheral Formations

Amin, Samir. *The Maghreb in the Modern World.* London, 1970.

Bettelheim, Charles. *India Independent.* London, 1968; New York, 1969.

Clairmonte, Frederick. *Economic Liberalism and Underdevelopment.* Bombay, 1960.

Cook, M.A., ed. *Studies in the Economic History of the Middle East.* London, 1970; New York, 1970.

de Planhol, Xavier. *Les Fondements géographiques de l'histoire de l'Islam.* Paris, 1968.

Dutt, Rajani Palme. *India Today.* London, 1940.

Dutt, Romesch C. *Economic History of India.* 1906; reprint ed., New York, n.d.

Fistie, Pierre. *La Thaïlande contemporaine.* Paris, 1967.

Furnivall, John S. *Netherlands India. A Study in Plural Economy.* London, 1930.

Haccou, J.-F., and Scholte, G. "Le développement économique de l'Indonésie." Institut de Science Economique Appliquée, *Cahiers de l'I.S.E.A.,* no. 87 (1959).

Hilan, Rizkalla. *Culture et développement en Syrie et dans les pays arabes.* Paris, 1969.

Hussein, Mahmoud. *Class Conflict in Egypt: 1945-1970.* New York, 1974.

Issawi, Charles, ed. *Economic History of the Middle East.* Chicago, 1966.

———. "Egypt Since 1800: A Study in Lopsided Development." *Journal of Economic History,* March 1961.

———. *Growth and Structural Change in the Middle East.* Columbia University Conference on Economic Development, 1971.

Issawi, Charles, ed. "Middle East Economic Development 1815-1914. The General and the Specific." In M.A. Cook, ed., *Studies in the Economic History of the Middle East.* London, 1970; New York, 1970.

Laroui, Abdullah. *L'Idéologie arabe contemporaine.* Paris, 1967.

Mukherjee, Ramkrishna. *The Rise and Fall of the East India Company.* 1958; London and New York, 1974.

Riad, Hassan. *L'Egypte nassérienne.* Paris, 1964.

Thorner, Daniel. *Peasant Unrest in South-East Asia.* Bombay, 1968.

The African Peripheral Formations

Afana, Osende. *L'Economie de l'Ouest africain.* Paris, 1966.

Ameillon, B. *La Guinée, bilan d'une indépendance.* Paris, 1964.

Amin, Samir. *L'Afrique de l'Ouest bloquée.* Paris, 1971.

———. *Le Développement du capitalisme en Côte d'Ivoire.* Paris, 1968.

Amin, S., and Coquery, Catherine. *Histoire économique du Congo, 1880-1968.* Paris, 1969.

Arrighi, Giovanni. "The Political Economy of Rhodesia." In Giovanni Arrighi and John Saul, *Essays on the Political Economy of Africa.* New York and London, 1973.

Arrighi, Giovanni, and Saul, John. "Socialism and Economic Development in Tropical Africa." In ibid.

Balandier, Georges. *Daily Life in the Kingdom of the Kongo: From the Sixteenth to the Eighteenth Century.* New York, 1968.

Barry, Boubacar. *Le Royaume de Waalo.* Paris, 1972.

Bénot, Yves. *Idéologies des indépendances africaines.* Paris, 1969.

Berg, Elliot J. "The Economics of the Migrant Labor System." In Hilda Kuper, ed., *Urbanization and Migration in West Africa.* Los Angeles, 1965.

Brunschwig, Henri. *L'Avènement de l'Afrique noire du XIXe siècle à nos jours.* Paris, 1963.

Coquery, Catherine. "De la traite des esclaves à l'exportation de l'huile de palme et des palmistes au Dahomey, XIXe siècle." In Claude Meillassoux, ed., *The Development of Indigenous Trade and Markets in West Africa.* London, 1971.

———. *Le Congo au temps des compagnies concessionnaires, 1890-1930.* Paris, 1973.

Cournanel, Alain. "Le Capitalisme d'Etat en Guinée." Unpublished Ph. D. thesis, Paris, 1969.

Crowder, Michael. *West Africa Under Colonial Rule.* London, 1968; Evanston, Ill., 1968.

De Andrade, Mario, and Olliver, Marc. *La Guerre en Angola*. Paris, 1971.

Dike, Kenneth Onwuka. *Trade and Politics in the Niger Delta. 1830-1885*. Oxford, 1956.

Fitch, Bob, and Oppenheimer, Mary. *Ghana: The End of an Illusion*. New York and London, 1966.

Gann, L.H., and Duignan, Peter. *Colonialism in Africa, 1870-1960. Vol. I: The History and Politics of Colonialism, 1870-1914*. Cambridge, 1969.

Gérard-Libois, J. "The New Class and Rebellion in the Congo." *Socialist Register 1966*. London, 1966.

Hill, Richard Leslie. *Egypt in the Sudan, 1820-1881*. London, 1959.

Holt, P.M. *The Mahdist State in the Sudan, 1881-1898*. Oxford, 1958.

Horwitz, Ralph. *The Political Economy of South Africa*. London, 1967.

Lewis, W. Arthur. "Economic Development with Unlimited Supplies of Labor." *The Manchester School*, May 1954.

Markovitz, Irving, ed. *African Politics and Society*. New York, 1970.

Meillassoux, Claude, ed. *The Development of Indigenous Trade and Markets in West Africa*. London. 1971.

Merlier, Michel. *Le Congo de la colonisation belge à l'indépendance*. Paris, 1962.

Oliver, Roland, and Mathew, Gervase, eds. *History of East Africa*. Oxford, 1963.

Pankhurst, Richard. *An Introduction to the Economic History of Ethiopia, from Early Times to 1800*. London, 1961; Atlantic Highlands, N.J., 1961.

Person, J.-Y. *Samori*. Dakar, IFAN, 1970.

Ranger, T.O., ed. *Aspects of Central African History*. London, 1968; Evanston, Ill., 1968.

Rey, Pierre-Philippe. *Colonialisme, néo-colonialisme et transition au capitalisme. L'expérience de la Comilog au Congo*. Paris, 1971.

Rodney, Walter. "African Slavery and Other Forms of Social Oppression on the Upper Guinea Coast in the Context of the Atlantic Slave Trade." *Journal of African History*, vol. 7, no. 3 (1966).

Rweyemamu, Justinian F. "The Political Economy of Tanzania." Unpublished Ph.D. thesis, Harvard University, 1971.

Szereszewski, R. *Structural Changes in the Economy of Ghana, 1891-1911*. London, 1965.

Trimingham, John S. *Islam in the Sudan*. 2nd ed. London, 1949.

Thion, Serge. *Le Pouvoir pâle: Essai sur le système sud-africain*. Paris, 1969.

Van Haeverreke, André. *Rémunération du travail et commerce extérieur. Essor d'une économie paysanne exportatrice et termes de l'échange des producteurs d'arachides au Sénégal*. Louvain, 1970.

Vansina, Jan. *Introduction à l'ethnographie du Congo.* Kinshasa, 1966.

————. "Long-distance Trade-routes in Central Africa." *Journal of African History,* vol. 3, no. 3 (1962).

————. "Notes sur l'origine du royaume de Kongo." *Journal of African History,* vol. 4, no. 1 (1963).

2. The General Characteristics of Peripheral Formations

The Predominance of Agrarian Capitalism

Amin, Samir. "Le Développement du capitalisme en Afrique noire." In Victor Fay, ed., *En partant du "Capital."* Paris, 1968.

Bergmann, Theodor. "Réforme agraire et révolution verte: le cas de l'Inde." *Economie Rurale,* no. 88 (April-June 1971).

Bondestam, Lars. *Agriculture Development in Awash Valley.* Economic National Institute, Addis Ababa, 1971.

Boserup, Ester. *The Conditions of Agricultural Growth: The Economics of Agrarian Change Under Population Pressure.* London, 1965; Chicago, 1965.

Brown, Lester R. "The Green Revolution, Rural Employment and the Urban Crisis." New York: Columbia Conference on International Economic Development, February 1970.

Chayanov, A.V. *On the Theory of Peasant Economy.* Homewood, Ill., 1966.

Delbard, Yves. "Les Dynamismes sociaux au Sénégal." Dakar: Institut de Science Economique Appliquée, 1964 (mimeo).

Dikoume, Cosme. *Les Problèmes fonciers du Cameroun oriental.* Duala: I.P.D., 1970.

Dobb, Maurice. *Studies in the Development of Capitalism.* London, 1946; rev. ed., New York, 1964.

Dumont, René. "Notes sur les implications sociales de la révolution verte dans quelques pays d'Afrique." Geneva: United Nations Research Institute for Social Development, 1971 (mimeo).

————. *Paysanneries aux abois: Ceylan, Tunisie, Sénégal.* Paris, 1972.

Dumont, René, and Mazoyer, Marcel. *Socialisms and Development.* New York, 1973.

Gutelman, M. *L'Agriculture socialisée à Cuba.* Paris, 1967.

————. *Réforme et mystification agraires en Amérique latine. Le cas du Mexique.* Paris, 1971.

Hill, Polly. *Studies in Rural Capitalism in West Africa.* London, 1970.

Jacoby, Erich H. *Man and Land: The Fundamental Issue in Development,* London, 1971.

Karim, A.K.N. *Changing Society in India and Pakistan*. Dacca, 1950.

Mukherjee, Ramkrishna. *The Dynamics of a Rural Society: A Study of the Economic Structure in Bengal Villages*. Berlin, 1957.

Myrdal, Gunnar. *Asian Drama: An Inquiry into the Poverty of Nations*. London, 1968; New York, 1971.

N'Dongala, E. "Mutations structurelles de l'économie traditionnelle dans le Bas-Congo sous l'impact de la colonisation." In *Cahiers Economiques et Sociaux* (Leopoldville), vol. 4, no. 1 (March 1966); and "Développement rural et fonction coopérative dans l'agriculture congolaise avant la décolonisation." in ibid., vol. 4, no. 4 (December 1966).

O'Brien, Donald B. *The Mourides of Senegal*. Oxford, 1971.

Post, Kenneth. *On "Peasantisation" and Rural Class Differentiation in Western Africa*. The Hague, 1970.

Raulin, Henri. *La Dynamique des techniques agraires en Afrique tropicale du nord*. Paris, 1967.

Saul, John, and Woods, Roger. "African Peasantries." In Giovanni Arrighi and John Saul, eds., *Essays on the Political Economy of Africa*. New York, 1973.

Schumaker, E.J. "Bureaucracy, Party and Rural Commercial Reform in Senegal, 1957-1968." New Haven: Yale University, Ph.D. dissertation.

Thorner, Daniel. *Peasant Unrest in South-East Asia*. Bombay, 1968.

Thorner, Daniel, and Thorner, Alice. *Land and Labor in India*. New York, 1962.

United Nations Research Institute for Trade and Development. "A Selection of Readings on the Green Revolution." Geneva, 1971 (mimeo).

Warriner, Doreen. *Land Reform and Development in the Middle East*. 2nd ed. London, 1962.

The Limits Imposed by Foreign Capital

Amin, Samir. *Le Développement du capitalisme en Côte d'Ivoire*. Paris, 1968.

———. *Les Revenus susceptibles d'épargne et leur utilisation en Egypte, 1938-1952*. Thesis, Paris, 1965.

Esseks, J., ed. *African States' Quest for Economic Independence. The First Decade*. To be published by Northern Illinois University Press.

Frank, Andre Gunder. *Lumpenbourgeoisie: Lumpendevelopment: Dependence, Class and Politics in Latin America*. New York, 1972.

Robinson, Ivor. *The Petit-Bourgeoisie. An Analysis of Its Socioeconomic Origins and Its Contemporary Role in the Political Economy of Kenya*. University of Nairobi, January 1971 (mimeo).

Shivji, Issa. *Class Struggles in Tanzania*. London, 1976; New York, 1976.

Verhaegen, Benoit. "Social Classes in the Congo." *Revolution,* no. 10 (1964).

Wallerstein, Immanuel. *The Colonial Era in Africa. Changes in the Social Structures.* Montreal: McGill University, 1972 (mimeo).

Waterman, Peter. *Nigeria as a Neo-colony.* Zaria (Nigeria): Ahmadu Bello University, 1971 (mimeo).

Who Controls Industry in Kenya? East African Publishing House, Nairobi, 1968.

Contemporary Tendencies Toward the Development of National Bureaucracies

Alavi, Hamza. "The State in Post-Colonial Societies: The Case of Pakistan and Bangladesh." In Kathleen Gough and Hari P. Sharma, eds., *Imperialism and Revolution in South Asia.* New York, 1973.

Althabe, G. *Oppression et libération dans l'imaginaire. Les communautés villageoises de la côte orientale de Madigascar.* Paris, 1969.

Arrighi, Giovanni. "International Corporations, Labor Aristocracies and Economic Development in Tropical Africa." In Giovanni Arrighi and John Saul, *Essays on the Political Economy of Africa.* New York, 1973.

Arrighi, Giovanni, and Saul, John S. "Nationalism and Revolution in Sub-Saharan Africa." In ibid.

———. "Socialism and Economic Development in Tropical Africa." In ibid.

Aron, Raymond. *La Lutte des classes.* Paris, 1964.

Bézy, F. "La situation économique et sociale du Congo-Kinshasa." *Cultures et Développement,* no. 3 (1969).

Burnham, James. *The Managerial Revolution.* London, 1942; reprint ed., Westport, Conn., 1972.

Galbraith, John K. *The New Industrial State.* New York, 1967.

———. *The Affluent Society.* Boston, 1958.

Ryelandt, Bernard. *L'Inflation au pays sous-développé; Congo, 1960-1969;* Kinshasha, 1970.

Silva Michelena, José. *The Illusion of Democracy in Dependent Nations.* Boston, 1971.

Proletarianization and Marginalization

Allen, Christopher. *Unions, Income and Development.* University of Edinburgh (mimeo).

Amin, Samir. *Le Développement du capitalisme en Côte d'Ivoire.* Paris, 1968.

————. *L'Economie du Maghreb.* Paris, 1966.

Axelson, Sigbert. *Culture Confrontation in the Lower Congo.* Falkoping, Sweden, 1970.

Bagú, Sergio. *Industrialización, sociedad y dependencia en América latina.* Santiago de Chile: Facultad Latino-Americana de Sciencias Sociales, 1970.

Boserup, Ester. *The Conditions of Agricultural Growth: The Economics of Agrarian Change Under Population Pressure.* London, 1965; Chicago, 1965.

Cardoso, F.H. *Comentario sobre os conceitos de superpopulação relativa e marginalidade,* Estudo I, São Paulo: Centro Brasileiro de Plavejamento, 1972.

Clairmonte, Frederick. *Zambia: Wages, Income and Employment.* Addis Ababa: United Nations Economic Commission for Africa, 1972 (mimeo).

Cline, William R. *Potential Effects of Income Redistribution on Economic Growth: Latin American Cases.* New York, 1972.

de Navarrete, Ifigenia Martínez. *La Distribución del ingreso y el desarrollo económico de México.* Mexico, 1960.

International Labor Organization. *A Program of Action for Ceylon.* Geneva, 1971.

————. *Towards Full Employment: A Program for Colombia.* Geneva, 1970.

Nun, José. "Sobrepoblación relativa, ejército industrial de reserva y masa marginal." *Revista Latino-Americana de Sociología,* vol. 5, no. 2 (July 1969).

Quijano, Anibal. *Redefinición de la dependencia y marginalización en América latina.* Santiago de Chile: Centro de Estudios Sociales, 1970 (mimeo).

Stewart, Frances, and Streeten, Paul. "Conflicts Between Output and Employment Objectives in Developing Countries." *Oxford Economic Papers,* vol. 23, no. 2 (1971).

Thorbecke, Erik. *Unemployment and Underemployment in the Developing World.* New York: Columbia Conference on International Economic Development, 1970 (mimeo).

Turnham, David, and Jaeger, Ingelies. *The Employment Problem in Less Developed Countries.* Paris, 1971.

United Nations Economic Commission for Latin America. *Estudios sobre la distribución del ingreso en América latina.* 1967.

New Central and Peripheral Formations

Arrighi, Giovanni. "The Political Economy of Rhodesia." In Giovanni Arrighi and John Saul, *Essays on the Political Economy of Africa.* New York, 1973.

Chaunu, Pierre. *L'Amérique et les Amériques.* Paris, 1964.

Gray, John Richard. *The Two Nations: Aspects of the Development of Race Relations in the Rhodesias and Nyasaland.* London, 1960.

Hanegbi, H., Machover, M., and Orr, A. "The Class Nature of Israeli Society." *New Left Review,* February 1971.

Horwitz, Ralph. *The Political Economy of South Africa.* London, 1967.

Jiryis, Sabri. *The Arabs in Israel, 1948-1966.* New York, 1976.

North, Douglass C. *Economic Growth of the United States, 1790-1860.* Englewood Cliffs, N.J., 1961.

Thion, Serge. *Le Pouvoir pâle: Essai sur le système sud-africain.* Paris, 1969.

3. For a Strategy of Transition

The Soviet Mode of Production

Amon, Pierre. "La Révolution culturelle et le marxisme." *Que faire,* no. 5 (November 1970).

Barone, E. "The Ministry of Production in the Collectivist State (1908)." In F.A. Von Hayek, ed., *Collectivist Economic Planning.* London, 1935.

Bettelheim, Charles. *Economic Calculation and Forms of Property.* London, 1976; New York, 1976.

Brus, Wlodzimierz. *The Market in a Socialist Economy.* London, 1972; Boston, 1972.

Critiques de l'économie politique, no. 6 (1972). See article by Roman Rosdolsky. In nos. 7 and 8 (1972), see articles by G. Tibert, B. Jobic, M. Ducombs, Tatsuo Tomochika, E. Germain, and C. Samary.

Denis, Henri, and Lavigne, M. *Le Problème des prix en Union soviétique.* Paris, 1965.

Horvat, Branko. *An Essay on Yugoslav Society.* New York, 1969.

Jakubowsky, F. *Les Superstructures idéologiques dans la conception matérialiste de l'histoire.* Paris, 1972.

Rossanda, Rossana. "Mao's Marxism." *Socialist Register 1971.* London, 1971.

Socialist Register 1965-1971. See articles by Miliband, Hodges, Johnstone, Merrington, Deutscher, Rossanda, Sartre, Draper, Meszaros, and Arblaster. London, 1965-1971.

The Spontaneous Tendencies of the System

Capitalism in the 70's. Tilburg Conference, September 1970 (mimeo).

Imperialism. Elsinore Conference, Danish Institute for Peace and Conflict Research, April 1971 (mimeo).

Lewis, Oscar. *The Children of Sanchez: Autobiography of a Mexican Family.* London, 1962; New York, 1961.

Mattick, Paul. *Marx and Keynes.* London, 1971; New York, 1973.

Mauro Marini, Ruy. *Subdesarrollo y revolución.* Mexico, 1969.

Mumford, Lewis. *Technics and Civilization.* London, 1934; New York, 1963.

Richta, Radovan. *Civilization at the Crossroads: Social and Human Implications of the Scientific and Technological Revolution.* White Plains, N.Y., 1969.

Tsuru, Shigeto, ed. *Has Capitalism Changed?* Tokyo, 1961.

Ward, Barbara, and Dubos, René. *Only One Earth.* New York, 1972.

The Problematic of Transition

Abdel Fadil, Mahmoud. "Modèles dynamiques d'intraversion dans les pays en voie de développement." *Economie appliquée,* no. 4 (1971).

Amon, Pierre. "La Révolution culturelle et le marxisme." *Que faire,* no. 5 (November 1970).

———. "Révolution culturelle et dialectique du centre et de la peripherie." *L'Homme et la Société,* no. 21 (1971).

Bettelheim, Charles. *La Transition vers l'économie socialiste.* Paris, 1968.

Falkowski, M. *Problèmes de la croissance du Tiers Monde, vus par les économistes des pays socialistes.* Paris, 1968.

Mahalanobis, P.C. *The Approach of Operational Research to Planning in India.* Calcutta, 1963.

Meadows, Donella H. et al. *The Limits to Growth.* London, 1972; New York, 1972.

Müller-Plantenberg, Urs. "Technologie et dépendance." *Critiques de l'économie politique,* no. 3 (1971).

Socialist Register, 1965: see article by Hamza Alavi; 1968: article by K.S. Karol; and 1970: article by V.G. Kiernan. London, 1965, 1968, 1970.

Sweezy, Paul M., and Bettelheim, Charles. *On the Transition to Socialism.* New York and London, 1971.

Index

Abbas, Ferhat, 316
Abbasids, 37, 40, 324
Abdel Kader, 29, 315
Abdullah, Caliph, 323
Abdullah ibn-Husein, 311
Abyssinia, 332
Afghanistan, 239, 300, 369
Africa, *see* Black Africa
"African" mode of production, 17
Aftalion, A., 89, 107
Agriculture
  in Arab world, 37, 44, 47
  capitalist displacing feudal,
    34-36, 63-66, 68, 76, 156,
    243
  decline of population in, 240
  European feudal development
    and, 55
  industrial progress and, 165-66
  in periphery, 167, 168, 171,
    183-84, 186, 193, 200, 204-06,
    246, 259, 282, 288, 296, 297,
    298-99, 310, 312-13, 315,
    325, 334-38, 349-50, 354, 381

  as productive labor sphere, 244
  productive output of, 215
Ahali club, 311
Alaouites, 41, 47
Albania, 118
Aleppo, 42
Alexander the Great, 20, 45
Alexandria, 45
Algeria, 29, 37, 242
  investment in, 207
  social formation in, 315-17
Ali Bey, 29, 302
Ali Pasha, 302, 304
Alienation
  of capitalist relations, 25-26, 62,
    70, 72, 376
  of Soviet production, 373, 374,
    378
Almohades, 43
Almoravides, 43
American Indians, 355, 367
Amin, Samir, 315-17
Anatolia, 301
Anglo-Egyptian treaty (1936), 307